JAVA™ AND JMX

JAVA™ AND JMX

Building Manageable Systems

Heather Kreger
Ward Harold
Leigh Williamson

Addison-Wesley

Boston • San Francisco • New York • Toronto • Montreal
London • Munich • Paris • Madrid
Capetown • Sydney • Tokyo • Singapore • Mexico City

The publisher offers discounts on this book when ordered in quantity for bulk purchases and special sales. For more information, please contact:

U.S. Corporate and Government Sales
(800) 382-3419
corpsales@pearsontechgroup.com

For sales outside of the U.S., please contact:

International Sales
(317) 581-3793
international@pearsontechgroup.com

Visit Addison-Wesley on the Web: www.awprofessional.com

Library of Congress Cataloging-in-Publication Data

Kreger, Heather.
Java and JMX : building manageable systems / Heather Kreger, Ward Harold, Leigh Williamson.
p. cm.
ISBN 0-672-32408-3 (Paperback : alk. paper)
1. Java (Computer program language) 2. Computer software--Development--Management. I. Harold, Ward. II. Williamson, Leigh. III. Title.

QA76.73.J38 K74 2003
005.13'3--dc21 2002014486

ISBN: 0-672-32408-3
Text printed on recycled paper
1 2 3 4 5 6 7 8 9 10—CRS—0605040302
First printing, December 2002

Dedicated to my husband, Ken,
and my daughters, Jennifer and Jessica,
for the sacrifices they made so that
I could do something I just had to do.

H. K.

This one, the first, is for my parents,
Cloyce and June Harold.
Thanks for everything, Mom and Dad.

W. H.

Dedicated to my family, whose support
and patience is boundless.

L. W.

CONTENTS

PREFACE

Introduction

Welcome! You have just opened your key to the secret art of management. This book is your comprehensive guide to the development of manageable application software using the Java Management Extensions (JMX). Now that Java has made the leap from cool to critical, every developer who has deployed a mission-critical application knows it is not enough just to write great code; to be truly useful, critical applications must be manageable as well. With the publishing of the JMX specification and the availability of multiple JMX implementations, Java programmers have a standard mechanism with which to instrument and manage their software products. This book will provide you with the information necessary to leverage JMX to create a new generation of better-instrumented, more manageable, and therefore more reliable mission-critical Java applications.

At the moment the two biggest growth areas for Java are enterprise and embedded systems. Tens of thousands of IT developers are now or soon will be using J2EE technologies to create mission-critical business systems. The major J2EE vendors, including IBM WebSphere and BEA WebLogic application servers, are using JMX to provide their own management, as well as to enable yours. The J2EE 1.4 standard is being extended to include management interfaces using JMX as defined by JSR (Java Specification Request) 77. At the other end of the spectrum, thousands more developers will be using Java to create embedded applications, from set-top boxes to remote pumping-station monitors.

It is essential that these applications, which run unattended on "invisible computers" for the most part, be as self-monitoring and self-managing as possible. JMX provides a substrate upon which to construct such self-monitoring/managing applications, and a copy of this book will substantially reduce your JMX learning curve.

JMX is also being accepted by the telephony industry as a management infrastructure for Java for the Advanced Intelligent Network (JAIN). As these specifications for the use of Java in telephony service environments emerge, whole new industries will need to become familiar with JMX. The probability that you will encounter JMX in one form or another, as part of your own designs or as the instrumentation mechanism for components of your infrastructure, is very high. This book will give you the foundation and technical details you need to make effective use of JMX wherever you find it.

Although it is well known that JMX is continuing to evolve, its basic architecture and interfaces will remain consistent. There is more to using JMX than understanding the architecture and interfaces; you also need to understand how it connects to management systems, the role it plays in the management industry, appropriate use of the technology, and management design patterns. In short, you need to understand how to create a manageable system.

This book has been written in a comprehensive manner by experts in that space. It also will give you an in-depth understanding of the application of JMX in hot technologies: J2EE and Web services. You will find this book to be useful long after new versions of JMX become available because the concepts introduced here are classic applications of management concepts and technologies to the Java family. This book will do more than help you write MBeans; it will help guide you build manageable systems.

This Book's Intended Audience

Our primary goal in writing this book is to explain Java-based management, manageability (i.e., enabling resources to be managed), and JMX in detail, and to make it easy to understand.

Architects and developers involved in the design and implementation of mission-critical Java applications are the primary audience for this book. They understand that their biggest challenges come well after the first successful installation of a new piece of software, when their client's business becomes critically dependent on that software. Then it is essential that administrators be able to monitor and manage the application day and night to keep the business in business. Until recently, each Java-based product had to develop its own ad hoc management solution. That changed with publication of the *Java Management Extensions Instrumentation and Agent Specification, v1.0.*

This book has been written especially for Java developers who find themselves in a situation where they must enable their application to be managed by an "outside" management system. Other Java developers and architects who will find this book useful include

- Those who are going to help create a new administrative or management system for their Java application
- Those who need to integrate their application into an existing JMX-based administrative or management system
- Those who want to develop some management functions to interact with an application that supports JMX
- Curious folks who just like to know what all the Java acronyms stand for

This book assumes that you do not have a background in systems or applications management and provides a comprehensive overview of the history of the management industry and the forces that combined to make JMX the ubiquitous management technology for Java resources across the Java community. Java resources deployed in the micro, standard, and enterprise editions of the JDK can all use JMX.

The authors have extensive firsthand experience with JMX from nearly every angle. Heather Kreger was an original member of the JMX Expert Group and personally contributed the specification, reference implementation (RI), and Technology Compatibility Kit (TCK) for model MBeans. She is now involved in Web services and applying management to this emerging space. Ward Harold is a member of the current JMX Expert Group (JSR 160), the lead architect for Tivoli's implementation of JMX and TMX4J, as well as Tivoli's Web Component Manager product, which uses JMX to manage resources. Leigh Williamson was a member of JSR 77 ("J2EE Management") and the architect for WebSphere's JMX support and JSR 77 support. This book represents our experience with JMX from all these projects: We bring you a unique insider perspective on the intent, implementation, application, and even pitfalls of JMX. All of this JMX experience is in the context of our extensive experience in all aspects of management systems and middleware.

This book will be valuable for developers of applications that should be managed, developers of middleware, and developers of management systems. We hope that you will find it useful not only as an introduction to JMX, but also as a frequent desktop reference as you connect your application to an existing management system or start to develop your own management application.

What You Need to Know before Reading This Book

This book assumes that you are familiar with developing applications using Java. We do not assume that you have experience with management systems. As such, the first chapter introduces management concepts, disciplines, and architectures. If you are familiar with management systems, then you may skip this chapter and start with Chapter 2 (Introduction to JMX).

Chapter 10 (J2EE and JMX) explains JSR 77 ("J2EE Management") in depth, as well as how it relates to JMX. This chapter assumes that you have a high-level understanding of the components of the J2EE specification and its realization in J2EE application servers.

Chapter 11 (Web Services and JMX) explains how JMX can be used to develop manageable Web service applications. It will be helpful to have a general understanding of what a Web service is, and familiarity with common Web service architectures.

What You Will Learn from Reading This Book

This book will provide you with the necessary information, insight, and examples for using JMX to build manageable mission-critical applications or provide a standard management interface to homegrown and third-party management applications.

It is sometimes as important to understand the context of Java technologies as it is to understand the technology itself. This is the case with JMX. Therefore, this book gives you almost two chapters (1 and 2) detailing the history of management systems, management architectures, applications, and technologies. In these chapters we also explain the forces that combined to make JMX so important for the Java community. This book gives you the background you need to understand and enter into conversations in the management industry.

Specifically, you will learn to develop standard and dynamic MBeans to represent JMX manageable resources in their applications. You will understand how and when to use the model MBean to rapidly develop extensible instrumentation and how to represent interdependent management components using the JMX relation service. Because instrumentation inevitably requires monitoring, this book discusses the use of JMX's various monitors and its notification model in detail. In addition, this book provides working sample code to illustrate the application of JMX technology in various settings, including J2EE and Web services.

Software Needed to Complete the Examples

All of the examples in this book, along with extras not in the book, can be downloaded from Addison-Wesley's Web site for this book: http://www.awprofessional.com/titles/0672324083. At a minimum, you will need to have a J2SE JDK and a JMX implementation installed on your computer to compile and run the samples shown throughout this book. These samples have been tested with the TMX4J. Some have also been tested with MX4J implementations. TMX4J is 100 percent Java code and should run on any platform, but it has been tested on a Windows operating system. TMX4J can be downloaded for free from the IBM alphaWorks Web site at http://alphaworks.ibm.com.

The examples in Chapter 10 demonstrate solutions based on J2EE application server products such as WebSphere Application Server. The J2EE servers that support JMX and JSR 77 are listed in the appendix. Complete product information for WebSphere Application Server may be found on the Web at http://www.ibm.com/products/websphere.

To run the examples in Chapter 11, you will need a Web services runtime including a Web server, servlet engine, SOAP engine, and JMX implementation. The samples in this chapter were tested with the IBM Web Services Tool Kit, which is available for free from the IBM alphaWorks Web site at http://alphaworks.ibm.com.

How This Book Is Organized

We have arranged the content of this book into three broad sections. Part I introduces management and JMX. Part II provides detailed and comprehensive coverage of the JMX architecture, APIs, programming techniques, and pitfalls. We even provide an entire chapter on design and implementation suggestions, along with our favorite pitfalls. Part III lays out the application of JMX in two fast-growing fields: J2EE and Web services.

We recognize that each reader will be interested in different portions of the book, and not everyone will need to read every chapter. Readers who are already familiar with management systems may skip Chapter 1 (Management Concepts), which introduces management concepts, disciplines, and architectures. We encourage everyone to read at least Chapter 2 (Introduction to JMX). You should feel free to read those chapters that most interest you or are most immediate to your needs. If you have a general understanding of JMX, then the rest of the chapters of the book can stand alone, so it is not necessary to read the book straight through.

The following is a quick summary of the contents of each of the three sections of the book:

- **Part I: JMX Introduction.** The first part of the book, Chapters 1 and 2, introduces you to the management world and JMX. JMX is a management technology, and effective use of it requires some fundamental understanding of the aspects of management and JMX's role in each. Chapter 1 (Management Concepts) describes the basic concepts and vocabulary of system and applications management. It starts by highlighting the history of management technologies, and it explains management disciplines, applications, architectures, and information. Chapter 2 (Introduction to JMX) describes why and how JMX came about, and then introduces each of the fundamental elements of JMX, MBeans, MBeanServer, and notifications. We give you a hands-on tour of JMX, using a simple server and then instrumenting it for management using JMX to illustrate each of the elements. If you are new to management and JMX, we recommend that you read the chapters in this part first to provide common background material and terminology for the remainder of the book.
- **Part II: JMX Details.** Part II is the meat of this book. This section gives you the comprehensive coverage of JMX along with practical examples and advice, including how to relate security to JMX. The management beans that you will need to be able to implement are introduced with extensive examples and advice in Chapter 3 (All about MBeans) and Chapter 4 (Model MBeans). Chapter 5 (The MBeanServer) describes the MBeanServer that is central to JMX's agent architecture and key to its flexibility. This chapter describes the interfaces and services that the MBeanServer provides: the MBean registry and object naming scheme, the generic MBean interface, the query mechanism, and the notification support. Chapter 6 (Monitors and Monitoring) and Chapter 7 (JMX Agent Services) will help you understand the standard services that JMX provides and how to use them. Chapter 8 (Securing JMX) covers a crucial topic that the JMX specification is silent on. This chapter describes the security exposures presented by the management domain and offers a transparent security layer based on the one designed for TMX4J. Finally, Part III closes with the pure gold of Chapter 9 (Designing with JMX). In this chapter, all the authors share their experiences with JMX and how these experiences can be used in real systems. Included are discussions on deployment models, instrumentation patterns, best practices, and pitfalls.
- **Part III: Application of JMX.** Part III is where we see JMX positioned as a fundamental technology for new and fast-growing industries. Chapter

10 (J2EE and JMX) provides great detail, from one who was there, about how JMX's management of J2EE systems has been standardized with JSR 77. It includes examples of how JMX works in real-world application server products. The section ends with a look to the future in Chapter 11 (Web Services and JMX). This chapter gives a brief description of Web services and the management issues associated with them. It then illustrates how JMX can be used to make Web service–based applications manageable. It lays out how to manage the registry, the Web service execution environment, and the Web service itself.
- **Appendix**. The appendix provides a reference for implementers and users of JMX technology, including lists of JMX implementations, JMX-enabled management platforms, and JMX-instrumented products.

Where to Download the Associated Code for This Book

The associated code files described in this book are available on Addison-Wesley's Web site at http://www.awprofessional.com. To access these files, enter this book's ISBN (without the hyphens) in the search box and click **Search**. When the book's title is displayed, click the title to go to a page where you can download the code. Or go directly to http://www.awprofessional.com/titles/0672324083.

Conventions Used in This Book

The following typographic conventions are used in this book:

- Code lines, commands, statements, variables, and any text you see onscreen appears in a `mono` typeface. **`Bold mono`** typeface is often used to represent user types.
- Placeholders in syntax descriptions appear in an *`italic mono`* typeface. Replace the placeholder with the actual file name, parameter, or other element that it represents.
- *Italic* typeface highlights technical terms when they're being defined.
- Indentation is used for lines of code that are really a continuation of the preceding line. Sometimes a line of code is too long to fit as a single line on the page. If a line of code is indented, remember that it's part of the line immediately above it.
- The book also contains notes, tips, and cautions to help you spot important or useful information more quickly. Some of these are useful shortcuts to help you work more efficiently.

About the Cover

The drawing on the cover of this book shows a snapshot in time of the sport of team penning. In team penning, an arena contains 15 to 30 cows with numbers on their backs. There are three cows assigned to each number. Three riders have up to 1-1/2 minutes to isolate the three cows with their assigned number (and *only* those cows) from the herd and put them through a gate into a small pen. The fastest time, usually less than 30 seconds, wins a cash prize. Team penning is a fun and exciting sport for horsemen of all ages and skill levels. This is true mostly because the cows are the great equalizers between the professionals and the amateurs. The cows are not cooperative in this sport. The cows do *not* want to leave their friends *or* go into that little pen where there is no food. After a few events, the cows are *not* afraid of the horses and actually don't mind going right under your horse's nose or belly to avoid the pen. Even the more cooperative cows are slow about it and don't help you win the money. In fact, it seems that the more highly skilled the horse and rider, the less inclined the more determined the cows are not to go into the pen. Beginner's luck reigns supreme and often cows happily trot into the pen in front of an 8-year-old on a stubborn pony. And of course, we can't leave out the horse, who has a mind of its own as well, chasing with us one minute and standing over us (while we lay on the ground) the next. Herding cows under a time deadline is a lot like herding cats.

There are many analogies between chasing unruly cows and managing IT infrastructures. No matter how skilled you are at managing your applications and infrastructure, something will go wrong to keep you from reaching your system availability targets. Application developers hand you uncooperative applications to manage. Your management systems, which are supposed to help you wrestle the applications into a highly available, high performing work of beauty, are often as much trouble as the applications you are trying to manage. And so, on the cover of a technical programming book, is a picture of team penners, the brave and skillful cowboy, er, IT administrator, riding his trusty horse, I mean, using his management systems, to efficiently move cows, um, applications, into the pen, rather, managed environment,... where they will all be well behaved and controllable. And what does JMX have to do with this? We hope that this book and JMX will help you make your horse behave, your cows cooperative, and your penning time faster. Oh wait, we mean your management systems more efficient, your applications more easily managed and your IT infrastructure more stable.

(Heather Kreger is an avid amateur team penner, Ward Harold was raised on a ranch in Kansas and appreciated the analogy having chased many cows from horseback as well. Leigh Williamson doesn't chase cows, but believed Heather and Ward's analogy.)

Acknowledgments

I'd like to thank my family, whom I bribed with four-wheelers with the advance money, in order to make losing a lot of Mom's time and attention worth it to them too. I especially want to thank my oldest daughter, Jennifer, for learning to make SpaghettiOs and hot dogs for herself and her sister so that Mommy could work on her book. I'd like to thank my youngest daughter, Jessica, for not letting me forget who is most important. And finally, I'd like to thank my husband, Ken, who really didn't understand why I needed to write this book but put up with it, and the never-ending crunching schedules, anyway . . . even when it didn't seem worth the four-wheelers anymore.

Thanks also to my manager and my friend, Carolyn Ruby, who made this book part of "my job" and has always been so supportive in helping me achieve my goals and find my killer instinct. Thanks to Janet Farrell and Vera Plechash, my cheerleaders. Thanks to Ward Harold for catching the JMX vision and for buddying up with me so that I could see my name in print. Thanks to Leigh for championing JMX in WebSphere and the JCP. And finally, thanks to Shelley Kronzek for continuing to nag until we were doing something we really wanted to do in the first place and for being the mediator between us technical chickens and the big scary publishing world.

— Heather Kreger

Wow, I'm writing acknowledgements. That must mean this project is almost complete. Saints be praised! Thanks to St. Heather for introducing me to JMX and, especially, for handling all the "lead author" administration chores. Our editor, St. Shelley Kronzek, persevered with us on this project through a series of trying circumstances and *still* bought us dinner in San Francisco. Thanks for your patience and dedication, Shelley.

Although I got to write the book, there is a fantastic group of people in Rome, Italy, who did most of the hard work of bringing JMX to life within Tivoli as TMX4J. To Kenneth Barron, Alfredo Cappariello, Raimondo Castino, Eliseba Costantini, Marco de Gregorio, Paola Diomede, Roberto Longobardi, Attilio Mattiocco, Marco Melillo, Alessio Menale, Chiara Montecchio, Massimiliano (Max) Parlione, Maurizio Simeoni, Massimo Tarquini, and Cosimo (Mimmo) Vampo, *mille grazie ragazzi*! My heartfelt thanks also go to Cesare Giuliani, the best development manager I've ever worked with, for turning my fuzzy musings into working code and never complaining when I didn't come back from Sabaudia when I said I would, and to Maurizio Piatti, who is simply my favorite Italian.

Finally, special thanks to my wife Diana and our kids Matthew, Aaron, and Kelly Rose for putting up with the constant presence of Daddy's laptop and the absence of his homemade bread for all these months. You guys make it all worthwhile.

— Ward Harold

I would like to thank my wife and daughter, Cheryl and Claire, for their patience and support. You are my compass and my light. I would also like to thank my coauthors, Heather and Ward, for their continued support and enthusiasm. Thanks go to all of the members of the JSR 77 expert group who worked so hard to produce the specification. Thanks to the management at IBM, Michelle Swenson and Diane Copenhaver, for encouragement and resources. And I would also like to thank the folks at Addison-Wesley, Shelley and all of the reviewers, for their excellent comments and suggestions.

— Leigh Williamson

PART I

JMX Introduction

CHAPTER 1

Management Concepts

The term *management* is grossly overused in the computer industry. It is often the responsibility of a *management* system to take care of installation and configuration of a resource into a computer system. After a resource is installed, the *management* system should be able to start it, monitor it to be sure it is performing well, change its behavior through reconfiguration or operations, and stop it. The first thing this book is going to do is define management and the terms to describe management, and then identify the aspects of management that are addressed by Java Management Extensions (JMX)[1].

This chapter gives a short history of management systems and an overview of management architectures and technologies. Building on this basis, we will discuss the management lifecycle, resulting management disciplines, management data and operations, and then how all of these things are combined into management applications and systems.

Most of this chapter is not specific to JMX, and if you have a background in management and management technologies, you may choose to move on to Chapter 2 (Introduction to JMX). If you are new to management, having a basic understanding of management technology will help you understand the terminology used in this book, in the JMX specification, and by management system vendors. It will also give you the background you may need to develop or integrate with a management system.

Resources use JMX to make themselves manageable by a management system. JMX is an isolation and mediation layer between manageable resources and management systems. Why do we need this decoupling of the manager and the managed? A quick look at the history of management systems and technologies will make clear how we came to need JMX for the Java platform.

1.1 Progress of Management

1.1.1 Why Invest in Management?

The basic motivation for corporations to invest in enterprise management systems is growth. This growth creates pain points that can be eased by network and systems management. Some of the more common scenarios that cause pain:

- When the IT resources become too numerous for computer operations staff to track with internally developed tools.
- When the IT resources become too distributed to control from a single systems console.
- When the IT resources are of diverse types causing console proliferation in the operations center, which cannot be staffed.
- When the IT resources need to ensure that they are highly available.

All of these scenarios result in workloads that ultimately overwhelm operations staff, like the poor fellow in Figure 1.1, causing stress and decreasing their ability to do their job of keeping the IT infrastructure available.

Figure 1.1 Harried Operators Can't Possibly Keep Up

As an example, these pain points are all felt by the leading-edge corporations building business-to-customer and business-to-business applications, also known as e-business, over the Internet. These applications are distributed not only geographically, but also across corporations. Each partner may be running his side on different platforms, servers, and networks. Each partner can manage only part of the application. Each partner may be using several consoles to manage the network, server, middleware, and application. And finally, these applications must be available 24 hours a day, 7 days a week, or else both partners may lose revenue by the minute.

1.1.2 The Natural Evolution of Management

The first businesses invested in computer systems to make themselves more competitive. These first systems were expensive, to say the least. In order to maximize the return on their investment, corporations had to make sure that all of the mainframe's resources were in use around the clock. This meant that these systems had to be *highly available*. At first, because a corporation had only a few such systems, a computer operations and administration staff were able to monitor and operate them with sufficient efficiency.

Then, as the number of mainframes in use by a single corporation increased, the systems also became more complex. It became difficult for the staff to efficiently distribute the work and monitor the systems. The mainframes needed management systems in order to be highly available and efficiently used. The requirements of highly available systems resulted in management systems that were tightly coupled with the target operating systems.

These management systems were responsible for providing interfaces and status on every detail of the system's lifecycle. The systems monitored themselves and notified operators when they required intervention. They provided operators ways to configure the system before and during execution, to operate the systems during execution, to monitor the status of the system, and to recover from failures. The operations staff was responsible for starting the system, managing the system's workload and throughput, backing up the system, stopping the system, and maintaining the system. Because the number of mainframes deployed within a company was still fairly small, having one management system per mainframe and an operations staff to monitor it was a reasonable way to provide a highly available, efficiently used system.

Two forces upset this short-lived balance. Large enterprises began deploying large numbers of mainframes that were dispersed across the company's locations. At the same time, applications began to emerge that could be used by many employees simultaneously. Inexpensive 3270[2] terminals were deployed to "bring the computer to the user." Networks were created to connect mainframes to each other and their far-flung users. Operations staffs were now responsible for monitoring and managing the network along with the systems.

The volume and distribution of the systems to be managed stressed operations staff. Many companies split the operations staff's responsibilities and organization between network operations and system operations. The resulting network control centers (NCCs) and operations control centers (OCCs) became distinct organizationally and geographically. Nonetheless, in the mid-1980s it became obvious that although all of the management consoles necessary to manage the complexes might fit within a large computer operations center, the number of human operators required to interact with these consoles could not fit into that same room. Likewise, the sheer volume of systems, networks, and applications to be monitored constantly by the operators guaranteed that problems would be missed and availability would be compromised. The split into NCC and OCC often made finding the root cause of a service outage an exercise in finger-pointing (see Figure 1.2), which merely exacerbated the frequency and length of the outages.

In answer to the need for more reliable management with fewer operators, new enterprise systems management products were developed by companies like IBM,[3] Candle,[4] and Computer Associates.[5] These products were written to manage a particular operating system or network, but they were not as tightly coupled as the original management systems. At the same time, as the networks grew larger and spanned greater distances, the demand for network management products rose sharply.

Figure 1.2 Problem Analysis Triggers Finger-Pointing

Up to this point, enterprise computing systems were fairly homogeneous. A single vendor's hardware, operating system, and networking hardware would be deployed and managed by a single management system. The introduction of UNIX[6]-based systems from Sun Microsystems[7] and Hewlett-Packard[8] allowed affordable alternatives to IBM's expensive mainframes. IBM introduced its own line of UNIX systems to compete. Smaller businesses could now afford to use computing to make business more efficient. Likewise, smaller branches and independent departments of large enterprises could afford to own and operate their own computers.

This adoption of computing by "grassroots" businesses that did not have dedicated, professional IT staff caused management applications to focus on ease of use. The results were new, non-management-oriented, improvements:

- **User interfaces.** Graphical, more intuitive user interfaces that were easier to use for the non-IT professional, who had another *real* job to do
- **Automation.** Automated recovery by the management system of a failed or badly performing resource
- **Recommendation.** Problem determination and correction recommendations that were made available to users within the management system
- **Administration.** Ease of installation, administration, and maintenance of the management system itself

The isolated departmental computer systems didn't stay isolated for very long. Within enterprises it became necessary to connect these systems to each other and the mainframes that were the backbone of the enterprise. This connection made networks a critical aspect of the IT infrastructure to be managed. Not only were there more systems to be managed, but these were simple systems and not always designed and built to be manageable. Now the enterprise IT staffs were facing the challenge of managing large volumes of systems using many different hardware platforms, operating systems, and network technologies. This variety exponentially increased the complexity of keeping the systems available, highly utilized, connected, and with reasonable response time.

The advent of TCP/IP[9] networking made connecting large numbers of these disparate systems and their clients much easier. This new ease of connection triggered the development and deployment of distributed computing environments. Businesses began deploying applications in these distributed computing environments. Applications were no longer focused on one system, but across many systems. They were also no longer dependent on one well-managed system, but a whole slew of reasonably managed systems and the network between them. Applications in this environment, as well as the distributed-computing environments across which they executed, became much more complex. It was absolutely critical that this new type of extremely complex environment be managed to ensure high availability and utilization.

Operations staffs now had to learn to manage many different types of systems. This diversity meant that there was a desperate need for external management systems that could manage many different systems from many different vendors. These managers not only needed to do what their predecessors did—start, stop, monitor, and control the systems and network—but they had the added requirement of normalizing all of these disparate systems so that operations staff were protected from the incessant learning curve. Tivoli Systems,[10] Computer Associates, and BMC Software[11] are a few of the companies that have stepped up to supply management products for these challenges.

1.2 Management Architectures

Let's look now at the architectures of the management systems that were successful during this history.

The initial management systems were tightly coupled with the operating systems and resources to be managed. Typically, the resource to manage was running on the same host as the management system. In such cases the resources to be managed interacted directly with the management system. Later, management systems were developed by vendors that had not developed the operating system. These vendors had to support the management of a variety of resources that were not on the same host as the management system.

Management architectures consist of four parts:

1. **Organizational model.** The *organizational model* defines the entities and roles involved in the architecture and their composition. In this section we will discuss the manager-agent model, which contains the roles of managed resource, agent, subagent, midlevel manager, and management system.
2. **Information model.** The *information model* defines the structure of the management information so that the different entities can understand the management interfaces exposed by instrumentation to enable manageability.
3. **Communication model.** The *communication model* defines the operations and protocol for accessing the information model.
4. **Functional model.** The *functional model* defines generic management services that can be used to manage any resource.

Most management systems today use variations of a manager-agent management architecture. Let's look at the details of this particular architecture.

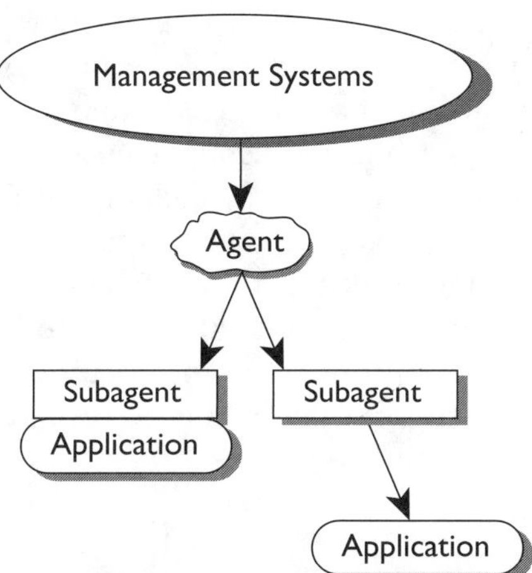

Figure 1.3 Manager-Agent Architecture

We will then look at some management standards and the parts of this architecture that they support. As Figure 1.3 shows, this architecture always contains the managed resource, agent, and management system roles. Subagent and midlevel manager are often seen as well.

Sections 1.2.1 through 1.2.5 examine the details of each role in the manager-agent architecture.

1.2.1 Managed Resource

The computer system, network, or application component that needs to be managed is the *managed resource*. Not all resources in an IT environment need to be managed. Some groups of resources are managed as a functional unit rather than individually. Looking specifically at Java[12] technology, managed resources can be stand-alone applications, client-server applications, and Web applications. The components of these applications can be managed resources as well. Such components may include Java Virtual Machines (JVMs), containers, servlets, and Enterprise JavaBeans (EJBs) on the server, or browsers and containers on the client.

The managed resource is responsible for exposing appropriate management data for use by a management system mapped into the information model supported by that management system. At a minimum, the managed resource should expose a description of itself, its configuration data, and some performance metrics and status indicators that reflect its health.

The managed resource is also responsible for interacting with the management system via its agent using the communication model, operations, and protocol that the management system and its agent support. Such interactions include responding to requests from and sending unsolicited events to the management agent. Requests from agents may include getting data, changing configurations, or executing operations. The resource determines which requests it will support and to what degree these requests are supported. The managed resource should also recognize internal errors and log them or notify the management system. The management patterns discussed later in this chapter illustrate common types of support that managed resources can provide.

1.2.2 Agent

The management *agent* is provided by a management system and supports the communication model and information model of the management system. The agent communicates with both the management system and the managed resources. It is usually running on the same host as a daemon[13] or in the same process as the resource it is managing. The agent may support one or more managed resources. Agents embedded in a resource can support only that instance of the resource.

The agent sends data and events from the resource to the management system. It also relays data and command requests from the management system to the resource, gathers the responses, and returns them to the management system. The agent usually provides a programming interface, which may expose or wrap the communication model for the managed resource to use to communicate with it. Some management agents require that the managed resource implement a particular programming interface that the agent invokes to have a request honored.

Standards bodies have specified some standard management architectures that define information models and communication models used for the creating agents in the manager-agent architecture. The three most common are the Management Information Bases (MIBs) and SNMP,[14] Managed Object Format (MOF) and CMIP,[15] and Common Information Model (CIM) and Web-Based Enterprise Management (WBEM)[16] specifications. Some enterprise management systems, such as those from Tivoli and Computer Associates, depend on their own, internal proprietary agent infrastructures.

1.2.3 Subagent

Management architectures in which one agent must support many managed resources use *subagents*. The subagent is tightly coupled with the resource.

Sometimes, it may actually be embedded within the resource. The subagent registers its presence and availability to the agent and then communicates between the resource and the agent. The subagent typically provides two programming interfaces—one to interact with the resource, and one to interact with the agent. The subagent may transform the managed resource's data from its native format and interfaces to the information model expected by the agent and management system.

It is usually the responsibility of the resource to register its subagent with the agent. The IETF has Request for Comments (RFC) documents for three subagents for SNMP, SMUX,[17] DPI,[18] and AgentX,[19] although none of these are official standards.

1.2.4 Midlevel Manager

The first manager-agent architectures had problems handling the massive numbers of managed resources that could be reporting to a single management system. This became a pain point for network managers in large enterprises using SNMP. To increase their scalability, they needed to reduce the amount of incoming data and events, as well as the number of systems they had to poll directly for availability. To accomplish this they introduced intermediate systems called *midlevel managers* (*MLM*s) into their architectures.

MLMs interact with management systems and a set, or *domain*, of agents and the management system. MLMs are responsible for aggregating and filtering the information from the managed resource and forwarding pertinent or summary information to the management system. They also poll the managed resources in their domain for availability and forward exceptions to the management system. MLMs increase the quality of information while reducing the rate and quantity of incoming messages that the management systems must handle.

The domaining aspect of architectures using MLMs allows resources to be managed as logical groups according to physical characteristics, like location or type, or by business characteristics, like division or business application. Sometimes architectures that use midlevel managers are called hierarchical management architectures or *cascaded agent* architectures.

1.2.5 Management System

The *management system* supports the information model and communication model—that is, operations and protocols—of the manager-agent management architecture. The management system may range widely in the amount of functionality it provides. Regardless of the comprehensiveness of that functionality, the management system interacts with the agents to receive and gather information about the managed resources. The management system uses the information to accomplish some of its purpose. This purpose can include all or some of the management applications described in Section 1.8. Management system–initiated requests to the managed resource go through the agent as well.

The management system can be a sophisticated enterprise manager that manages all the distributed, disparate, critical resources, like those available from Tivoli or Computer Associates. The management system may be a domain-specific management system (tightly or loosely coupled) designed to fully manage a particular resource, such as IBM's WebSphere Administration Console.[20] Another common type of management system is the resource-specific management system designed to manage a business system like banking, accounting, or customer management.

The management system is responsible for providing the infrastructure and user interfaces to manage the resources. A typical management system receives events from agents, displays them to operators, and takes any defined automated actions. The management system initiates a request to agents to control the resource. It requests data from the agent (which then requests it from the resource) for polling, monitoring, identifying trends, or determining problems. Advanced management systems that use pervasive standard management technologies, like SNMP, may also automatically discover resources in order to reduce management system configuration requirements and produce accurate topology and inventory information.

Management systems generally allow their resource management services to be customized. Examples of customizable features include commands, available statistics, threshold values used to indicate problems, automated actions, and operational policies. With more sophisticated management applications, service-level agreements and business system contexts can be defined as well. Let's take a look at the proprietary and standard management technologies that have developed and how they support the roles in this architecture.

1.3 Management Technologies

Several different types of management systems are currently available: vendor-specific management systems that manage a particular product set, homogenizing management systems that hide management of dissimilar systems under a standard interface, and network management systems that manage the connections between systems and users. All of these types of management systems from different vendors have been implemented through different protocols and technologies. This variety is illustrated by a survey of proprietary and standard management technologies in use by management products today.

1.3.1 Proprietary Technologies

Many vendor management systems use proprietary technologies. Many operating systems, such as IBM's System/390[21] and Microsoft's SMS[22] have their own proprietary, and usually tightly coupled, management system and infrastructure. They provide their own information model, communication model, and services.

The dominant enterprise management systems by Tivoli, Computer Associates, and BMC Software are homogenizing management systems that manage diverse and distributed resources. They each use their own, proprietary technology for their distributed management infrastructure, including manager-to-agent communications. These enterprise management system vendors compete on three fronts:

1. The management system infrastructure and capabilities
2. The services for installation and customization
3. The set of products and applications they can monitor and manage

Management systems that use proprietary technologies may use any of the management architectures already described or their own unique organizational models.

1.3.2 Standard Technologies

1.3.2.1 SNMP

Data network management systems for TCP/IP networks use predominantly the *Simple Network Management Protocol* (*SNMP*).[23] SNMP is a de facto standard for device and network management. However, it has not been widely deployed for application management. It was developed as a temporary solution for management until CMIP was completed. It is part of the IETF's Management Architecture[24] which also defines the System Management Interface (SMI)[25] communication model and standardizes the information model in MIBs[26] for network, device, and some system resources. Hewlett-Packard's OpenView[27] and Tivoli's Netview[28] are popular SNMP-based network management products today. SNMP-based management systems use the manager-agent architecture, including the subagent and midlevel manager roles, that we have discussed.

1.3.2.2 CMIP

Telecommunications network management products often use *Common Management Information Protocol* (*CMIP*).[29] CMIP was developed by the International Standards Organization (ISO)[30] as a standard protocol for a larger standard management architecture called OSI/TMN.[31] TMN also has its own information model and operations model. It did not displace SNMP as expected. Sun Microsystems, BullSoft,[32] and Hewlett-Packard all provided network management products that support CMIP. CMIP-based management systems usually use manager-agent architectures.

1.3.2.3 CIM/WBEM

The Distributed Management Task Force (DMTF)[33] defines a *Common Information Model* (*CIM*) as a standard information model for describing management data about the devices, networks, systems, and applications of computer systems. An agent that supports this model is called a *CIM object manager* (*CIMOM*). The DMTF also defined the communication model to be *Web-Based Enterprise Management* (*WBEM*)[34] that defines CIM operations as an interface to the model, an XML representation (CIM.DTD) used to represent the CIM model in XML, and a mapping to transport the CIM operations with the XML CIM model data over HTTP. This entire combination of CIM and XML-based protocol to the CIMOM is collectively referred to as *CIM/WBEM*.

Although the device and system models are fairly complete, the application model is still a work in progress. This is still an emerging technology, but Microsoft's SMS[35] and Sun Solstice do provide support and managers for it. WBEMsource[36] is an open-source community for CIM/WBEM implementations in both C++ and Java. The Open Group publishes Pegasus,[37] an open-source C++ implementation of the CIM/WBEM standard. Sun and other vendors publish Java implementations that conform to the APIs defined by Sun's WBEM service Java Specification Request (JSR) 48.[38]

CIM/WBEM systems are generally implemented in a manager-agent architecture and don't use MLMs. Work is in progress to standardize an interface for resources to provide data to the CIMOM, a provider interface. When this work is complete, these providers will function in a subagent role and CIM/WBEM will support the manager-agent-subagent architecture as well.

1.3.2.4 JMX

Java Management Extensions (*JMX*) defines a Java technology that supports management services for any Java technology–based resource. JMX defines extensions of the Java language that will allow any Java technology–based resource to be inherently manageable, as well as Java interfaces to existing management technologies. JMX is used by the resource to make itself manageable by a management system. JMX is basically an isolation and mediation layer between manageable resources and management systems.

JMX-based management systems that are based on the current specification support the basic manager-agent architecture. Unlike SNMP and CIM/WBEM, JMX deliberately does not define a management information model. JMX provides the agent with the JMX agent, or MBeanServer—which will be discussed in detail later. Depending on the adapters available to other management agents, the JMX agent can be viewed in the agent role or subagent role. If the JMX adapter communicates directly with the management system, it is functioning in an agent role. If the JMX adapter communicates with an agent for the management system, then it is functioning in a subagent role. The JMX instrumentation API is the communication model and provides the interface used by the managed application, as well as the management system to communicate with the management agent. The JMX Expert Group is currently working to standardize connections between JMX agents and between JMX agents and managers. When this work is done, JMX will be able to support manager-MLM-agent-subagent architectures by federating JMX agents.

Sun Microsystem's JDMK[39] includes a JMX implementation and simple management console to support it. Tivoli's TMX4J[40] implements the JMX specification as well and is used by numerous other IBM products.

1.3.2.5 AIC

Application Information and Control (*AIC*),[41] from The Open Group's Enterprise Management program, is a C language and Java API for exposing application metrics and thresholds. AIC is not as comprehensive or as flexible as JMX. It does not support all the aspects of resource and application management that require relationships, operations, and resource grouping. It is a relatively new standard and has not seen any widespread adoption yet.

1.3.2.6 ARM

Application Response Measurement (*ARM*)[42] with a Java API is also from The Open Group's enterprise management program. It focuses on capturing the amount of time it takes to perform units of work inside applications. The ARM standard is supported by products from both Tivoli Systems and Hewlett-Packard, but widespread instrumentation of resources to report ARM data has yet to occur.

So far we have discussed just a few of the challenges and complexities facing enterprises trying to manage their information systems. And as if managing diversity and wide geographic distribution weren't enough, they also have to deal with understanding and deploying the different technologies used for management. Although there is a dominant technology for network management, that luxury does not exist for systems and application management. There is no broadly accepted or implemented technology, standard or otherwise, for managing Java applications. This situation begs for a unifying technology like JMX. As we introduce JMX in the next chapter, you'll see how it helps simplify some of this complexity.

1.4 Managing the Lifecycle

Given that such a wide variety of functionality is provided by management systems, it may be easier to think about them in terms of what parts of the lifecycle of IT resources they manage.

Nearly all computing resources have a similar lifecycle that needs to be managed (see Figure 1.4).

First the resource needs to be installed onto its platform. Then it needs to be started or somehow made available to those who need to use it. After it has been started, it is said to be executing. While it is executing, it needs to be monitored, operated, and configured. This is called *runtime management*. At some point the resource will need to be stopped to block its availability to its users. A stopped resource is "unavailable." When a resource is unavailable it

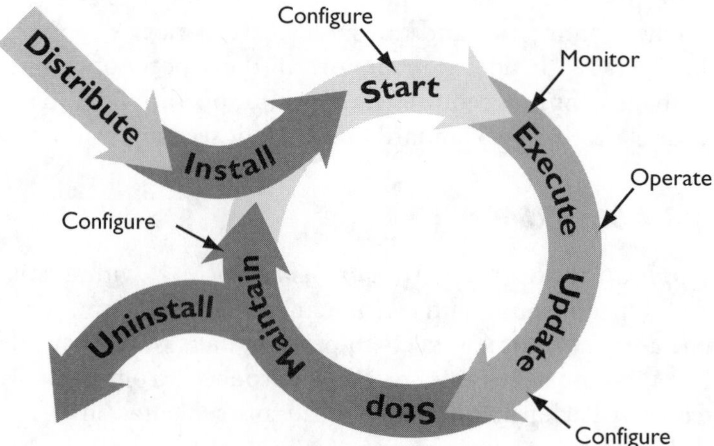

Figure 1.4 The Resource Management Lifecycle

can be maintained (updates and fixes) and configured. Given this generic scenario, we define the lifecycle of a resource to have the following stages:

1. **Distribute.** Move files that are the resource to the target system.
2. **Install.** Install a resource in the target system.
3. **Start.** Initialize a resource so that it will be executing.
4. **Execute.** Actively perform functions.
   - **Monitor.** Periodically check a resource to ensure that it is available and performing appropriately.
   - **Operate.** Invoke functions or operations while executing that do not permanently affect the state of the resource.
   - **Configure.** Permanently change configuration data while executing or while stopped.
5. **Stop.** Terminate a resource so that it is no longer executing.
6. **Maintain.** Apply code or configuration changes to a resource on a regular basis or as needed.
7. **Uninstall.** Remove a resource from the system.

The need to manage this lifecycle has spawned the various management disciplines. Most modern management applications provide support for one or more of these disciplines, but no single management application supports all of them.

1.5 Management Disciplines

The management disciplines emerged to support the application lifecycle outlined in the preceding section. The five management disciplines are distribute, install, configure, monitor, and control. All management applications will support at least some of these disciplines. Few support all of them. In Section 1.8 we will look at the management applications that have been developed to support these disciplines.

1.5.1 Distribute

The *distribute discipline*, also known as deploy, emerged to provide a scalable solution to the distribute, configure, and maintain lifecycle phases. Management applications that support the distribute discipline support moving the files that make up a product or application from a centralized "source" system to a set of distributed "target" systems (see Figure 1.5). The set of target systems may number in the tens of thousands. The software being distributed may be operating systems, products, applications, maintenance, new versions of installed software, or configuration updates. The distribution can

Figure 1.5 A Software Distribution System

be scheduled to occur at any time to minimize the impact on existing resource utilization.

Most management applications that support the distribute discipline allow scheduling and also manage initial installations. Many also handle the distribution and installation of upgrades and maintenance.

1.5.2 Install

The *install discipline* emerged to provide a scalable solution to the install and maintain lifecycle phases. Management applications that support the install discipline customize initial configuration files, update system files, and run installation programs for initial installation of resources, as well as maintenance installation for those same resources. Before they install any resources, they perform dependency checking. Dependency checking ensures that any software or resources that the installation requires are available. Dependency checking may include checking product versions, physical resources, and maintenance levels. For example, to install IBM's WebSphere 4.0,[43] 250MB of disk space must be available, DB2 7.1 fp2a must be installed, and the Windows NT operating system must be at maintenance level SP4. Installations can be scheduled for one or more products and coordinated across a set of systems.

1.5.3 Configure

Applications may potentially be configured during the install, start, execute, or update lifecycle phases. More specifically, configuration can be done at any of these configuration points:

- **Pre-installation.** Before the install phase, configuration changes may be needed to prepare the resource or target system for a new installation.
- **During installation.** During the install phase, configuration changes may be required to respond to installation processes.
- **Post-installation.** After the install phase, configuration changes may be required to customize the resource for the specific target systems and application needs.
- **Pre-execution.** Before the execute phase, configuration changes may be required to customize the resource for this particular run.
- **During execution.** During the execute phase, configuration changes may be required to tune or correct failures in the running application.

Configuration before or during the execute phase can happen multiple times on every iteration of the lifecycle.

The *configure discipline* emerged to provide a scalable solution to this repetitious task, like updating a single parameter in a configuration file on 40 systems (see Figure 1.6). Management applications that support the configure discipline may customize the configuration of resources during any of these configuration points.

We can change the configuration by updating a file or using configuration APIs supplied by the resource developer. File-based configuration changes—that is, *static reconfiguration*—usually requires that the application be stopped to make the changes or restarted for them to take effect. API-based configuration changes—termed *dynamic reconfiguration*—usually take effect as soon as the changes have been made. Some of the more advanced configuration systems support the definition and application of policy to drive the configuration values or the configuration distribution and application to a set of target systems.

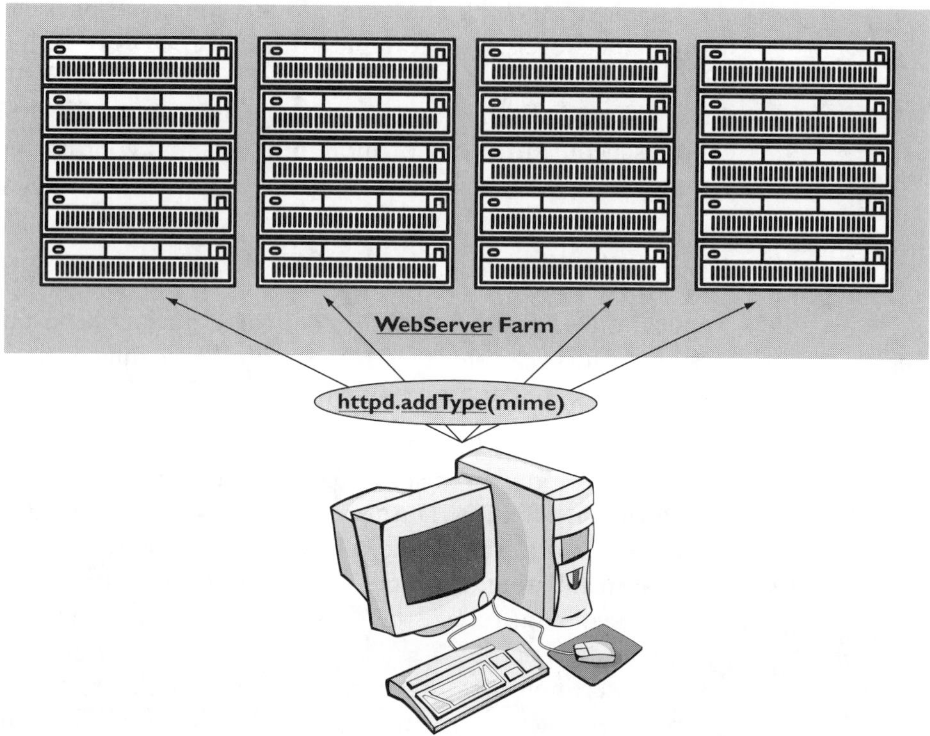

Figure 1.6 Large-Scale Configuration Change: Adding a MIME Type to a Web Server Farm

1.5.4 Monitor

The *monitor discipline* emerged to provide a scalable solution to the monitor lifecycle phase. Management applications that support the monitor discipline maintain knowledge of the current status of a computer resource, both hardware and software. If the status is unacceptable at any point, the management system notifies operations staff via a management console (see Figure 1.7) or correlation and automation software. The monitoring application gets its status in a variety of ways:

- Polling application metrics
- Polling operating system metrics
- Polling software logs
- Receiving unsolicited events from the software or system
- Receiving unsolicited status events from a peer management system

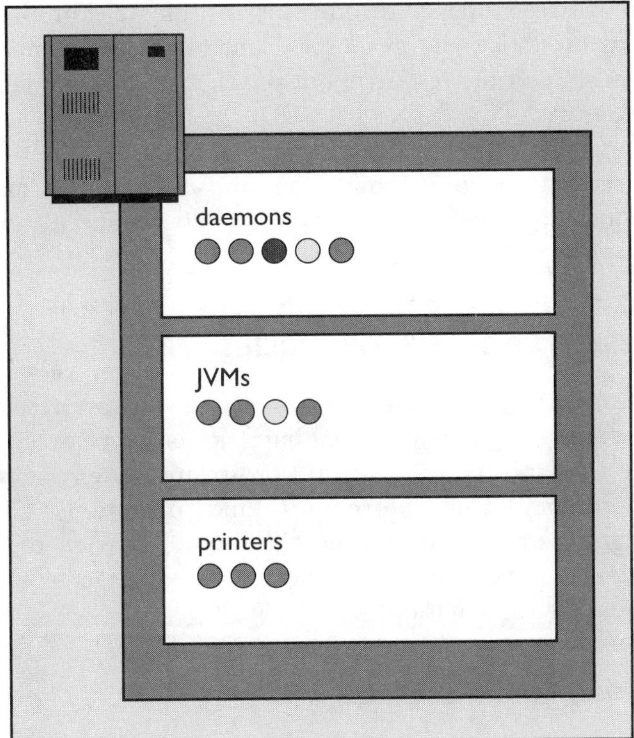

Figure 1.7 Status Console

The resource developer must define, maintain, and expose metric information through logs, events, commands, or APIs for the management system to monitor and interpret.

1.5.5 Control

The *control discipline* emerged to provide a scalable solution to the execute, operate, stop, and update lifecycle phases. Management applications that support the control discipline give computer operations and administration staff a user interface for controlling the execution of systems alone or in groups. They are used to change the way the resource is executing in order to prevent it from failing, to change the current state of the software (start or stop it), or to make the current configured software more efficient. A series of operations can be scripted together and scheduled to execute to sets of target systems. Control is different from configure in that configuration changes are preserved between phases throughout the lifecycle of the resource, even between two instances of a resource. Control causes an immediate change in the current state of the resource, but the change does not last over iterations of the resource.

JMX is applicable to the configure, monitor, and control disciplines. In the next section we will examine the kind of support a managed resource needs to include to be managed by management applications that support these disciplines.

1.6 Managed Resource Responsibilities

In order for management systems to manage software resources, they must have information (i.e., management data) about the resources they're managing, along with the ability to control or update those resources via management operations. This information and operations are provided by management instrumentation from inside and outside the resource itself. This section will explain management data, management operations, and management instrumentation.

1.6.1 Management Data

Management data is the information about a software resource that a management system uses. The management system must be able to determine the identity of the resource, how it has been defined to run, and what statistics are available to monitor it. The management data that management systems need access to generally falls into four categories:

1. **Identification data.** *Identification data* uniquely identifies the resource to be managed. This data must include the name of the resource and an identifier that allows a specific instance of the resource to be distinguished from other instances of the same type. Other data that is usually included is resource type, vendor, version, serial number, location, contact, installation date, last updated date, and address. This data is used by management systems with discovery, inventory, topology, and configuration components. If the management system cannot find this data for the resource, the resource must be manually defined to the discovery, inventory, topology, and configuration management systems.
2. **Configuration data.** *Configuration data* may include the complete configuration of the resource or a subset thereof. Read access alone is valuable for problem determination and dynamic management policy. It gives the

management system real-time management guidance about data for which thresholds should be established, logs and components that should be managed, and so on. If the configuration data can be set by the management system, an update to this data may cause the resource to dynamically update and behave in accordance with the new configuration values.

3. **Statistical data.** *Statistical data* is numerical data that generally represents the current state of the resource. Most management systems use resource statistics as the data to be monitored to determine resource health. Depending on the quality and quantity of statistical data available from the resource, management systems may also be able to use this data for load and resource balancing, tuning, trend analysis, capacity forecasting, billing, and understanding application usage. Service-level agreements and the systems that report and enforce them use statistical data to define the expectations, thresholds, and responses for the service-level agreements for an application.
4. **Status data.** *Status data* is information about the resource that indicates its health and current operational state. Typically status data is reported by enumerated values, like `Active`, `Degraded`, `Stopped`, `DependencyDown`, `Down`, or `Failed`. A resource may have status substates indicating the health and state of its components.

Some of this information (e.g., configuration data) can be obtained from logs and files. Some of this information must be obtained directly from the managed resource.

1.6.2 Management Operations

Management operations are used to control, locally or remotely, all components of a managed resource. Operations can be categorized as lifecycle control (start, stop, restart, refresh, and so on), query, configure, and custom. Some of these operations (e.g., start and stop) are provided by the platform that is hosting the managed resource. Some must be provided directly by the managed resource as commands or APIs. The management system will invoke these APIs and commands from scripts, programs, remote connections, command prompts, and agents in response to events, schedules, and user requests.

It is interesting to note that although user-driven interfaces like administration applications can be used to drive management operations, it is difficult for management systems to use them. Software resources should supply a user interface and command or APIs for the management operations.

1.6.3 Management Instrumentation

Management instrumentation is the way a resource provides its management data and operations to the management system. Resources provide two types of management instrumentation: external and internal.

Management disciplines need different kinds of instrumentation, depending on whether they need to interact directly with the executing resource. For example, the distribute discipline typically needs only external instrumentation, and operations are difficult to support without internal instrumentation. Most disciplines use a combination of both types of instrumentation, as illustrated by Figure 1.8.

JMX provides the infrastructure for Java resource developers to expose this management information. It also provides the APIs for management systems to gain access to the information and invoke the operations.

1.6.3.1 External Instrumentation

External instrumentation is management enablement that is defined and executed outside the resource itself. The external instrumentation consists of definitions describing the resource. The instrumentation is used to customize the management system so that it can effectively manage the resource. These definitions specify the directories, files, libraries, executables, installation processes, configurations, events, APIs, and policies that are required knowledge to manage the resource. The external instrumentation of the resource includes special files, programs, or utilities that may be necessary for the

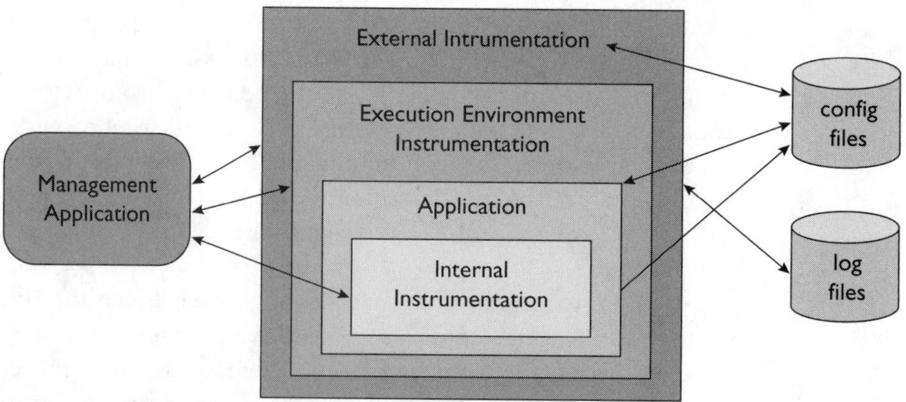

Figure 1.8 Internal and External Instrumentation

management system to access the data for or control the resource. The management disciplines of distribute, install, configure, monitor, and operate can be supported by this type of instrumentation.

Tivoli uses its Application Management Specification (AMS)[44] files as its external instrumentation. AMS files are generically defined as a software resource's management "definition file." Some management system vendors provide tools to facilitate the creation of a resource's management definition files. For SNMP, the MIB file represents this type of instrumentation. For CIM/WBEM, the instrumentation is defined as a schema in a MOF (Managed Object Format) file.[45]

1.6.3.2 Internal Instrumentation

Internal instrumentation is management enablement that is developed and executed directly as part of the resource by the vendor or developer. It consists of code specifically engineered to meet a management system's requirements. Basic instrumentation includes the provision of a command tool or a management agent that can invoke or perform the operations and that can obtain the application status and statistics. The monitor and control management disciplines may require this type of instrumentation. Extensive internal instrumentation may be required for communication with a single management system.

Monitoring and operating an executing application requires that the application support instrumentation for several different types of management data and functions. For example, an SNMP subagent must be developed for each application that supports a defined SNMP MIB. Likewise, with WBEM, a CIM provider may need to be developed to support the management schema for an application. There is currently no standard instrumentation data or API approach for applications to adhere to or take advantage of. This may not be true in the future, however, because a management model defining the data for managing executing applications is currently being developed in the DMTF.

In reality, a combination of external and internal instrumentation methodologies, as illustrated in Figure 1.8, is optimal. There are at least three good arguments for this:

1. External instrumentation is rarely sufficient in and of itself. Generally the resource will need to expose some specific metrics, operations, and events. You then have internal instrumentation.
2. Internal instrumentation is rarely sufficient in and of itself. There are frequently management tasks to perform within a system to keep it healthy

for the application to continue to function. Data space management by the rotation or clipping of logs, the compression of backup data, and the deletion of obsolete logs and data is an example of the second case for external instrumentation.

3. You will need to advertise the internal instrumentation's capabilities in external instrumentation used by the management system. Defining an SNMP MIB is an example. You are advertising your management data to an SNMP manager.

A single common application management API simplifies and minimizes the internal instrumentation required. This is the essence of the requirement for a common management system application-level API, as defined by the JMX API set and as described in this book.

JMX is designed to satisfy the requirements of managing the executing application from the resource developer's point of view, as well as the management vendor's point of view. JMX is an internal instrumentation API. It is used to expose and and provide access to the execution-time management information that is necessary for an application to be manageable by an arbitrary management system. Tools can be used to generate the external instrumentation for a specific management system from the information available through the JMX APIs.

1.7 Management Patterns

When developing a manageable resource, the developer is faced with many choices concerning how to interact with the management system and how to fit into a manager-agent architecture. The set of architectural patterns we present here[46] categorizes the common ways that managed resources interact with the management system. Each pattern is progressively more interactive from the management system to the managed resource. Patterns are differentiated by the flow of information and the placement of function.

1.7.1 Event Generator

The *Event Generator* pattern is applicable to resources whose processing contains events and metrics and whose service does not require operations or dynamic configuration control while executing. The resource contains instrumentation and sends management data via events to the management system. The events would represent failures, lifecycle changes, state changes, metric data, or configuration data changes. The resource would not support being invoked for operations or reconfiguration by the management system. It does not have to implement any facilities to listen for and respond to management requests or implement the generic API. This is the simplest and most basic way for a managed resource to interact with a management system.

1.7.2 Noninterruptible

In the *Noninterruptible* pattern, the managed resource contains instrumentation, and it sends events and publishes management information to a management system. Unlike the Event Generator pattern, in the Noninterruptible pattern the resource sends the management system a standard object, like an MBean, MIB object, or CIM object, that contains that resource's identity and metric information, as well as details of the current configuration. Notifications of changes to the managed object can be sent via events specified for that purpose or by the resending of the updated managed object to the management system.

This pattern is preferable to the Event Generator pattern when the management requires the data to be represented as a managed object or there is a great amount of potentially complex management data that may be frequently updated. When the management is not in real time, sending the entire managed object on a periodic basis rather than every time a value is updated *batches* the service's changes to the management system. It also allows a set of changes to be sent so that they are consistent with each other. This is better than sending a set of events, some of which may not arrive in order or at all, which would leave the management system's version of the managed object in an invalid or inconsistent state.

The Noninterruptible pattern should also be used when a particular management system requires the data in a particular format. The receiver of this information receives data already in the context of the managed object it understands. The resource does not support being invoked for operations or reconfiguration by the management system. It does not have to implement any facilities to listen for and respond to management requests, nor does it have to implement a particular API.

1.7.3 Queryable

The *Queryable* pattern is related to the Event Generator pattern in that the resource does not require configuration or operational control, but in this case the service sends events and implements an API that can be called by the management system. This is essentially *read-only* management because the managed resource supports being invoked by the management system to get current metric and configuration data, but not being controlled or altered. The management data may be represented as complex data types and objects.

Management systems typically retrieve the management data when they need it or poll for entire sets of related management data rather than one or two metrics. This approach works well for applications with a high rate of change of metric values or a number of complex metrics large enough that sending events to signal changes represents too much overhead. The managed resource implements facilities to listen for and respond to management requests and may implement the generic management API.

1.7.4 Operational

As in the Queryable pattern, in the *Operational* pattern the management system can retrieve configuration and metric data and get events from managed resources. However, in this pattern the management system can set configuration data and invoke operations on the managed resource. The managed resource implements facilities to listen for and respond to management requests and may implement the generic management API. In addition, the managed resource must be designed to allow for configuration changes during execution.

Figure 1.9 summarizes the essential characteristics of these four patterns. These patterns give increasing amounts of information and control over the resource to the management system. Any of the patterns may send events

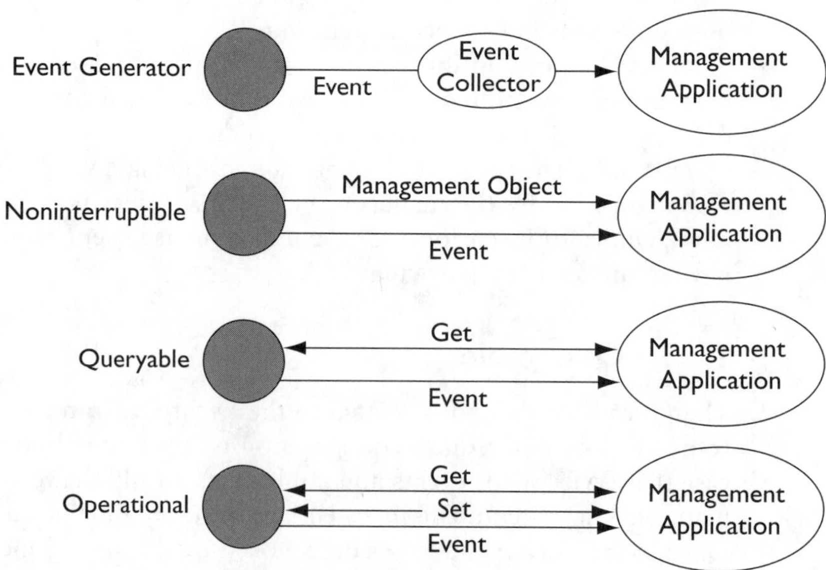

Figure 1.9 Management Patterns

directly to the management application or through an event collector. Both the Event Generator and the Noninterruptible patterns only send communications and do not implement any way for the management application to initiate communications with the resource. The Noninterruptible pattern sends a specific managed object and is much more dependent on a management application understanding that object. The Queryable and Operational patterns usually use a managed object as well. These two patterns must support two-way communications. They both require the implementation of a way for the management application to initiate communications with the resource. Only the Operational pattern allows the management system the ability to control the resource.

1.8 Management Applications

Management systems can be considered as a set of management applications. These management applications usually address one or more management disciplines. This section gives an overview some of the more common management applications.

1.8.1 Distribution Applications

Software distribution applications (Figure 1.10) address the transfer of the files that compose an application from a central software repository to target systems, both servers and clients, where they will be installed and used. Once these files have been transferred, the distribution application prompts the

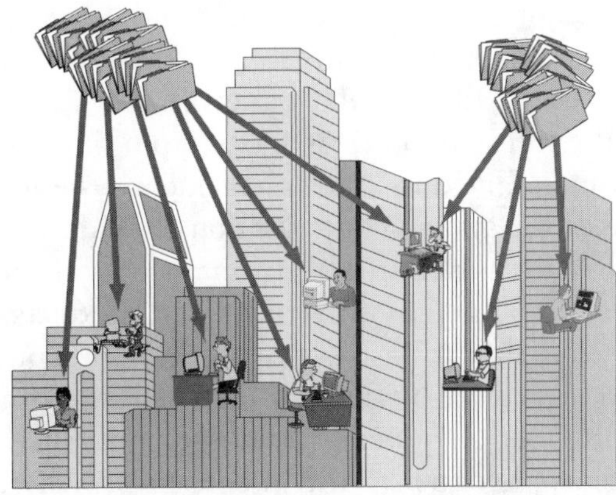

Figure 1.10 Software Distribution System

user for configuration information or distributes the initial configuration files as well. Then it checks that all the prerequisite software is already installed on each of the target systems. If there are missing prerequisites, a more advanced software distribution application will automatically distribute and install the prerequisites available to it. The software distribution application will then start the installation programs and scripts on the target systems.

Usually the distribution and installation are scheduled to run during "off-peak" (night) hours. Therefore, these systems should be able to run unattended from configuration files rather than requiring user interaction. Because the tasks for installing maintenance are similar to the tasks for initial installation of the software, most software distribution systems also provide support for distributing and installing maintenance for those applications. So you can see that software distribution applications support the distribution, installation, and maintenance phases of the management lifecycle.

Maintaining software on large numbers of systems in this manner allows professional systems administrators to take care of more systems than they could otherwise. Having administrators take care of systems relieves the laypeople or end users from having to understand and administer the system themselves along with their regular responsibilities. Professional administrators and help desks can count on a known set of product versions and configurations in their customers' systems. This consistency makes problem determination more predictable.

When existing products are upgraded or maintained, the entire product or set of files is usually replaced. This wholesale replacement maintains a consistent set of software across the enterprise. Central management of software upgrades reduces the chance that different systems will end up with different and incompatible versions of software.

The drawback of using software distribution management systems is that some of them remove control from the educated end user and do not accommodate the user with special needs. Some simpler distribution systems do not allow the end user to install additional products. A software distribution system may update all the software on the systems from time to time, and some or all of the files not maintained by the management system could be lost. In addition, some or all of the system configuration done during product installation may be lost. Finally, system problems may occur if there are resource conflicts between the distributed and user-installed products. These types of problems can be very difficult to resolve. Any customization or personalization of system or products done by the user may be lost during each update.

Some software distribution systems distribute only initial installations of products. These systems are easier to use in enterprises where the target systems may have different inventories of software on them. Such systems will move the files onto the target system and perhaps even run installation programs. However, customization and maintenance of the software are the responsibilities of the end user.

Software distribution products are available from a variety of vendors, including Tivoli, Marimba,[47] and Computer Associates.

1.8.2 Inventory Applications

Inventory management applications inspect and track the hardware and software resources available on all of the managed systems. For each resource, an inventory management application tries to keep a similar base of information: type, vendor, model, version, serial number, part number, owner, contact, and location. The more advanced inventory systems also discover and track changes in the inventories automatically. This process is easier if the inventory management application is well integrated with the software distribution or maintenance application. In this case whenever the software on the target systems is updated, the inventory management application is updated.

Inventory systems can also be coupled with resource discovery systems that find new resources on their own. Discovery systems poll the managed systems and network to verify and update the inventory data. For example, SNMP MIB-II provides a significant amount of information about the system, such as interfaces, TCP connections, UDP connections, ICMP connections,[48] and so on. The "Host Resources MIB" RFC[49] gives details about the installed software. The CIM models provide similar information.

An inventory management application usually maintains a database of this information that can be used by other management applications (like software distribution's prerequisite checking function) or by topology applications. Inventory management applications support the install, maintain, and monitor lifecycle phases.

The advantage of using an inventory management application is that it maintains a more accurate database of IT, systems, software, and maintenance resources than manually updated databases do. Besides being used to feed other management applications, this information can be used by business accounting systems for asset reporting, control, and depreciation. When warnings from vendors regarding flaws and fixes for their product are received, it is relatively simple to notify users within the company and schedule the appropriate corrective action. Knowing the age of the IT resources and scheduling the replacement of obsolete sources before they fail and are replaced in a panic can help us make predictions about expenses and capital.

The drawback of using these management applications is that all resources must be deployed by an application that automatically feeds the inventory application, or the resource information must be entered manually. Obsolete resources must be removed from the inventory manually. Manually entered information can quickly become inaccurate. Even in automatically updated installations, advanced users in an organization will circumvent controlled resource deployment and install their own hardware and software, causing more inaccuracy in the inventory.

1.8.3 Topology Applications

Topology management applications are the heart of most functionally complete management applications. Topology management applications, as illustrated in Figure 1.11, display the current status and relationships, both physical and logical, between managed systems and/or software components. Topology applications discover the current set of resources to be monitored and displayed. They can discover these resources from a configuration file,

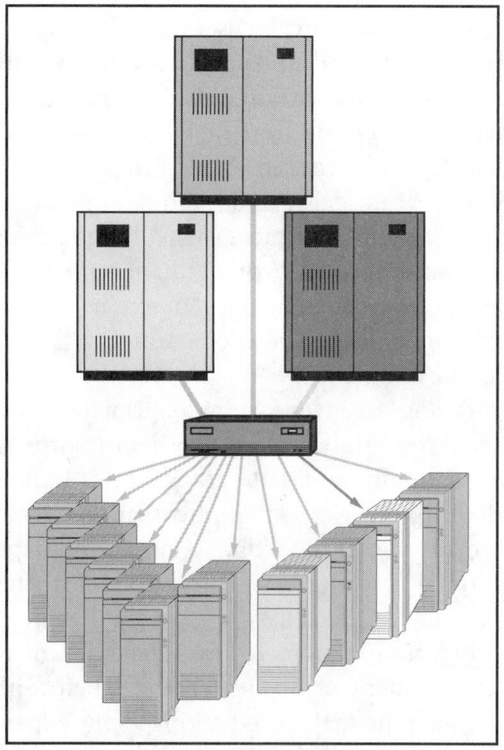

Figure 1.11 Topology Console

from an inventory management application, from queries to resources with knowledge about neighbors (gateways, routers, name servers, and so on), or from queries to the systems themselves.

Topology management applications allow administrators to define policy to or manually include or exclude resources for the displays. The display of the resources shows their name, type, relationship to other resources, and status. These applications should be able to provide different views of the resources by type, status, or relationships. Custom views and views defined by policies can be defined by the administrator.

Some topology management applications also support monitoring, operations, and configuration management. Most topology management applications contain or use monitoring management applications to get and maintain the status of the resources. Monitoring may be controlled by configuration files or policy. Ties to event management applications provide an additional asynchronous source of status information. The topology display is a convenient launch point to display and invoke available operations. It is also convenient to launch configuration displays from this screen.

Topology management applications support the monitor lifecycle phase as well. Monitoring applications can reflect any detected status changes in the topology management application. Using topology management applications that reflect status can help operations staff identify failing resources with a glance at the topology console. The effect of resource failures on the health of the infrastructure and the root causes of those failures can usually be determined faster. If operations are available, recovering those resources directly from the topology application can be the most efficient means to return the resource to a fully operational state.

The disadvantages of using topology management applications are similar to those of using an inventory management application. The topology is only as accurate as the resources it knows about and the status it can access. In addition, in a very large enterprise environment, the number of resources becomes unwieldy to represent on a single topology screen, and the screen is no longer meaningful, as shown in Figure 1.12.

Large enterprises may have to spend more time developing custom and policy-driven screens.

1.8.4 Configuration Applications

Configuration management applications support displaying the configuration of a resource. If the resource supports runtime reconfiguration or staged reconfiguration (loading a batch of configuration changes or a new configuration file and restarting the resource), then configuration management applications

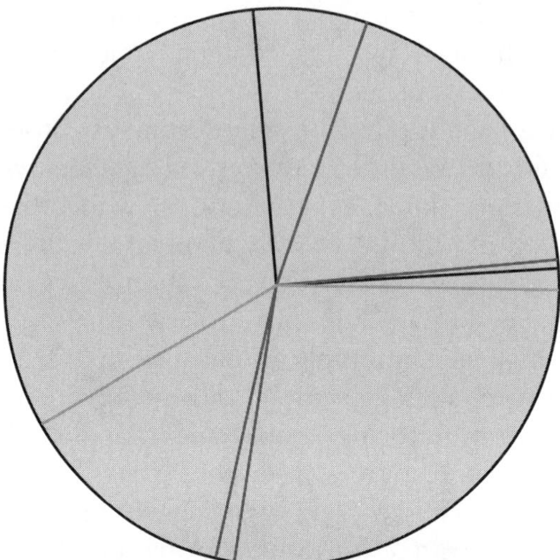

Figure 1.12 A Less-Than-Useful Topology Console. There Are So Many Resources That Each Resource Is Just a Shaded Line

can also support changing the configuration of a resource. Configurations may be changed automatically by policy or manually by an administrator. When configuration changes are applied, they should be validated against the state of the target system. This goes for dependent product configurations too. Side effects of the changes should be predicted and identified if possible. Configuration changes can be applied to a single resource or a group of resources. The group of target resources can be defined by the operator or by a policy.

Configuration management applications are often part of a topology management or an installation management application. Configuration management applications support the execute, configure, and operate phases of the management lifecycle.

Using configuration management applications can dramatically increase the number of systems that a single administrator can manage. This is the case not only because the configuration can be applied to large groups of resources at the same time, but also because it checks that the configuration change is valid before applying it, avoiding configuration problems. Using configuration management applications across the enterprise also helps ensure a consistent configuration of resources, making problem determination and tuning much easier. Configuration managers assign version numbers to the configurations they replace and install so that they can be used in problem determination on problems in deployment and upgrades. Having one centralized control over configuration of many distributed resources can simplify the administrator's job by eliminating the need for him to start and access multiple configuration utilities for each resource type or resource instance.

As with distribution management applications, the disadvantages of using configuration management applications is the freedom that they take from the users. If users customize their configuration at all, that customization may be lost or in conflict with centrally controlled configuration changes.

1.8.5 Operations Applications

Operations management systems provide a list of tasks or operations associated with each resource. Administrators can invoke these operations and see the responses. Operations may be simple or complex. *Simple operations* can usually be completed with one interaction with the resource. *Complex operations* invoke a series or set of operations, like a work flow or a script, on a resource or set of resources.

Different scopes of operations are available. *Singleton operations* are invoked for one resource. *Group operations* invoke the same operation on a set of similar resource types. *Cascaded operations* invoke the operation on a resource and all of its subresources or dependent resources.

A typical simple operation is "shutdown" or "stop." It is often invoked as a group and cascaded operation. A complex operation may be "failover," in which case in order to start executing a resource on a backup system after the primary system has failed, a series of operations must be executed successfully.

Operations management applications are often used in conjunction with distribution, installation, and automation management applications. Operations management applications support the start, execute, operate, and stop phases of the management lifecycle.

Like configuration management, operations management applications dramatically increase the number of resources an operator can be responsible for by supporting execution of an operation for an entire set of resources at the same time, as shown in Figure 1.13. Giving operators centralized control of resources saves them trying to find and keep track of an operations console for each resource type or instance. For operators responsible for many disparate resource types, operations management applications will simplify their lives by mapping their operations to some common operations.

1.8.6 Event and Automation Applications

Event management applications and automation management applications are nearly always delivered together.

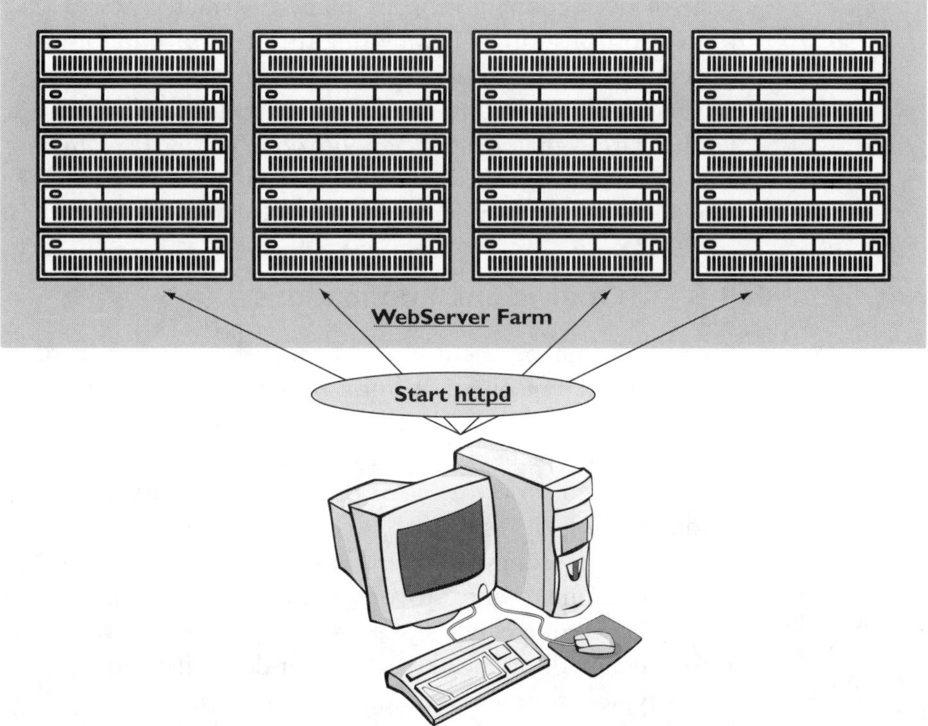

Figure 1.13 Sending a `Start` Operation to Large Numbers of Systems to Start a Web Server Farm

Event management applications receive, filter, categorize, and display events from resources to an administrator in near real time. The events may be forwarded to other management applications, such as an inventory management applications, topology management applications, or monitoring and performance management applications. Advanced event management applications correlate the events to filter duplicate events and determine the root cause of a failure. Event filters can be based on event types, severity, resource types, resource groups, or policy rules.

The events are also recorded in a log or database. These records are mined later by performance analysis, problem determination, and capacity planning applications.

Automation management applications detect conditions and perform response actions on the basis of predefined policies without administrator intervention, as illustrated in Figure 1.14. The conditions that are detected are called *triggers*. The most common trigger is an event. Other common

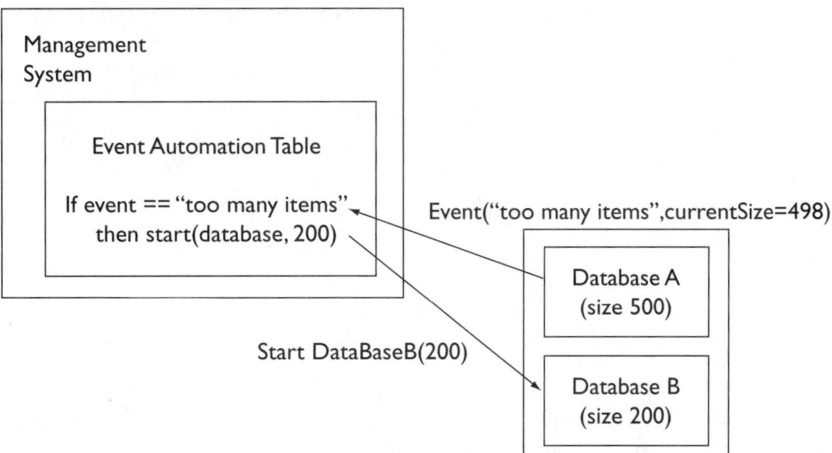

Figure 1.14 Event Automation: Expanding a Database When a Database Is Full

triggers are resource status changes, configuration changes, log updates, and monitored value changes (i.e., threshold exceptions).

Response actions can be to display or log the event, generate a new event, send the event to a new target, invoke an operation, or update the configuration. There can be multiple response actions.

Policies defined in the automation management application are generally based on rules. Simple rules may consist of simple comparisons and Boolean logic. Complex rules have multiple parts, may be order and time dependent, and may require program execution to provide values for parts of the rules.

Event and automation management applications are used by inventory, monitoring, and performance management applications. Event and automation management applications are used to support the execute, monitor, and maintain phases of the management lifecycle.

Using event and automation management applications can reduce the amount of problem determination and recovery that an operator has to do. Just having the events collected and displayed drastically reduces the amount of proactive monitoring of resource status that operators must do.

The only downside to using these management applications is that an operator needs to be tending to them or carrying a pager that the applications use to signal the operator so that critical events are seen and reacted to. Event and automation management applications need to be well customized and tuned. In a large enterprise without filtering, these applications can consume a fair amount of enterprise resource bandwidth.

1.8.7 Monitoring and Performance Applications

Monitoring and performance management applications monitor resources on a regular basis for the purpose of making sure the application is functional, catching problems before they become fatal, and gathering statistics for analysis. Monitoring can be used to provide availability tracking, health status, and events. Monitoring is usually done in a polling format, but passive, asynchronous event monitoring is also used.

Monitoring and performance applications may collect and use several types of management data. The collected data is usually logged or saved in a database for analysis later. Data processed after execution or a failure can be used to drive root cause analysis, capacity planning and management, trend identification, and usage reporting applications. The real-time management data can be used by management applications, such as topology, monitoring, and event managers, to determine availability, health, and events.

Availability management applications report when a resource is not available or responding. Resource availability in the eyes of the management application may be different from that experienced by users because the network status may be different between them and the resource. Availability may also be determined by support of `test` operations.

Performance and health status management applications report when resources are not performing within defined limits. They determine this by monitoring availability, as in Figure 1.15, and application statistics, or by running and measuring a resource `test` command that will exercise the critical resource functions that must perform well. Management applications can also test thresholds, analyze the quality of service guarantees, graph data, and identify trends of historical statistical data. The results of these activities indicate application health.

The monitoring and performance management application asynchronously receives or pulls events from the event management application or resource. An automation management application can be used to run recovery or tuning operations, to notify operators, to log, or to filter. Events indicating that the resource is healthy, rather than failing, are called *heartbeats*. Monitoring management applications should receive and accommodate heartbeats. Heartbeats should also drive status updates in related topology management applications. More sophisticated management systems may monitor application statistics to establish trend lines to guide tuning for optimal operational results over time.

Monitoring and performance management applications implement the monitor discipline and are used to support the execute and monitor phases of the management lifecycle.

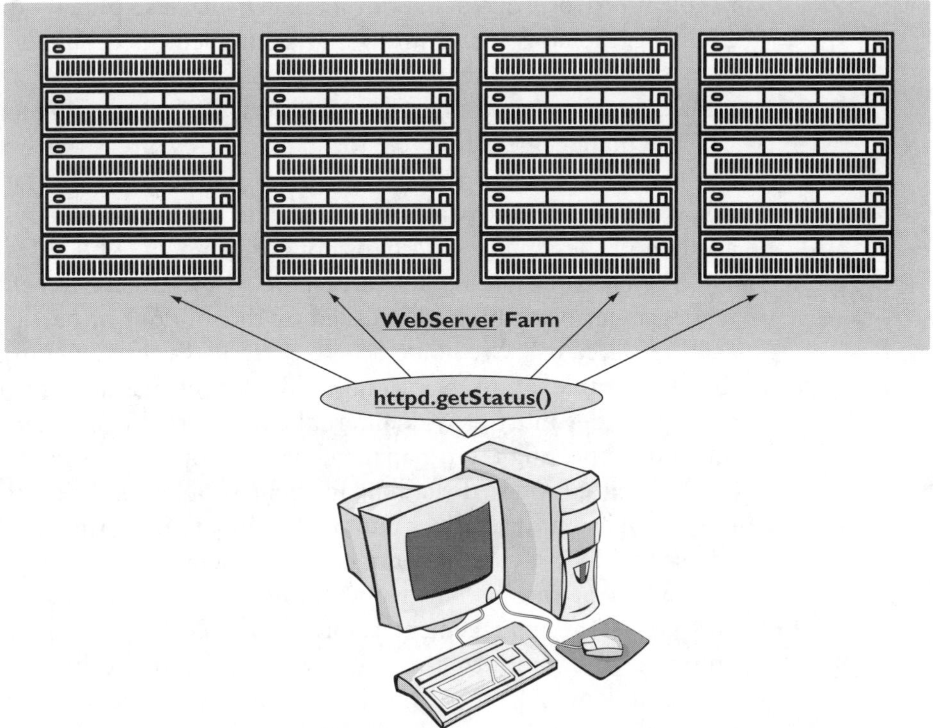

Figure 1.15 Performance Monitoring System for a Web Server Farm

Using monitoring and performance management applications can improve operator efficiency by removing the need to constantly survey resources. Performance management applications can warn operators early and allow them an opportunity to proactively tune resources, avoiding resource failure and outages.

Monitoring and performance management applications, like event and automation management applications, must be customized and tuned for large enterprises, or they may consume too much of the IT resources.

1.9 Summary

In this chapter we have introduced and defined the historical basis for today's application, network, and systems management solutions. We can see how the progression from centralized to distributed computing created the dominant management architecture—agent-manager. This progression created the problems to be solved by the management disciplines—distribute, install, configure, monitor, and control—that are implemented, supported, and deployed in today's management applications: distribution, inventory, topology, configuration, operations, event and automation, and monitoring and performance.

The management lifecycle for managed resources that we have defined is fairly pervasive across the IT industry: distribute, install, start, execute, monitor, configure, operate, stop, maintain, and uninstall. Some resources have only a subset of these phases, perhaps not requiring an explicit start or stop phase.

Managed resources can participate in their management in a variety of management patterns distinguished by the amount of participation the managed resource has. We named these patterns Event Generator, Noninterruptible, Queryable, and Operational. In order for managed resources to be well managed, they must provide internal and external instrumentation for exposing and supporting their management data, operations, and events.

Having considered the management problem in the large, let's establish the management disciplines and management applications in which JMX can be used. JMX provides a common set of metadata and APIs that can be used to implement internal instrumentation, generate external instrumentation, and access the management information. This consistent foundation helps automate and minimize the amount of system- or technology-specific definition that would have to be done to integrate the resource's management needs with an arbitrary management system.

Let's relate JMX to the topics we just discussed: management architectures, management lifecycle, management disciplines, management data, and management applications.

JMX can fulfill the requirements of the agent and subagent roles in management architectures. The MBeanServer is the agent, and MBeanServers can be cascaded into agent and subagent roles.

JMX is not best suited to help with the deploy, install, or maintain management lifecycle stages because it is a local management agent. It does not provide explicit support for system-to-system communication, moving files between systems, or version control.

JMX is best used to manage the management lifecycle from start to stop—start, execute, monitor, configure, operate, and stop—because it has explicit support for operations. It also has a presence in the runtime of your application and provides connectivity to control your application for system managers.

The same presence and connectivity also make JMX a natural to support the management disciplines of configure, operate, monitor, and control. JMX provides explicit support for access to management and configuration information through attributes on MBeans. JMX also provides support for local monitoring of MBean attributes via the monitoring service and by monitor MBeans.

JMX can be used to develop and support inventory, topology, configuration, monitoring and performance, or event and automation management applications. JMX's MBeanServer provides interfaces to list all MBeans that represent managed resources. The JMX relation service defines associations between MBeans that can be used to support topology applications. The notification support enables applications to send events to JMX, and JMX forwards them to event management and automation applications. Configuration, monitoring, and control applications are supported by JMX just like their respective disciplines: through MBean attributes and monitor MBeans.

The following chapters will explain the JMX technology and how it should be used to support and implement the management applications.

1.10 General References

Farrell, J., and H. Kreger, "Web Services Management Approaches," *IBM Systems Journal* 41:2 (June 2002), http://www.research.ibm.com/journal/sj/412/farrell.pdf.

Kreger, H., "Java Management Extensions for Application Management," *IBM Systems Journal* 40:1 (March 2001), http://www.research.ibm.com/journal/sj/401/kreger.pdf.

1.11 Notes

1. Source: "Java Management Extensions (JMX) Specification," JSR 3, http://www.jcp.org/jsr/detail/3.jsp, which was led by Sun Microsystems to create a management API for Java resources.

2. 3270 is the model of a line of user terminals made by IBM Corporation, Armonk, NY (http://www.ibm.com).

3. IBM Corporation, Armonk, NY (http://www.ibm.com).

4. Candle Corporation, 201 N. Douglas St., El Segundo, CA 90245 (http://www.candle.com).

5. Computer Associates International, Inc., One Computer Associates Plaza, Islandia, NY 11749 (http://www.cai.com).

6. For information about UNIX, see The Open Group's site at http://www.opengroup.org.

7. Solaris is Sun Microsystems' UNIX-based operating system. More information is available at http://www.sun.com/solaris.

8. Hewlett-Packard's UNIX-based operating system is called HP-UX. More information is available at http://www.hp.com/products1/unix/operating.

9. TCP/IP (Transmission Control Protocol/Internet Protocol) is an Internet protocol that has been defined as a standard by the Internet Engineering Task Force. Additional information is available at http://www.ietf.org.

10. Tivoli Systems Inc., 9442 Capital of Texas Highway North, Arboretum Plaza One, Austin, TX 78759 (http://www.tivoli.com). Tivoli is a trademark of Tivoli Systems in the United States, other countries, or both.

11. BMC Software, Inc., 2101 City West Blvd., Houston, TX 77042-2827 (http://www.bmc.com).

12. Java and all Java-based marks are trademarks or registered trademarks of Sun Microsystems, Inc., in the United States and other countries.

13. A daemon on a system is a long-running system process that is executing a program.

14. SNMP stands for Simple Network Management Protocol, which is an IETF standard. More information on SNMP is available at http://www.ietf.org.

15. CMIP stands for Common Management Information Protocol and is usually referred to in conjunction with CMIS (Common Management Information Services). This management standard was defined by OSI (Open Systems Interconnection) as an ISO (International Standards Organization) standard: ISO 9595/2 and 9596/2 (http://www.iso.ch). More information on CMIP/CMIS can be found at http://www.iso.ch.

16. CIM/WBEM stands for Common Information Model/Web-Based Enterprise Management. It is defined by the Distributed Management Task Force (DMTF). More information is available at http://www.dmtf.org.

17. SMUX stands for SNMP Multiplexing Protocol (IETF RFC 1227, http://www.ietf.org/rfc/rfc1227.txt?number=1227) and is used to allow an application to communicate with an SNMP agent for the purposes of satisfying a portion of the MIB. SMUX tends to predominate in UNIX systems.

18. The Distributed Program Interface (DPI) is designed for extending SNMP agents. It is predominant in IBM systems. Source: G. Carpenter and B. Wijnen, "SNMP-DPI: Simple Network Management Protocol Distributed Program

Interface," RFC 1228 (May 1991), http://www.ietf.org/rfc/rfc1228.txt?number=1228.

19. AgentX is a standard SNMP agent-to-subagent protocol, "Extensible SNMP Agent" specification from the IETF. Source: M. Daniele, B. Wijnen, M. Ellison, and D. Franciso (Eds.), "Agent Extensibility (AgentX) Protocol Version 1," RFC 2741 (January 2000), http://www.ietf.org/rfc/rfc2741.txt?number2741.

20. Information on IBM's WebSphere Administration Console is available at http://www.ibm.com/software/webservers/appserv. WebSphere is a trademark of IBM in the United States.

21. Information on IBM's System/390 series is available at http://www.s390.ibm.com. System/390 is a registered trademark of IBM in the United States.

22. Systems Management Server (SMS) is Microsoft's workstation management application. More information is available at http://www.microsoft.com/smsmgmt/default.asp?RLD=263. Microsoft, Windows, Windows NT, and the Windows logo are trademarks of Microsoft Corporation in the United States, other countries, or both.

23. See note 14.

24. More information is available at http://www.ietf.org.

25. Source: M. Rose and K. McCloghrie, "Structure and Identification of Management Information for TCP/IP-Based Internets," RFC 1065 (August 1988), http://www.ietf.org/rfc/rfc1065.txt?number=1065.

26. Source: M. Rose and K. McCloghrie, "Management Information Base for Network Management of TCP/IP-Based Internets," RFC 1066 (August 1988), http://www.ietf.org/rfc/rfc1066.txt?number=1066.

27. More information about Hewlett-Packard's OpenView is available at http://www.openview.hp.com?qt=OpenView, or from Hewlett-Packard, 3000 Hanover St., Palo Alto, CA 94304-1185.

28. Information about Tivoli NetView is available at http://www.tivoli.com/products/index/netview.

29. See note 15.

30. The URL for the International Standards Organization (ISO) is http://www.iso.ch.

31. OSI/TMN stands for Open System Interconnection/Telecommunication Management Network. OSI was defined as an ISO (International Standards Organization) standard: ISO ISO/IEC DIS 10165-1,2,3,4, 9595/2 and 9596/2 (http://www.iso.org).

32. Groupe Bull was the original company name for the representative. This company is now referred to as "Evidian, A Groupe Bull Company" (http://www.evidian.com).

33. The Distributed Management Task Force (DMTF) is a standards body that is responsible for DMI, CIM, and WBEM management standards. More information is available at http://www.dmtf.org.

34. See note 16.

35. See note 22.

36. WBEMsource, at http://www.wbemsource.org, is a group of open-source WBEM implementations sponsored by The Open Group. Implementations are available in Java and C++.

37. Pegasus is The Open Group's C++ implementation of the DMTF's WBEM and CIM operations specifications, and a CIMOM, for accessing CIM data through HTTP (http://www.opengroup.org/management, http://www.openpegasus.org).

38. JSR 48, "WBEM Services Specification," is Sun's Java implementation of the DMTF's WBEM and CIM operations specifications for accessing CIM data through HTTP. See http://www.jcp.org/jsr/detail/48.jsp.

39. JDMK stands for Java Dynamic Management Kit. JDMK 4.0 is available from Sun Microsystems, Inc., 901 San Antonio Rd., Palo Alto, CA 94303, http://java.sun.com/products/jdmk.

40. TMX4J is an implementation of the JMX specifiation from Tivoli Systems and is available for free on IBM's alphaWorks Web site: http://alphaworks.ibm.com.

41. Information about AIC is available at http://www.opengroup.org/management/aic.htm.

42. The Application Response Measurement (ARM) standard was developed by The Open Group, http://www.opengroup.org/management/arm.htm.

43. You can find more information about IBM WebSphere 4.0 at http://www.ibm.com/websphere. WebSphere is a trademark of IBM in the United States.

44. Tivoli's Application Management Specification is used to define the characteristics of a managed application.

45. MOF file stands for Managed Object Format file. This format is used to describe CIM information and is defined by the DMTF in the CIM specification. More information is available at http://www.dmtf.org/standards/cim_schema_v23.php.

46. Source: J. Farrell and H. Kreger, "Web Services Management Approaches," IBM Systems Journal 41: 2 (March 2002).

47. Marimba, Inc., 440 Clyde Ave., Mountain View, CA 94043. Additional information is available at http://www.marimba.com. Marimba is a trademark of Marimba, Inc., in the United States and other countries.

48. TCP stands for Transmission Control Protocol, UDP for User Datagram Protocol, and ICMP for Internet Control Message Protocol.

49. S. Waldbusser and P. Grillo. "Host Resources MIB," RFC 2790 (March 2000), http://www.ietf.org/rfc/rfc2790.txt?number=2790.

CHAPTER 2

Introduction to JMX[1]

The Java Management Extensions (JMX) specification[2] defines a Java optional package for J2SE[3] that provides a management architecture and API set that will allow any Java technology–based or accessible resource to be inherently manageable. By using JMX, you can manage Java technology resources. You can also use Java technology and JMX to manage resources that are already managed by other technologies, such as SNMP[4] and CIM/WBEM.[5]

JMX introduces a JavaBeans model for representing the manageability of resources. The core of JMX is the simple, yet sophisticated and extensible, management agent for your Java Virtual Machine (JVM) that can accommodate communication with private or acquired enterprise management systems. JMX also defines a set of services to help manage your resources. JMX is so easy to use and is so suited for the Java development paradigm that it is possible to make an application manageable in three to five lines of code.

Basically, JMX is to management systems what JDBC (Java Database Connectivity)[6] is to databases. JDBC allows applications to access arbitrary databases; JMX allows applications to be managed by arbitrary management systems. JMX is an isolation layer between the applications and arbitrary management systems. So why do we need this layer anyway?

2.1 Why We Need JMX

2.1.1 Choosing a Management Technology

As we saw in Chapter 1, many different management technologies are being used in different areas of the industry. CMIP[7] dominates the telephony management market. SNMP dominates the device and network management market. Because this book is about developing Java applications and systems, let's narrow our focus to those technologies used by Java-based resources. Most Java-based resources today will be part of applications.

Even though SNMP is supported by some applications and middleware, it is not widely used for application management. One of the most commonly cited reasons for this is that many application vendors and management vendors have felt that the granularity of security in SNMP is not sufficient to use it for configuration updates and sensitive information. Therefore SNMP is often seen as useful only for *read-only* management of more or less public data and events. SNMP also does not have a natural model for operations on managed resources. Operations must be represented as a settable attribute. Sometimes this can be a difficult representation to map. Dependencies and associations can also be difficult to represent in SNMP.

CIM defines a more natural way to represent management data and addresses some of the weaknesses just described. It has extensive models for systems and devices, but the application management models are still emerging. The fact remains that there is no dominant management technology for the management of applications.

This would not be such a big problem if there were a single, dominant management systems vendor. If that were the case, you could use the management technology chosen by that vendor. Unfortunately, life is not that simple. Today the enterprise and application management market is pretty evenly split between Tivoli Systems[8] and Computer Associates,[9] who use their own proprietary technology for their manager-agent infrastructure.

If you have to manage an application or resource that runs on only one operating system, or on one vendor's systems, then choosing a management technology can be guided (or dictated) by the preferences of that vendor. Microsoft's Windows,[10] IBM's AIX,[11] Sun's Solaris,[12] and Hewlett-Packard's HP-UX[13] each has its own management system. However, one of the great things about Java has been the ease in which applications can be ported to and supported on many different vendors' systems. This means that most Java-based applications run on many platforms. If you are developing managed software products, you may be pressured to support multiple management technologies and systems because every vendor will want you to make your Java resources manageable by its management system.

Just to add to the list of management technologies you need to support, customers may have installed enterprise management systems that they will want to use to manage your application. In fact, they may or may not buy your application, depending on whether or not it can be managed by their existing enterprise management software. Your customers cannot be expected to replace their existing enterprise management systems just to accommodate your application. If you supply your own management system, your customers may still not be happy. They may not want yet another management console to watch and understand just to manage your application. Adding another console mitigates the console consolidation benefits of their enterprise management systems.

If you are a developer or architect working for a vendor of cross-platform applications, you will find yourself between a rock and a hard place. The rock is that your marketplace may be demanding that your software be manageable. To appease that marketplace, the software will need support for multiple management technologies. The hard place is that the cost of developing support for one management technology is expensive. This cost includes the learning curve, design and development, and maintaining currency with those technologies as they continue to advance. The cost of developing support for multiple technologies may very well exceed the potential new sales. This makes the business case for creating manageable applications and systems very hard to maintain and contain.

As a result, the potential return on investment may not motivate you to instrument appropriately for manageability. In fact, you may choose to write your own application-specific management system to solve a particular problem quickly, and not implement it for any external management technology. You can see how this adds to the populations of unique, nonstandard management systems and unmanageable applications.

A single suite of uniform instrumentation for manageability, like JMX, makes it cost effective to develop new applications with management capability. You can use JMX to instrument your Java applications. You can also use JMX to provide access to the manageability capabilities of your non-Java applications via Java Native Interface (JNI) and wrappers. Because JMX is centered on an architecture for pluggable adapters that allow any management technology to manage your resources, you have the best of both worlds: instrumenting your application with one management technology, and being manageable by many different management systems.

2.1.2 Dealing with Diversity

One of the primary challenges in managing applications is their diversity. This diversity is also a challenge for developers! Applications today vary widely in purpose, size, architecture, and criticality. Very little is common across all application types. Application architecture trends are increasing the diversity rather than settling the industry on a few de facto standard approaches.

JMX can be used to enable management of a wide variety of application architectures. JMX allows you as a developer to build your skills on one management technology that you can then apply to lots of application projects, today and in the future. Using JMX to enable this variety of application types benefits management systems vendors as well. They can support JMX well and be able to manage a wide variety of applications. Some of the application types that JMX is suited for are centralized applications, distributed applications, Internet applications, e-business applications, and service-oriented applications.

2.1.2.1 *Centralized Applications*

Centralized applications, such as payroll and accounting, are backed by a database on a high-end server and usually accessed by a limited set of users, like a financial department. Managing centralized applications entails ensuring high availability and performance throughput because they can be a single point of failure. The clients of these distributed systems are usually other programs, which expect lightning-fast response times.

2.1.2.2 *Distributed Applications*

Distributed applications, such as mail systems, usually require groups of small and midrange server systems to be running at all times, and they are accessed throughout the enterprise. Managing distributed applications is often a scaling problem: Many, many servers must be managed (i.e., available, connected, and performing well), as well as the networks that connect them, in order to simply ensure the application is available to its users. Generally the clients require proprietary software, so client software distribution and configuration must be managed as well.

2.1.2.3 *Internet Applications*

The introduction of the intranet/Internet concept precipitated a new class of application that connects the end user to existing, traditional, centralized applications. The new application facilities range from Web-accessible corporate personnel directories to Web-based order-tracking systems that benefit customers and reduce order management costs. These types of applications make it easier to access corporate information inside traditional applications, and they reduce the number of personal contacts necessary. Managing Internet applications entails keeping several layers of applications available to each other and the network: Web servers, application servers, back ends. Browsers must be appropriately configured.

2.1.2.4 E-Business Applications

The next generation of autonomous, Web-based applications is rapidly being developed and deployed in the new business environment. These applications embody e-commerce in the form of catalogs, shopping, marketplaces, and auctions. The move of the supply chain to the Internet will drive the next set of critical, distributed business-based applications. These applications move the heart of the business—buying supplies and selling products—to the Internet. Managing e-business applications is challenging because applications may span enterprise boundaries and use unreliable protocols like HTTP.

2.1.2.5 Service-Oriented Applications

Service-based architectures are currently emerging where IT resources across the network appear, move, and disappear. Relationships between applications can be just-in-time and fleeting. Managing the dynamic topologies, dependencies, and availability of these applications in this environment will be difficult at best.

Each of these classes of applications has its own management challenges. However, all of these application types execute across multiple hosts, operating systems, and corporations. They incorporate existing traditional and emerging application models. They are no longer just client-server, they are now client-middleware-server. These new application types are business critical, creating the need for them to be uniformly controlled and managed by a business's existing management systems with the same diligence as traditional applications. JMX is flexible and extensible enough to be taken advantage of in all of these diverse types of application architecture.

2.1.3 Being Managed by Multiple Management Applications

As we discussed in Chapter 1, there are many different types of management applications: distribution, inventory, topology, configuration, operations, event, automation, monitoring, and performance. You will probably want your application to be managed by several of these. Without JMX, you might have to implement explicit support for each type of management application. If you're using JMX combined with JMX adapters, the same instrumentation can be used to support and interact with most or all of these applications.

2.1.4 Supporting Application-Specific Management Systems

Your application will need to be installed, configured, monitored, and maintained. This means that you must implement your own management system—that is, an application-specific management system—that supports these tasks. Otherwise, you will be dependent on a management system being available in your customer's environment. This dependency may limit sales if some of your customers have a different management system, or even no management system. Applications in the market today have their own proprietary instrumentations to communicate with their internal management systems, as well as instrumentation to connect to other management systems. We've seen how JMX can be used to interact with multiple management technologies and management applications. In the same vein, JMX can be used to drive an internal or application-specific management system, as well as an external management system.

2.2 Which Applications Should Be Manageable?

Not all Java applications and resources should be managed. Let's talk about some considerations for deciding whether or not you should enable your application to be managed by an external or third-party management system.

How extensive your application's manager is, and how well it is integrated with an enterprise management system, will depend on a number of different characteristics of your application. These include how critical your application is, how complex your application is, how scalable your application needs to be, what policy your corporation has on application management, and what your application's target market is.

2.2.1 Complex Applications

If your application has a very complex architecture or configuration, you may need a reasonably extensive and comprehensive management application. It doesn't necessarily need to be integrated with enterprise management systems, unless they are mission critical or if several of them might be executing simultaneously. J2EE application servers[14] are a good example of mission-critical, complex applications that must have their own managers and be integrated with an enterprise management system.

2.2.2 High-Volume Applications

If your application will have a great many simultaneously executing installations in an enterprise, it may require distributed management support. Such applications are also excellent candidates for integration with the enterprise management system because they will benefit from both software distribution and centralized configuration. Because there will be so many images, operations staff will need topologies with status indicators and event management systems to distill the management information into events they can take action on.

2.2.3 Mission-Critical Applications

If your application is mission critical, you are going to need availability and performance management. Your application may be mission critical if it is an integral part of a business-critical system, like a database, router, application server, or name server. Mission-critical applications may be singletons or one of many instances. Your mission-critical application will need to have its own manager and be very well integrated with the enterprise management system. It must have very good availability and performance monitoring, with status reflected in a topology application.

2.2.4 Corporate Applications

If your application is being developed for use in a specific organization, corporate policies may dictate the degree of management support that you need to develop for the application. If the application is being developed for an organization that has invested in an enterprise management system, certain business policies may govern which applications are supported by the enterprise management system, and how extensive that support must be.

2.2.5 Applications with Expectant Customers

If your application is being developed to sell, you must consider the needs and expectations of your target market. Some applications have a target customer base that expects application management. These customers may buy *only* manageable applications. For example, owners of mainframes will expect applications that execute on those mainframes to be integrated with the management systems on those mainframes. If you are developing an application intended to execute on a mainframe, you must plan on enabling it to be well managed by the appropriate management application. If a large percentage of your target market uses a particular enterprise management system, then your application should be supported by the same system. If your target market expects that one or more enterprise managers will support your application, you will want to be sure that your application satisfies those expectations.

To summarize, if your application has a large, diverse target market, you may be forced to support multiple management systems on multiple platforms. This diversity can lead to significant, perhaps unsupportable, development costs. Developing and maintaining support for any one of the standard or proprietary management technologies requires you to tackle a steep learning curve and commit to a significant development effort. JMX mitigates your investment in management during application development by allowing you to concentrate on supporting one management technology: JMX. Multiple enterprise management systems can interact with the JMX agent in order to manage your application.

2.3 The Goals of JMX

There has been incredible growth in the number of mission-critical Web-based and Java applications being developed. The Web applications bring new business to the enterprise. Java e-business applications actually conduct business transactions on the Web, including catalog and shopping cart applications. E-business applications that generate income for the enterprise become mission critical in a hurry. When these applications are not available or responding quickly, customers shop elsewhere and income is lost. Therefore, enterprises are demanding end-to-end application manageability for e-business applications. The manageability requirement applies to the device, system, network, middleware, and any other applications that the e-business applications depend on.

In order for Java applications to make this transition from "cool" Web applications to "critical" e-business applications, they must be well behaved, reliable, and manageable. These requirements, along with the need for end-to-end management of these applications, mean that customers and developers will demand that products be manageable out of the box. These products include application servers, distributed application infrastructures, component toolkits, and the applications themselves.

Ideally, development tools and environments would provide wizards and tools to make it easy to develop manageability along with the product. These tools need a standard, portable, flexible API in order to be able to generate or modify applications so that they are manageable.

JMX defines a set of APIs to address management of and through Java. Three main influencing forces on the success of JMX are (1) having a simple API for the developer, (2) ensuring enough information for management systems to manage the resource "generically," and (3) providing an architecture to support the management of diverse, dynamic applications. Figure 2.1 shows the relationship of the JMX MBeanServer to the resources it manages and the management systems it communicates with. The following paragraphs will explain further.

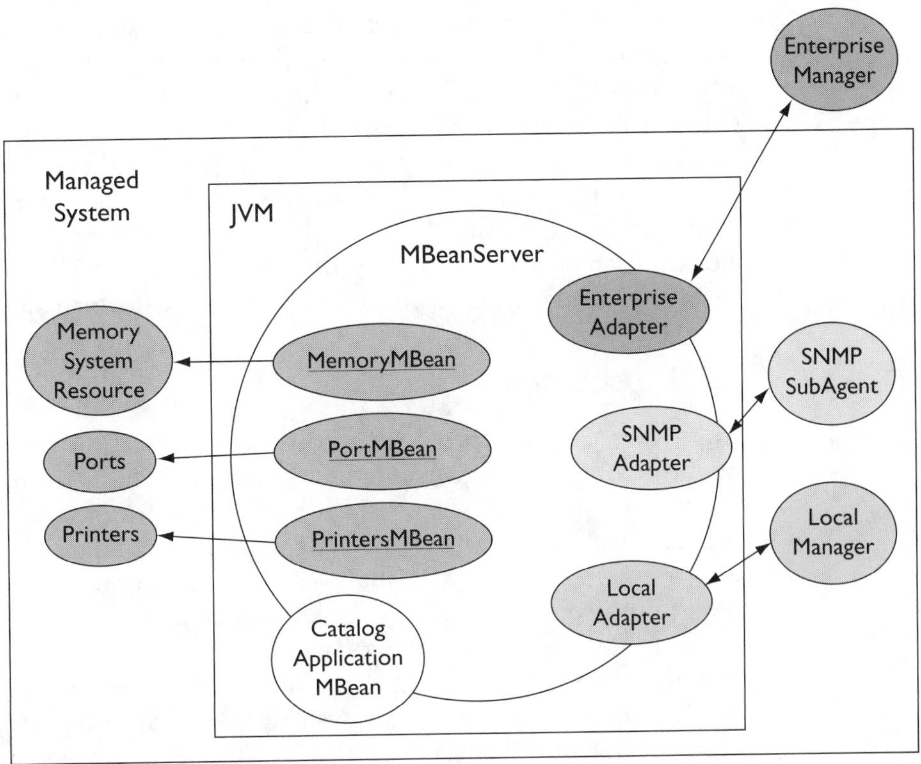

Figure 2.1 JMX Overview

2.3.1 Simple API

JMX provides a simple, straightforward management API for Java application developers. You can use this API to bring attributes, operations, and notifications to management systems from within your application. The API is easy to understand because it is similar to one you already know: JavaBeans. JMX uses Management Beans (MBeans) to represent the management interface for the managed resource (see Section 2.5.2). As you can see in Figure 2.1, the MBeans interact with the resources they manage: memory, ports, and printers. You can use your existing JavaBeans as MBeans, like the catalog MBean in Figure 2.1, or you can easily develop new ones as facades for your existing Java applications.

2.3.2 Dynamic Management

JMX provides a "management container" called an *MBeanServer.* The MBeanServer is a registry and a "traffic cop" in that it is always between the MBeans and their users. You can see this relationship in Figure 2.1. You can register your MBean with the MBeanServer at any time. You can also deregister your MBean at any time. Therefore, the MBeanServer represents an accurate inventory of all the resources to be managed. If resources are permanently removed from the system, you can remove them from JMX without reconfiguring or recycling the MBeanServer. JMX also provides for management services to be registered as MBeans. This means that additional functionality can be added or removed at any time. This flexibility makes JMX a dynamic and easily extensible architecture to use for management.

2.3.3 Isolation

The MBeanServer acts as the isolation or mediation layer between your application and management system vagaries, including protocols, behavior, platforms, and so on. The management system is encapsulated away from the managed resources by JMX adapters. JMX adapters, as seen in Figure 2.1, translate from the MBeanServer's MBeans to the management systems' native protocols and object models, and back again.

In fact, these adapters don't have to be provided by the management system; they could be developed by anyone. If the adapters communicate with a local management agent on the system, like an SNMP agent, then the management system will never "see" JMX. This means that the management system may not be aware if JMX is providing access to the manageability of your application.

2.3.4 Generic Management

Many current management systems require a custom module to be written for every application they are to manage. This module integrates the application's management into the management system. One of the goals of JMX was to provide sufficient information to the management systems so that management support could be generated or provided generically (i.e., without developers having to create custom integration modules for their applications for every management system). Ideally, the management system would provide a tool, along with its adapter, that would generate these integration modules if they were needed.

When information is being provided to management systems, either a management model or metadata must be supplied. JMX is a model-less management architecture; it deliberately does not define an information model or the structure of management information (SMI) like the IETF did for its Network Management Framework.[15] Instead, JMX provides metadata in `MBeanInfo` objects associated with every MBean. Management system adapters and tools can use the information in the `MBeanInfo` object to create integration modules or feed dynamic management architectures.

2.4 History

This section presents a historical perspective on JMX, covering the precursor specifications and products, Sun's JMAPI and JDMK, the JMX JSR and current specifications, compliance levels, and a review of some of the current implementations.

2.4.1 JMAPI

Java Management API (JMAPI) was an effort led by Sun. It was intended to arrest the proliferation of management platforms by developing a standard Java management platform infrastructure. There were two parts to JMAPI:[16] the Admin View Module and the Admin Runtime Module. The Admin View Module was an infrastructure to be used to build management consoles. The Admin Runtime Module was an API and infrastructure to be used to build management systems and applications. Most of the management system vendors were involved, including Tivoli and Computer Associates. An early implementation of this specification was developed and used by a few vendors. In late 1998 this work stalled. An "arms race" developed among the vendors to get their management agents on the most systems. JMAPI was not focused on helping developers make their resources manageable. But that is precisely where JMX is focused.

2.4.2 JDMK

Java Dynamic Management Kit (JDMK) 2.0[17] was a Sun product that was the precursor to JMX and provided the starting point for the JMX specification. Today it is Sun's product version of JMX. The JMX Reference Implementation is independently licensed and contains quite a bit of additional functionality that is not in the specification. It contains a remote JMX manager, tools to support the creation of MBeans from SNMP MIBs, and Java SNMP manager APIs.

2.4.3 JMX

Sun opened JSR 3[18] in December 1998 using its then brand-new Java Community Process.[19] JMX's initial name was Java Management API (JMAPI) 2.0, although it had no relationship to the first JMAPI's goals, APIs, or implementation (see Section 2.4.1). The first action of the JMX Expert Group was to change the name to Java Management Extensions to eliminate confusion between JMX and JMAPI.

The expert group consisted of Sun, IBM/Tivoli, Computer Associates, Groupe Bull (Evidian),[20] TIBCO,[21] and Powerware.[22] Eventually Borland,[23] Motorola,[24] BEA,[25] IONA,[26] Lutris,[27] and JBoss[28] also joined, as it became obvious that this new technology could be very relevant to J2EE application servers. The interesting thing about this expert group was its cross-industry mix. Not only were enterprise management system vendors represented, but so were telecommunications device and system vendors, as well as application server vendors. This diversity created a very important balance in interests and a willingness to focus on the needs of the Java resource developer rather than the management system.

The initial specification contribution from Sun was based on its Java Dynamic Management Kit (JDMK) 3.0[29] product, which was gaining some following in the telecommunications industry. Sun intended the next release of JDMK (4.0)[30] to be the first JMX-compliant product.

The JMX mailing list is jmx-forum@java.sun.com, and the Web site is http://java.sun.com/products/JavaManagement. The JMX Reference Implementation and Technology Compatibility Kit (TCK) are available from Sun Microsystems through this same site.

Sun was the specification lead and is now the maintenance lead. Here are some of the JSRs that pertain to JMX:

- **JMX 1.5.**[31] JSR 160: "Java Management Extensions (JMX) Remoting 1.2" (http://www.jcp.org/jsr/detail/160.jsp), led by Sun Microsystems. This specification extends the JMX 1.0 specification by adding distributed capabilities to support remote JMX managers, remote MBeans, and JMX agent discovery. At the time of this writing, this expert group is actively working on a new specification that should be available in 2002.
- **JMX and CIM/WBEM.**[32] JSR 146: "WBEM Services: JMX Provider Protocol Adapter" (http://www.jcp.org/jsr/detail/146.jsp), led by Sun Microsystems. This specification defines how JMX instrumentation can be mapped to CIM and provides the definition of a JMX provider protocol adapter for WBEM Services. This JSR provides a bridge from JMX into WBEM though a JMX adapter. Although an expert group has formed, little progress is being made on this specification and there are currently no reliable availability dates.
- **JMX and TMN.**[33] JSR 71: "JMX-TMN Specification" (http://www.jcp.org/jsr/detail/071.jsp), led by Evidian. This specification specifies interoperability between the Telecommunication Management Network (TMN) standards and JMX. This JSR defines bidirectional integration between JMX and TMN. In the end, a JMX-manageable application would be manageable by a TMN manager or agent. Likewise, a JMX manager would be able to manage a TMN environment. This JSR was withdrawn in June 2001.
- **JMX and IIOP.**[34] JSR 70: "IIOP Protocol Adapter for JMX Specification" (http://www.jcp.org/jsr/detail/070.jsp), led by IONA. This specification will establish an IIOP-based[35] adapter for the JMX agent, to allow CORBA[36] clients to access JMX agents. This specification will allow non-Java environments, such as CORBA applications, access to JMX information using IIOP. This expert group has been formed; however, when a specification and reference implementation will be available is unknown.
- **JMX and SNMP.** A JSR for an adapter from JMX to SNMP agents was discussed frequently within the JMX Expert Group, but the JSR was never opened. There is quite a bit of SNMP support available in the JMX Reference Implementation, and from products such as Sun's JDMK and AdventNet.

Figure 2.2 shows how the adapters being defined by these JSRs are related to the JMX MBeanServer and the original management systems. The Mof2MBean and MIBGen tools take other definitions of management objects (for CIM and SNMP, respectively) and generate JMX MBeans to match them. The data going over the network is in the native management system's format.

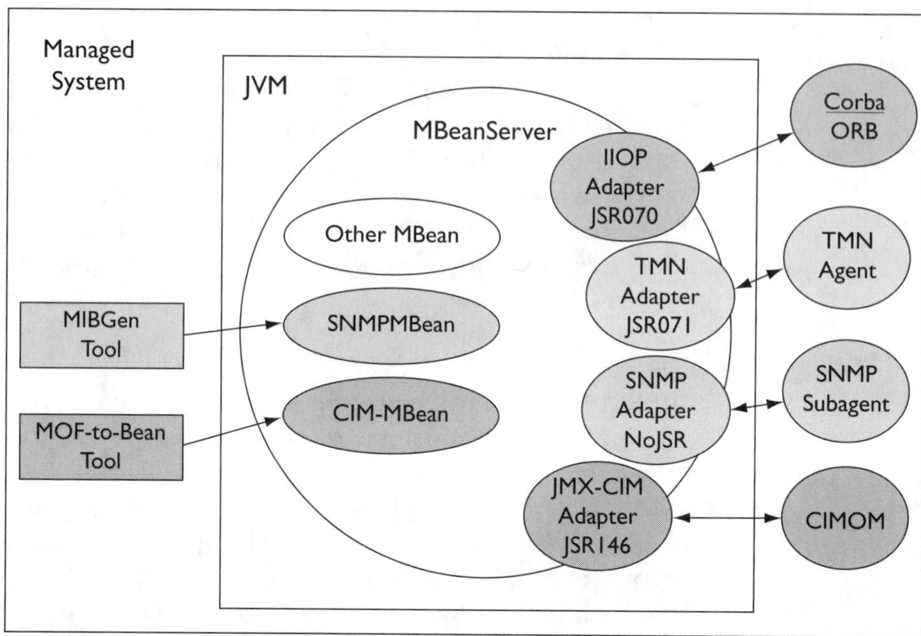

Figure 2.2 JSR Adapters

Other JSRs use or reference JMX as well, including the Java Integrated Networks (JAIN) JSRs and "J2EE Management" (JSR 77).[37]

2.4.4 The Specification and Compliance

The final *Java Management Extensions (JMX) v1.0 Specification* is available from http://jcp.org/aboutJava/communityprocess/final/jsr003. This specification was narrowed to define only the agent and instrumentation layers. The JMX 1.1 maintenance release specification and reference implementation are available at http://java.sun.com/products/JavaManagement. This release fixed specification ambiguities and reference implementation problems. Future versions of the specification (hopefully JMX 1.5) will address the distributed management layers.

The agent layer defines the MBeanServer and service MBeans that cooperate to implement the agent role in the manager-agent architecture. The instrumentation layer consists of the MBeans that are used by resources to expose their manageability.

The manager layer in the original JMX specification included Java APIs for communicating with agents and managers that are based on existing management technologies. These APIs do not communicate with JMX MBeanServers directly. In order for these APIs to communicate with an MBeanServer, an adapter to communicate with the native management technology would need to be loaded. For example, if you had an MBean you wanted to access using the Java SNMP manager APIs, you would communicate with an SNMP agent, which would communicate with an SNMP subagent that is also a JMX adapter, which would communicate with the MBean. This chain of communication is illustrated in Figure 2.2. The JMX Expert Group considered three Java APIs for managers, the Java API for interacting with SNMP agents, the Java API for interacting with a CIMOM using WBEM, and the Java API for interacting using TMN managers.

Some of these "manager APIs" in the original specification were spun off into separate JSRs so that they would have their own specification and reference implementation because they had no direct dependency on the JMX agent or MBeanServer. Figure 2.3 shows the relationship of these manager

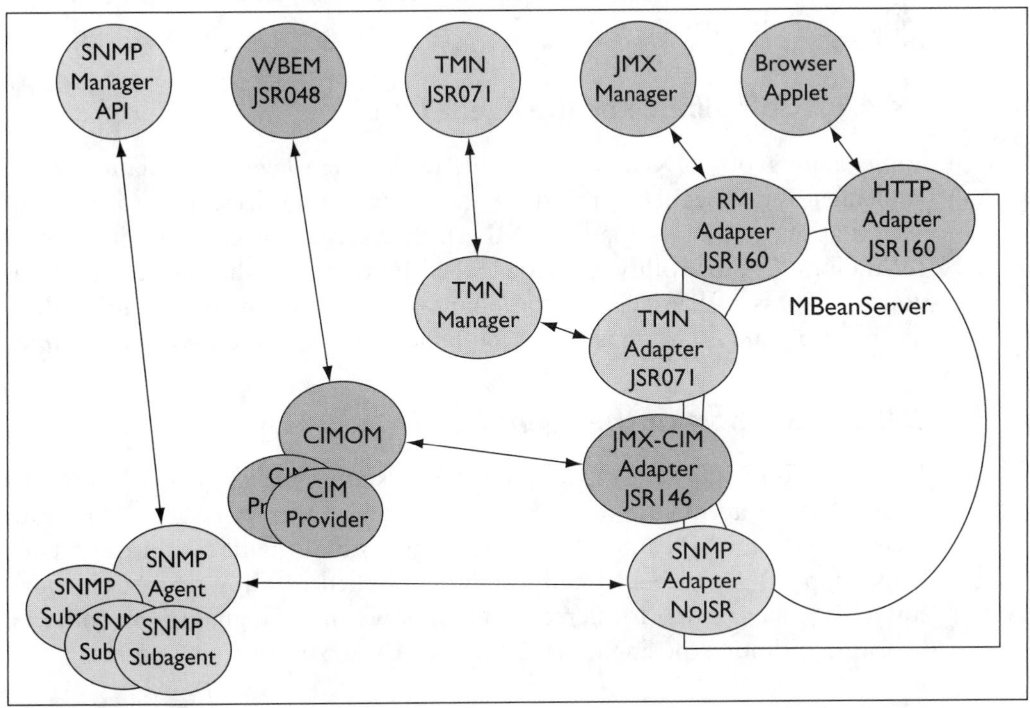

Figure 2.3 Manager-Level API JMX JSRs

JSRs to the MBeanServer. The JMX Java APIs for WBEM specification and libraries became JSR 146.[38] The JMX Java APIs for TMN became JSR 71.[39] The JMX Java APIs for SNMP are not associated with a JSR. However, JDMK does ship the SNMP Manager Java APIs.

JMX *compatibility* is defined to be an implementation of some or all of the JMX 1.0 specification that has not passed Sun's JMX TCK test suite. JMX *compliance* is defined in levels. These levels are defined in terms of what parts of JMX are supported. We will cover these terms and components in depth throughout this book, so if you are new to JMX, this section will make more sense when you revisit it.

2.4.4.1 Compliance at the Instrumentation Level

Resources and applications that want to be managed through JMX and claim JMX compliance must implement an MBean and provide for its registration with an MBeanServer. The application can provide any of the four types of MBeans: standard MBean, dynamic MBean, open MBean, or model MBean.

The JMX Technology Compatibility Kit (TCK) does not test for accurate compliance of MBeans. But the JMX Reference Implementation does come with an MBean verifier.

2.4.4.2 Compliance at the Agent Level

Implementers of JMX agents can be JMX agent-level compliant if they implement the MBeanServer and the four required services: monitoring, timing, relation, and class loading (MLet). There is a formal compliance test Technology Compatibility Kit from Sun Microsystems that an implementation must pass to be declared compliant. If you implement the entire JMX specification and do not pass the compliance tests, you are JMX *compatible*.

2.4.4.3 Support at the Agent Level

There is also the concept of providing JMX support at the agent level. This means that the agent supports managing resources through MBeans, but not necessarily as an MBeanServer. There is no formal qualification or test for JMX support. This level of support was specified to allow existing proprietary product agents to detect and support new management objects, MBeans, without exposing their agents as MBeanServers to adapters.

2.4.4.4 Compliance at the Distributed Services Level

This level of JMX has not yet been defined. The recently opened JSR "Java Management Extensions (JMX) Remoting 1.2" (JSR 160) is considering defining this level. The distributed services level would define how JMX agents work cooperatively across a distributed network, as well as how a manager would discover and interact with groups of agents and cascaded agents.

2.4.4.5 Compliance at the Management Level

JMX was intended to be an umbrella JSR and include a set of manager-side management APIs. The previous three levels describe JMX for instrumentation and management. The management APIs define Java APIs for management of other existing management technologies using Java. Currently Java APIs are being defined for SNMP, WBEM, and TMN. These Java APIs will be defined in other JSRs.

2.4.5 The Reference Implementation

Version 1.0 of the JMX Reference Implementation from Sun Microsystems was released in December 2000. The reference implementation source code[41] is licensed under the Sun Community Source License (SCSL).[41] The binary version of the reference implementation is available for free. The JMX Technology Compatibility Kit (TCK)[42] must be purchased from Sun, and the price can be substantial. Vendors who implement the JMX agent specification must purchase and pass the TCK in order to claim JMX compliance.

JMX 1.1, a maintenance release, is available from the same Web site. For more information and access to the source or binary versions of the reference implementation, see http://java.sun.com/products/JavaManagement.

Sun also provides a Web site called the JMXperience at http://java.sun.com/products/JavaManagement/JMXperience.html, where Sun and other vendors can contribute interesting tools, MBeans, and components for JMX. Sun has contributed a remoting component that provides a remote MBeanServer for use by JMX clients (usually JMX managers) and an Mof2MBean tool that generates MBean skeletons from CIM MOF (Managed Object Format) files.

The appendix of this book lists a short summary of some of the JMX agent implementation vendors, including Sun's JDMK, Tivoli's TMX4J, AdventNet's Agent ToolKit, and MX4J. The appendix also lists JMX manager vendors, including those from Tivoli, Dirig Software, AdventNet, and

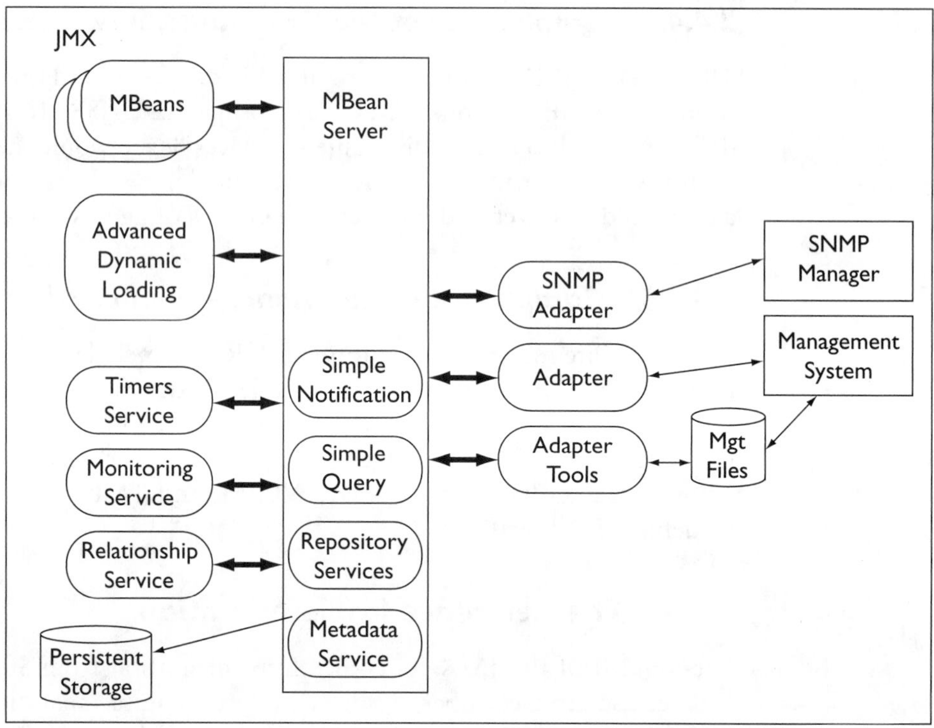

Figure 2.4 JMX Architecture

Jamie. In addition, the appendix lists some of the JMX manageable products, including WebSphere, WebLogic, iPortal, JBoss, SonicXQ, hawkEye, and Pramati Server.

2.5 JMX Overview

In its instrumentation and agent specification, the JMX architecture consists of four components (see Figure 2.4) that map to the management system components discussed earlier:

1. **Managed resources and management beans** (**MBeans**) that expose the management interfaces that make up the instrumentation level.
2. **Agents**, including MBeanServers and the monitoring, timing, relation, and class-loading services, that constitute the agent level.
3. **Adapters** that translate between JMX capabilities and APIs, and between their respective management systems.

4. **Adapter tools** that generate the files required by the management system through JMX APIs. Examples of these file types are Tivoli's AMS file,[43] SNMP's MIB file,[44] and CIM's MOF file.[45]

   Let's take a closer look at each of these elements.

2.5.1 JMX-Managed Resources

JMX-managed resources are instrumented with management beans (MBeans). You, the application developer, use MBeans to expose the management interface of the managed resource. The management interface of a resource consists of the attributes, operations, and notifications that are used to manage it.

2.5.2 MBeans

JMX specifies four types of MBeans: standard MBean, dynamic MBean, open MBean, and model MBean. Each MBean has metadata in `MBeanInfo`. `MBeanInfo` defines the attributes, operations, and notifications supported by the MBean.

2.5.2.1 *Standard MBeans*

A *standard MBean* can be any JavaBean or JavaBean-style program that has been registered with the MBeanServer. You, the application developer, define these MBeans and their management interfaces at development time. The only requirement is that your MBean class must implement a Java interface named `classnameMBean` that you must define for them. For example, an MBean class named `CatalogManager` would implement an interface called `CatalogManagerMBean`. This interface defines the management interface for the MBean. The interface might include all or just a subset of the methods in the actual MBean class.

When your MBean is registered with the MBeanServer, the MBeanServer will create an `MBeanInfo` metadata object for it by introspecting the `classnameMBean` interface. It will create attributes and operations in the MBean by looking for the JavaBean pattern. Each `getAttributeName()` method with a matching `setAttributeName(attributeValue)` method will create an attribute for the MBean. All other public methods will create operations for the MBean. The MBeanServer will use `MBeanInfo` to make sure only the attributes and operations you have exposed are invoked on your MBean.

Standard MBeans can be useful if your application already has management-oriented classes to support its own manager. You can simply register these instances with the MBeanServer after minor modifications to add "implements MBean." Chapter 3 explains standard MBeans thoroughly.

2.5.2.2 Dynamic MBeans

Dynamic MBeans allow your application or domain-specific manager to define or generate the management interface for your resource at runtime. This provides a simple way for you to wrap existing nonbean-style or even non-Java resources.

A dynamic MBean can be any Java class that implements the dynamic MBean interface. The dynamic MBean interface is similar to the CORBA Dynamic Invocation Interface (DII).[46] The most important thing to remember about dynamic MBeans is that they must provide their own management interfaces during runtime by maintaining their own `MBeanInfo` objects. The MBeanServer requests `MBeanInfo` from your dynamic MBean whenever it needs that information. This means that a `classnameMBean` interface is not used by the MBeanServer to create an `MBeanInfo` object. Your dynamic MBean is also responsible for implementing and validating correct invocation of the interfaces it defines in `MBeanInfo`. The MBeanServer delegates invocations of `getAttribute()`, `setAttribute()`, and `invoke()` directly to your dynamic MBean. Your dynamic MBean satisfies the request and returns it to the MBeanServer.

You can develop dynamic MBean implementations for your applications directly, have them generated, or allow a management application developer to create them. You can also develop an MBean service that will instantiate or generate the dynamic MBeans.

The next two types of MBeans we will look at are standardized types of dynamic MBeans: open MBeans and model MBeans. However, the fact that JMX defines standard types of dynamic MBeans does not mean that you cannot write your own dynamic MBeans, nor does it in any way restrict how you implement them. See Chapter 3 for a more detailed discussion of diagnostic MBeans.

2.5.2.3 Open MBeans

Open MBeans are dynamic MBeans that are restricted to accepting and returning a limited number of data types. If you use open MBeans and these basic data types, you eliminate the need for class loading. Removing the need for class loading can make it easier for you to deploy the MBean and support a highly distributed system. However, it does not remove the need for your application or a management application to understand the semantics of the data to be passed or returned. The open Mbean data types that are allowed are

- **Primitive data types:** `int`, `boolean`, `float`, `double`, and so on

- **Class wrappers for primitive data types:** `Integer`, `Boolean`, `Float`, `Double`, `String`, and so on
- **Table:** An array of rows of the same type
- **Composite:** An object that can be decomposed into other open data types

Your open MBeans must return an `OpenMBeanInfo` object from the `getMBeanInfo()` method. `OpenMBeanInfo` extends `MBeanInfo`, adding some additional metadata that you may supply, such as legal values, and default values. The open MBean support is optional in JMX 1.0, and the classes are not available in the current Sun JMX 1.0 Reference Implementation. See Chapter 3 for an explanation of open MBeans.

2.5.2.4 Model MBeans

A *model MBean* is an extension of a dynamic MBean. However, where you *must* write all of a dynamic MBean, you don't have to implement the model MBean. A model MBean is more than a set of interfaces; it is a customizable, standardized, dynamic MBean implementation. An implementation class of a model MBean named `RequiredModelMBean` must come with the JMX agent. This model MBean instance is immediately useful because your application can instantiate and customize a `RequiredModelMBean` instance with its own management interface information. This reuse of an existing implementation drastically reduces the amount of code you need to write to achieve manageability, and it protects your resource from JVM version and JMX agent implementation variances. Using `RequiredModelMBean` instances can allow your managed resources to be installed in a range of JVMs, from embedded environments to enterprise environments, without affecting your instrumentation.

The MBeanServer functions as a factory and delegator for `RequiredModelMBean` instances. Because `RequiredModelMBean` instances are created and maintained by the JMX agent, the `RequiredModelMBean` class implementation can vary, depending on the needs of the environment and the JVM in which the JMX agent is installed. An application that requests the instantiation of a `RequiredModelMBean` object does not have to be aware of the implementation specifics of a `RequiredModelMBean` class. The `RequiredModelMbean` class is responsible for implementing and managing the implementation differences between JMX and JVM environments internally. These differences may include persistence, transactional behavior, caching, performance requirements, location transparency, and remotability.

Because the `RequiredModelMBean` model MBean implementation is provided by the JMX agent, your application does not have to implement `RequiredModelMBean`; it just needs to instantiate it, customize it, and use it.

Your instrumentation code is consistent and minimal. Your application gains the benefit of support for and default policies concerning logging events, data persistence, data caching, and notification handling. Your application initializes its `RequiredModelMBean`'s `ModelMBeanInfo` with its identity, management interface, and policy overrides.

You can add custom attributes to the model MBean during execution. Your application-specific information can be modified without interruption during runtime. The `RequiredModelMBean` instance then sets the behavior interface for the MBean and does any setup necessary for event logging and handling, data persistence and currency, and monitoring for your application's model MBean instance. The model MBean default behavior and simple APIs will satisfy the management needs of most applications, but they will also allow complex application management scenarios. More details on the model MBean are given in Chapter 4.

2.5.3 JMX Agents

Your managed resources will communicate data and events to management systems with their MBeans through the JMX agent. JMX agents consist of an MBeanServer and a set of service MBeans.

2.5.3.1 The MBeanServer

The MBeanServer runs in the JVM local to the managed resources' MBeans. The MBeanServer is a registry for MBeans. It is also a repository of the current set of MBean names and references, but it is not necessarily a repository for your MBeans. The MBeanServer provides a query service for the MBeans. Upon a query, it returns the names of the MBeans, not the references. Because only names are returned, all operations on all MBeans must go through the MBeanServer. The MBeanServer acts as a delegator to the MBeans, returning the results to the requester.

The MBeanServer can be a factory for any MBean, even those you create. You have the option of instantiating MBeans directly and then registering them, or having the MBeanServer return an instance of the MBean to your application. The MBeanServer should always be a factory for `RequiredModelMBean` instances. The MBeanServer also provides access to the metadata about the MBeans in the `MBeanInfo` instance. The metadata includes the attributes, operations, and notifications provided by the MBean. The MBeanServer provides notification registration and forwarding support to MBeans representing adapters, services, and resources. The MBeanServer is discussed thoroughly in Chapter 5.

2.5.3.2 Required Services

The JMX agent includes a set of required services: the monitoring service, the timer service, the relation service, and the MBean class loader. Services are MBeans registered with the MBeanServer that provide some generic functionality that can be used by MBeanServers, MBeans, and adapters. Additional management services can be added dynamically as service MBeans by applications or management systems, making the JMX agent flexible and extensible.

- The **monitoring service** runs monitoring MBeans on a scheduled basis. It must support basic monitoring MBeans, including `Gauge`, `Counter`, `StringMatch`, and `StateChange`. Additional or specialized monitoring MBeans can also be developed and used.
- The **timer service** executes an operation on a timed basis. It is used by the monitoring service.
- The **relation service** supports relationship MBeans. Relationship MBeans contain the names of a set of MBeans that are related in some way. Some kinds of possible relationships include "contains" and "depends on."
- The MLet (management applet) service is an **MBean class-loading service** that loads an MBean across a network when an `MLET` tag in an HTML page is encountered.

These services are covered in more detail in Chapter 7.

2.5.4 JMX Adapters

Adapters communicate between the JMX agent and their corresponding management systems. The adapter is responsible for translating from JMX MBean types to its manager's types and taking care of any remoteness issues. Because the adapter can be implemented to mimic the manager's supported agent technology, the management system may not even be aware that JMX is in the picture. Generally, there is at least one specific adapter for each management protocol or technology required to support different management systems.

Adapters are also MBeans, and they are registered with the MBeanServer. Given that this is the case, it is possible to find out all of the adapters that are currently registered with an MBeanServer. Because adapters are MBeans, they can register for JMX notifications from the MBeanServer or other MBeans. In this case the adapter would have to implement the `NotificationListener` interface, and it might provide a filter to limit the notifications it receives.

Because the MBeanServer returns only names of MBeans and not instances, adapters invoke methods on MBeans only through the MBeanServer. The type of MBean that represents the resource does not affect how the adapter invokes operations on the MBean. The type of MBean does affect how much data is available to the adapter in `MBeanInfo`. Adapters use the MBeanServer's interface directly. Adapters are responsible for "translating" JMX management information to their native representation of the management information, so JMX provides some hints on how to do that translation using `ProtocolMap` instances for attributes in model MBeans. Common, though nonstandard, adapters are RMI,[47] HTTP,[48] and SNMP.[49] CIM and IIOP adapters are in the process of standardization. Adapters are discussed in depth in Chapter 5.

2.5.5 Adapter Tools

Adapter tools typically accompany a particular adapter for a particular management system. Adapter tools will interact with the MBeanServer to create any files to represent the available management data in the MBeans in a format that the management system can consume. For example, an SNMP adapter tool might create a MIB file from the available `MBeanInfo` instance. This MIB file would be used by an SNMP management system to represent the management data on its console.

2.6 Quick Tour of JMX

The easiest way to understand JMX is with a simple but thorough example. This example uses Tivoli's TMX4J JMX implementation, but the code should be identical regardless of who the JMX vendor is. The remainder of this chapter is dedicated to demonstrating the major features of JMX—MBeans, the MBeanServer, monitors, and notifications—via the design and implementation of a simple manageable server application.[1]

2.6.1 todd, the Time of Day Daemon

todd is a simple daemon that does a simple job. It accepts client connections and sends them the current date and time whenever they ask for it. Figure 2.5 shows todd's static structure.

Three classes form todd's core: `Server`, `Listener`, and `Session`. The `Server` class is responsible for starting a listener and assigning sessions to

---

1. Please note that whenever you see ". . ." there is code missing for illustrative purposes. Complete code examples are available at http://www.awprofessional.com/titles/0672374083.

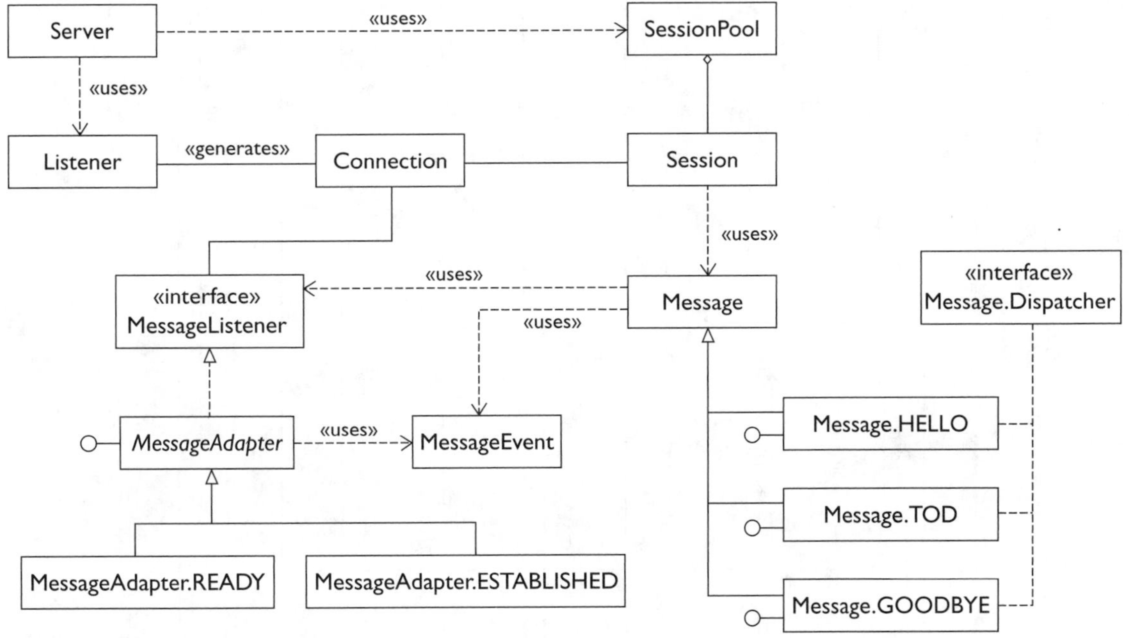

Figure 2.5 Class Structure of the Unmanaged Time of Day Daemon

incoming connections. The `Listener` class accepts incoming connections and queues them for the server. The `Session` class is responsible for responding to client messages received via a connection. Figure 2.6 illustrates the interaction among todd's classes.

2.6.2 todd Management

todd satisfies its basic functional requirements by accepting client connections and supplying the current date and time on demand, but it's not *manageable*. We have no way of knowing the total number of sessions that todd has handled, how many sessions are active, how many connections are queued, how long each session has been running, and so on. We can't stop and start the listener without killing todd, and any active sessions along with it. We can't change the size of the connection queue or session pool without recompiling the code. If todd were to become a popular service, our administrator colleagues would not be happy with us.

JMX lets us build manageability into our Java applications. MBeans capture the *management interface* of the resources that management systems

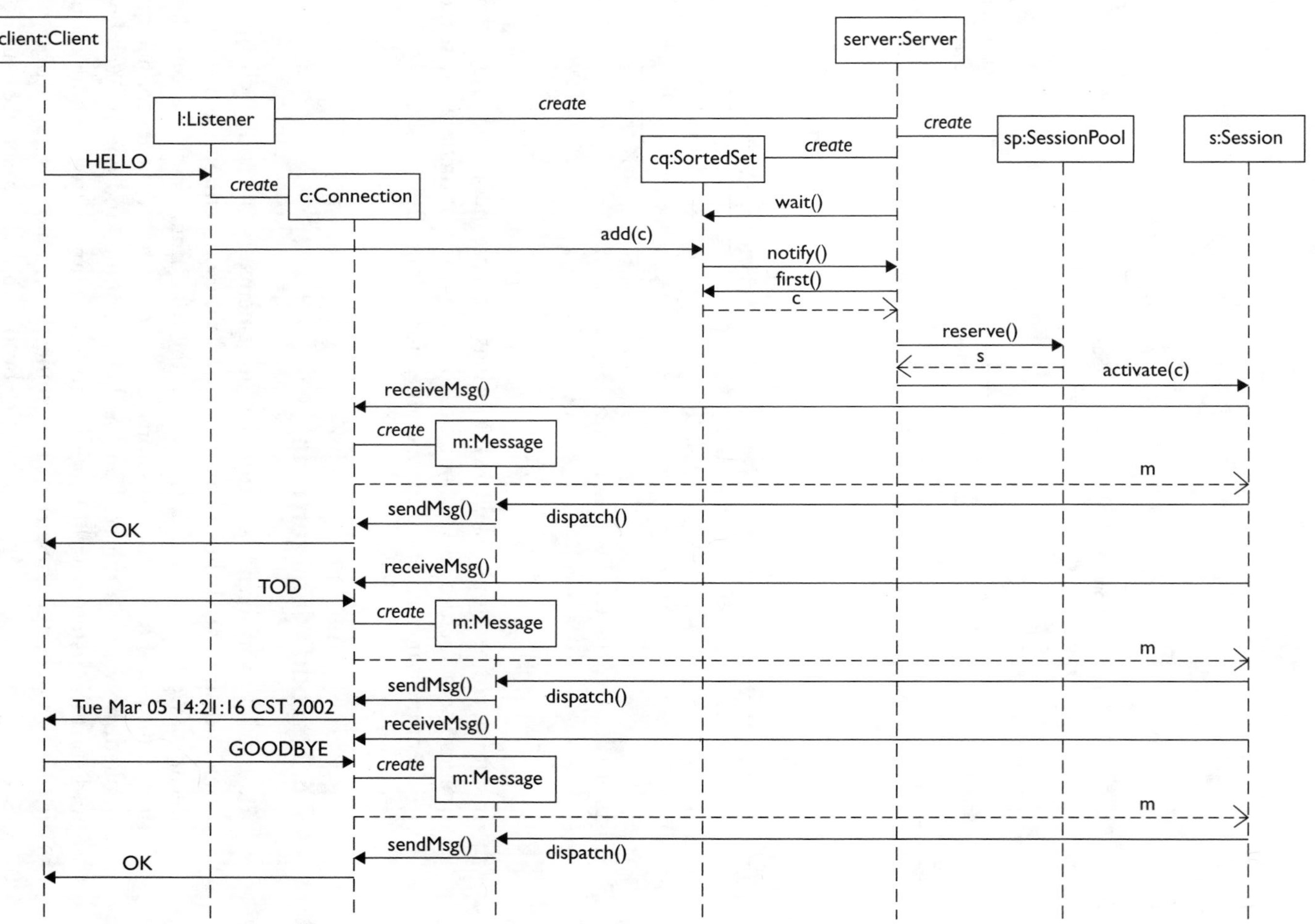

Figure 2.6 todd Component Interactions During a Client Session

need to monitor and control. The MBeanServer provides a common registry and naming model for all of an application's MBeans. MBean services exist to autonomously monitor MBean attribute values and fire notifications when constraints are violated. Notifications provide both a means to alert an administrator of a problem, and an implicit invocation mechanism that developers can use to make an application self-managing.

In the next few sections we will apply JMX to todd and transform it into a manageable application that will delight the system administration staff, or at least keep them from paging us in the middle of the night. Because the goal of this tour is to demonstrate the major features of JMX in an application, we will introduce them without a lot of explanation. Subsequent chapters will provide details of all the features we use in our example.

Before we start, it would be good to have an idea of the sort of manageability requirements the new version of todd has to satisfy. Table 2.1 provides a minimal list. Modifying todd to satisfy these requirements will involve the following activities: designing and implementing the necessary MBeans, incorporating an MBeanServer into todd, and wiring up the monitors and `NotificationListener` instances that are needed to complete the implementation.

Table 2.1 Basic todd Management Requirements

Aspect	**Requirement**	**Description**
Server control	Stop/start	Stop and start the server without killing the todd process or any active sessions.
	Shutdown	Shut down the server, killing the todd process and any active sessions.
Server data	Total connections	Show how many connections the server has handled so far.
	Uptime	Show how long the server has been running.
	Active sessions	Show how many sessions are currently active.
Session pool management	Grow pool	Increase the size of the session pool by a specified amount.
	Empty pool management	Stop the server when the pool becomes empty; restart the server when the pool contains at least two sessions.

2.6.3 todd's MBeans

From the requirements in Table 2.1, it's pretty clear that we're concerned with only a couple of todd's resources: the server itself, and the pool of sessions that todd uses to service connections. Because JMX uses MBeans to represent managed resources, it follows that we need to make the `Server` and `SessionPool` classes MBeans. There are several ways to accomplish that goal; the simplest is to make them standard MBeans. In general a standard MBean for a given resource is defined by a Java interface named `MyResourceMBean` and a Java class, `MyResource`, which implements the `MyResourceMBean` interface. `MyResourceMBean` defines the MBean's *management interface*—that is, the attributes and methods that JMX makes available to management applications.

It's clear from the requirements what the server's management interface should look like:

```
public interface ServerMBean {
  void shutdown();
  void start();
  void stop();
  Integer getConnections();
  Integer getSessions();
  Long getUptime();
}
```

A JMX management interface contains attributes and operations. In a standard MBean those attributes and operations are expressed as methods in a Java interface. Methods that have the following form:

```
AttributeType getAttributeName();
void setAttributeName();
```

define an attribute named `AttributeName` that takes values of type `AttributeType`. If the `setAttributeName()` method is missing, the attribute is read-only; if the `getAttributeName()` method is missing, the attribute is write-only. Any method in the MBean interface that doesn't define an attribute defines an operation for the management interface.

The first three methods in the `ServerMBean` interface define operations that a management application can invoke on `ServerMBean` instances. The remaining methods define attributes; specifically they define three read-only attributes: `Connections`, `Sessions`, and `Uptime`.

The implementation of the `ServerMBean` interface in the `Server` class is straightforward:

```
public class Server implements ServerMBean, NotificationListener {
  private SessionPool sessions;
  private SortedSet connectionQueue;
  private Listener listener;
  private int connections;  // incremented for each new connection
  private int tzero;   // System.currentTimeMillis at Server start
  ...
  // Other Server methods that aren't part of the MBean interface

  /**
   * Shut down the server, killing the process and any active sessions
   */
  public void shutdown() {
    System.exit(0);
  }

  /**
   * Start a listener thread that will queue incoming connections
   */
  public void start() {
    listener = new Listener(connectionQueue);
    listener.start();
  }

  /**
   * Stop the server's listener thread; active sessions continue to
   * handle requests
   */
  public void stop() {
    listener.stopListening();
  }

  /**
   * Connections attribute getter
   * @returns total number of connections handled
   */
  public Integer getConnections() {
    return new Integer(connections);
  }

  /**
   * Sessions attribute getter
```

```
   * @returns number of active sessions
   */
  public Integer getSessions() {
    int as = sessions.getAvailableSessions().intValue();
    int sz = sessions.getSize().intValue();
    return new Integer(sz - as);
  }

  /**
   * Uptime attribute getter
   * @returns number of milliseconds since the server was started
   */
  public Long getUptime() {
    return new Long(System.currentTimeMillis() - tzero);
  }
}
```

The shape of the SessionPool management interface requires a little more thought. Clearly it needs a *grow* operation to satisfy the first session pool management requirement. What about the empty pool management requirement? We could specify a monitorPoolSpace operation that would provide the necessary behavior, but as we'll see in a moment, that would be reinventing a perfectly good JMX wheel. Instead, let's just satisfy the underlying data requirement by providing access to the number of sessions left in the pool. A glance back at the ServerMBean implementation will reveal that we've already assumed that this information, along with the session pool size, is available, so we have this:

```
public interface SessionPoolMBean {
  void grow(int increment);
  Integer getAvailableSessions();
  Integer getSize();
}
```

todd uses java.util.Set as the underlying data structure for the SessionPool implementation:

```
public class SessionPool implements SessionPoolMBean {
  private static final int DEFAULT_POOLSIZE = 8;
  private Set sessions;
  private int size;
```

```
/**
 * Default constructor creates a SessionPool instance of size
 * DEFAULT_POOLSIZE
 */
public SessionPool() {
  this(DEFAULT_POOLSIZE);
}

/**
  * Creates a SessionPool instance of the specified size and
  * fills it with Session instances
  */
public SessionPool(int size) {
  this.size = size;
  sessions = new HashSet(size);
  fill();
}

/**
 * Increase the number of Session instances in SessionPool by
 * increment
 * @param increment the number of Session instances to add to
 * the pool
 */
public synchronized void grow(int increment) {
  for (int i = 0; i < increment; i++) {
    Session s = new Session(this);
    sessions.add(s);
  }
  size = size + increment;
}

/**
 * AvailableSessions attribute getter
 * @returns number of sessions remaining in the pool
 */
public Integer getAvailableSessions() {
  return new Integer(sessions.size());
}

/**
 * Size attribute getter
 * @returns size of the session pool
 */
```

```
  public Integer getSize() {
    return new Integer(size);
  }
   ...
   // Other SessionPool methods that are not part of the MBean
   // interface
}
```

You've probably noticed that all of our attribute getters return Java numeric wrapper types—`Integer`, `Long`, and so on. We do that so that we can use JMX monitors such as `GaugeMonitor`, which we'll use in the implementation of the empty pool management requirement, to observe the values taken by those attributes. Note also that we have kept the operations in the `ServerMBean` and `SessionPoolMBean` interfaces very simple.

2.6.4 Incorporating an MBeanServer

Now that we've got some MBeans, what do we do with them? Because a JMX-based management application can access MBeans only if they are registered with an MBeanServer, we should register them. Unfortunately, we don't have an MBeanServer in todd to register any MBeans with at the moment. That problem can be solved with a single line of code in todd's `main()` method:

```
MBeanServer mbs = MBeanServerFactory.createMBeanServer();
```

In the interest of minimizing the impact of incorporating the MBeanServer, we will instantiate both the `Server` and the `SessionPool` MBeans and then register them, rather than creating and automatically registering them via the MBeanServer. `Server` is instantiated in `main()`, and `SessionPool` is created as part of the `Server` instantiation:

```
public static void main(String[] args) throws Exception {
  MBeanServer mbs = MBeanServerFactory.createMBeanServer();

  Server server = new Server(mbs);
  ObjectName son = new ObjectName("todd:id=Server");
  mbs.registerMBean(server, son);

...
```

```
    while (server.isActive()) {
      Connection k = server.waitForConnection()
      server.activateSession(k);
    }
  }

public Server(MBeanServer mbs) throws Exception {
    this.mbs = mbs;

    connectionQueue = new TreeSet();
    connections = 0;

    sessions = new SessionPool();
    ObjectName spon = new ObjectName("todd:id=SessionPool");
    mbs.registerMBean(sessions, spon);

    active = true;
    tzero = System.currentTimeMillis();
  }
```

The MBeanServer associates an `ObjectName` instance with each MBean. We've registered `Server` and `SessionPool` under the names `todd:id=Server` and `todd:id=SessionPool`. The portion of the name to the left of the colon is the *domain*, which is an arbitrary string that is opaque to the MBeanServer but may have meaning to one or more management applications. On the right are the *key properties*, a set of name/value pairs that help distinguish one MBean from another. Together they must form a unique name, within a given MBeanServer, for the associated MBean.

2.6.5 Monitoring todd

We still haven't satisfied the `SessionPool` empty pool management requirement. The `SessionPool` MBean tells us how many sessions are left in the pool. What we need is a way to react to these two events: (1) `AvailableSessions` has become zero, and (2) `AvailableSessions` has increased from zero to one or more.

In JMX, events are called *notifications*. Every JMX notification has a class and a type; its class is either `javax.management.Notification` or one of its subclasses; its type is `String` expressed in dot notation—for example, `jmx.mbean.registered`. Notifications are handled by calls to one of the MBeanServer's `addNotificationListener()` methods:

```
public void addNotificationListener(ObjectName objname,
                                    NotificationListener listener,
                                    NotificationFilter filter,
                                    Object handback);

public void addNotificationListener(ObjectName objname,
                                    ObjectName listener,
                                    NotificationFilter filter,
                                    Object handback);
```

The only difference between the two method calls is the second parameter. In the first version the second parameter is a reference to a `NotificationListener` instance—that is, an instance of a class that implements the `NotificationListener` interface. In the second version the second parameter is the `ObjectName` instance of an MBean that implements `NotificationListener`.

Careful readers will have noticed that the `Server` class implements `ServerMBean` *and* `NotificationListener`. Satisfying the empty pool management requirement involves stopping and starting the server that makes the `Server` class. These actions provide the `stop()` and `start()` methods with a natural place to handle the notifications that trigger those actions. The `NotificationListener` interface declares a single method, `handleNotification()`. Here is the `Server` implementation of the method:

```
public void handleNotification(Notification n, Object hb) {
  String type = n.getType();
  if (type.compareTo
       (MonitorNotification.THRESHOLD_LOW_VALUE_EXCEEDED) == 0) {
    stop();
  } else if (type.compareTo
       (MonitorNotification.THRESHOLD_HIGH_VALUE_EXCEEDED) == 0) {
    if (isActive() == false) start();
  }
}
```

Now all that's required is a mechanism for generating notifications at the appropriate times. We need something that will monitor `SessionPool`'s `AvailableSessions` attribute, send a notification when it becomes zero, and then send another notification later when `AvailableSessions` increases to one or more.

The JMX GaugeMonitor class provides just such a mechanism. A `GaugeMonitor` instance is configured to monitor a specific attribute of an MBean registered with the MBeanServer. The `GaugeMonitor` class has two thresholds: high and low. A `MonitorNotification` instance with type `jmx.monitor.threshold.high` is sent when the attribute value increases to or past the high threshold value. Similarly, when the attribute value decreases to or below the low threshold value, a `MonitorNotification` instance with type `jmx.monitor.threshold.low` is sent.

The `Server.configureMonitor()` method sets up a `GaugeMonitor` instance that completes the implementation of the empty pool management requirement:

```
public static void configureMonitor(MBeanServer mbs) throws
  Exception {
  ObjectName spmon = new ObjectName("todd:id=SessionPoolMonitor");
  mbs.createMBean("javax.management.monitor.GaugeMonitor",
spmon);

  AttributeList spmal = new AttributeList();
  spmal.add(new Attribute("ObservedObject", new
    ObjectName("todd:id=SessionPool")));
  spmal.add(new Attribute("ObservedAttribute",
    "AvailableSessions"));
  spmal.add(new Attribute("GranularityPeriod", new Long(10000)));
  spmal.add(new Attribute("NotifyHigh", new Boolean(true)));
  spmal.add(new Attribute("NotifyLow", new Boolean(true)));
  mbs.setAttributes(spmon, spmal);

  mbs.invoke(
    spmon,
    "setThresholds",
    new Object[] { new Integer(1), new Integer(0)},
    new String[] { "java.lang.Number", "java.lang.Number" });

  mbs.addNotificationListener(
    spmon,
    new ObjectName("todd:id=Server"),
    null,
    new Object());

  mbs.invoke(spmon, "start", new Object[] {}, new String[] {});
}
```

The first two lines here create and register a `GaugeMonitor` MBean named `todd:id=SessionPoolMonitor`. The next seven lines set attributes that tell `GaugeMonitor` which attribute of which MBean should be monitored (`ObservedAttribute` or `ObservedObject`), how often (`GranularityPeriod`, in milliseconds), and whether or not to send a notification on high-threshold and low-threshold violations. Then we invoke the `setThresholds()` method, via the MBeanServer, to set the actual high and low threshold values. Finally, we make the server listen for session pool monitor notifications and start the gauge monitor.

2.6.6 Browser Control

The new version of todd satisfies all of the management requirements specified in Table 2.1. There is, however, one more issue to address: We would like to be able to control todd interactively. For example, an administrator should be able to connect to todd from home to check the values of key MBean attributes, stop the server, increase the size of the session pool, and restart the server if necessary.

Although there are as many ways to address this issue as there are communication protocols, most JMX implementations provide an HTTP adapter that allows a user to "surf" an MBeanServer—inspecting MBean attributes, invoking operations, and so on—using a standard Web browser. Here's the code necessary to start the TMX4J HTTP adapter:

```
ObjectName httpon = new ObjectName("adapters:id=Http");
mbs.createMBean("com.tivoli.jmx.http_pa.Listener", httpon);
mbs.invoke(httpon, "startListener",
new Object[] {}, new String[] {});
```

Once the adapter has been started, you can connect to the MBeanServer via a Web browser. In the case of the TMX4J HTTP adapter, you would direct your browser to http://<your-server>:6969. You can change the port the adapter listens on in the `jmx.properties` file that the TMX4J implementation reads on startup. Figure 2.7 shows the TMX4J view of the todd MBeans.

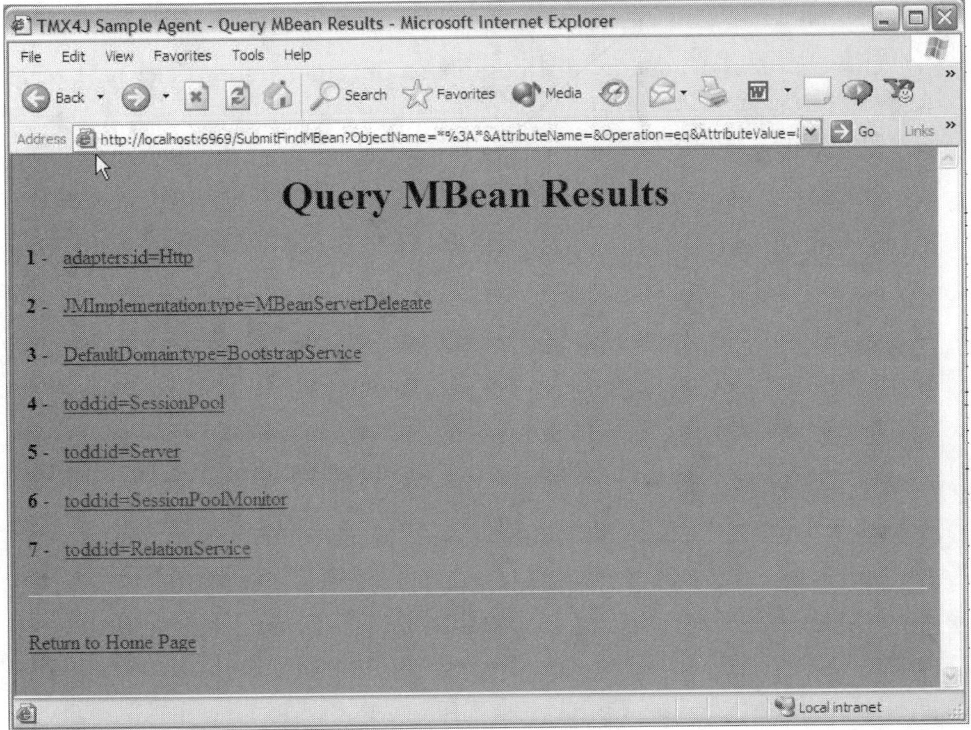

Figure 2.7 The TMX4J HTTP Adapter's MBean View

2.7 Summary

In the course of this tour we have illustrated the use of JMX in the context of a simple Java-based service. Although the service itself may be straightforward, the process we went through to make it manageable is a common approach and does work in practice. Working with a set of management requirements, we developed a set of resources that we must monitor and control to satisfy those requirements. We reflected the management interface for each of our managed resources in an appropriate MBean, and then brought instances of those MBeans together in an MBeanServer. Finally, we used JMX services like monitors and notification to implement the policy mechanism that enabled us to satisfy our management requirements.

2.8 Notes

1. This chapter is generally attributable to the following article: H. Kreger, "Java Management Extensions for Application Management," *IBM Systems Journal* 40(1) (March 2001), http://www.research.ibm.com/journal/sj/401/kreger.pdf.

2. "Java Management Extensions (JMX) Specification," JSR 3, http://www.jcp.org/jsr/detail/3.jsp.

3. J2SE stands for Java 2 Platform, Standard Edition, which is Sun Microsystems' Java platform. More information is available at http://java.sun.com/j2se. Java and all Java-based marks are trademarks of Sun Microsystems, Inc., in the United States and other countries.

4. SNMP stands for Simple Network Management Protocol, which is an IETF (Internet Engineering Task Force) standard. More information on SNMP is available at http://www.ietf.org.

5. CIM/WBEM stands for Common Information Model/Web-Based Enterprise Management. It is defined by the Distributed Management Task Force (DMTF). More information is available at http://www.dmtf.org.

6. JDBC (Java Database Connectivity) is an API that isolates database clients from database vendors. It is a Sun Microsystems technology. JDBC is a trademark of Sun Microsystems, Inc., in the United States and other countries.

7. CMIP stands for Common Management Information Protocol and is usually referred to in conjunction with CMIS (Common Management Information Services). This management standard was defined by OSI (Open Systems Interconnection) as an ISO standard: ISO 9595/2 and 9596/2 (http://www.iso.ch). More information on CMIP/CMIS can be found at http://www.iso.ch.

8. Tivoli Systems, Inc., 9442 Capital of Texas Highway North, Arboretum Plaza One, Austin, TX 78759 (http://www.tivoli.com). Tivoli is a trademark of Tivoli Systems in the United States, other countries, or both.

9. Computer Associates International, Inc., One Computer Associates Plaza, Islandia, NY 11749 (http://www.cai.com).

10. Microsoft Windows is Microsoft's workstation operating system family, including Windows 95, Windows 98, Windows NT, Windows 2000, and Windows XP. More information is available at http://www.microsoft.com. Microsoft, Windows, Windows NT, and the Windows logo are trademarks of Microsoft Corporation in the United States, other countries, or both.

11. IBM AIX is a UNIX-based operating system available from IBM Corporation, Armonk, NY (http://www.ibm.com/servers/aix).

12. Solaris is Sun Microsystems' UNIX-based operating system. More information is available at http://www.sun.com/solaris.

13. HP-UX is Hewlett-Packard's UNIX-based operating system. More information is available at http://www.hp.com/products1/unix/operating.

14. J2EE stands for Java 2 Platform, Enterprise Edition, which is Sun Microsystems' Java platform. J2EE application servers are vendor products that support the J2EE specification. More information is available at http://java.sun.com/j2ee. Java and all Java-based marks are trademarks of Sun Microsystems, Inc., in the United States and other countries.

15. RFC 1514 (http://www.ietf.org/rfc/rfc1514.txt) dictates that, "The Internet-standard Network Management Framework consists of three [four] components. They are: STD 16, RFC 1155 [1] which defines the SMI, the mechanisms used for describing and naming objects for the purpose of management. http://www.ietf.org/rfc/rfc1155.txt; STD 16, RFC 1212 [2] defines a more concise description mechanism, which is wholly consistent with the SMI. http://www.ietf.org/rfc/rfc1212.txt; STD 17, RFC 1213 [3] which defines MIB-II, the core set of managed objects for the Internet suite of protocols.; STD 15, RFC 1157 [4] which defines the SNMP, the protocol used for network access to managed objects."

16. JMAPI .08, Java Management API specification. These specifications are no longer available from Sun Microsystems; however, this book contains an overview of the JMAPI technologies: "Java 1.2 Unleashed," Sams Publishing (http://www.szptt.net.cn/9810dnwl/new/jdk1.2/index.htm). This chapter covers JMAPI (see http://www.szptt.net.cn/9810dnwl/new/jdk1.2/ch36/ch36.htm).

17. JDMK 2.0 is available from Sun Microsystems, Inc., 901 San Antonio Rd., Palo Alto, CA 94303. More information is available at http://java.sun.com/products/jdmk.

18. Source: "Java Management Extensions (JMX) Specification," JSR 3, http://www.jcp.org/jsr/detail/3.jsp, which was led by Sun Microsystems to create a management API for Java resources.

19. Java Community Process (http://www.jcp.org) is Sun Microsystem's process for allowing the Java community to participate in the development of Java language extensions and new Java APIs.

20. Groupe Bull was the original company name for the representative. This company is now referred to as "Evidian: A Groupe Bull Company" (http://www.evidian.com).

21. TIBCO Software is a provider of business integration solutions (http://www.tibco.com).

22. Powerware, an Invensys Company, Powerware Corporation, designs and manufactures innovative, end-to-end power protection and management solutions (http://www.powerware.com).

23. Borland Software Corporation is a provider of technology used to develop, deploy, and integrate software applications (http://www.borland.com).

24. Motorola, Inc., is a provider of integrated communications solutions and embedded electronic solutions (http://www.motorola.com).

25. BEA Systems, Inc., is an application infrastructure software company (http://www.bea.com).

26. IONA iPortal J2EE is an application server by IONA. According to IONA, the iPortal Application Server has been incorporated into the Orbix E2A Application Server Platform as the Orbix E2A J2EE Technology Edition. More information is available at www.iona.com.

27. Produced by Lutris Technologies, Lutris EAS 4 is a J2EE application server that introduces a services architecture, in which J2EE services are pluggable modules, that incorporates JMX manageability into every service, as well as full versioning of service components for complete configuration and product packaging control. More information is available at http://www.lutris.com.

28. JBoss is an open-source J2EE application server. It is inherently JMX based. More information is available at http://www.jboss.org.

29. Java Dynamic Management Kit (JDMK) 3.0 is available from Sun Microsystems, Inc., 901 San Antonio Rd., Palo Alto, CA 94303, http://java.sun.com/products/jdmk.

30. Java Dynamic Management Kit (JDMK) 4.0 is available from Sun Microsystems, Inc., 901 San Antonio Rd., Palo Alto, CA 94303 (http://java.sun.com/products/jdmk).

31. "Java Management Extensions (JMX) Remoting 1.2," JSR 160, http://www.jcp.org/jsr/detail/160.jsp, led by Sun Microsystems.

32. JSR 146: "WBEM Services: JMX Provider Protocol Adapter" (http://www.jcp.org/jsr/detail/146.jsp), led by Sun Microsystems.

33. JSR 71: "JMX-TMN Specification," (http://www.jcp.org/jsr/detail/071.jsp), led by Evidian.

34. JSR 70: "IIOP Protocol Adapter for JMX Specification," (http://www.jcp.org/jsr/detail/070.jsp), led by IONA.

35. IIOP stands for Internet Inter-Operability Protocol. More information is available at http://www.omg.org and http://www.omg.org/technology/documents/corba_spec_catalog.htm.

36. CORBA stands for Common Object Request Broker Architecture. More information is available at http://www.omg.org and http://www.omg.org/gettingstarted/corbafaq.htm.

37. The specification in JSR 77, "J2EE Management" (http://www.jcp.org/jsr/detail/077.jsp), led by Sun, defines the object model and JMX implementation for managing J2EE application servers.

38. JSR 146: "WBEM Services: JMX Provider Protocol Adapter" (http://www.jcp.org/jsr/detail/146.jsp), led by Sun Microsystems.

39. JSR 71: "JMX-TMN Specification," (http://www.jcp.org/jsr/detail/071.jsp), led by Evidian.

40. *Java Management Extensions Instrumentation and Agent Specification v1.0* (Final Release, April 2000), Sun Microsystems, Inc., 901 San Antonio Road, Palo Alto, CA 94303; available at http://java.sun.com/products/JavaManagement.

41. According to the Free Software Foundation (http://www.gnu.org/philosophy/license-list.html#SunCommunitySourceLicense) and numerous editorials at the time of the SCSL release, this license is not well thought of in the free-software and open-source communities.

42. *Java Management Extensions Technology Compatibility Kit 1.0* (April 2000), Sun Microsystems, Inc., 901 San Antonio Road, Palo Alto, CA 94303; available at http://java.sun.com/products/JavaManagement.

43. Tivoli's Application Management Specification is used to define the characteristics of a managed application.

44. The MIB file is the Management Information Base data format used by SNMP to describe its object model. Source: M. Rose and K. McCloghrie,

"Concise MIB Definitions," STD 16, RFC 1212 (March 1991), http://www.ietf.org/rfc/rfc1212.txt?number=1212.

45. MOF stands for Managed Object Format. This format is used to describe CIM information and is defined by the DMTF in the CIM specification. More information is available at http://www.dmtf.org/standards/cim_schema_v23.php.

46. The Dynamic Invocation Interface for CORBA description can be found at http://www.omg.org. Java and all Java-based marks are trademarks or registered trademarks of Sun Microsystems, Inc., in the United States and other countries.

47. RMI stands for Remote Method Invocation, a Java API to support distributed programming with Java technology. More information is available at http://java.sun.com/products/jdk/rmi.

48. HTTP stands for Hypertext Transfer Protocol. See "Hypertext Transfer Protocol -- HTTP/1.1," RFC 2068 (January 1997), http://www.ietf.org/rfc/rfc2068.txt?number=2068.

49. SNMP stands for Simple Network Management Protocol, the protocol used for network access to managed objects. The SNMP is defined in RFC 1157 ("A Simple Network Management Protocol (SNMP)," May 1990, http://www.ietf.org/rfc/rfc1157.txt).

PART II

JMX Details

CHAPTER 3

All about MBeans

MBeans are the raw material of JMX-based management. Management systems monitor and control resources: a router, a server, an EJB, or a JVM. To perform their monitoring and control duties, management systems need information about the resources they are responsible for and a means of affecting the operation of those resources. In JMX, MBeans provide the information about, and operations on, resources that management systems require.

The instrumentation layer of the JMX architecture is all about MBeans: standard MBeans, dynamic MBeans, open MBeans, and model MBeans. This chapter describes standard and dynamic MBeans in detail and gives an overview of the principles and interfaces of open MBeans. Model MBeans are the topic of Chapter 4. Here we define what MBeans are, discuss the various aspects of their design, and describe their implementation. Throughout we pay special attention to the management interface that MBeans expose to the rest of the management system.

3.1 MBean Fundamentals

An MBean represents a resource that a management system will monitor and control. The resource in question could be a device like a network card, a system resource such as a file or process, or an application component like a server-side container or service. In each case the MBean *is* the resource as far as the management system is concerned.

The JMX specification defines an MBean as a concrete Java class that

- Has one or more public constructors
- Implements its own corresponding MBean interface or the `DynamicMBean` interface
- Optionally implements the `NotificationBroadcaster` interface

3.1.1 The Management Interface

An MBean's constructors, the attributes and operations defined by the MBean interface that it implements, and the notifications that it generates make up the MBean's *management interface*. The MBean's Java class may have behavior beyond that exposed in the management interface but that behavior is not available to the management system.

Management systems access MBeans via an MBeanServer. Figure 3.1 illustrates the relationship among the three components. Note that there are two distinct interfaces in this picture. The management system has direct access to the MBeanServer interface, but it needs access to the MBean's management interface to manage the resource that the MBean represents. One of the MBeanServer's principal functions is to provide access to any MBean's management interface via a standard interface of its own.

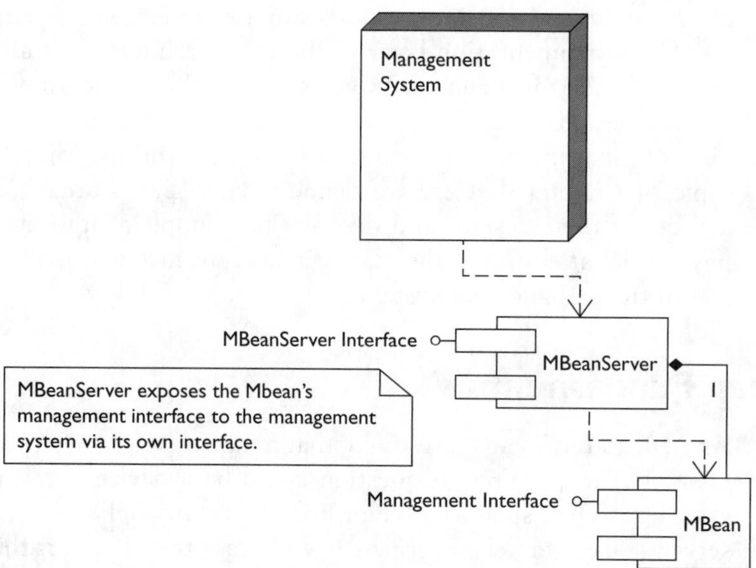

Figure 3.1 The MBeanServer Mediates Access to MBeans

The MBeanServer will be described in detail in Chapter 5. Here we will focus on just its *MBean access methods* in order to understand how MBean's management interfaces are exposed to management systems. There are six MBean access methods in the MBeanServer interface:

```
Object getAttribute(ObjectName objname, String attrname);
AttributeList getAttributes(ObjectName objname,
  String[] attrnames);
MBeanInfo getMBeanInfo(ObjectName objname);
Object invoke(ObjectName objname, String method, Object[] params,
  String[] signature);
void setAttribute(ObjectName objname, Attribute attribute);
AttributeList setAttributes(ObjectName objname,
  AttributeList attributes);
```

The `ObjectName` parameters in these APIs refer to MBeans registered with the MBeanServer. The `getAttribute()` and `getAttributes()` methods return the values of the specified MBean's attributes, `setAttribute()` and `setAttributes()` set the values of the specified MBean's attributes, and `invoke()` executes an operation on the specified MBean.

The `MBeanInfo` object returned by the `getMBeanInfo()` method encapsulates metadata that describes the management interface of the MBean registered under the specified name. Figure 3.2 presents the static structure of this information.

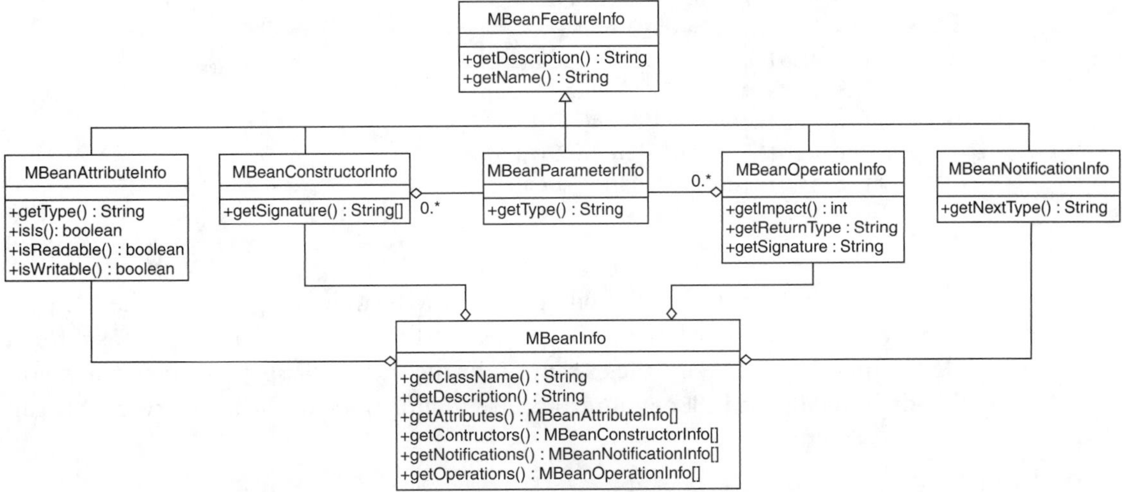

Figure 3.2 Static Structure of the Metadata That Describes an MBean's Management Interface

The MBeanServer uses an MBean's MBeanInfo to implement its MBean access methods. The MBeanServer makes sure that no methods are invoked or attributes retrieved or updated that are not described in MBeanInfo. Management systems can use getMBeanInfo() to retrieve a complete description of an MBean's management interface. For example, management system consoles commonly use MBeanInfo to display MBeans in their GUIs.

3.1.2 The Introspection Algorithm

The MBeanServer uses a two-step process to collect MBean information for each MBean as it is registered:

1. It determines the kind of MBean being registered.
2. It asks a dynamic MBean for its MBean info or derives a standard MBean's MBean info via introspection.

There are two main kinds of MBeans: standard and dynamic. Here is the pseudocode for the algorithm that determines a given MBean's kind:

```
Let the MBean's Java class be C
if C is abstract or C has no public constructors
  throw NotCompliantMBeanException
if C implements both CMBean and DynamicMBean
  throw NotCompliantMBeanException
if C implements CMBean
  return C is a CMBean StandardMBean
if C implements DynamicMBean
  return C is a DynamicMBean
for each superclass S of C
  if S implements both SMBean and DynamicMBean
    throw NotCompliantMBeanException
  if S implements SMBean
    return C is an SMBean StandardMBean
  if S implements DynamicMBean
    return C is a DynamicMBean
```

Once it has determined what kind of MBean it is registering, the MBeanServer has to record the MBean's MBeanInfo. That is a simple task for a dynamic MBean. With the exception of the ObjectName parameter, the methods in the DynamicMBean interface are identical to the MBeanServer's MBean access methods:

```
public interface DynamicMBean {
  Object getAttribute(String attrname);
  AttributeList getAttributes(String[] attrnames);
  MBeanInfo getMBeanInfo();
  Object invoke(String method, Object[] params, String[] signature);
  void setAttribute(Attribute attr);
  AttributeList setAttributes(AttributeList attrs);
}
```

So the MBeanServer just has to ask the MBean for its `MBeanInfo`.

Things are a little more complex for a standard MBean. Because the MBeanServer can't depend on the presence of a `getMBeanInfo()` method, it uses another level of introspection and the "lexical design patterns" defined by the JMX specification to derive `MBeanInfo` from the MBean's `MBean` interface. Don't be confused by the words *design pattern*, we're not talking about object-oriented design patterns here; *lexical design pattern* is just another way of saying *naming convention*. These lexical design patterns are used to distinguish MBean attributes from MBean operations. An attribute is identified by the following pattern:

```
public AttrType getAttrName();              // attribute "getter"
public void setAttrName(AttrType val);      // attribute "setter"
```

`AttrType` may be any Java type, but see the design considerations outlined in Section 3.3. `AttrName` is case sensitive, so `getconnections()` and `getConnections()` define two different attributes: `connections` and `Connections`, respectively. If both the attribute getter and setter are present, the attribute is a *read/write* attribute; if only the getter is present, the attribute is *read-only*; and if only the setter is present, the attribute is *write-only*. Finally if `AttrType` is `boolean`, the attribute getter may be defined by the pattern

```
public boolean isAttrName();
```

Note that only one form of getter is allowed for an attribute; that is, a Boolean attribute may have either a `getAttrName()` getter or an `isAttrName()` getter, but not both.

Methods defined by a standard MBean interface that don't match one of the attribute design patterns are taken to be operations. Like attributes, operations may take parameters of any valid Java type and return as a result a value of any valid Java type.

3.2 MBean Construction

Now that we understand the place of MBeans in the world, we're ready to work through the details of implementing them. We'll look at standard MBeans first because their construction is straightforward; then we'll explore the implementation of dynamic MBeans.

3.2.1 Standard MBeans

According to the JMX specification, the Java class of a standard MBean "must implement a Java interface named after the class." We've already seen a couple of standard MBeans in Chapter 2's Quick Tour of JMX (Section 2.6). Let's take another look at the todd `Server` MBean. The Unified Modeling Language (UML) diagram in Figure 3.3 shows these two components and the relationship between them.

The first thing to note is that like every other standard MBean, the `Server` MBean has two components. The first is the Java class, in this case named `Server`, and the second is the interface whose name is the corresponding Java class name followed by *MBean*—thus `ServerMBean` in this instance—which defines the MBean's management interface. Here is the `ServerMBean` interface:

```
public interface ServerMBean {
  void shutdown();
  void start();
  void stop();
  Integer getConnections();
  Integer getSessions();
  Long getUptime();
}
```

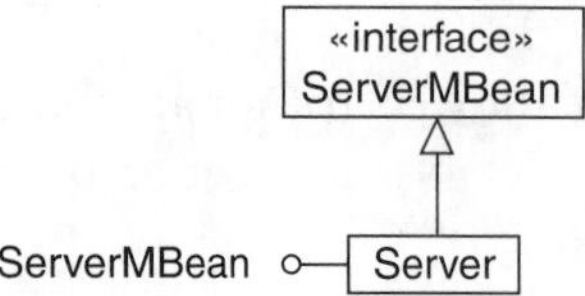

Figure 3.3 The Two Components of a Standard MBean: The Java Class That Represents the Managed Resource and the Interface That Defines the Management Interface to That Resource

Applying the JMX specification's lexical design patterns to this interface yields three attributes.

1. `Connections`, an `Integer`-valued, read-only attribute
2. `Sessions`, an `Integer`-valued, read-only attribute
3. `Uptime`, a `Long`-valued, read-only attribute

Figure 3.4 illustrates the application of the lexical design patterns to the interface declarations.

Because the other three methods in the `ServerMBean` interface—`shutdown()`, `start()`, and `stop()`—don't fit the attribute pattern, they become the management interface's operations.

The `MBeanInfo` structure that describes the `Server` MBean is illustrated in Figure 3.5.

Note that all of the *Description* fields are null. This is one of the drawbacks of standard MBeans: There is no way to provide descriptive information about the management interface—an attribute's units, its upper or lower bounds, valid parameter values, and so on. This limitation makes it difficult for a GUI to present a useful view of a standard MBean.

Another thing to note about the `Server` MBean is that it provides a management interface to a resource that exists in the same JVM. That is, the `Server` class, along with its management interface, is an essential part of the todd application. This arrangement is a common one, but it is not the only possibility. Management applications often need to monitor and control resources "from the outside"; that is, the management application runs in a separate process and accesses the resource via the management interfaces native to the resource, which may include proprietary remote interfaces,

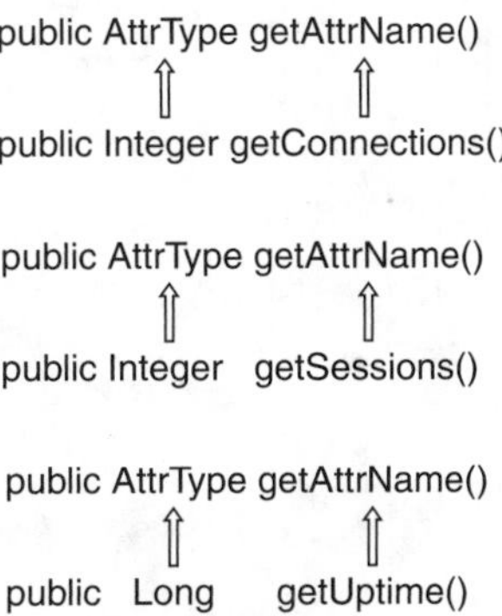

Figure 3.4 Derivation of MBean Attributes and Their Types

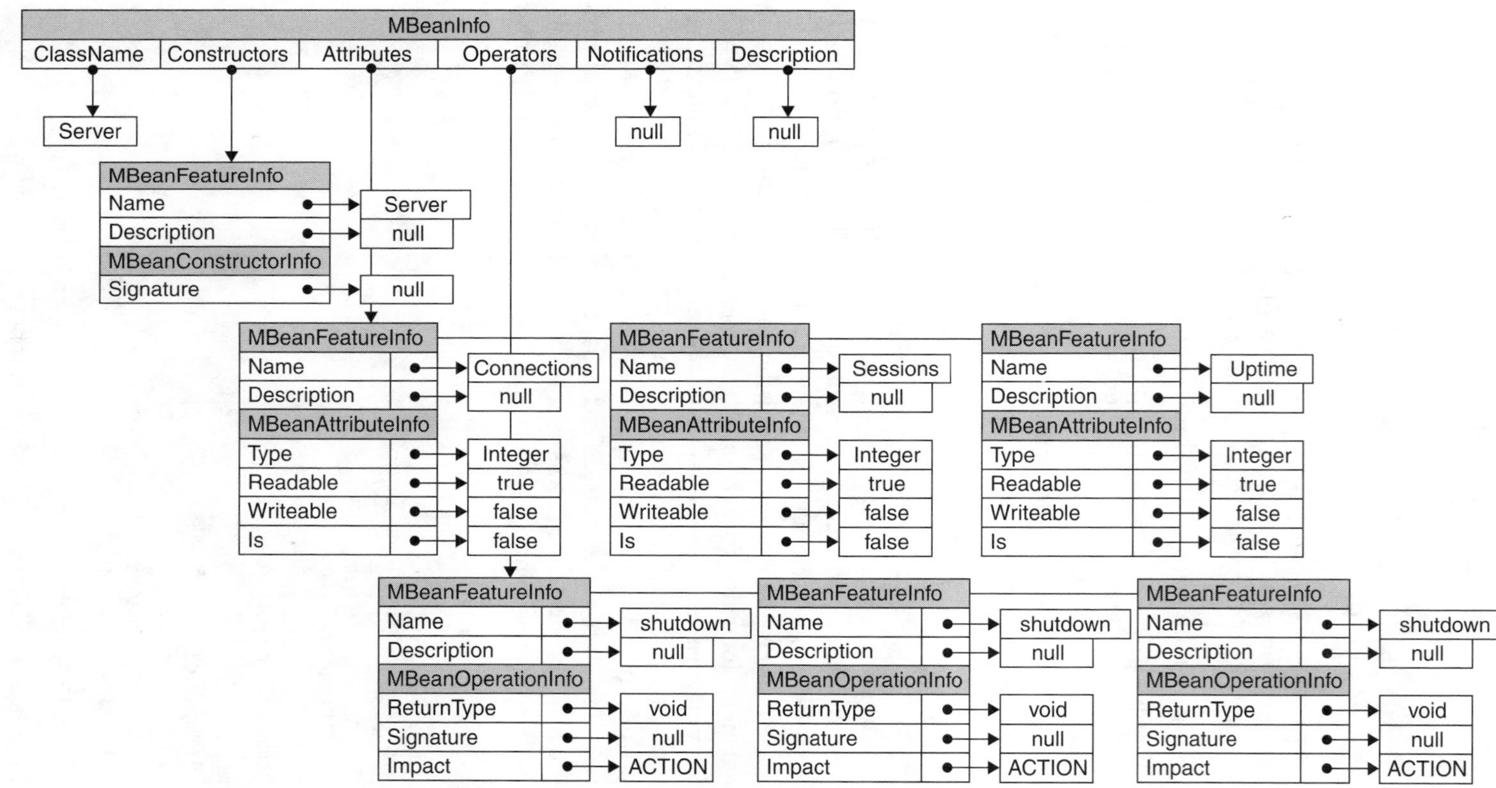

Figure 3.5 The `MBeanInfo` Object That Describes the `Server` MBean's Management Interface

command-line utilities, and so on. Mapping those native management interfaces into MBeans provides a uniform access mechanism for management applications.

To see how this works in practice, we'll develop an MBean for the Apache HTTP daemon. Note that although Apache isn't even written in Java, we can use its native management information to create an MBean that provides a JMX-based management application with a wealth of information about a running Apache instance. So exactly what native management information does Apache provide, and how do we access it? The Apache HTTP daemon provides a module, `mod_status`, that allows administrators to check on the server's performance via a Web browser. When a browser accesses the "server status" page on an Apache server, the server returns an HTML page with the current server statistics. For example, entering the URL http://www.apache.org/server-status in a browser returned the following results:

```
Current Time: Saturday, 01-Jun-2002 11:30:42 PDT
Restart Time: Saturday, 25-May-2002 18:46:07 PDT
Parent Server Generation: 9
Server uptime: 6 days 16 hours 44 minutes 35 seconds
Total accesses: 20035080 - Total Traffic: 1189.8 GB
CPU Usage: u149.07 s279.266 cu278.867 cs45.4219 - .13% CPU load
34.6 requests/sec - 2.1 MB/second - 62.3 kB/request
149 requests currently being processed, 43 idle workers
```

To simplify things further, you can request the status information in a more "machine-friendly" format by appending *?auto* to the URL. Entering http://www.apache.org/server-status?auto in a browser yielded this response:

```
Total Accesses: 16019131
Total kBytes: 1297434471
CPULoad: .0984651
Uptime: 520751
ReqPerSec: 30.7616
BytesPerSec: 2551260
BytesPerReq: 82936.6
BusyWorkers: 200
IdleWorkers: 25
Scoreboard: KWKCWWWWWCW_KWWKKKW_WWWWWWWWKWKWWKKW_...
```

Because fetching URLs is simple in Java and the machine-friendly format is easily parsed, creating a very useful Apache MBean is pretty straightforward. As usual, we start by defining the Apache management interface:

```
package net.jnjmx.ch3;

public interface ApacheMBean }
  public String DOWN = "DOWN";
  public String NOT_RESPONDING = "NOT_RESPONDING";
  public String RUNNING = "RUNNING";
  public String UNKNOWN = "UNKNOWN";
  public int getBusyWorkers() throws ApacheMBeanException;
  public int getBytesPerSec()throws ApacheMBeanException;
  public float getBytesPerReq()throws ApacheMBeanException;
  public long getCacheLifetime();
  public float getCpuLoad()throws ApacheMBeanException;
  public int getIdleWorkers()throws ApacheMBeanException;
  public float getReqPerSec()throws ApacheMBeanException;
  public String getScoreboard()throws ApacheMBeanException;
  public String getServer();
  public String getState();
  public int getTotalAccesses()throws ApacheMBeanException;
  public long getTotalKBytes()throws ApacheMBeanException;
  public long getUptime(throws ApacheMBeanException);
  public boolean isCaching();
  public void setCacheLifetime(long lifetime);
  public void setCaching(boolean caching);
  public void setServer(String url) throws MalformedURLException,
    IllegalArgumentException;
  public int start()throws ApacheMBeanException;
  public int stop()throws ApacheMBeanException;
}
```

The bulk of the management interface expressed by ApacheMBean consists of attributes. Most of the ApacheMBean attributes—BusyWorkers, BytesPerReq, BytesPerSec, CpuLoad, IdleWorkers, ReqPerSec, Scoreboard, TotalAccesses, TotalKBytes, and Uptime–are read-only attributes that reflect the values returned by the server-status?auto request. Table 3.1 describes the other four ApacheMBean attributes.

The impact of management on a resource should be minimized whenever possible; resources exist to provide a business function, not to generate data for management applications. To that end the Apache MBean supports caching of the results of a mod_status request; when caching is in effect, requests

Table 3.1 ApacheMBean Attributes Not Associated with mod_status Information

Attribute	Type	Description
CacheLifetime	Read/write	Gives the length of time, in milliseconds, that the Apache MBean caches information returned by a mod_status request.
Caching	Read/write	Indicates whether or not information returned by a mod_status request will be cached by the Apache MBean. Its value is true by default.
State	Read-only	Represents the Apache MBean's current assumption about the execution state of the Apache server that it's associated with.
Server	Read/write	Holds the URL of the server that the Apache MBean's mod_status requests are directed toward.

for Apache-related attribute values that occur close together can be satisfied from the cache, reducing the load that the management application imposes on the server and improving the management application's performance. The Caching attribute determines whether or not mod_status results are cached, and the CacheLifetime attribute indicates how long the results are valid.

The State attribute provides a "best guess" at the state of the Apache server with which the MBean is associated. When the MBean is created, the value of the State attribute is ApacheMBean.UNKNOWN. When mod_status results are successfully retrieved, the MBean's State attribute changes to ApacheMBean.RUNNING. What happens when an error—for example, "unable to connect" or "connection timeout"—occurs in the course of making a mod_status request? The first time an error occurs, the value of the State attribute becomes ApacheMBean.NOT_RESPONDING; after three consecutive errors the MBean's State attribute changes to ApacheMBean.DOWN.

Finally, we need a way to tell the Apache MBean where to send its mod_status requests. The Server attribute holds the URL of the Apache instance with which an Apache MBean is associated. The Server attribute is read/write, so this association can change over the course of an Apache MBean's lifetime.

The management interface also specifies two operations: start() and stop(). These methods perform the actions that their names imply, but only if the server is running on the same machine as the management application.

Now that the management interface is fully defined, all we have to do is implement it:

```
import java.io.BufferedReader;
import java.io.IOException;
import java.io.InputStreamReader;
import java.net.MalformedURLException;
import java.net.URL;
import java.net.URLConnection;
import java.util.HashMap;
import java.util.StringTokenizer;

public class Apache implements ApacheMBean {
  // String constants for each of the Apache-related attributes
  private static final String BUSY_WORKERS = "BusyWorkers";
  private static final String BYTES_PER_REQ = "BytesPerReq";
  private static final String BYTES_PER_SEC = "BytesPerSec";
  private static final String CPU_LOAD = "CPULoad";
  private static final String IDLE_WORKERS = "IdleWorkers";
  private static final String REQ_PER_SEC = "ReqPerSec";
  private static final String SCOREBOARD = "Scoreboard";
  private static final String TOTAL_ACCESSES = "Total Accesses";
  private static final String TOTAL_KBYTES = "Total kBytes";
  private static final String UPTIME = "Uptime";

  private static final int MAX_FAILURES = 3;

  private boolean caching = true;
  private int failures = 0;
  private long lifetime = 1000;
  private String state = ApacheMBean.UNKNOWN;
  private HashMap status;
  private long tzero;
  private URL url;

  public Apache(String url) throws MalformedURLException,
      IllegalArgumentException {
    setServer(url);
  }
```

There are a couple of things to notice about this part of the implementation. The first is that we create a set of `String` constants, one for each of the Apache attributes that `mod_status` returns. These constants will be used as keys into the hash map (`java.util.HashMap`) that contains the attribute values. The second is that we have to associate the Apache MBean with an Apache instance when we create it.

Next comes the implementation of the methods specified by the ApacheMBean interface:

```
public int getBusyWorkers() throws ApacheMBeanException {
  return getIntValue(BUSY_WORKERS);
}

public int getBytesPerSec() throws ApacheMBeanException {
  return getIntValue(BYTES_PER_SEC);
}

public float getBytesPerReq() throws ApacheMBeanException {
  return getFloatValue(BYTES_PER_REQ);
}

public long getCacheLifetime() {
  return this.lifetime;
}

public float getCpuLoad() throws ApacheMBeanException {
  return getFloatValue(CPU_LOAD);
}

public int getIdleWorkers() throws ApacheMBeanException {
  return getIntValue(IDLE_WORKERS);
}

public float getReqPerSec() throws ApacheMBeanException {
  return getFloatValue(REQ_PER_SEC);
}

public String getScoreboard() throws ApacheMBeanException {
  return getStringValue(SCOREBOARD);
}

public String getServer() {
  return this.url.toString();
}

public int getState() {
  return this.state;
}
```

```
public int getTotalAccesses() throws ApacheMBeanException {
  return getIntValue(TOTAL_ACCESSES);
}

public long getTotalKBytes() throws ApacheMBeanException {
  return getLongValue(TOTAL_KBYTES);
}

public long getUptime() throws ApacheMBeanException {
  return getLongValue(UPTIME);
}

public boolean isCaching() {
  return this.caching;
}

public void setCacheLifetime(long lifetime) {
  this.lifetime = lifetime;
}

public void setCaching(boolean caching) {
  this.caching = caching;
}

public void setServer(String url) throws MalformectURLException,
    IllegalArgumentException {
  this.url = new URL(url);
  if (isStatusUrl(this.url) == false) {
    throw new IllegalArgumentException(url.toString()));
  }
  this.status = new HashMap();
  this.state = ApacheMBean.UNKNOWN;
}
```

There's not much to the implementation of the attribute-related methods. For the most part either they return the value of an instance variable or they call a `get`*Type*`Value()` method; we'll look at the latter in a moment. The most interesting attribute method is `setServer()`, which is responsible for checking whether the given URL is an appropriate `mod_status` URL and initializing the hash map of attribute values and the `State` attribute. Note that in the interest of simplicity, this implementation is not thread-safe; if one thread sets the `Server` attribute while another thread is fetching attributes, the latter thread will get inconsistent results.

The ApacheMBean management interface has only two operations:

```
public int start() {
  // platform-specific code to exececute a command shell and
  // start Apache
  return RUNNING;
}

public int stop() {
  // platform-specific code to exececute a command shell and
  // start Apache
  return DOWN;
}
```

The Apache MBean operations start() and stop() work only if the Apache instance the MBean is associated with is running on the same machine as the MBean. If the Apache MBean and its associated Apache instance are collocated, then we can use java.lang.Runtime's exec() method to execute the appropriate shell command to start or stop the instance.

Now let's look at the private methods where all the work gets done:

```
private boolean isStatusUrl(URL url) {
  return url.toString().endsWith("server-status?auto");
}
```

The isStatusUrl() method just checks to see if the URL under consideration ends in *server-status?auto*.

The getValue() method is responsible for making mod_status requests, via fetchStatus(), when necessary and retrieving the specified attribute from the hash map of attribute values:

```
private String getValue(String value)
 throws ApacheMBeanException, NoSuchFieldException, IOException
{
  String result;
  if (updateStatus()) fetchStatus();
  if ((result = (String) this.status.get(value)) == null) {
    throw new NoSuchFieldException(value);
  }
  return result;
}
```

```
private float getFloatValue(String value) throws
      ApacheMBeanException {
  float result;
  try {
    result = Float.parseFloat((String) getValue(value));
  } catch (IOException x) {
    throw new ApacheMBeanException(x);
  } catch (NoSuchFieldException x) {
    throw new ApacheMBeanException(x);
  }
  return result;
}

private int getIntValue(String value) throws
      ApacheMBeanException {
  int result;
  try {
    result = Integer.parseInt((String) getValue(value));
  } catch (IOException x) {
    throw new ApacheMBeanException(x);
  } catch (NoSuchFieldException x) {
    throw new ApacheMBeanException(x);
  }
  return result;
}

private long getLongValue(String value) throws
      ApacheMBeanException {
  long result;
  try {
    result = Long.parseLong((String) getValue(value));
  } catch (IOException x) {
    throw new ApacheMBeanException(x);
  } catch (NoSuchFieldException x) {
    throw new ApacheMBeanException(x);
  }
  return result;
}

private String getStringValue(String value) throws
      ApacheMBeanException {
  String result;
  try {
    result = (String) getValue(value);
  } catch (IOException x) {
```

```
      throw new ApacheMBeanException(x);
    } catch (NoSuchFieldException x) {
      throw new ApacheMBeanException(x);
    }
    return result;
  }
```

The get*Type*Value() methods call getValue() to retrieve the required attribute and then transform the resulting String value into the appropriate return type. As we saw in the implementation of the Apache-related attribute methods, this suite of methods is the core of the Apache MBean implementation.

Last but not least is the code that actually sends the mod_status request and parses the result into the hash map of attribute values:

```
  private void fetchStatus() throws ApacheMBeanException,
        IOException {
    URLConnection k = establishConnection();
    readStatus(k);
  }

  private URLConnection establishConnection()
    throws IOException, ApacheMBeanException {
    URLConnection k = this.url.openConnection();
    try {
      k.connect();
      this.failures = 0;
      this.state = ApacheMBean.RUNNING;
    } catch (IOException x) {
      if (++this.failures > MAX_FAILURES) {
        this.state = ApacheMBean.DOWN;
      } else {
        this.state = ApacheMBean.NOT_RESPONDING;
      }
      throw new ApacheMBeanException("state: " + this.state);
    }
    return k;
  }

  private void readStatus(URLConnection k) throws IOException {
    BufferedReader r = new BufferedReader
        (new InputStreamReader(k.getInputStream()));
    for (String l = r.readLine(); l != null; l = r.readLine()) {
      StringTokenizer st = new StringTokenizer(l, ":");
```

```
      this.status.put(st.nextToken().trim(),
        st.nextToken().trim());
    }
    r.close();
    this.tzero = System.currentTimeMillis();
  }

  private boolean updateStatus() throws IOException {
    boolean result = true;
    if (this.caching) {
      long now = System.currentTimeMillis();
      result = ((now - this.tzero) > this.lifetime);
    }
    return result;
  }
}
```

The `establishConnection()` method is responsible for setting up a `URLConnection` object and for managing the value of the `ApacheMBean State` attribute on success and failure. The `readStatus()` method parses the response and populates the hash map. Note that we have hard-coded each of the `mod_status` attribute labels into our implementation; if they ever change, our code will need to be updated and recompiled.

3.2.2 Dynamic MBeans

Now let's look at dynamic MBeans. To be recognized as a dynamic MBean, the underlying Java class, or one of its ancestors, must implement the `DynamicMBean` interface. As we saw earlier, this interface consists of six methods that get and set an attribute, or sets thereof, invoke a method, and retrieve the MBean's `MBeanInfo` metadata.

Standard MBeans assume that the management information associated with the resources they represent is well known in advance—that is, at development time—and is relatively static. By contrast, a dynamic MBean can support resource management information that is known only at runtime and is relatively dynamic.

3.2.2.1 MBeanInfo Classes

Figure 3.5 depicts the `MBeanInfo` structure associated with an MBean. The MBeanServer uses the introspection algorithm described in Section 3.1.2 to construct this structure for standard MBeans. A dynamic MBean is responsible for building its own `MBeanInfo` structure. This added responsibility creates extra work for developers, but it also makes it possible to present a more flexible management interface. For example, a dynamic MBean representing a service might make a `start` operation available only when the service is not running and a `stop` operation available when the service is running. This section describes the classes that dynamic-MBean developers use to construct an `MBeanInfo` structure that represents a dynamic MBean's management interface.

The `MBeanInfo` class itself is just a collection of arrays, along with the name of the class that implements the `DynamicMBean` interface and a human-readable description of the MBean:

```
public class MBeanInfo implements Cloneable, Serializable {
  public MBeanInfo(String classname,
                   String description,
                   MBeanAttributeInfo[] attributes,
                   MBeanConstructorInfo[] constructors,
                   MBeanOperationInfo[] operations,
                   MBeanNotificationInfo[] notifications)
  { … }

  public Object clone() { … }
  public MBeanAttributeInfo[] getAttributes() { … }
  public MBeanContsturctorInfo[] getConstructors() { … }
  public String getDescription() { … }
  public MBeanNotificationInfo[] getNotifications() { … }
  public MBeanOperationInfo[] getOperations() { … }
}
```

All the management interface information is supplied in the constructor and then returned by the getters.

There is a separate array for each of the features of an MBean: attributes, constructors, notifications, and operations. A single base class, `MBeanFeatureInfo`, captures the information that is common to each of these MBean features—that is, the feature name and a human-readable description of it:

```
public class MBeanFeatureInfo implements Serializable {
  public MBeanFeatureInfo(String name, String description) { … }

  public getDescription() { … }
  public getName() { … }
}
```

The `MBeanAttributeInfo` class extends `MBeanFeatureInfo` with information about the attribute's type and indications of the kind of access—read, write, or both—that is provided for the attribute's value:

```
public class MBeanAttributeInfo extends MBeanFeatureInfo
    implements Cloneable, Serializable {
  public MBeanAttributeInfo(String name,
                            String descriptions,
                            Method getter,
                            Method setter)
  { … }
  public MBeanAttributeInfo(String name,
                            String type,
                            String description,
                            boolean isReadable,
                            boolean isWriteable,
                            boolean isIs)
  { … }

  public Object clone() { … }
  public String getType() { … }
  public boolean isIs() { … }
  public boolean isReadable() { … }
  public boolean isWriteable() { … }
}
```

The first constructor is the only mysterious part of this class definition. It allows developers to supply a reference to the MBean's get and set methods shift the responsibility for figuring out the attribute's type and accessibility to the constructor.

The `MBeanConstructorInfo` class extends `MBeanFeatureInfo` with information about the signature of the MBean's constructor:

```
public class MBeanConstructorInfo extends MBeanFeatureInfo
    implements Cloneable, Serializable {
  public MBeanConstructorInfo(String description,
    Constructor constructor) { … }
  public MBeanConstructorInfo(String name,
                              String description,
                              MBeanParameterInfo[] parameters)
  { … }
```

```
  public Object clone() { … }
  public MBeanParameterInfo[] getSignature() { … }
}
```

Again the first constructor takes a reference to the MBean's actual constructor, leaving it up to the `MBeanConstructorInfo` constructor to figure out the signature information. Note that the signature information is expressed as an array of `MBeanParameterInfo` instances. The `MBeanParameterInfo` class extends `MBeanFeatureInfo` with information about the parameter's type:

```
public class MBeanParameterInfo extends MBeanFeatureInfo
    implements Cloneable, Serializable {
  public MBeanParameterInfo(String name,
                            String type,
                            String description)
  { … }

  public Object clone() { … }
  public String getType() { … }
}
```

The `MBeanNotificationInfo` class extends `MBeanFeatureInfo` with information about the notification types that the MBean may send:

```
public class MBeanNofiticationInfo extends MBeanFeatureInfo
    implements Cloneable, Serializable {
  public MBeanNotificationInfo(String[] types,
                               String name,
                               String description)
{ … }

  public Object clone() { … }
  public String[] getNotifTypes() { … }
}
```

We will discuss JMX Notifications in detail at the end of this chapter.

Finally, the `MBeanOperationInfo` class extends `MBeanFeatureInfo` with information about the operation: its *impact*, its return type, and its signature:

```
public class MBeanOperationInfo extends MBeanFeatureInfo
    implements Cloneable, Serializable {
  public MBeanOperationInfo(String description, Method method) { … }
  public MBeanOperationInfo(String name,
                            String description,
                            MBeanParameterInfo[] signature,
                            String returnType,
                            int impact)
  { … }

  public Object clone() { … }
  public int getImpact() { … }
  public String getReturnType() { … }
  public MBeanParameterInfo[] getSignature() { … }
}
```

Like `MBeanAttributeInfo` and `MBeanConstructorInfo`, the first `MBeanOperationInfo` constructor takes a `Method` reference, so it makes the constructor responsible for determining the signature and return type information. As with constructors, an operation's signature is described by an array of `MBeanParameterInfo` instances. What about the *impact* aspect of `MBeanOperationInfo`? The `impact` attribute indicates the impact of the operation on the MBean and can have one of four values:

- `MBeanOperationInfo.ACTION` indicates that the operation modifies the MBean's state in some way, typically by modifying a value or altering the configuration.
- `MBeanOperationInfo.ACTION_INFO` indicates that the operation modifies the MBean as described for the `ACTION` impact, and that it returns information regarding the modification. For example, an operation that sets the value of a particular field and returns the field's old value has `ACTION_INFO` impact.
- `MBeanOperationInfo.INFO` indicates that the operation returns some information about the MBean without altering its state.
- `MBeanOperationInfo.UNKNOWN` indicates that the nature of the operation's impact is unknown.

We'll see how these classes are used to create a dynamic MBean's `MBeanInfo` in the next section. Basically we will just use the various constructors to build up the appropriate arrays. Management consoles typically use the get methods provided by these classes to obtain the information they need to create graphical representations of a system's MBeans.

3.2.2.2 Using Dynamic MBeans

Suppose that the resource we're interested in managing is a server-side container that provides a context for services like an HTTP daemon, a servlet engine, or an e-mail transfer agent. Let's suppose further that containers are not one-size-fits-all; a given container might provide features beyond hosting services—for example, replication, fault tolerance, security.

Using standard MBeans, either we could design a lowest-common-denominator MBean interface, or we could create MBean interfaces that capture each of the extended feature sets. A lowest-common-denominator approach wouldn't allow the management system to manage replication or security features effectively, and the separate-interfaces approach works only if the features can't be composed—that is, you can't have a secure, replicated container.

The DynamicMBean interface allows us to extend the Container management interface as we extend the feature set. Here is one possible structure for this approach:

```
public class Container implements DyanmicMBean {
  // Container class and instance variables
  ...
  // data structures describing the Container management interface
  ...

  public Container() {
    // initialize the instance variables for the base Container
    // features
    // initialize the data structures for the base management
    // interface
  }

  // Implement the DynamicMBean interface by mapping the data
  // structures describing the container management interface into
  //  the corresponding MBeanInfo structures
  public Object getAttribute(String attrname) { … }
  public AttributeList getAttributes(String[] attrnames) { … }
  public MBeanInfo getMBeanInfo() { … }
  public Object invoke(String method, Object[] params,
    String[] signature) { … }
  public void setAttribute(Attribute attr) { … }
  public AttributeList setAttributes(AttributeList attrs) { … }
```

```
  // other Container-specific methods used by server applications
  ...
}

public class SimpleSecureContainer extends Container {
  // SecureContainer class and instance variables
  ...

  public SecureContainer() {
    super();
    // initialization of SecureContainer
    // Add information about SecureContainer's management
    // interface to the management interface data structures
    // The DynamicMBean methods inherited from the base class
    // will reflect this additional information in the
    // management interface they present to clients
  }

  // SecureContainer methods
  ...
}

public class ExtendedContainer extends SecureContainer {
  // ExtendedContainer class and instance variables
  ...

  public ExtendedContainer(ContainerExtensionList extensions) {
    super();
    // initialization of ExtendedContainer
    // Add information about ExtendedContainer's management
    // interface to the management interface data structures
    // The DynamicMBean methods inherited from the base class
    // will reflect this additional information in the
    // management interface they present to clients
}

  // ExtendedContainer methods
  ...
}
```

Each `Container` subclass is an MBean and so can be registered with an MBeanServer. Once a subclass is registered, its `MBeanInfo` is available to management systems that connect to its MBeanServer. A management console could use `MBeanInfo` to render a different GUI for `SecureContainer` and `ExtendedContainer` objects. Container-aware management systems could inspect `MBeanInfo` and take advantage of additional capabilities like replication if they are part of the management interface.

Another, simpler, use of the `DynamicMBean` interface is to implement a management interface for a class that doesn't follow the lexical design patterns of standard MBeans. Recall that the time of day daemon (todd) in the previous chapter's Quick Tour of JMX (Section 2.6) used a queue, implemented by `java.util.SortedSet`, to hold incoming connection requests. Suppose we wanted to monitor the number of pending requests in the queue so that we could grow the session pool when that number passed a specified threshold. We could create a subclass of `SortedSet`, making it a standard MBean, or we could use the `DynamicMBean` interface:

```
public class ConnectionQueue implements DynamicMBean {
  private SortedSet queue;
  private int capacity;

  /**
   * Construct a new ConnectionQueue instance
   * @param queue - a SortedSet that holds incoming connection
   * requests
   * @param capacity - the maximum capacity of the queue
   */
  public ConnectionQueue(SortedSet queue, int capacity) {
    this.queue = queue;
    this.capacity = capacity;
  }

  /**
   * Retrieve the value of the named attribute
   * @param attr - name of the attribute of interest
   * @return value associated with the named attribute
   * @exception AttributeNotFoundException
   */
  public Object getAttribute(String attr) throws Exception {
    Object value = null;
    if (attr.compareTo("Length") == 0)
        value = new Integer(queue.size());
    else if (attr.compareTo("Capacity") == 0)
        value = new Integer(capacity);
    else throw new AttributeNotFoundException(
        "No such attribute: " + attr);
    return value;
  }
```

```
/**
 * Retrieve the values of the named attributes
 * @param attrs - array of names of attributes of interest
 * @return AttributeList containing an Attribute for each value
 * retrieved
 */
public AttributeList getAttributes(String[] attrs) {
  AttributeList result = new AttributeList();
  for (int i = 0; i < attrs.length; i++) {
    try {
      result.add(new Attribute(attrs[i],
          getAttribute(attrs[i])));
    } catch (AttributeNotFoundException x) {
      System.err.println("No such attribute: " + attrs[i]);
    } catch (Exception x) {
      System.err.println(x.toString());
    }
  }
  return result;
}

/**
 * Retrieve the MBeanInfo metadata for this MBean
 * @return ConnectionQueue MBeanInfo instance
 */
public javax.management.MBeanInfo getMBeanInfo() {
  MBeanAttributeInfo[] attributes = attributeInfo();
  MBeanConstructorInfo[] constructors = constructorInfo();
  MBeanOperationInfo[] operations = operationInfo();
  MBeanNotificationInfo[] notifications = notificationInfo();
  return new MBeanInfo("net.jmx.todd.ConnectionQueue",
    "todd ConnectionQueue MBean",
    attributes,
    constructors,
    operations,
    notifications);
}

/**
 * Invoke the named operation
 * @param operation - name of the operation to invoke
 * @param params - array of parameters to be passed to named
 * operation
 * @param signature - fully qualified type names for each
 * parameter
```

```
 * @return result of invocation or 'null' if the operations
 * return type is void
 */
public Object invoke(String operation, Object[] params,
      String[] signature)
  throws Exception {
  if (operation.compareTo("clear") == 0) {
    queue.clear();
  }
  return null;
}

/**
 * Update the value of the named attribute
 * @param attr - attribute name and value
 */
public void setAttribute(Attribute attr) throws Exception {
  if (attr.getName().compareTo("Length") == 0) {
    throw new MBeanException(
        new IllegalArgumentException("Length is read-only"));
  } else if (attr.getName().compareTo("Capacity") == 0) {
    capacity = ((Integer) attr.getValue()).intValue();
  } else throw new AttributeNotFoundException(
        "No such attribute: " + attr.getName());
}

/**
 * Update the values of the named attributes
 * @param attrs - AttributeList of attribute names and values
 * @return AttributeList of the updated names and values
 */
public AttributeList setAttributes(AttributeList attrs) {
  AttributeList attrsSet = new AttributeList();
  ListIterator li = attrs.listIterator();
  while (li.hasNext()) {
    try {
      Attribute attr = (Attribute) li.next();
      setAttribute(attr);
      attrsSet.add(attr);
    } catch (Exception x) {
      System.err.println(x.toString());
    }
  return attrsSet;
}
```

```
  private MBeanAttributeInfo[] attributeInfo() {
    MBeanAttributeInfo[] attributes = new MBeanAttributeInfo[2];
    attributes[0] = new MBeanAttributeInfo("Capacity",
            "java.lang.Integer",
            "Capacity of the Connection queue",
            true,
            true,
            false);
    attributes[1] = new MBeanAttributeInfo("Length",
            "java.lang.Integer",
            "Number of entries currently in the Connection queue",
            true,
            false,
            false);
    return attributes;
  }

  private MBeanConstructorInfo[] constructorInfo() {
    MBeanConstructorInfo[] constructors = new
        MBeanConstructorInfo[1];
    MBeanParameterInfo[] signature = new MBeanParameterInfo[2];
    signature[0] = new MBeanParameterInfo("requestQueue",
            "java.util.SortedSet",
            "The Connection queue");
    signature[1] = new MBeanParameterInfo("Capacity",
            "int",
            "The Connection queue capacity");
    constructors[0] = new MBeanConstructorInfo("ConnectionQueue",
            "Constructor for ConnectionQueue MBeans",
            signature);
    return constructors;
  }

  private MBeanNotificationInfo[] notificationInfo() {
    return null;
  }

  private MBeanOperationInfo[] operationInfo() {
    MBeanOperationInfo[] operations = new MBeanOperationInfo[1];
    operations[0] = new MBeanOperationInfo("clear",
            "Remove all entries from the Connection queue",
            null,
            "void",
            MBeanOperationInfo.ACTION);
    return operations;
  }
}
```

In the time of day daemon (todd) code, after the Connection queue was instantiated we would register the ConnectionQueue MBean as follows:

```
mbs.registerMBean("net.jmx.todd.ConnectionQueue",
                  cqobjname,
                  new Object[] { connectionQueue },
                  new String[] { "java.util.SortedSet" });
```

Once that was done, we could add a monitor that would trigger a notification if the ConnectionQueue's Length attribute exceeded a specified threshold.

The thing to note here is that the DynamicMBean interface has allowed us to expose certain aspects of the connection queue to a management system without requiring any change to the implementation of the connection queue itself or the code that uses it.

3.2.3 Active MBeans

So far all the MBeans we have seen have been "passive" MBeans. They provide attributes and operations that management systems can use, but they don't take any initiative themselves. For example, the ConnectionQueue class that we created in the previous section doesn't do anything when its capacity is exceeded. If a management system wanted to react to that situation, it would have to create a monitor to check the Capacity attribute periodically. In many cases this sort of separation of concerns reflects a good design. But sometimes an MBean needs to be proactive.

MBeans become "active" through implementation of the NotificationBroadcaster interface:

```
public interface NotificationBroadcaster {
  void addNotificationListener(NotificationListener listener,
                               NotificationFilter filter,
                               Object handback);
  MBeanNotificationInfo[] getNotificationInfo();
  void removeNotificationListener(NotificationLIstener listener);
}
```

Listeners, classes that implement the NotificationListener interface that we will describe momentarily, may register and deregister interest in an MBean's notifications via the addNotificationListener() and removeNotificationListener() methods. The getNotificationInfo() method returns information about the notifications that an MBean may generate.

JMX provides an implementation of NotificationBroadcaster called NotificationBroadcasterSupport that provides a standard implementation of each of the NotificationBroadcaster methods and an additional sendNotification() method:

```
void sendNotification(Notification notification);
```

Active MBeans can take advantage of NotificationBroadcasterSupport by using it as a base class that they extend with the methods defined by their MBean interface. We'll see how to do just that with the Apache MBean in a moment. First we need to explain the JMX notification model.

3.2.3.1 JMX Notifications

The JMX notification model has four components:

1. Notification, a generic class that can be used to signal any sort of management event
2. NotificationListener, an interface that is implemented by objects that want to receive MBean notifications
3. NotificationFilter, an interface that is implemented by objects that filter notifications before they are delivered to listeners
4. NotificationBroadcaster, the interface that we just discussed

The Notification class extends the java.util.EventObject class and serves as a base class for all the other notification subclasses that the JMX specification defines: AttributeChangeNotification, MBeanServerNotification, MonitorNotification, RelationNotification, and TimerNotification. The subclasses will be described in later chapters; the Notification class has the following form:

```
public class Notification extends java.util.EventObject {
  public Notification(String type, Object source, long seqno) {}
  public Notification(String type, Object source, long seqno,
    long timestamp) {}
  public Notification(String type, Object source, long seqno,
    long timestame, String msg) {}
  public Notification(String type, Object source, long seqno,
    String msg) {}

  public String getMessage() {}
```

```
  public long getSequenceNumber() {}

  public Object getSource() {}
  public long getTimeStamp() {}
  public String getType() {}
  public Object getUserData() {}

  public void setSequenceNumber(long seqno) {}
  public void setSource(Object source) {}
  public void setTimeStamp(long timestamp) {}
  public void setUserData(Object userdata) {}
}
```

Here are the pertinent aspects of this set of methods:

- The **source** of the message is a reference to either the MBean that is sending the notification or the object name of the MBean sending the notification. Which one it is depends on whether the listener to which the notification is being delivered registered its interest via the MBean itself or via the MBeanServer. In the former case, the source is an object reference; in the latter it is an object name.
- The **message** can be any string that the sending MBean wants to deliver to the listener.
- The **user data** likewise can be any Java object that the sending MBean wants to deliver to the listener.
- The **time stamp** has the obvious meaning: the time, in milliseconds, when the notification was sent.
- The **sequence number** requires a little more explanation. The JMX specification defines it as "a serial number identifying a particular instance of notification in the context of the notification broadcaster."
- Finally, we have the **type** of the notification. The type string provides a mechanism that distinguishes one kind of notification from another. The JMX specification defines the type as a set of components separated by dots (.). Taken together, the components convey the meaning of the particular notification. For example, the notification type `jmx.monitor.counter.threshold` indicates that a counter monitor threshold has been exceeded. All notifications defined by the JMX specification are prefixed by *jmx*; with the exception of that prefix, MBean developers are free to define additional notification types as appropriate for their applications.

The `NotificationListener` interface defines a single method:

```
public interface NotificationListener {
  void handleNotification(Notification notification,
    Object handback);
}
```

When an MBean sends a notification, `handleNotification()` is called on each of the objects that have expressed interest in the MBean's notifications. The notification that the MBean sent is passed as the first argument, and the object that the listener passed in when it registered its interest is "handed back" to the listener in the second parameter. The listener can use the handback to create additional context regarding the source of the notification.

A listener might not be interested in every notification that an MBean may send. The `NotificationFilter` interface can be used to filter out notifications that are not of interest:

```
public interface NotificationFilter {
  boolean isNotificationEnabled(Notification notification);
}
```

When a listener registers interest in an MBean's notifications, it may specify a filter, a class that implements `NotificationFilter`. Before a notification is delivered to any listener, the MBean checks to see if the listener has an associated filter. If it does, the notification is delivered only if `isNotificationEnabled()` returns `true`.

3.2.3.2 Activating the Apache MBean

Although our `Apache` MBean is a perfectly good standard MBean, it would be even more useful if a management application could be notified immediately of changes in the `State` attribute. For example, we might want to page an administrator if the value of the `State` attribute became `ApacheMBean.DOWN`. The `NotificationBroadcasterSupport` class makes it easy to get that behavior:

```
public class Apache extends NotificationBroadcasterSupport
  implements ApacheMBean {

... // Only the establishConnection method requires a change
```

```
  private URLConnection establishConnection() throws IOException,
        ApacheMBeanException {
    String oldstate = this.state;
    URLConnection k = this.url.openConnection();
    try {
      k.connect();
      this.failures = 0;
      this.state = ApacheMBean.RUNNING;
    } catch (IOException x) {
      if (++this.failures > MAX_FAILURES) {
        this.state = ApacheMBean.DOWN;
      } else {
        this.state = ApacheMBean.NOT_RESPONDING;
      }
      throw new ApacheMBeanException("state: " + this.state);
    } finally {
      if (this.state.compareTo(oldstate) != 0) {
        Notification n = new Notification("apache.state." +
            this.state,
            this,
            0);
        sendNotification(n);
      }
    }
    return k;
  }
}
```

The `ApacheMgr` code shows how listening works in this simple example:

```
import java.text.DateFormat;
import java.util.Date;

import javax.management.Attribute;
import javax.management.MBeanServer;
import javax.management.MBeanServerFactory;
import javax.management.Notification;
import javax.management.NotificationListener;
import javax.management.ObjectName;

public class ApacheMgr {
  public static void main(String[] args) throws Exception {
    // Create an MBeanServer to host an ApacheMBean; then create
    // an ApacheMBean instance
```

```
    MBeanServer mbs = MBeanServerFactory.createMBeanServer();
    ObjectName apacheon = new ObjectName(
        "book/ch3:id=ApacheExample");
    mbs.createMBean("net.jnjmx.ch3.Apache",
      apacheon,
      new Object[] { "http://www.apache.org/server-status?auto" },
      new String[] { "java.lang.String" });

    // apacheListener will receive the ApacheMBean State change
    // notification
    NotificationListener apacheListener =
        new NotificationListener() {
        public void handleNotification(Notification notification,
            Object handback) {
            // Do something useful here when the notification is
            // received
        }};

    // Listen for the ApacheMBean's State change notification
    mbs.addNotificationListener(apacheon, apacheListener, null,
        new Object());

    // At this point the value of State is ApacheMBean.UNKNOWN;
    // successfully fetching one of the Apache-related attributes
    // will cause it to become ApacheMBean.RUNNING and will
    //  result in a notification that will trigger apacheListener
    int accesses = mbs.getAttribute(apacheon, "TotalAccesses");

    … // remainder of the ApacheMgr application
  }
}
```

The `main()` method of the `ApacheMgr` class creates an MBeanServer and then creates an instance of `Apache`–that is, an `Apache` MBean—in the MBeanServer. After that it creates an instance of `NotificationListener` to respond to `Apache` MBean `State` change notifications. In this simple example we just used an anonymous inner class; in a more complex example we might have created a separate class.

3.2.4 Open MBeans

Open MBeans and model MBeans are both types of dynamic MBeans. Model MBeans will be covered in Chapter 4. JMX implementations (1.0 and 1.1) are not required to implement support for open MBeans. The open-MBean interfaces may change in JSR 160 and subsequent JSRs. The JMX 1.0 reference implementation does not provide an implementation of open MBeans. We will give an overview of open MBeans in this chapter, but we will not provide working examples. Programming with open MBeans is much like programming with other dynamic MBeans.

Open MBeans are dynamic MBeans that restrict the allowed data types for their attributes, constructors, and operations to Java primitive types, their respective wrapper objects, `String`, `CompositeData`, `TabularData`, `ObjectName`, and `ArrayType`. Using these limited basic types enables serialization and mapping to XML representations. It also removes the need for class loading and proxy coordination between the MBeanServer and remote users of the MBeans. However, it does not remove the need for the program that is processing the open MBean to understand the semantics of the fields. The `getMBeanInfo()` method of open MBeans returns instances that implement the `OpenMBeanInfo` interface, which is a specialization of the `MBeanInfo` class. `OpenMBeanInfo` adds additional metadata for attributes, operations, and parameters, and it restricts the allowed data types.

3.2.4.1 Basic Data Types

Open MBeans restrict their data to the basic data types, which must be described by `OpenType` instances in `OpenMBeanInfo`. The `OpenType` class is defined as follows:

```
public abstract class OpenType extends Object implements
  Serializable {
    protected OpenType(String className, String typeName, String
      description) {}
    abstract boolean equals(Object obj) {}
    String getClassName(){}
    String getDescription(){}
    String getTypeName(){}
    abstract int hashCode(){}
    abstract boolean isArray(){}
    abstract String toString(){}
```

The basic data types for open MBeans can be divided into four categories: primitives, primitive objects, aggregate types, and `ObjectName`.

Primitives

Valid primitive Java data types, or scalars, are valid open MBean basic data types, including `void`, `null`, `integer`, `byte`, `short`, `long`, `double`, `float`, `bool`, and `char`. We describe primitives using the `SimpleType` class. Here is `SimpleType`'s definition:

```
public final class SimpleType extends OpenType implements
Serializable {
    public static SimpleType VOID
    public static SimpleType BOOLEAN
    public static SimpleType CHARACTER
    public static SimpleType BYTE
    public static SimpleType SHORT
    public static SimpleType INTEGER
    public static SimpleType LONG
    public static SimpleType FLOAT
    public static SimpleType DOUBLE
    public static SimpleType STRING
    public static SimpleType BIGDECIMAL
    public static SimpleType BIGINTEGER
    public static SimpleType OBJECTNAME
    public boolean isValue(Object obj)  {}
    public boolean equals(Object obj) {}
    public int hashCode() {}
    public String toString() {}
    public Object readResolve() throws ObjectStreamException  {}
}
```

Primitive Objects

Any of the object wrappers for the Java primitive objects are valid open-MBean basic data types. We describe wrappers using the `SimpleType` class as well. Here is the list of the supported object wrappers:

- `java.lang.Void`
- `java.lang.Byte`
- `java.lang.Short`
- `java.lang.Integer`
- `java.lang.Long`
- `java.lang.Double`
- `java.lang.Float`
- `java.lang.Boolean`
- `java.lang.Character`
- `java.lang.String`

Aggregate Types

The aggregate types allow the representation of complex data types. Aggregate data types may contain *only* other basic data types, including other aggregate types. Therefore aggregate data types can be predictably decomposed into the Java primitive types. Because these are required, standard interfaces and a known set of contained types, programs can process and parse aggregate types, and therefore open MBeans, without having access to any classes beyond the ones supported by JMX itself. This reduces the coordination of class distribution and installation. All aggregate types inherit from the `OpenType` abstract class. The `OpenType` interface describes the basic data type and gives you access to its type, description, and class name.

These are the aggregate types:

- **Composite.** Hash tables are represented by instances of `javax.management.openmbean.CompositeData`. Composites may contain any valid basic data type. Values are retrieved by a `String` name. Values can be set only during instantiation, meaning that once `CompositeData` is instantiated, it is immutable. `CompositeData` also contains a method to get the type of the value elements in the hash table. Each value element must be a basic data type. The JMX reference implementation contains an implementation called `CompositeDataSupport`. `CompositeDataSupport` has one complete constructor that contains all of its initialization values and one that accepts a `Map` instance. Here is the `CompositeData` interface:

```
Public interface CompositeData {
    public CompositeType getCompositeType()
    public Object get(String key) throws
    IllegalArgumentException, InvalidKeyException
    public Object[] getAll(String[] keys) throws
      IllegalArgumentException, InvalidKeyException
    public Collection values()
    public boolean containsKey(String key)
    public boolean containsValue(Object value)
    public boolean equals(Object obj)
    public int hashCode()
    public String toString()
}
```

- These methods are all typical of hash table implementations. Values are retrieved via `get()`, `getAll()`, and `values()`. The `values()` method returns a collection of the basic data types in the `CompositeData` instance. The containsValue() and containsKey() methods test if a value or key exists in the CompositeData instance.

- CompositeData is described by the CompositeType instance that is returned by the getCompositeType() method. CompositeType has one full constructor:

```
CompositeType (String typeName,
    String description,
    String[] itemNames,
    String[] itemDescriptions,
    OpenType[] itemTypes)
```

The CompositeType interface is

```
Public interface CompositeType {
    public OpenType getType(String itemName)
    public String getDescription(Stirng itemName);
    public boolean containsKey(String key)
    public boolean isValue(Object obj)public Collection
        values()
    public boolean equals(Object obj)
    public int hashCode()
    public Set keySet()
    public String toString()
}
```

- **Table.** Tables are represented by instances of javax.management.openmbean.TabularData. Tables are arrays of CompositeData data types. Tables can be modified after instantiation. The TabularData interface is

```
public interface TabularData {
    public TabularType getTabularType();
    public Object[] calculateIndex(CompositeData value);
    public int size();
    public boolean isEmpty();
    public boolean containsKey(Object[] key);
    public boolean containsValue(CompositeData value);
    public CompositeData get(Object[] key);
    public void put(CompositeData value);
    public CompositeData remove(Object[] key);
    public void putAll(CompositeData[] values);
    public void clear();
```

```
    public Set keySet();
    public Collection values();
    public boolean equals(Object obj);
    public int hashCode();
    public String toString();
}
```

These methods are typical methods for accessing tables. The few interesting methods are `values()`, which returns a collection of the `CompositeData` instances, and `getTabularType()`, which returns a `TabularType` instance. The `TabularType` instance describes the data in the table. It is immutable for an instance of `TabularData`.

- **Array.** Java array types are described with `javax.management.openmbean.ArrayType`. All elements in the array must be of the same type. Here is the definition of the class `ArrayType`:

```
public class ArrayType extends OpenType, implements Serializable {
    ArrayType(int dimension, OpenType elementType) throws
      IllegalArgumentException,
      OpenDataException {}
    public int getDimension() {}
    public OpenType getElementOpenType(){}
    public boolean isValue(Object obj) {}
    public boolean equals(Object obj) {}
    public int hashCode() {}
    public String toString() {}
}
```

ObjectName

The `ObjectName` type is the `javax.management.ObjectName` class. This means that open MBeans can refer to other MBeans.

3.2.4.2 OpenMBeanInfo

Open MBeans have their own extension of the `MBeanInfo` implementation: `OpenMBeanInfo`. `OpenMBeanInfo` is an interface with the same methods as `MBeanInfo`. Because `MBeanInfo` does not have an interface to accompany it, some strange interfaces are created for `OpenMBeanInfo` classes that now must define the methods of `MBeanInfo` and `OpenMBeanInfo`. This arrangement of interfaces may change in the next major version of JMX, where appropriate interfaces can be developed for the `MBeanInfo` classes. An `OpenMBeanInfo` implementation—OpenMBeanInfoSupport, for example—must extend MBeanInfo and implement OpenMBeanInfo.

The MBeanAttributeInfo, MBeanOperationInfo, and MBeanConstructorInfo arrays returned by the OpenMBeanInfo instance must be implementations of OpenMBeanAttributeInfo, OpenMBeanOperationInfo, and OpenMBeanConstructorInfo interfaces, respectively. Likewise, MBeanParameterInfo instances returned by MBeanOperationInfo and MBeanConstructorInfo must implement the OpenMBeanParameterInfo interface. However, the MBeanNotificationInfo array still returns MBeanNotificationInfo instances. MBeanNotificationInfo was not extended by the open MBean specification.

One notable quirk of open MBeans is that the OpenMBeanAttributeInfo interface extends the OpenMBeanParameterInfo interface. This relationship between MBeanAttributeInfo and MBeanParameterInfo does not exist in the base MBeanInfo class. Another important quirk is that the OpenMBeanInfo variation consists of a set of interfaces. This is different from MBeanInfo and ModelMBeanInfo, each of which is strictly a set of classes, except for the ModelMBeanInfo interface itself. All OpenMBeanInfo implementations should provide a fully defined constructor:

```
OpenMBeanInfoSupport(String className,
  String description,
  OpenMBeanAttributeInfo[] openAttributes,
  OpenMBeanConstructorInfo[] openConstructors,
  OpenMBeanOperationInfo[] openOperations,
  MBeanNotificationInfo[] notifications);
```

Note that the arrays passed in must be of the OpenMBeanInfo types. Here is the OpenMBeanInfo interface:

```
public interface OpenMBeanInfo {
  public String getClassName();
  public String getDescription();
  public MBeanAttributeInfo[] getAttributes();
  public MBeanOperationInfo[] getOperations();
  public MBeanConstructorInfo[] getConstructors();
  public MBeanNotificationInfo[] getNotifications();
  public boolean equals(Object obj);
  public int hashCode();
  public String toString();
}
```

Let's look at the extensions that have been added to the metadata in each of the MBeanInfo elements, MBeanParameterInfo, MBeanAttributeInfo, MBeanConstructorInfo, and MBeanOperationInfo.

- OpenMBeanParameterInfo

  Some of the methods in this interface reflect the attributes that were already in the MBeanParameterInfo class: name and description. The type attribute in MBeanParameterInfo has been replaced by OpenType. Here is the interface for OpenMBeanParameterInfo:

```
public interface OpenMBeanParameterInfo {
    public String getDescription();
    public String getName();
    public OpenType getOpenType();
    public Object getDefaultValue();
    public Set getLegalValues();
    public Comparable getMinValue();
    public Comparable getMaxValue();
    public boolean hasDefaultValue();
    public boolean hasLegalValues();
    public boolean hasMinValue();
    public boolean hasMaxValue();
    public boolean isValue(Object obj);
    public boolean equals(Object obj);
    public int hashCode();
    public String toString();
}
```

  You can see that the open MBean adds the DefaultValue, LegalValues, MaxValue, MinValue, and OpenType attributes to MBeanPropertyInfo. In the model MBean, these attributes are captured in the descriptor. The model MBean also adds some simple testers: hasLegalValues(), hasMaxValue(), and hasMinValue(). One interesting method is isValue(), which validates an input object as a legal value for this parameter; it does *not* test if the parameter has a value. OpenMBeanParameterInfo is used to describe the input parameters for the constructors and operations described by OpenMBeanConstructorInfo and OpenMBeanOperationInfo. Any implementation of OpenMBeanParameterInfo must inherit from MBeanParameterInfo and implement OpenMBeanParameterInfo.

- OpenMBeanAttributeInfo

  OpenMBeanAttributeInfo inherits from OpenMBeanParameterInfo. The OpenMBeanAttributeInfo interface defines the attributes supported by

MBeanAttributeInfo: name, description, type, getter, and setter; and operations: isIs(), isReadable(), isWritable(). The OpenMBean-AttributeInfo interface adds these operations as extensions to OpenM-BeanParameterInfo:

```
Public interface OpenMBeanAttributeInfoSupport
      extends OpenMBeanParameterInfo {
      public boolean isReadable();
      public boolean isWritable();
      public boolean isIs();
      public boolean equals(Object obj);
      public int hashCode();
      public String toString();
}
```

The effect is to add the ability to define metadata about attributes like we can about parameters: legal values, default values, minimum value, and maximum value. The operation isValue() also applies to attributes, which permits validation of the attribute values before they are being set. Any implementation of OpenMBeanAttributeInfo must inherit from MBeanAttributeInfo and implement OpenMBeanAttributeInfo.

- OpenMBeanConstructorInfo

  The OpenMBeanConstructorInfo interface defines all the methods that were defined in MBeanConstructorInfo. No additional metadata is added to MBeanConstructorInfo by OpenMBeanConstructorInfo. Here is the interface for OpenMBeanConstructorInfo:

```
public interface OpenMBeanConstructorInfo {
    public String getDescription();
    public String getName();
    public MBeanParameterInfo[] getSignature();
    public boolean equals(Object obj);
    public int hashCode();
    public String toString();
}
```

You should instantiate and use OpenMBeanConstructorInfoSupport implementations just as you do ModelMBeanConstructorInfo implementations. Note that the input signature to the constructor—that is, the MBeanParameterInfo array—must contain instances that implement the

OpenMBeanParameterInfo array. Any implementation of OpenMBeanConstructorInfo must inherit from MBeanConstructorInfo and implement OpenMBeanConstructorInfo.

- OpenMBeanOperationInfo

  OpenMBeanOperationInfo defines all the methods from the ModelMBeanInfo class and adds one piece of additional metadata: ReturnOpenType. Here is the interface for OpenMBeanOperationInfo:

```
public interface OpenMBeanOperationInfo {
public String getDescription();
public String getName();
public MBeanParameterInfo[] getSignature();
public int getImpact();
public String getReturnType();
public OpenType getReturnOpenType();
public boolean equals(Object obj);
public int hashCode();
public String toString();
}
```

Note that the input signature—that is, the MBeanParameterInfo array—must contain instances that implement the OpenMBeanParameterInfo array. Any implementation of OpenMBeanOperationInfo must inherit from MBeanOperationInfo and implement OpenMBeanOperationInfo.

3.2.4.3 Using Open MBeans

Programming with open MBeans is very similar to programming with other dynamic MBeans, except that additional data is supplied to the OpenMBeanInfo instance construction. All attributes, constructor parameters, operation parameters, and operation return types must be compliant with the open-MBean basic data types described earlier. It is the responsibility of the developer who creates the open MBeans to comply with these restrictions.

To summarize, the restricted data types and extended metadata facilitate several kinds of functions:

- Decomposability into Java primitives ensures that open MBeans are easily mapped into XML for portability and remote access.
- Extended metadata for value checking and validation means that open MBeans are easier to represent in generated management consoles.

- A limited set of well-understood data types makes open MBeans easier to understand by remote applications without having to import special classes and address the remote class-loading issues for the open MBean

Once the open MBeans specification is finalized and a required part of the specification, they will be a very valuable tool for building MBeans.

3.3 Design Guidelines

MBeans are Java classes, so all the normal rules of good class design apply directly to their design. There are, however, a few special considerations to keep in mind when you're designing MBeans to represent resources:

- Keep the management interfaces for similar resources similar. Creating radically different interfaces for resources that aren't that different will make achieving consistency in your management applications difficult.
- Remember that your resource's management interface will be exposed to management applications. Making application functionality—for example, the `release()` and `reserve()` methods of the "Quick Tour's" `SessionPool`–part of the management interface will at best confuse administrators and at worst make your resource unstable.
- Keep the attribute types and operation parameters simple. Administrators may be accessing your MBean via a GUI where it isn't feasible to input complex objects.

3.4 Summary

MBeans connect JMX-based management applications to the real world; they model the resources that management monitors and controls. There are two basic kinds of MBeans—standard and dynamic—and we have seen examples of both in this chapter. We have also discussed the MBean's management interface, its definition and its formal representation, in detail. This information should enable you to design and implement MBeans for the resources that require management in your own applications. Before you start coding, however, read the discussion of model MBeans in Chapter 4. You just might get away with writing less code than you thought.

CHAPTER 4

Model MBeans

4.1 Introduction

Creating instrumentation with MBeans from scratch can be time-consuming and tedious. The JMX model MBean specification[1] provides generic instrumentation that can be quickly customized for many resources. This chapter describes the model MBean in detail and provides multiple examples of its use in practice.

A model MBean is a fully customizable dynamic MBean. The `RequiredModelMBean` class, which implements the `ModelMBean` interface, is guaranteed to exist on every JMX agent. A model MBean implements the `ModelMBean` interface that extends a set of interfaces including `DynamicMBean`, `PersistentMBean`, and `ModelMBeanNotificationBroadcaster`.

Like the open MBean, the model MBean has it's own extended `MBeanInfo` interface called `ModelMBeanInfo`. `ModelMBeanInfo` associates new, extensible metadata objects called *descriptors* with the management interface. Descriptors add additional information about the managed resource and are also used to customize the behavior of a `RequiredModelMBean` instance. In this chapter, when we say simply "model MBeans" we are referring to implementations of the model MBean or `RequiredModelMBean`. When we are referring to the `ModelMBean` interface, we will say "the `ModelMBean` interface."

Model MBeans were added to JMX for several reasons:

- **Ease of use for developers.** Because model MBeans have an actual implementation class, `RequiredModelMBean`, as part of every JMX implementation, developers don't need to write their entire MBean and address all of the accompanying support for logging, notifications, errors, persistence, and so on. All of this is provided as part of the `RequiredModelMBean` implementation. Because it is an actual implementation, you can create subclasses for it and override its behavior with your own. Model MBeans make it possible to instrument your managed resource in as little as five lines of code (not including configuration of the model MBean).
- **Ease of support by development tools.** Because model MBeans are fully configurable through metadata kept in descriptors, the creation of `ModelMBeanInfo` requires either a lot of programmatic setting of metadata or a lot of XML[2] in a file. However, the use of metadata with a portable XML file or API to create it makes it much easier to create and maintain model MBeans with development tools. Part of the intent for model MBeans was to enable the creation of management objects during development by development tools and wizards. Eventually we hope that developing the management objects and interfaces for your application will be as much a part of your application development cycle as developing remote interfaces and logging or tracing support.
- **Common services.** Model MBeans support a common set of behaviors in all implementations, including logging, generic notifications, attribute change notifications, persistence, and value caching. These behaviors can be customized and overridden.
- **Dynamic behavior.** Model MBeans are completely customized during development or during runtime. During development, the `ModelMBeanInfo` class supports APIs to customize the management interface and behavior of the model MBean. During runtime, external files, properties files, or XML files can be used to customize the model MBean. Likewise the resource may use the `ModelMBeanInfo` APIs to customize the model MBean so that it conforms to its own runtime factors.
- **Isolation.** Model MBeans isolate the application manageability instrumentation from differences in Java runtimes and JMX implementations. Manageable components today may be installed and used in different editions of Java: J2SE,[3] J2EE,[4] and eventually J2ME.[5] These different JVMs may use different approaches when providing common services to model MBeans. For example, a J2SE JMX `RequiredModelMBean` implementation may support persistence by writing the data to files. If persistence to a database were required, then `RequiredModelMBean` would use

JDBC[6] directly. However, a J2EE JMX `RequiredModelMBean` may be implemented as a local EJB[7] or wrapped as a remote EJB and use container-managed persistence. As JMX becomes more pervasive in the J2ME JVMs, these differences in MBean behavior will become more apparent.

In a J2ME JVM, persistence and logging may not be allowed at all if the JVM is run on a diskless device. Even value caching in memory may be too costly. If you were writing your own MBeans for your component, you would have to write very different MBeans for each of these scenarios. However, because you use the MBeanServer as a factory to instantiate the `RequiredModelMBean` class that has been supplied by the JMX implementation, your use of the MBean in your managed resource does not change. The JMX implementation is required to make sure that the `RequiredModelMBean` implementation is appropriate for the installation and current JVM environment. Your investment in instrumentation of your managed resources is protected and requires less development and maintenance.

4.1.1 The Simplest Model MBean Example

In this section we will look at a simple example of how to use a model MBean. This example shows how to make a resource manageable in as little as five lines of code. In this example we expose attributes and operations of the managed resource and send a notification upon an error condition.

Recall from Chapter 3, on MBeans, that the Apache server application had its own standard MBean. Let's look at what it would take to create a model MBean for the Apache server. We will have to write a Java utility, `ApacheServer`, to get the information from the Apache module and return it to the model MBean. In our scenario, the `ApacheServer` class is similar to the `Apache` implementation, but it does not implement the `ApacheMBean` class, and it does not have to support value caching (see Code Block 3 in the text that follows). The model MBean will provide caching support at a much finer grain. The caching policy will be defined in the attribute descriptors in `ModelMBeanInfo`. Therefore, we don't support the `isCaching()`, `getCacheLifetime()`, `setCacheLifetime()`, `getCaching()`, and `setCaching()` methods in the original standard MBean interface. The `ApacheServer` class is the managed resource.

The first code block that follows shows how to find the MBeanServer, instantiate the model MBean, instantiate `ApacheServer`, associate it with the model MBean, configure the model MBean, and send a notification if the server is down at this time. The second code block shows how to configure the model MBean through `ModelMBeanInfo`. Notice that we can selectively cache the data from the Apache server, choosing not to cache some of the more time-sensitive counters. The third code block shows the slightly modified Apache class from Chapter 3. All of the examples in this book (plus some others) are available on the book's Web site: http://www.awprofessional.com/titles/0672324083.

Code Block 1

```
package jnjmx.ch4;

import javax.management.*;
import javax.management.modelmbean.*;
import java.lang.reflect.Constructor;
import java.util.ArrayList;

/**
 * @author Heather Kreger
 * Chapter 4:  Java and JMX Building Manageable Systems
 * ApacheServerManager: Manages the ApacheServer as a managed
 * resource using a model MBean.
 *
 * ModelMBeanInfo is created using ModelMBeanInfo APIs
 * rather than an XML file.
 */

public class ApacheServerManager {

  public static void main(String[] args) {
    boolean tracing = false;
    String serverURL = "";
    try {

      if (args.length != 0) {
        System.out.println(args[0]);
        if (args[0] != null)
          serverURL = serverURL.concat(args[0]);
        else
          serverURL = "http://www.apache.org/server-status?auto";
      }
      // This serverURL default mechanism is just for this example
      // We would not recommend this in a real application
      if (!serverURL.startsWith("http"))
        serverURL = "http://www.apache.org/server-status?auto";

      /** Find an MBeanServer for our MBean */
      MBeanServer myMBS = MBeanServerFactory.createMBeanServer();
```

```
/** Instantiate an unconfigured RequiredModelMBean in the MBeanServer */
RequiredModelMBean apacheMMBean =
  (RequiredModelMBean) myMBS.instantiate(
    "javax.management.modelmbean.RequiredModelMBean");

/** Create a name for the MBean
 * domain = apacheManager
 * one attribute: id = ApacheServer*/
ObjectName apacheMBeanName =
  new ObjectName("apacheManager: id=ApacheServer");

/** Instantiate the ApacheServer utility to be delegated to */
jnjmx.ch4.ApacheServer myApacheServer =
  new jnjmx.ch4.ApacheServer(serverURL);

/** Set the configuration of the ModelMBean through the ModelMBeanInfo
 ** This method is below */
ApacheServerManager asmgr = new ApacheServerManager();
ModelMBeanInfo apacheMMBeanInfo =
  asmgr.createApacheModelMBeanInfo(
    myApacheServer,
    apacheMBeanName);
apacheMMBean.setModelMBeanInfo(apacheMMBeanInfo);

// ** Set the ApacheServer as the managed resource
apacheMMBean.setManagedResource(myApacheServer, "ObjectReference");

// ** Register the ModelMBean instance that is now ready to run with the
// MBeanServer
ObjectInstance registeredApacheMMBean =
  myMBS.registerMBean((Object) apacheMMBean, apacheMBeanName);

// ** Use the ModelMBean to send the notification into JMX where it gets
// sent to a manager adapter that is registered for notifications from the
// Apache MBeans and sends them to a pager system

String apacheStatus =
  (String) apacheMMBean.invoke("getState", null, null);

if ((apacheStatus.equals("DOWN"))
  || (apacheStatus.equals("NOT_RESPONDING"))) {
  System.out.println("Apache Server is Down");
  apacheMMBean.sendNotification("Apache Server is Down");
  /*  You could create monitor to notify when up
   * again so Web traffic can be routed back to it */
```

```
    } else
      System.out.println("Apache Server is " + apacheStatus);
  } catch (Exception e) {
    System.out.println(
      "Apache Server Manager failed with " + e.getMessage());
  }
  System.exit(0);
}
```

Because model MBeans support the `NotificationBroadcaster` interface, when the `getStatus()` method returns `Down` or `Not Responding`, we have the model MBean send a notification to the MBeanServer, which in turn sends it to all registered notification listeners. This is fairly simple to do; we merely

1. Find our `MBeanServer`.
2. Instantiate the `RequiredModelMBean` class using the MBeanServer.
3. Customize `RequiredModelMBean` in two steps:
   a. Set up the `ModelMBeanInfo instance.`
   b. Associate the model MBean with the access to the actual managed resource.
4. Register `RequiredModelMBean` with the MBeanServer.
5. Invoke the model MBean to get the `Status` attribute.
6. Send the notification if the status is `Down` or `Stopped`. In the downloadable examples for the book, we provide an example of a notification listener for this event that you can experiment with.

Here's how we set the `ModelMBeanInfo` instance that we used to customize this model MBean. The `ModelMBeanInfo` object created for the ApacheServer managed application used in the Apache model MBean defines the following:

- `String` attributes that are read-only: `BusyWorkers`, `BytesPerSec`, `BytesPerReq`, `IdleWorkers`, `ReqPerSec`, `Scoreboard`, `State`, `TotalAccesses`, `TotalKBytes`, and `Uptime`
- `String` attributes that are read/write: `Server`
- Operations: `start` and `stop`
- Notification: ApacheServer `Down`
- Operations to support the attributes on the `ApacheServer` class: `getBusyWorkers()`, `getBytesPerReq()`, `getBytesPerSec()`, `getIdleWorkers()`, `getReqPerSec()`, `getScoreboard()`, `getServer()`, `getState()`, `getTotalAccesses()`, `getTotalKBytes()`, `getUptime()`, `setServer(String URL)`

Code Block 2 illustrates the programmatic way to create a ModelMBeanInfo instance. ModelMBeanInfo can also be initialized from data saved in a file. This is shown in the XML primer examples later in this chapter (see Section 4.7). It is much simpler code, but it requires the use of an XML service that is not a standard service of JMX. This entire method is relatively lengthy, but it is very simple to program and it is easy for tools to generate. The method in its entirety is listed here. We will explain how to set an attribute, an operation, and a notification in the next section.

Code Block 2

```
// Create the ModelMBeanInfo for the Apache server
  ModelMBeanInfo createApacheModelMBeanInfo(
    ApacheServer managedApache,
    ObjectName apacheMBeanName) {

    // Set the ApacheServer's class name, there are other
    // more flexible ways to do this
    Class apacheClass = null;
    try {
      apacheClass = Class.forName("jnjmx.ch4.ApacheServer");
    } catch (Exception e) {
      System.out.println("ApacheServer Class not found");
    }

    // Set the MBean's descriptor with default policies
    // MBean name is apacheMBeanName
    // logging notifications to jmxmain.log
    // caching attributes for 10 seconds
    Descriptor apacheDescription =
      new DescriptorSupport(
        new String[] {
          ("name=" + apacheMBeanName),
          "descriptorType=mbean",
          ("displayName=ApacheServerManager"),
          "type=jnjmx.ch4.ApacheServer",
          "log=T",
          "logFile=jmxmain.log",
          "currencyTimeLimit=10" });

    // Define attributes in ModelMBeanAttributeInfo instances

    ModelMBeanAttributeInfo[] apacheAttributes =
      new ModelMBeanAttributeInfo[11];
```

```
// Declare BusyWorkers attribute
// cache BusyWorkers for 3 seconds,
// use get method
Descriptor busyWorkersDesc =
  new DescriptorSupport(
    new String[] {
      "name=BusyWorkers",
      "descriptorType=attribute",
      "displayName=Apache BusyWorkers",
      "getMethod=getBusyWorkers",
      "currencyTimeLimit=3" });

apacheAttributes[0] =
  new ModelMBeanAttributeInfo(
    "BusyWorkers",
    "int",
    "Apache Server Busy Workers",
    true,
    false,
    false,
    busyWorkersDesc);

// Declare BytesPerSec attribute
// Cache ByetesperSec for 10 seconds
Descriptor bytesPerSecDesc =
  new DescriptorSupport(
    new String[] {
      "name=BytesPerSec",
      "descriptorType=attribute",
      "displayName=Apache BytesPerSec",
      "getMethod=getBytesPerSec",
      "currencyTimeLimit=10" });

apacheAttributes[1] =
  new ModelMBeanAttributeInfo(
    "BytesPerSec",
    "int",
    "Apache Server Bytes Per Sec",
    true,
    false,
    false,
    bytesPerSecDesc);

// Declare BytesPerReq attribute
Descriptor bytesPerReqDesc =
  new DescriptorSupport(
```

```
    new String[] {
      "name=BytesPerReq",
      "descriptorType=attribute",
      "displayName=Apache BytesPerReq",
      "getMethod=getBytesPerReq",
      "currencyTimeLimit=10" });

apacheAttributes[2] =
  new ModelMBeanAttributeInfo(
    "BytesPerReq",
    "int",
    "Apache Server Bytes Per Request",
    true,
    false,
    false,
    bytesPerReqDesc);

// Declare IdleWorkers attribute
Descriptor idleWorkersDesc =
  new DescriptorSupport(
    new String[] {
      "name=IdleWorkers",
      "descriptorType=attribute",
      "displayName=Apache IdleWorkers",
      "getMethod=getIdleWorkers",
      "currencyTimeLimit=10" });

apacheAttributes[3] =
  new ModelMBeanAttributeInfo(
    "IdleWorkers",
    "int",
    "Apache Server Idle Workers",
    true,
    false,
    false,
    idleWorkersDesc);

// Declare ReqPerSec attribute
Descriptor reqPerSecDesc =
  new DescriptorSupport(
    new String[] {
      "name=ReqPerSec",
      "descriptorType=attribute",
      "displayName=Apache ReqPerSec",
      "getMethod=getReqPerSec",
      "currencyTimeLimit=5" });
```

```
apacheAttributes[4] =
  new ModelMBeanAttributeInfo(
    "ReqPerSec",
    "int",
    "Apache Server Requests Per Second",
    true,
    false,
    false,
    reqPerSecDesc);

// Declare Scoreboard attribute
Descriptor ScoreboardDesc =
  new DescriptorSupport(
    new String[] {
      "name=Scoreboard",
      "descriptorType=attribute",
      "displayName=Apache Scoreboard",
      "getMethod=getScoreboard",
      "currencyTimeLimit=10" });

apacheAttributes[5] =
  new ModelMBeanAttributeInfo(
    "Scoreboard",
    "java.lang.String",
    "Apache Server Scoreboard",
    true,
    false,
    false,
    ScoreboardDesc);

// Declare TotalAccesses attribute
// Do not cache TotalAccesses
Descriptor totalAccessesDesc =
  new DescriptorSupport(
    new String[] {
      "name=TotalAccesses",
      "descriptorType=attribute",
      "displayName=Apache TotalAccesses",
      "getMethod=getTotalAccesses",
      "currencyTimeLimit=-1" });

apacheAttributes[6] =
  new ModelMBeanAttributeInfo(
    "TotalAccesses",
    "int",
```

```
        "Apache Server total accesses",
        true,
        false,
        false,
        totalAccessesDesc);

    // Declare TotalKBytes attribute
    // Do not cache TotalKBytes
    Descriptor totalKBytesDesc =
      new DescriptorSupport(
        new String[] {
          "name=TotalKBytes",
          "descriptorType=attribute",
          "displayName=Apache TotalKBytes",
          "getMethod=getTotalKBytes",
          "currencyTimeLimit=-1" });

    apacheAttributes[7] =
      new ModelMBeanAttributeInfo(
        "TotalKBytes",
        "int",
        "Apache Server total KiloBytes",
        true,
        false,
        false,
        totalKBytesDesc);

    // Declare Uptime attribute
    Descriptor uptimeDesc =
      new DescriptorSupport(
        new String[] {
          "name=Uptime",
          "descriptorType=attribute",
          "displayName=Apache Uptime",
          "getMethod=getUptime",
          "currencyTimeLimit=10" });

    apacheAttributes[8] =
      new ModelMBeanAttributeInfo(
        "Uptime",
        "java.lang.String",
        "Apache Server Up Time",
        true,
        false,
```

```
        false,
        uptimeDesc);

    // Declare State attribute
    // State has a getMethod
    Descriptor stateDesc =
      new DescriptorSupport(
        new String[] {
          "name=State",
          "descriptorType=attribute",
          "displayName=Apache State",
          "getMethod=getState",
          "currencyTimeLimit=10" });

    apacheAttributes[9] =
      new ModelMBeanAttributeInfo(
        "State",
        "java.lang.String",
        "Apache Server state",
        true,
        false,
        false,
        stateDesc);

    // Declare Server attribute
    // Server has a getMethod and a setMethod
    Descriptor serverDesc =
      new DescriptorSupport(
        new String[] {
          "name=Server",
          "descriptorType=attribute",
          "displayName=Apache Server URL",
          "getMethod=getServer",
          "setMethod=setServer",
          "currencyTimeLimit=10" });

      apacheAttributes[10] =
        new ModelMBeanAttributeInfo(
          "Server",
          "java.lang.String",
          "Apache Server Busy Workers",
          true,
          true,
          false,
          serverDesc);
```

```
// Declare constructors for the managed resource
// one constructor which accepts one parameter,
// a String URL
Constructor[] myConstructors = apacheClass.getConstructors();

ModelMBeanConstructorInfo[] apacheConstructors =
  new ModelMBeanConstructorInfo[1];

MBeanParameterInfo[] constructorParms =
  new MBeanParameterInfo[] {
    (new MBeanParameterInfo("serverURL",
    "java.lang.String",
    "Apache Server URL"))};

Descriptor apacheBeanDesc =
  new DescriptorSupport(
    new String[] {
      "name=ApacheServer",
      "descriptorType=operation",
      "role=constructor" });

apacheConstructors[0] =
  new ModelMBeanConstructorInfo(
    "Apache",
    "ApacheServer(): Constructs an ApacheServer utility class",
    constructorParms,
    apacheBeanDesc);

// Define operations in ModelMBeanOperationInfo instances
/* Operations: getBusyWorkers, getBytesPerSec, getBytesPerReq,
  * getIdleWorkers, getReqPerSec, getScoreboard, getTotalAccesses,
  * getTotalKBytes, getUptime are satisfied by getValue, getState,
  * getServer, setServer(String URL), start, stop have own operations */

// Declare getValue operation String getValue()
// Set parameter array
ModelMBeanOperationInfo[] apacheOperations =
  new ModelMBeanOperationInfo[6];

MBeanParameterInfo[] getParms = new MBeanParameterInfo[0];

MBeanParameterInfo[] getValueParms =
  new MBeanParameterInfo[] {
    (new MBeanParameterInfo("FieldName",
    "java.lang.String",
    "Apache status field name"))};
```

```
Descriptor getValueDesc =
  new DescriptorSupport(
    new String[] {
      "name=getValue",
      "descriptorType=operation",
      "class=ApacheServer",
      "role=operation" });

apacheOperations[0] =
  new ModelMBeanOperationInfo(
    "getValue",
    "getValue(): get an apache status field",
    getValueParms,
    "java.lang.String",
    MBeanOperationInfo.INFO,
    getValueDesc);

Descriptor getStateDesc =
  new DescriptorSupport(
    new String[] {
    "name=getState",
    "descriptorType=operation",
    "class=ApacheServer",
    "role=operation" });


apacheOperations[1] =
  new ModelMBeanOperationInfo(
    "getState",
    "getState(): current status of apache server",
    getParms,
    "java.lang.String",
    MBeanOperationInfo.INFO,
    getStateDesc);

Descriptor getServerDesc =
  new DescriptorSupport(new String[] { "name=getServer",
     "descriptorType=operation",
     "class=ApacheServer",
     "role=operation" });

apacheOperations[2] =
  new ModelMBeanOperationInfo("getServer",
    "getServer(): URL of apache server",
```

```
        getParms,
        "java.lang.Integer",
        MBeanOperationInfo.INFO,
        getServerDesc);

    MBeanParameterInfo[] setParms =
      new MBeanParameterInfo[] {
        (new MBeanParameterInfo("url",
        "java.lang.String",
        "Apache Server URL"))};

    Descriptor setServerDesc =
      new DescriptorSupport(new String[] { "name=getServer",
         "descriptorType=operation",
         "class=ApacheServer",
         "role=operation" });

    apacheOperations[3] =
      new ModelMBeanOperationInfo("setServer",
        "getServer(): URL of apache server",
        setParms,
        "java.lang.String",
        MBeanOperationInfo.ACTION,
        setServerDesc);

    MBeanParameterInfo[] startParms = new MBeanParameterInfo[0];

    Descriptor startDesc =
      new DescriptorSupport(new String[] { "name=start",
        "descriptorType=operation",
        "class=ApacheServer",
        "role=operation" });

    apacheOperations[4] = new ModelMBeanOperationInfo("start",
      "start(): start apache server",
      startParms,
      "java.lang.Integer",
      MBeanOperationInfo.ACTION,
      startDesc);

    MBeanParameterInfo[] stopParms = new MBeanParameterInfo[0];
    Descriptor stopDesc = new DescriptorSupport(new String[] { "name=stop",
       "descriptorType=operation",
       "class=ApacheServer",
       "role=operation" });
```

```
apacheOperations[5] = new ModelMBeanOperationInfo("stop",
  "stop(): start apache server",
  stopParms,
  "java.lang.Integer",
  MBeanOperationInfo.ACTION,
  stopDesc);

/* getters/setters for operations */
//    MBeanParameterInfo[] getParms = new MBeanParameterInfo[0];

Descriptor bytespsDesc =
  new DescriptorSupport(new String[] { "name=getBytesPerSecond",
  "descriptorType=operation",
  "class=ApacheServer",
  "role=operation" });

apacheOperations[6] =
  new ModelMBeanOperationInfo("getBytesPerSecond",
    "number of bytes per second processed",
    getParms,
    "int",
    MBeanOperationInfo.ACTION,
    bytespsDesc);

// Define notifications in ModelMBeanNotificationInfo
// declare an "Apache Server Down" notification
ModelMBeanNotificationInfo[] apacheNotifications =
  new ModelMBeanNotificationInfo[1];

Descriptor apacheDownEventDesc =
  new DescriptorSupport(
    new String[] {
      "descriptorType=notification",
      "name=jmx.ModelMBean.General.Apache.Down",
      "severity=1",
      "MessageId=Apache001" });

apacheNotifications[0] =
  new ModelMBeanNotificationInfo(
    new String[] { "jmx.ModelMBean.General.Apache.Down" },
    "jmx.ModelMBean.General",
    "Apache Server Down",
    apacheDownEventDesc);
```

```
    // Create the ModelMBeanInfo
    ModelMBeanInfo apacheMMBeanInfo =
      new ModelMBeanInfoSupport(
        "Apache",
        "ModelMBean for managing an Apache Web Server",
        apacheAttributes,
        apacheConstructors,
        apacheOperations,
        apacheNotifications);

    // Set the MBean's Descriptor for the ModelMBeanInfo
    try {
      apacheMMBeanInfo.setMBeanDescriptor(apacheDescription);
    } catch (Exception e) {
      System.out.println("CreateMBeanInfo failed with " + e.getMessage());
    }
    return apacheMMBeanInfo;
  }
```

Finally, just to complete the example, even though this is basically what's in Chapter 3 as the `Apache` class, here is the `ApacheServer` class for getting the data for the Apache server resource we are managing:

Code Block 3

```
package jnjmx.ch4;

/**
 * @author Heather Kreger
 * Chapter 4:  Java and JMX: Building Manageable Systems
 * ApacheServer: interacts with an Apache server through a URL
 */

import java.io.BufferedReader;
import java.io.IOException;
import java.io.InputStreamReader;
import java.net.MalformedURLException;
import java.net.URL;
import java.net.URLConnection;
import java.util.HashMap;
import java.util.StringTokenizer;
import javax.management.*;
```

```
public class ApacheServer {
  // String constants for each of the Apache-related attributes
  private static final String BUSY_WORKERS = "BusyWorkers";
  private static final String BYTES_PER_REQ = "BytesPerReq";
  private static final String BYTES_PER_SEC = "BytesPerSec";
  private static final String CPU_LOAD = "CPULoad";
  private static final String IDLE_WORKERS = "IdleWorkers";
  private static final String REQ_PER_SEC = "ReqPerSec";
  private static final String SCOREBOARD = "Scoreboard";
  private static final String TOTAL_ACCESSES = "Total Accesses";
  private static final String TOTAL_KBYTES = "Total kBytes";
  private static final String UPTIME = "Uptime";

  private static final int MAX_FAILURES = 3;

  // state constants for the Apache Server (brought over from ApacheMBean interface
  public String DOWN = "DOWN";
  public String NOT_RESPONDING = "NOT_RESPONDING";
  public String RUNNING = "RUNNING";
  public String UNKNOWN = "UNKNOWN";

  private int failures = 0;
  private String state = UNKNOWN;
  private long tzero;
  private URL url;

  // constructor that accepts the URL for the Apache server to be managed
  public ApacheServer(String url)
    throws MalformedURLException, IllegalArgumentException {
    setServer(url);
    // test the ability to communicate using the URL
    try {
      getValue(UPTIME);
    } catch (Exception e) {
      System.out.println(
        "Apache server at " + url + " does not respond.");
    }
  }

  // Return the URL of the Apache server being managed
  // Server is a readable and writable attribute because
  // it has a getter and setter
  public String getServer() {
    return this.url.toString();
  }
```

```
// Set the URL of the Apache server being managed
public void setServer(String url)
  throws MalformedURLException, IllegalArgumentException {
  this.url = new URL(url);
  // test to be sure the URL is really an Apache server URL
  if (isStatusUrl(this.url) == false) {
    throw new IllegalArgumentException(url.toString());
  }
  this.state = ApacheMBean.UNKNOWN;
}

// return the current state of the Apache server
public String getState() {
  return this.state;
}

// Example operation for start
// If this were running in the same JVM, this is
// where the apache process initialzation would go
public String start() {
  this.state = RUNNING;
  return this.state;
}

// Sample operation for stop
// If this were running in the same JVM, this is
// where the Apache process initialization would go
public String stop() {
  this.state = DOWN;
  return this.state;
}

// Validate that the URL is an Apache server status URL
private boolean isStatusUrl(URL url) {
  return url.toString().endsWith("server-status?auto");
}

// Get methods for metrics retrieved via the Apache URL
// These are read-only attributes because no "setters" are
// defined for them

public int getBusyWorkers() throws ApacheMBeanException {
  return getIntValue(BUSY_WORKERS);
}
```

```
public int getBytesPerSec() throws ApacheMBeanException {
  return getIntValue(BYTES_PER_SEC);
}

public float getBytesPerReq() throws ApacheMBeanException {
  return getFloatValue(BYTES_PER_REQ);
}

public float getCpuLoad() throws ApacheMBeanException {
  return getFloatValue(CPU_LOAD);
}

public int getIdleWorkers() throws ApacheMBeanException {
  return getIntValue(IDLE_WORKERS);
}

public float getReqPerSec() throws ApacheMBeanException {
  return getFloatValue(REQ_PER_SEC);
}

public String getScoreboard() throws ApacheMBeanException {
  return getStringValue(SCOREBOARD);
}

public int getTotalAccesses() throws ApacheMBeanException {
  return getIntValue(TOTAL_ACCESSES);
}

public long getTotalKBytes() throws ApacheMBeanException {
  return getLongValue(TOTAL_KBYTES);
}

public long getUptime() throws ApacheMBeanException {
  return getLongValue(UPTIME);
}

// These methods are used as internal utilities by the getter methods
// There is one for each type returning the base Java type

private String getValue(String value)
  throws ApacheMBeanException, NoSuchFieldException, IOException {
  String result;
  URLConnection k = establishConnection();

  result = (String) readStatus(k, value);
```

```
    if (result == null) {
      throw new NoSuchFieldException(value);
    }
    return result;
  }

  private float getFloatValue(String value) throws ApacheMBeanException {
    float result;
    try {
      result = Float.parseFloat((String) getValue(value));
    } catch (IOException x) {
      throw new ApacheMBeanException(x);
    } catch (NoSuchFieldException x) {
      throw new ApacheMBeanException(x);
    }
    return result;
  }

  private int getIntValue(String value) throws ApacheMBeanException {
    int result;
    try {
      result = Integer.parseInt((String) getValue(value));
    } catch (IOException x) {
      throw new ApacheMBeanException(x);
    } catch (NoSuchFieldException x) {
      throw new ApacheMBeanException(x);
    }
    return result;
  }

  private long getLongValue(String value) throws ApacheMBeanException {
    long result;
    try {
      result = Long.parseLong((String) getValue(value));
    } catch (IOException x) {
      throw new ApacheMBeanException(x);
    } catch (NoSuchFieldException x) {
      throw new ApacheMBeanException(x);
    }
    return result;
  }

  private String getStringValue(String value) throws ApacheMBeanException {
    String result;
    try {
```

```
    result = (String) getValue(value);
  } catch (IOException x) {
    throw new ApacheMBeanException(x);
  } catch (NoSuchFieldException x) {
    throw new ApacheMBeanException(x);
  }
  return result;
}

// Establishes the connection to the URL
// If the connection fails, then the state
// is changed to DOWN or NOT_RESPONDING

private URLConnection establishConnection()
  throws IOException, ApacheMBeanException {
  URLConnection k = this.url.openConnection();
  try {
    k.connect();
    this.failures = 0;
    this.state = ApacheMBean.RUNNING;
  } catch (IOException x) {
    if (++this.failures > MAX_FAILURES) {
      this.state = DOWN;
    } else {
      this.state = NOT_RESPONDING;
    }
    throw new ApacheMBeanException("state: " + this.state);
  }
  return k;
}

// Parses the data returned from the URL

private String readStatus(URLConnection k, String value)
  throws IOException {
  BufferedReader r =
    new BufferedReader(new InputStreamReader(k.getInputStream()));
  for (String l = r.readLine(); l != null; l = r.readLine()) {
    StringTokenizer st = new StringTokenizer(l, ":");
    if (st.nextToken().trim().equals(value)) {
      // if it's the right value
      return (String) (st.nextToken().trim()); // get wanted value
    } else {
      st.nextToken(); // past unwanted value
    }
```

```
    }
    return "";
  }

}
```

Now, let's look at the capabilities of model MBeans in detail.

4.2 The ModelMBean Interface

The model MBean implementation, including RequiredModelMBean, must implement the ModelMBean interface, which extends three other JMX interfaces: DynamicMBean, PersistentMBean, and ModelMBeanNotificationBroadcaster. Here's how these interfaces are used in the model MBean.

4.2.1 DynamicMBean

Because it is a dynamic MBean, the model MBean must implement the DynamicMBean interface, which consists of the getAttribute(), setAttribute(), invoke(), and getMBeanInfo() methods. The getMBeanInfo() method returns a ModelMBeanInfo instance that extends MBeanInfo. The model MBean uses the additional information in the descriptors in ModelMBeanInfo to delegate and map these operations to the correct operations on your managed resources. You do not need to implement these methods unless you need to override the default behavior. The DynamicMBean and basic MBeanInfo interfaces were explained fully in Chapter 3.

4.2.2 PersistentMBean

The model MBean is also responsible for its own persistence and therefore must implement the PersistentMBean interface. The PersistentMBean interface is simply the load() and the store() methods. This does not mean that a model MBean *must* persist itself. Some implementations of the JMX agent may be completely transient in nature. In this situation, the load() and store() methods would be empty. The load() method is invoked when the model MBean is instantiated. The store() method is invoked according to the policy defined in the descriptors in the ModelMBeanInfo of the MBean (to be discussed later in this chapter).

In a simple implementation, the model MBean may be saved to a file. Alternatively, it may be saved to a database through JDBC (a.k.a., the Java

Database Connectivity API). In a more complex environment, the JMX agent may handle persistence on behalf of the model MBean. If you are using an implementation of JMX that has an implementation of `RequiredModelMBean` that does not support persistence and you need support for persistence, then you must override and implement the `load()` and `store()` methods. Here is the `PersistentMBean` interface:

```
interface PersistentMBean {
        void load();
        void store();
}
```

The model MBean constructor will attempt to prime itself by calling the model MBean `load()` method. The model MBean `load()` method must determine if this model MBean has a persistent representation. It can do this by invoking the `findInPersistent()` method; this is not a JMX standard, but it is a common practice. Then the `load()` method must determine where this data is located, retrieve it, and initialize the model MBean. The model MBean can, through JDBC operations, persist data to and populate the model MBeans from any number of data storage options, such as an LDAP[8] server, a DB2[9] application, a flat file, an NFS[10] file, or an internal high-performance cache. If the model MBean were implemented as an EJB object, object loading might be managed by the EJB container and the `load()` method would do nothing.

Because the `load()` method is not typically used by the application or adapter, the JMX agent can be independent and ignorant of data locale information and knowledge. Thus, data location may vary from one installation to another, depending on how the JMX agent and managed resource are installed and configured. Data locale independence also permits application configuration data to be defined within the directory service for use by multiple application instances or JMX agent instances. In this way, data locale has no impact on the interaction between the application, its model MBean, the JMX agent, the adapter, or the management system. As with all data persistence issues, the platform data services characteristics may have an impact on performance and security.

4.2.3 ModelMBeanNotificationBroadcaster

The `ModelMBeanNotificationBroadcaster` interface extends the `NotificationBroadcaster` interface and adds support for issuing generic text notifications and attribute change notifications. These events are sent only if at least one

NotificationListener instance is registered with the model MBean. Generic text notifications are simple to use, accepting any text string and sending it as a notification. Attribute change notifications are sent by the model MBean whenever one of its attribute's values changes. The MBean can also send an attribute change notification to the managed resource itself. For example, if a configuration program has just changed an attribute in the MBean and a setter does not exist for that attribute, the MBean could send an attribute change notification to the managed resource, given that the managed resource implements the NotificationListener interface. The managed resource would detect the change in its external configuration (held by the MBean), and it would make the internal adjustments necessary to comply. Application-specific notifications are supported like they are for any other MBean. Here is the ModelMBeanNotificationBroadcaster interface:

```
    interface ModelMBeanNotificationBroadcaster extends
    NotificationBroadcaster {
    addAttributeChangeNotificationListener(
            javax.management.NotificationListener inlistener,
            java.lang.String inAttributeName,
            java.lang.Object inhandback);
    removeAttributeChangeNotificationListener(
            javax.management.NotificationListener inlistener,
            java.lang.String inAttributeName);
    sendAttributeChangeNotification(
            javax.management.Attribute inOldVal,
            javax.management.Attribute inNewVal);
    sendAttributeChangeNotification(
            javax.management.AttributeChangeNotification ntfyObj);
    sendNotification(javax.management.Notification ntfyObj);
    sendNotification(java.lang.String ntfyText);
}
```

The ModelMBean interface has two additional methods:

```
void setManagedResource(java.lang.Object managedResourceReference,
        java.lang.String managedResourceReference_type);
void setModelMBeanInfo(ModelMBeanInfo ModelMBeanInfo_instance);
```

Let's look at how these methods are used to customize your model MBean.

4.3 Managed Resources

As illustrated in Figure 4.1, when attributes are retrieved or operations are invoked on a model MBean, it will delegate those requests to a managed resource. The managed resource is a runtime object associated with a model MBean via the `setManagedResource()` method. The `setManagedResource()` method sets the default managed resource for the entire model MBean. A different managed resource can be set per operation and attribute as well. The model MBean delegates operations to the managed resource associated with it.

Because attribute setter and getter methods are represented as operations in the model MBean, attribute values may be retrieved from or set to different managed resources as well. This capability eliminates the need to write a management facade or delegation class if your application's management characteristics are distributed across several classes or instances of the same class. The model MBean can be customized to perform as that facade.

If you want to stay simple and set one managed-resource object for your entire model MBean, you can use the `ModelMBean` interface's `setManagedResource()` method:

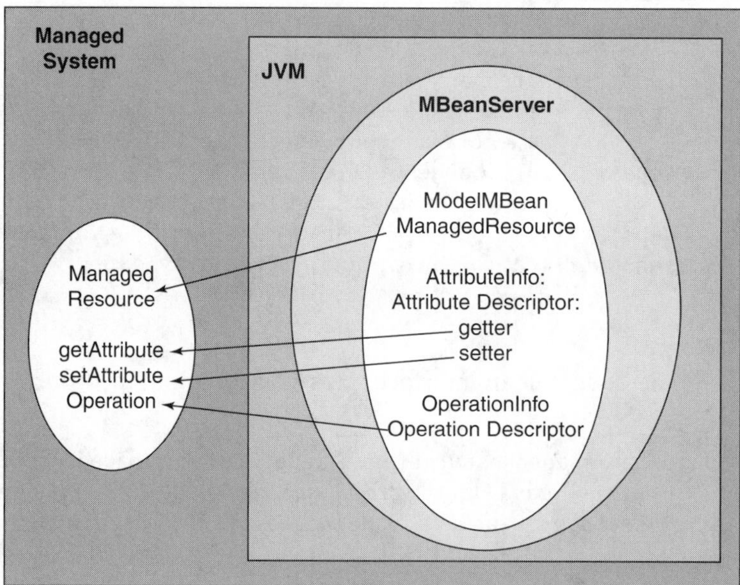

Figure 4.1 JMX Model MBeans and a Managed Resource

```
void setManagedResource(
        java.lang.Object managedResourceReference,
        java.lang.String managedResourceReference_type)
```

The first parameter is the reference of your managed resource class. The second parameter indicates the type of reference you are passing. It can be set to one of the following strings: "ObjectReference", "Handle", "IOR", "EJBHandle", "RMIReference". Although "ObjectReference" is always supported, an MBeanServer does not have to support all of these types. You should read the documentation for your JMX implementation to determine which of these types, or any additional types, are valid for your implementation.

Think back to the earlier ApacheServer example. The statement

```
apacheMMBean.setManagedResource(myApacheServer, "ObjectReference");
```

causes the `ApacheServer` instance, `myApacheServer`, to be the managed resource for the model MBean. This managed resource, `myApacheServer`, will now be the default managed resource for executing all operations in this model MBean—that is, `start()`, `stop()`, all get methods (including `getServer()`), and `setServer()`. You can override this default on a particular attribute or operation by using the descriptors in `ModelMBeanInfo` for that particular operation. We will show how to do this in the next section.

4.4 ModelMBeanInfo

The model MBean uses a `ModelMBeanInfo` class for metadata. `ModelMBeanInfo` extends the `MBeanInfo` class by adding a descriptor to each of the elements of the management interface: attributes, operations, and notifications. Descriptors are a list of name/value pairs that describe additional metadata about the resource and behavioral policy for the model MBean instance. The descriptors control how attribute values are cached or persisted, which attributes are retrievable from other objects, whether notifications are logged, where logs are located, along with other descriptive data. This is the `ModelMBeanInfo` interface:

```
interface ModelMBeanInfo {
  Object clone():
  Descriptor getMBeanDescriptor();
  void setMBeanDescriptor(Descriptor inDescriptor );
```

```
    Descriptor getDescriptor(String inDescriptorName,
                             String inDescriptorType );
    Descriptor[] getDescriptors (String inDescriptorType );
    void setDescriptor(Descriptor inDescriptor,
                       String inDescriptorType );
    void setDescriptors(Descriptor[] inDescriptors );

    ModelMBeanAttributeInfo getAttribute(String inAttrName );
    ModelMBeanNotificationInfo getNotification(String inNotifName );
    ModelMBeanOperationInfo getOperation(String inOperName );
    MBeanAttributeInfo[]getAttributes();
    MBeanNotificationInfo[]getNotifications() ;
    MBeanOperationInfo[]getOperations();
    MBeanConstructorInfo[]getConstructors() ;
    String getClassName();
    String getDescription();
}
```

In addition, `ModelMBeanInfo` is required to support the following constructors:

- `ModelMBeanInfo();`

  The default constructor constructs a `ModelMBeanInfo` instance with empty component arrays and a default MBean descriptor.

- `ModelMBeanInfo (ModelMBeanInfo);`

  The copy constructor constructs a `ModelMBeanInfo` instance that is a duplicate of the one passed in.

- ```
  ModelMBeanInfo (className, String description,
      ModelMBeanAttributeInfo[], ModelMBeanConstructorInfo[],
      ModelMBeanOperationInfo[], ModelMBeanNotificationInfo[])
  ```

  The `MBeanInfo`-compliant constructor creates a `ModelMBeanInfo` instance with the provided information, but the MBean descriptor contains default value. Because the MBean descriptor must not be `null`, the default descriptor will contain at least the `name` and `descriptorType` fields. The name will match the MBean name.

- ```
  ModelMBeanInfo (className, String description,
      ModelMBeanAttributeInfo[], ModelMBeanConstructorInfo[],
      ModelMBeanOperationInfo[], ModelMBeanNotificationInfo[],
      MBeanDescriptor)
  ```

  The full constructor creates a `ModelMBeanInfo` instance with the provided information. The MBean descriptor is verified: If it is not valid, an exception will be thrown and a default MBean descriptor will be set. You can see that there is a descriptor associated with the model MBean itself. It must not be `null`.

The normal `MBeanInfo` methods return model MBean extensions of the `AttributeInfo`, `OperationInfo`, and `NotificationInfo` classes respectively. Each of the model MBean extensions implements the `DescriptorAccess` interface. The `DescriptorAccess` interface gives you access to `attribute descriptor`, `operation descriptor`, and `notification descriptor`, which are associated with `AttributeInfo`, `OperationInfo`, and `NotificationInfo`, respectively. This is the `DescriptorAccess` interface:

```
interface DescriptorAccess {
  Descriptor getDescriptor();
  void setDescriptor(Descriptor inDescriptor);
}
```

The descriptor also defines the method signatures that will be executed by the model MBean on its managed resource to satisfy the `getAttribute()`, `setAttribute()`, and `invoke()` operations. As Figure 4.2 shows, defining the managed resource and method signature in the operation descriptor allows

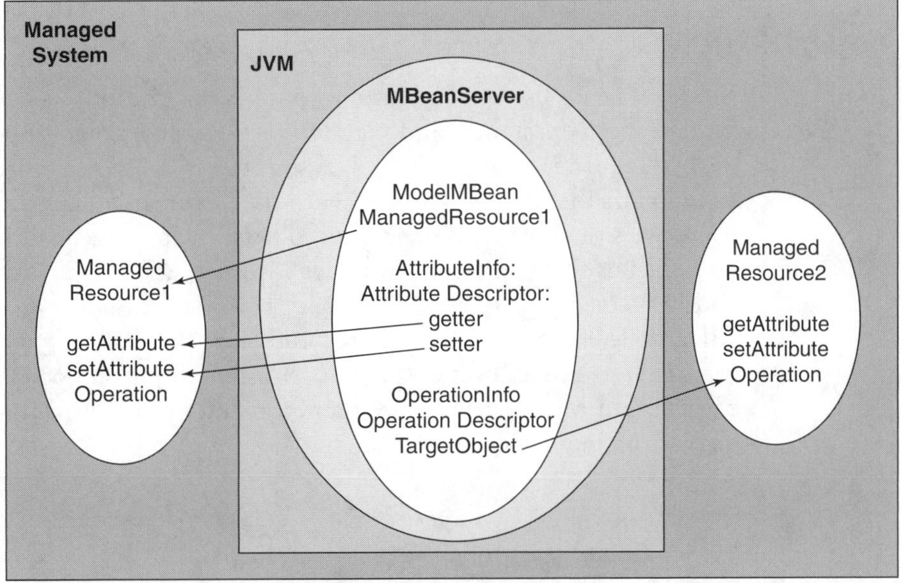

Figure 4.2 JMX Model MBeans and Multiple Managed Resources

the actual methods called for an operation to have different signatures and to be delegated to a wide range of objects at runtime. This flexibility enables the management of distributed, dynamic applications directly from a model MBean.

The descriptor-oriented methods in `ModelMBeanInfo` allow you to list and update any descriptor in the model MBean without having to retrieve the specific `ModelMBeanAttributeInfo`, `ModelMBeanOperationInfo`, `ModelMBeanConstructorInfo`, or `ModelMBeanNotificationInfo` class for it first. This is strictly a convenience for the programmer.

You can customize the model MBean during development by defining the `ModelMBeanInfo` instance in the program with the `ModelMBeanInfo` interface. Defining an instance of `MBeanInfo` directly in a program creates a static model MBean. You can also create model MBeans more dynamically. The descriptor values and `ModelMBeanInfo` attributes and operations can be loaded from the application or a file at runtime. This means that you can update or upgrade the management data along with your application without having to remove and reinstantiate all of the data. You could also use an Interface Definition Language (IDL)[11] or Managed Object Format (MOF)[12] file. Using external files whose formats are defined by standards permits management interfaces to be defined in a language-independent manner. The JMX specification does not define how to use XML, IDL, or MOF files for `MBeanInfo` data, but we include an example at the end of this chapter to illustrate the use of an XML service to load `ModelMBeanInfo` from an XML file.

4.5 Descriptors

Model MBeans use the descriptors to support additional metadata and policy for caching, persistence, and logging for the management interface defined in `ModelMBeanInfo`. Simply put, a descriptor is a set of unordered `keyword=value` pairs that can be accessed with the `Descriptor` interface.

Copies of descriptors are retrieved from the management interface element with the `DescriptorAccess` interface. A different descriptor type is defined for and implemented by `ModelMBeanOperationInfo`, `ModelMBeanConstructorInfo`, `ModelMBeanAttributeInfo`, and `ModelMBeanNotificationInfo`. You can also retrieve and set descriptors from methods on `ModelMBeanInfo`. You can get and set descriptors by name or descriptor type (`mbean`, `attribute`, `operation`, `notification`):

```
interface Descriptor {
  java.lang.Object clone();
  java.lang.String[] getFieldNames();
```

```
   java.lang.String[] getFields();
   java.lang.Object getFieldValue(java.lang.String fieldName);
   java.lang.Object[] getFieldValues(java.lang.String[] fieldNames);
   boolean isValid();
   void removeField(java.lang.String fieldName);
   void setField(java.lang.String fieldName,
                 java.lang.Object fieldValue);
   void setFields(java.lang.String[] fieldNames,
      java.lang.Object[] fieldValues);
}
```

The `Descriptor` interface allows a variety of accesses. You can retrieve one descriptor field, a specific set of descriptor fields, or all descriptor fields. The `Descriptor` interface also provides a method that can be used to validate that the current value of the descriptor is valid for its descriptor type.

A set of descriptor keywords are defined by the JMX specification to ensure standard and uniform functionality and treatment. We will cover these in detail later in this section.

Note that you can set values for descriptors as well. You can replace an entire field value. In the `setField()` method the `fieldValue` parameter is copied into the descriptor. New keywords can be added by applications or adapters at any time (see Section 4.8.3).

The `Descriptor` interface is implemented by the `DescriptorSupport` class. You can use this class to create descriptors in a variety of ways. Choose the one that's easiest for you because there is no difference in the net effect:

- Instantiate with an array of `name=value` strings:

```
// Instantiate Descriptors using the array
Descriptor timeStateDescA =
     new DescriptorSupport(new String[] {
          "name=Time",
          "descriptorType=attribute",
          "displayName=currentTime",
          "getMethod=getTime",
          "setMethod=setTime",
          "currencyTimeLimit=20" });
```

This style does not support setting object values for the descriptor.

- Make a series of `setField()` method calls:

```
// Instantiate Descriptors using the field setters
Descriptor timeStateDescF = new DescriptorSupport();
timeStateDescF.setField("name","Time");
timeStateDescF.setField("descriptorType","attribute");
timeStateDescF.setField("displayName","currentTime");
timeStateDescF.setField("getMethod","getTime");
timeStateDescF.setField("setMethod","setTime");
timeStateDescF.setField("currencyTimeLimit","20");
```

This style is somewhat less efficient in processing, but it is easier to adjust during development because you can just comment out the statements for the fields you no longer want to set. This is the style you should use if the type for the field is `Object` and you need to save an object value as the descriptor value. Here is how to set a value for an object attribute that reflects the start date for an application:

```
Date currDate = new Date();
timeStateDescF.setField("value", currDate);
```

- Call the `setField()` method with an array of names and values:

```
Descriptor timeStateDescFA = new DescriptorSupport();
String[] fieldnames = new String[] {"name",
        "descriptorType",
        "displayName",
        "getMethod",
        "setMethod",
        "currencyTimeLimit"} ;
Object[] fieldvalues = new Object[] {
        new String("Time"),
        new String("attribute"),
        new String("currentTime"),
        new String("getTime"),
        new String("setTime"),
        new String("20") } ;
timeStateDescFA.setFields(fieldnames,fieldvalues);
```

This style does support object values.

The `Descriptor` interface also supports a `clone()` operation that is very convenient for creating new descriptors from existing ones as templates. The `remove()` and `setField()` methods make it very simple to selectively modify the descriptor.

Sections 4.5.1 through 4.5.5 cover the standard descriptor keywords supported by all model MBeans. These descriptor keywords are defined in the JMX specification[13] as well. Section 4.6 then discusses caching and persistence behavior in the model MBean.

4.5.1 Model MBean Descriptors

Descriptors at the MBean level define default policies for the attributes, operations, and notifications for persistence, caching, and logging. Table 4.1 shows the descriptors that are valid for model MBeans.

Table 4.1 Valid Model MBean Descriptors

Descriptor	Meaning
`name`, `displayName`	The logical and displayable names of the model MBean.
`descriptorType`	Must be "mbean" to signal that this descriptor applies to the model MBean.
`version`	The version of this model MBean.
`export`	If this is set to a value, then the model MBean is exported to a registry (like JNDI) or somehow made visible to entities outside the MBeanServer. The value is used to assist with the export. If the value is `null`, then an export is not performed. See Section 4.6.6.3 (Export).
`persistPolicy`, `persistPeriod`, `persistLocation`, `persistName`	See Section 4.6.4 (Persistence).
`currencyTimeLimit`, `lastReturnedValue`, `lastUpdatedTimeStamp`	See Section 4.6.1 (Caching).
`log`, `logFile`	See Section 4.6.5 (Logging).
`visibility`	See Section 4.6.6.2 (Visibility).
`presentationString`	See Section 4.6.6.1 (Presentation String).

Looking back at the Apache server example again, we can see an example of the model MBean descriptor. Here is another example for an Apache server that also defines a persistence policy:

```
//   Set MBean descriptor example
  Descriptor mmbDescription = new DescriptorSupport(new String[] {
    "name=apacheServerManager",         // server MBean name
    "descriptorType=mbean",             // MBean descriptor
    "displayName=apache server MBean", // screen name of MBean
    "log=T",                            // log all notifications
    "logFile=jmxmain.log",              // log in jmxmain.log
    "currencyTimeLimit=10",             // cache all attribute
                                        // values for 10 seconds
    "persistPolicy=noMoreOftenThan",    // persist on change
    "persistPeriod=10",                 // no more often than
                                        // 10 seconds
    "persistLocation=jmxRepository",    // save in jmxRepository
                                        // directory
    "persistName=serverMBean"});        // save in file called
                                        // serverMBean
```

The `descriptorType` field is set to "mbean" to indicate that this is an MBean descriptor. The `displayName` field is set to "serverMBean". The line `log=T` indicates that all notifications will be logged into the file named in the `logFile` field: `jmxmain.log`. The line `currencyTimeLimit=10` means that all attributes in this model MBean will be cached for up to 10 seconds. After a value is 10 seconds old, it will be retrieved from the managed resource again. The `persistPolicy` field is set to `noMoreOftenThan` with a `persistPeriod` value of `10`. This means that the attribute values will be saved to a directory called `jmxRepository` in a file called `serverBean` whenever they are updated, but no more often than every 10 seconds. This restriction prevents high rates of updates that are not meaningful.

4.5.2 Attribute Descriptors

The model MBean attribute descriptor includes policy and configuration for managing its persistence, caching, protocol mapping, and handling of get and set requests. When the model MBean is created by the managed resource, the managed resource defines the operations that will be executed by the model MBean that will satisfy the get and set of the attribute. By defining operations, the actual methods called to satisfy `getAttribute()` and `setAttribute()` requests are allowed to vary and to be delegated to a wide range of objects at runtime. This flexibility enables management of distributed, dynamic applications. If an attribute has no operation associated with it, the values are maintained in the value descriptor field in the model MBean.

Let's look at the implications of this a little more closely. If an attribute has no method signature associated with it, then no managed-resource method can be invoked to satisfy it. This means that for `setAttribute()`, the value is simply cached in the model MBean and any `AttributeChangeNotification` listeners are sent an attribute change notification—that is, an `AttributeChangeNotification` instance. For `getAttribute()`, the currently cached value for the attribute in the model MBean itself is simply returned. In this case there is no delegation to a managed resource. This can be useful for static information and helps minimize the interruption of managed resources to retrieve static resource information.

When attribute value caching is supported, if the data requested is current, then the model MBean returns its cached value and the managed resource is not interrupted with a data retrieval request. Because direct interaction with the managed resource is not required for each interaction with the management system, the impact of management activity on runtime application resources and performance is minimized.

Table 4.2 shows the descriptors that are supported in the `ModelMBeanAttributeInfo` descriptor.

This attribute descriptor example is based on the `State` attribute of the Apache model MBean example and illustrates most of the fields:

```
// Set attribute descriptor examples
ModelMBeanAttributeInfo[] aAttributes = new
  ModelMBeanAttributeInfo[3];
// State
Descriptor stateDesc = new DescriptorSupport();

stateDesc.setField("name","State");
stateDesc.setField("descriptorType","attribute");
stateDesc.setField("displayName","Apache Server State");
stateDesc.setField("getMethod","getState");
stateDesc.setField("setMethod","setState");
stateDesc.setField("currencyTimeLimit","20");
aAttributes[0] = new ModelMBeanAttributeInfo("State",
        "java.lang.String",
        "State: state string.",
        true,
        true,
        false,
        stateDesc);
```

Table 4.2 ModelMBeanAttributeInfo Descriptors

Descriptor	Meaning
name, displayName	The logical and displayable names of the model MBean attribute. The displayable name should be human readable and may be internationalized. If displayName is not set, the name descriptor field will be used.
descriptorType	Must be set to attribute.
value, default, legalValues	See Section 4.6.2 (Values and Validation).
protocolMap	See Section 4.6.6.4 (Protocol Map).
getMethod, setMethod	See Section 4.6.3 (Delegation).
persistPolicy, persistPeriod	See Section 4.6.4 (Persistence).
currencyTimeLimit, lastUpdatedTimeStamp	See Section 4.6.1 (Caching).
iterable	Defines if this attribute must be iterated over. The default is false.
visibility	See Section 4.6.6.2 (Visibility).
presentationString	See Section 4.6.6.1 (Presentation String).

In this example the name of the attribute is State, but the displayed name will be "Apache Server State". The getMethod descriptor field defines getState() as the get method. The setMethod descriptor field defines setState() as the set method. The value 20 in the currencyTimeLimit field means that this attribute value will be cached for 20 seconds.

In the following ModelMBeanAttributeInfo instance for total accesses to the Apache server, we have added an example for the use of default and protocolMap fields:

```
// TotalAccesses
Descriptor totalAccessesDesc = new DescriptorSupport();
    totalAccessesDesc.setField("name","TotalAccesses");
    totalAccessesDesc.setField("descriptorType", "attribute");
```

```
    totalAccessesDesc.setField("default", "0");
    totalAccessesDesc.setField("displayName",
                                    "Total Accesses on Server");
    totalAccessesDesc.setField("getMethod","getTotalAccesses");
    totalAccessesDesc.setField("setMethod","setTotalAccesses");
    Descriptor TotalAccessesMap =
       new DescriptorSupport(new String[] {
          "SNMP=1.3.6.9.12.15.18.21.0",
          "CIM=ManagedResource.Version"});
    totalAccessesDesc.setField("protocolMap",(TotalAccessesMap));

aAttributes[1] = new ModelMBeanAttributeInfo("TotalAccesses",
    "java.lang.Integer",
    "TotalAccesses: number of times the State string",
    true,
    false,
    false,
    totalAccessesDesc);
```

A value of `0` in the `default` field means that the default value for `TotalAccesses`, if it is not set, should be `0`. The protocol map contains two hints to the protocol adapters. One is for an SNMP adapter indicating that when the MIB object ID (OID) 1.3.6.9.12.15.18.21.0 is requested, the value in `TotalAccesses` should be returned. The other is for a CIM adapter indicating that this same attribute and value is equivalent to the `Version` attribute in the CIM class `ManagedResource`.

In the following example we are defining a static attribute, the maximum thread pool to be used in each JVM for an Apache server. The `value` field of the descriptor is set to 99. The `currencyTimeLimit` descriptor field is set to −1, which means that the value never becomes stale. Notice that no get or set methods have been defined:

```
// MaxPool static value
Descriptor maxPoolHardValueDesc = new DescriptorSupport();
maxPoolHardValueDesc.setField("name","maxPool");
maxPoolHardValueDesc.setField("descriptorType","attribute");
maxPoolHardValueDesc.setField("value", new Integer("99"));
maxPoolHardValueDesc.setField("displayName",
  "maximum Thread Pool for Apache Server, a Hard Coded Value");
maxPoolHardValueDesc.setField("currencyTimeLimit","-1");

aAttributes[2] = new ModelMBeanAttributeInfo("maxPoolHardValue",
  "java.lang.Integer",
```

```
"maxPool: static maximum thread pool value for the Apache server",
true,
false,
false,
maxPoolHardValueDesc);
```

Just for the sake of completeness, if we needed to define a static value that contained a Date object, in this case the time that the Apache server was started, the setting of the descriptor would look like this:

```
// StartDate as a static value
  Descriptor startDateDesc = new DescriptorSupport();
  startDateDesc.setField("name","startDate");
  startDateDesc.setField("descriptorType","attribute");
  startDateDesc.setField("displayName","ApacheServerStartTime");
  startDateDesc.setField("value", new Date());
  startDateDesc.setField("currencyTimeLimit","-1");
```

And the setting of the ModelMBeanAttributeInfo object would look like this:

```
// Set the attribute info
  aAttributes[3] =
     new ModelMBeanAttributeInfo("startDateHardValue",
     "java.util.Date",
     "startDate of ApacheServerHardValue: static Date value",
     true,
     false,
     false,
     startDateDesc);
```

Here is how you would get these attributes using the model MBean myMMBean:

```
// Retrieving these attributes using the model MBean myMMBean:
RequiredModelMBean myMMBean = new RequiredModelMBean();
// Set ModelMBeanInfo and managedResource here
String myState = (String) myMMBean.getAttribute("State");
String myAccesses = (String) myMMBean.getAttribute("TotalAccesses");
Integer myPool = (Integer) myMMBean.getAttribute("maxPool");
```

4.5.3 Constructor Descriptors

Every MBean must have a public constructor. It is also recommended that a default constructor—that is, a constructor that accepts no parameters—be provided. If you define constructors that require parameters, then you must define the constructor with an `MBeanConstructorInfo` instance. The `ModelMBeanInfo` descriptor for the constructor defines the constructor to be an operation with a method role of constructor, as opposed to operation, getter, or setter, examples of which we will see later. Constructor signatures are defined just like operation signatures (which are discussed in the next section):

```
  // Constructor descriptor example

ModelMBeanConstructorInfo[] aConstructors =
  new ModelMBeanConstructorInfo[1];
Class apacheServerClass = null;
try {
  apacheServerClass = Class.forName("jnjmx.ch4.ApacheServer");
} catch(Exception e) {
  System.out.println("Apache Server Class not found");
}

Constructor[] constructors = apacheServerClass.getConstructors();

Descriptor apacheServerDesc = new DescriptorSupport();
apacheServerDesc.setField("name","ApacheServer");
apacheServerDesc.setField("descriptorType", "operation");
apacheServerDesc.setField("role","constructor");

aConstructors[0] = new ModelMBeanConstructorInfo(
    "ApacheServer(): Constructs an apache server query tool",
     constructors[0],
     apacheServerDesc);
```

In this example we see that a default constructor has been defined for the model MBean. Table 4.3 gives the details of all the descriptors standardized for `ModelMBeanConstructorInfo`.

4.5.4 Operation Descriptors

For operations, the method signature must be defined in `ModelMBeanOperationInfo`. For each operation defined, a target object must be identified on which to invoke the operations. This target object can be set for the model MBean as a whole (by the `setManagedResource()` method) or per operation in the `targetObject` descriptor field. You can even have different target objects for different operations. This flexibility allows distributed, component-based applications to be supported by the model MBean. It also supports management of applications that do not already have a management facade. Like attributes, the model MBean supports caching the last returned value of the operation. Caching can reduce the interruptions to the managed application. Table 4.4 lists the descriptors that are supported in `ModelMBeanOperationInfo`.

Table 4.3 `ModelMBeanConstructorInfo` Descriptors

Descriptor	Meaning
`name`, `displayName`	The logical and displayable names of the model MBean constructor. The displayable name should be human readable and may be internationalized. If `displayName` is not set, then the `name` descriptor field will be used.
`descriptorType`	Must be set to “operation”.
`role`	Set to “constructor”, “operation”, “getter”, or “setter”, depending on how the operation is used.
`Class`	Class where method is defined (fully qualified).
`visibility`	See Section 4.6.6.2 (Visibility).
`presentationString`	See Section 4.6.6.1 (Presentation String).

Table 4.4 `ModelMBeanOperationInfo` Descriptors

Descriptor	Meaning
`name`, `displayName`	The logical and displayable names of the model MBean operation. The displayable name should be human readable and may be internationalized. If `displayName` is not set, then the `name` descriptor field will be used.
`DescriptorType`	Must be set to ”operation”.
`role`	Set to “constructor”, “operation”, “getter”, or “setter”, depending on how the operation is used.

Descriptor	Meaning
`targetObject`, `targetType`	See Section 4.6.3 (Delegation).
`currencyTimeLimit`, `lastReturnedValue`, `lastUpdatedTimeStamp`	See Section 4.6.1 (Caching).
`Iterable`	Defines if this attribute must be iterated over. The default is `false`.
`visibility`	See Section 4.6.6.2 (Visibility).
`presentationString`	See Section 4.6.6.1 (Presentation String).

The following example illustrates a simple `Integer start()` operation. A value of `3` in the `currencyTimeLimit` descriptor field specifies that the value returned from the operation will be valid in the cache for three seconds. The value of `jnjmx.ch4.ApacheServer for the class` field defines what the class for the target object will be. Then we can see where we are creating an `apacheServerInitiator` instance. This object is set as the target object for *just* the start operation because it must use a command line to start the Apache process. The `targetObjectType` descriptor field must be set to `objectReference`. The `stop()method` is still invoked on the default target object for the model MBean.

```
  // Operation descriptor example
ModelMBeanOperationInfo[] dOperations =
  new ModelMBeanOperationInfo[1];
MBeanParameterInfo[] params = null;

Descriptor stopDesc = new DescriptorSupport();
stopDesc.setField("name","stop");
stopDesc.setField("descriptorType","operation");
stopDesc.setField("class","jnjmx.ch4.ApacheServer");
stopDesc.setField("role","operation");

dOperations[0] = new ModelMBeanOperationInfo("stop",
     "stop(): stop the apache server",
     params ,
     "void",
```

```
        MBeanOperationInfo.ACTION,
        stopDesc);

Descriptor startDesc = new DescriptorSupport(new String[] {
        "name=start",
        "class=jnjmx.ch4.ApacheServerInitiator",
        "descriptorType=operation",
        "role=operation",
        "currencyTimeLimit=3"} );

// Create an instance of ApacheServerInitiator just for the
// start operation
ApacheServerInitiator asf =
  new ApacheServerInitiator("http://www.apache.org");
startDesc.setField("targetObject",asf);
startDesc.setField("targetObjectType","objectReference");

aOperations[1] = new ModelMBeanOperationInfo("start",
        "start(): start the apache server",
        params,
        "java.lang.Integer",
        MBeanOperationInfo.INFO,
        startDesc);
```

Here is how you would invoke the start operation on the model MBean myMMBean where it has no parameters:

```
// invoking the operation
Integer startRC = (Integer) apacheMMBean.invoke("start", null,
    null);
```

4.5.5 Notification Descriptors

The model MBean notification descriptor defines a severity value, visibility value, and message ID for national language support, as well as whether the notification should be logged. A response operation may also be defined. Table 4.5 lists the descriptor keywords supported in the model MBean notification descriptor.

Table 4.5 `ModelMBeanNotificationInfo` Descriptors

Descriptor	Meaning
`name`	The logical and displayable name of the notification.
`descriptorType`	Must be "notification".
`severity`	The `severity` integer ranges from `0` to `6`. Here are the meanings of these numbers: `0`: Unknown, indeterminate `1`: Nonrecoverable `2`: Critical, failure `3`: Major, severe `4`: Minor, marginal, or error `5`: Warning `6`: Normal, cleared, or informative The `severity` descriptor field can be used with a `notificationListener` notification filter or to influence logging. The assignment of `severity` values is very subjective and should be done by someone with an understanding of the managed resource, the notification, and how the management systems might be using `severity` to guide their reaction to the notification.
`messageId`	The ID of the notification. This value can be used to translate the message into another language. It should be unique per notification; it is not intended to be unique per message instance. This descriptor field can be used such that only the message ID is sent to the listeners and the message text is assigned by the listener. Using `messageID` minimizes the bytes on the wire and ensures that the appropriate language is displayed in a log or on a console. A resource file could be used to do this.
`log`	A Boolean. If `true`, then all of these notifications should be logged if `log` is set to `true` at the model MBean descriptor level.

Table 4.5 `ModelMBeanNotificationInfo` Descriptors *(continued)*

Descriptor	Meaning
`logFile`	The name of the file where these notifications should be logged. Note that if the log file is not defined, even if the log Boolean is set to `true`, nothing will be logged. If the model MBean descriptor contains a log file name for the entire MBean, then it is not necessary to define it on every notification as well. However, if you define a different log file name here, then these notifications will be logged in the new file and the rest will be in the model MBean default log file.
`visibility`	See Section 4.6.6.2 (Visibility).
`presentationString`	See Section 4.6.6.1 (Presentation String).

Here is a notification descriptor example from the Apache model MBean:

```
// Declare an "Apache Server Down" notification
ModelMBeanNotificationInfo[] apacheNotifications =
  new ModelMBeanNotificationInfo[1];

Descriptor apacheDownEventDesc =
  new DescriptorSupport(
    new String[] {
      "descriptorType=notification",
      "name=jmx.ModelMBean.General.Apache.Down",
      "severity=1",
      "MessageId=Apache001",
      "log=T",
      "logfile=jmx.apachelog" });

apacheNotifications[0] =
  new ModelMBeanNotificationInfo(
    new String[] { "jmx.ModelMBean.General.Apache.Down" },
    "jmx.ModelMBean.General",
    "Apache Server is Down",
    apacheDownEventDesc);
```

In this case the name of the notification is `jmx.ModelMBean.General.Apache.Down`. The severity of the notification is set to `1`, and the message ID is "Apache001". This notification will always be logged in the file `jmx.apachelog`.

Here is how you would send this notification from the myMMBean model MBean:

```
apacheMMBean.sendNotification("Apache Server is Down");
```

4.6 Behavior of the Model MBean

Model MBeans provide support for some common MBean requirements—caching, persistence, logging—and a host of miscellaneous other services. This section describes the processing that model MBeans perform in these services. Remember, because RequiredModelMBean is an actual concrete class (and you have the source for it), you can extend it and override its behavior.

4.6.1 Caching

Caching is supported for both attribute values and operation responses. In general, if the data requested is current, then the model MBean returns the cached value and does not retrieve the value from or invoke the operation on the managed resource. The value is cached in the value descriptor field of ModelMBeanAttributeInfo or the lastReturnedValue field of ModelMBean-OperationInfo. Caching policy is defined by two descriptor fields: currency-TimeLimit and lastUpdatedTimeStamp. This is the algorithm for caching; it is relatively straightforward:

```
if (currencyPeriod < 0)
{  /* if currencyTimeLimit is -1, then value is always current */
   returnCachedValue = true;
   resetValue = false;
} else if (currencyPeriod == 0)
{  /* if currencyTimeLimit is 0, then value is never current */
   returnCachedValue = false;
   resetValue = true;
} else
{  /* if now < currencyTimeLimit + LastUpdateTimeStamp */
   String tStamp = (String)
       descr.getFieldValue("lastUpdatedTimeStamp");
   if (tStamp == null)
   {
     tStamp = "0";
   }
   long lastTime = (new Long(tStamp)).longValue();
```

```
   long now = (new Date()).getTime();
   if (now < (lastTime + currencyPeriod))
   {
     returnCachedValue = true;
     resetValue = false;
   } else
   { /* value is expired */
     returnCachedValue = false;
     resetValue = true;
   }
}

if (resetValue == true)
  { /* value is not current, so remove it */
    descr.setField("lastUpdatedTimeStamp", "0");
    descr.setField("value", null);
    response = null;
  }

If (returnCachedValue == true) {
  response = descr.getFieldValue("value");

} else {
  response = getAttribute();
  descr.setField("lastUpdatedTimeStamp", now);
  descr.setField("value", response);
}


return response;
```

For attributes, if `getAttribute()` is called for an attribute with a stale value (or no value), then the `getMethod` defined in the attribute's descriptor will be invoked and the returned value will be recorded in `value` for the attribute, and the `lastUpdatedTimeStamp` field will set to the current time. The requester will be handed the new value. If no `getMethod` descriptor field is defined and the `value` field in the attribute descriptor is not set, then the value in the `default` descriptor field from the attribute's descriptor will be returned. Note that the cached value is set lazily; that is, it is not updated just because it is stale; someone must ask for it to trigger the update. Here is an example of caching descriptor fields for an attribute:

```
"getMethod=getMyOwnAttribute"
"currencyTimeLimit=30"
```

```
"lastUpdatedTimeStamp=03302002120905003"
"value=highspeed"
```

Similarly for operations, if an `invoke()` method is executed for an operation with a stale value (or no value) set in the `lastReturnedValue` field of the descriptor, then the `invoke()` method is executed for the operation and the returned value will be recorded in the `lastReturnedValue` field for the operation. Likewise, `lastUpdatedTimeStamp` will be set to the current time. The requester will be handed the new value. This cached value is also maintained lazily:

```
"name=getRateOfSpeed"
"currencyTimeLimit=30"
"lastUpdatedTimeStamp=03302002120905003"
"lastReturnedValue=30mph"
```

The `currencyTimeLimit` descriptor field may be in the model MBean's descriptor. When `currencyTimeLimit` is set here, it applies to all attributes and operations. If `currencyTimeLimit` is not defined, then the default is to do no caching. We can override the model MBean's default policy by defining it in the attribute or operations descriptor. As in the preceding examples, `currencyTimeLimit` is set to the number of seconds that a cached value is current. If `currencyTimeLimit` is set to `0`:

```
"currencyTimeLimit=0"
```

then no caching is performed and the value is retrieved or operation invoked for every request.

If `currencyTimeLimit` is set to –1:

```
"currencyTimeLimit=-1"
```

then the value is never stale. This is appropriate for static information or information that the managed resource populates in the model MBean. These types of managed resources may not be able to support or tolerate interruptions.

4.6.2 Values and Validation

The attribute descriptor contains three fields that govern the attribute's value outside of the caching algorithm: value, default, and legalValues. The value field is set by a setAttribute() operation and by caching support. It can be set statically and not updated from a managed resource, or it can be set on every iteration of getAttribute(). The default field defines the default value to be returned on getAttribute() for this attribute if there is no current data in the value field and a value cannot be retrieved from the managed resource. The legalValues field defines an array of values that are legal for the attribute. This field was meant to be a hint to a generated console or model MBean user. These values are not enforced by the model MBean or the descriptor. It is up to the model MBean user to consult and use them. Likewise it is up to the console developer to use legalValues appropriately.

```
"defaultValue=True"
"legalValues=True,False"
```

4.6.3 Delegation

Model MBeans delegate getAttribute() and setAttribute() method calls, as well as operations, to your managed resource. In every case the method invoked on your managed resources can be any method with any signature. The attribute descriptor contains a getMethod field and a setMethod field. These fields contain the names of the operations (in the same ModelMBeanInfo instance) that are to be executed to satisfy the get or the set. The operation's ModelMBeanOperationInfo instance defines the method signatures to be invoked on the managed resource. The managed resource is set for an entire model MBean with the setManagedResource() method on the model MBean itself.

The interesting thing here is that the operation descriptor allows the definition of its own target object. The targetObject descriptor field overrides setManagedResource() for just that operation. The override causes the MBean to send the invoke() command to a new object instance, perhaps even a different class of object. This is a very powerful feature of model MBeans and allows a great deal of flexibility for defining model MBeans for existing applications.

Figure 4.3 shows an MBean with its management interface and how attributes delegate to operations and operations delegate to methods on different target objects.

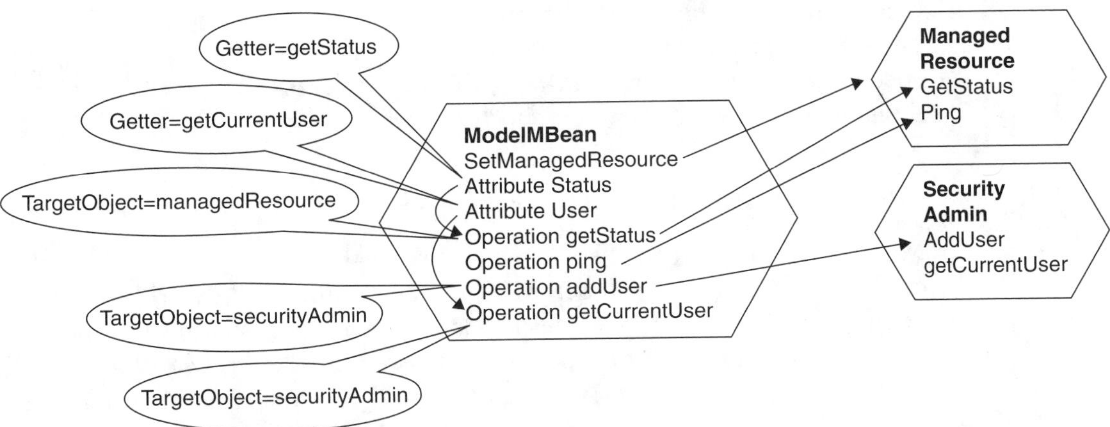

Figure 4.3 Operation Delegation to Target Objects

During initialization of the MBean itself, we would use a dashboard object as the default target for all methods:

```
setManagedObject(dashboard)
```

On the attribute descriptor for `Rate`, we would have

```
"name=Rate"
"getMethod=getRateOfSpeed"
```

Then on the operation descriptor for `getRateOfSpeed`, we would see

```
"name=getRateOfSpeed"
"targetObject=" + mphGauge
"targetObjectType=ObjectReference"
```

This means that whenever the value of the `Rate` attribute is requested, the model MBean will invoke the `mphGauge.getRateOfSpeed()` method.

Now, the `targetObjectType` descriptor field identifies what type of reference the `targetObject` field's value is. The `targetObjectType` field may be set to `ObjectReference`, `IOR`, `EJBHandle`, or `RMIReference`. It may be set to other values as well, as long as the model MBean implementation recognizes the type and can deal with the reference appropriately. The JMX reference implementation supports only `ObjectReference`, which means that the reference in `targetObject` must be a local one. However, you can see that it was designed to work with remote objects as well.

4.6.4 Persistence

Model MBeans are responsible for persisting themselves. Persistence policy can be defined in the model MBean's descriptor and overridden in the attribute's descriptor. If a model MBean supports persistence, then some or all of the attributes may be persisted. This is important if you have highly volatile attributes (like counters) that have no meaning when they are saved. Using selective persistence, you can avoid the overhead of saving unstable, unusable data, like `currentThreadPoolSize` or `currentSessionCount`. Persistence is useful when the attributes that are persisted may be used to prime the next instantiation of the application or its model MBeans. For example, configuration attributes like `traceState` or long-running counters like `totalNumberOfInvocationsOfApplicationInJuly` would be good candidates for persistence. Persistence policy is defined by four descriptor fields: `persistName`, `persistLocation`, `persistPolicy`, and `persistPeriod`.

The `persistName` and `persistLocation` descriptor fields are defined only in the MBean-level descriptor. The `persistName` field defines the name of the model MBean in the persistence medium. If file persistence is being used, this is the file name. If database persistence is being used, the name is the primary key for the record. The `persistLocation` field defines where the model MBean is persisted. For file-based persistence this is the fully qualified directory. For database-based persistence this is the database name.

The persistence policy descriptor field, `persistPolicy`, can be set in the model MBean descriptor or attribute descriptor. It may be set to one of four policies:

1. `persistPolicy=Never` to switch persistence off
2. `persistPolicy=OnTimer` to force persistence at checkpoint intervals
3. `persistPolicy=OnUpdate` to allow persistence whenever the model MBean is updated
4. `persistPolicy=NoMoreOftenThan` to throttle the update persistence so that it does not write out the information any more frequently than a certain interval

If policies `OnTimer` or `NoMoreOftenThan` are defined, then the interval must be defined in the `persistPeriod` descriptor field. If the value of `persistPolicy` is not `OnTimer` or `NoMoreOftenThan`, then the `persistPeriod` field is ignored. The following combinations are valid in any MBean descriptor or attribute descriptor:

```
"persistPolicy=Never"
```

```
"persistPolicy=OnTimer"
"persistPeriod=180"
```

```
"persistPolicy=OnUpdate"
```

```
"persistPolicy=NoMoreOftenThan"
"persistPeriod=10"
```

When persistence policy is defined in the MBean descriptor, the directory and file names (or database and key, depending on the implementation) for the MBean are required. In such cases the descriptor would contain the following:

```
"persistPolicy=OnTimer"
"persistPeriod=180"
"persistName=MBean_File_Name"
"persistLocation=MBean_Directory_Name"
```

The algorithm that the model MBean uses is predictable. Whenever a model MBean detects that an attribute has been updated, or when a checkpoint time has been reached, it will invoke its own `store()` method. The model MBean `store()` method must determine where the data should reside and store it there appropriately. If, for example, the model MBean were implemented as an `EJBObject` instance with container-managed persistence, the `store()` method might do nothing, instead relying on the EJB container to provide the persistence on transaction boundaries. If the model MBean is implemented as an `EJBObject` instance through bean-managed persistence, the `store()` method might be responsible for writing the data to the appropriate data store.

The model MBean's `load()` method is invoked when a model MBean is being constructed and is set to prime itself from the saved data. Later in this chapter there is an example of how to override the model MBean's `load()` and `store()` methods to use XML-formatted files.

The MBeanServer's persistence setting applies to all of its model MBeans unless a model MBean defines overriding policies.

4.6.5 Logging

The descriptors that are used for setting logging policy are `log` and `logFile`. Logging policy can be set in the model MBean's descriptor to define default policy for all notifications in the model MBean. The log descriptor field is a Boolean value set to `T` (`true`) or `F (false)`. If the field is set to `T`, then the `logFile` descriptor field must be set to a valid, fully qualified file name (including the drive if appropriate) in the system. If the file does not exist, then one is created. If log is set to `T` and `logFile` is not set, no logging will occur. The default logging policy, if log is not specified, is `F`, or no logging. The default logging policy can be overridden by the logging policy of any notification's descriptor. Different notifications can be directed to different log files:

```
"log=T",
"logFile=jmx.log"
```

These descriptor fields on the MBean or notification descriptors will log the notification to the `jmx.log` file. If the descriptor were

```
"log=F",
"logFile=jmx.log"
```

then the notification would not be logged to any file, even if one were defined. The `logFile` descriptor would be ignored.

4.6.6 Miscellaneous Descriptors

4.6.6.1 Presentation String

The `presentation` descriptor field was intended to hold XML fragments that describe how to display the model MBean, attribute, operation, or notification. This information is useful to a generic or third-party console only if this XML fragment is standardized to some degree. This standardization, or agreement on what the important elements were, was not done for the first release of the JMX specification. However, the `presentation` field can still be very useful for building specific management systems for applications. Some information that we thought would be in this string was a GIF or a BMP file name for a small or large icon. If it were a configuration field, it might contain information on whether a list box, radio dial, range, or text box should be used to set the value. Here is an example of a `presentation` string that associates a GIF file with an attribute:

```
"presentation=tooFast.gif"
```

4.6.6.2 Visibility

Because JMX was intended to support both third-party, enterprise class management systems and application-specific management systems, it quickly became obvious that the amount of information an enterprise manager wants to display could be much less in volume and much coarser grained than the information displayed and managed by an application-specific management system. Even within application-specific management systems, in order to support the goal for allowing console generation for applications, some rating was needed about the granularity of this information.

This rating was used to decide whether to put the attribute or operation information on the "first page" (i.e., the resource status or summary page), or on a detail page where the user had to click on something in order to access the page. The `visibility` descriptor was meant to help express this concept. It allows attributes, operations, and notifications to be ranked from 1 to 4. The value `1` is supposed to indicate the coarsest-grained, most often visible elements, and `4` is supposed to indicate the finest-grained, more advanced, least often visible elements. An enterprise manager may ask only for model MBeans with a `visibility` value of `1`. Or if displaying a resource summary page, the enterprise manager would display only attributes with a `visibility` value of `1`. If the resource were clicked on, another page would be displayed that contained all of the attributes and operations regardless of visibility. Of course, assigning `visibility` values is very subjective and should be done by someone who understands the resource and the management systems managing that resource.

4.6.6.3 Export

The `export` field is valid only in theMBean-level descriptor. It signifies to the MBeanServer and model MBean constructor that this model MBean should be advertised so that other MBeanServers or remote management systems can find it. This field was intended to allow a management system to locate an MBean without necessarily knowing which MBeanServer houses it beforehand. One common place that an MBean may be exported to is a directory accessible via JNDI. If the `export` field's value is set to `null`, then the MBean is not exported. If it is not null, then its value is used by the export support in the MBeanServer of the model MBean itself to perform the export. So, for example, if the MBean were to be registered via JNDI, the export descriptor's value would contain the JNDI directory URI (Uniform Resource Identifier) and the JNDI name to be used. If the MBean were to be simultaneously registered with several MBeanServers, the export value might be the MBeanServer's host name and domain name. Here is an example:

```
"export=jndiserver:8080:SpeedBean"
```

Not all MBeanServers support the export of model MBeans. In fact, the JMX reference implementation does not. If the MBeanServer and model MBean implementations do not support it, this field is simply ignored. The default value for export is null.

4.6.6.4 Protocol Map

JMX was intended to allow the translation of MBean data and data models into other management technologies and their data models. This translation cannot always be generated. Sometimes JMX management data must be mapped to a specific data model in a specific technology. For example, you might define a set of MBeans for your HTTP Web server. The IETF[14] has also defined a MIB for managing Web servers.[15]

If you know that you want your MBean attributes to be accessed by SNMP[16] managers through the HTTP MIB,[17] then you can define a protocol map in the attribute descriptor that will define the protocol and object to map to. You can define multiple mappings for your attribute in the protocol map. The same attribute can be mapped to an SNMP MIB and a CIM[18] object property.

The protocolMap descriptor contains a reference to a protocolMap object. The protocolMap object is actually a descriptor with name/value pairs. The name is the protocol name, and the value is the mapped object name for the protocol for this attribute.

So for an MBean attribute status with SNMP and CIM maps, you would have the following name/value pairs:

```
"SNMP=1.3.6.1.1.1.3.1.1.5.1" // maps to this SNMP OID
"CIM=cim_service.status"     // maps to the status attribute of
                             // the cim_service abstract class
```

Adapters will be the ones accessing and using the protocol map to translate the attributes into their own data model correctly. The adapters will have to recognize the protocol names as hints for their translation.

Attributes do not have to have specific protocol maps for all potential protocols that might make the attributes available through adapters. The adapter could generate a generic mapping for all attributes in all MBeans. The mapping would be realized and enforced by the adapter, not by the definition of a protocol map. For example, a MIB generator could be executed when new JMX MBeans were registered. This MIB generator would create a new SNMP MIB that would be loaded by the SNMP management system and used by the SNMP adapter. This is convenient because all the MBean's protocol map descriptors do not have to be updated whenever a new adapter to a new management protocol is registered with the MBeanServer.

4.7 XML Service: Priming ModelMBeanInfo from XML Files

Creating `ModelMBeanInfo` instances in your code using the available `ModelMBeanInfo` APIs is very tedious. Using the API also means that your management instrumentation code has to be updated every time you have a slight change in your attributes or operations that you want to make available. It makes some sense to provide `ModelMBeanInfo` customization data in a separate file that accompanies the managed application. This file could be formatted as a properties file; however, choosing an XML format allows more tooling support and portability. This file would be used to customize `ModelMBeanInfo` at runtime. Support for creating MBeans from XML files and writing MBeans to XML files is not part of the JMX specification or reference implementation. Using an XML file does illustrate a more convenient and robust means to customize your model MBeans. It is also a useful illustration of how to create and use MBean services. We will illustrate one technique for providing XML services support here.

In this case we have created a service MBean: `XMLService`. A *service MBean* is an MBean that is used by other MBeans as a utility and doesn't actually represent a managed resource. The `XMLService` MBean can create an XML file from a model MBean, or it can read an XML file and return a model MBean, or `ModelMBeanInfo` instance. It is possible to choose a number of different XML DTDs (document type definitions) to guide the file's format.

One choice is to use the DTD used by CIM.[19] Reasons to use the CIM DTD include the following: It is freely available; it is a generally accepted standard for management data representation; and it defines a mechanism to express management objects, attributes, and operations, as well as metadata (qualifiers) about them. One drawback to using the CIM DTD is that you will have to modify it to add support for expressing notifications. These features make the CIM DTD an easy fit for JMX MBean representation.

An alternative representation for the XML file is the DTD used by the Apache Jakarta Project's Commons Modeler version 1.0.[20] The modeler uses a special DTD (at http://jakarta.apache.org/commons/modeler/mbeans-descriptors.dtd) that is a relatively straightforward use of XML elements for each of the `MBeanInfo` information types. At the time of this writing, the implementation of the Modeler did not fully support descriptors in `ModelMBeanInfo` objects. We were able to add that support and an updated version of the modeler with the support is available as part of the downloadable examples for this book on the book's Web site: http://www.awprofessional.com/titles/0672324083. Full support of descriptors is required to run these examples. The full source for these examples and the `XMLService` MBean are available on the Addison-Wesley Web site for this book. The Modeler reads XML files and creates `ModelMBean` instances. It does not provide support for creating the XML files. In order to create the XML Service envisioned here, we created our own interface that supports creating `ModelMBean` instances from an XML file, creating `ModelMBeanInfo` instances from an XML file, variations with and without the managed object, and writing an XML file.

Here is the API for the `XMLService` MBean:

```
package jnjmx.ch4;
import javax.management.*;
import javax.management.modelmbean.*;

public interface XMLServiceMBean {
  Object createMBeanFromXMLFile(String fileName,
                                ObjectName mbName);
  MBeanInfo createMBeanInfoFromXMLFile(String fileName,
    String name);

  Object createMBeanFromXMLFile(String fileName, ObjectName mbName,
                                Object managedResource);
  MBeanInfo createMBeanInfoFromXMLFile(String fileName, String name,
                                Object managedResource);

  Object createMBeanFromXMLFile(String fileName, String mbName,
                                Object managedResource);
  void writeXMLFile( ModelMBean mb, String fileName);
}
```

First let's look at how to use XMLService to create a model MBean for the Apache model MBean:

```
/** Create a name for the MBean */
ObjectName apacheMBeanName = new ObjectName
  ("apacheManager: id=ApacheServer");

/** Instantiate the ApacheServer utility to be the
* managed resource */
serverURL = "http://www.apache.org/server-status?auto";
Apache myApacheServer = new Apache(serverURL);

/** Instantiate a model MBean from the XML file */
ModelMBean apacheMMBean = (ModelMBean)
  XMLPrimer.createMBeanFromXMLFile(
    "jnjmx.ch4/apachembeans.xml",  // name of XML file
    apacheMBeanName,               // name of MBean in XMl file
    myApacheServer);               // managed resource

/ ** Register the model MBean that is now ready
* to run with the MBeanServer */
  ObjectInstance registeredApacheMMBean =
        myMBS.registerMBean(apacheMMBean,
        apacheMBeanName);
//** Write the XML file
writeXMLFile( apacheMMBean, "jnjmx.ch4/apachembeans.xml");
```

You can see that first we create the XMLService MBean. Then we use XMLService's createMBeanFromXMLFile() method to read the file and instantiate a model MBean. We also use XMLService to write the MBean's ModelMBeanInfo to a file called apachembeans.xml. This would be important to do if some of the configuration of the model MBean had been changed—that is, caching or logging policy—that needed to be persisted for the next instantiation of this model MBean.

Now we are going to look at how to use the XML service as a service MBean. Here is how to instantiate an XMLService MBean:

```
/** Find an MBeanServer for our MBean */
MBeanServer myMBS = MBeanServerFactory.createMBeanServer();
// Create a JMX object name for the XML service
ObjectName sn = new ObjectName("todd:id=XMLPrimer");
// Instantiate the XML service
```

```
XMLPrimer = new XMLService();
ObjectInstance registeredXMLService =
  mbs.registerMBean(XMLPrimer, sn);
```

We created an instance of XMLService, created an object name for it, and registered it with the MBeanServer.

Here is how another adapter or JMX manager can use the same XMLService MBean to create a model MBean. In this case we have used a variation of the API that does not require the managed resource. The managed resource is associated with it later:

```
/** Find an MBeanServer for our MBean */
MBeanServer myMBS = MBeanServerFactory.createMBeanServer();

/** Instantiate the ApacheServer utility to be the managed
* resource */
serverURL = "http://www.apache.org/server-status?auto";
Apache myApacheServer = new Apache(serverURL);

/** Create the XML service's name */
XMLServiceName=("todd:id=XMLPrimer");
/** Instantiate an ModelMBean using the already registered
* XMLService */
ModelMBean apacheMMBean = (ModelMBean) mbs.invoke(
  xmlServiceName, "createMBeanFromXMLFile",
  new Object[] { "jnjmx.ch4/apachembeans.xml", // name of XML file
                 "id=ApacheServer"); // name of MBean in XMl file
  new String[] { "java.lang.String",
                 "java.lang.String"} );
/** Assign the managed resource to the MBean, since we didn't pass
* it in this time */
apacheMMBean.setManagedResource(myApacheServer,"ObjectReference");
/** Register the model MBean that is now ready to run with the
* MBeanServer */
ObjectInstance registeredApacheMMBean =
  myMBS.registerMBean(apacheMMBean,
                      apacheMBeanName);
```

The XML file containing the ModelMBeanInfo data using the Jakarta Modeler DTD is listed in full at the end of this chapter.

4.8 Using Model MBeans

Let's review what we know about model MBeans, and then we'll go over some examples and strategies for using them.

The MBeanServer functions as a factory for model MBeans. Therefore, model MBean instances should be created and maintained by the MBeanServer. Using the factory allows the `RequiredModelMBean` class implementation to vary depending on the needs of the environment in which the MBeanServer is installed. Your application that requests the instantiation of `RequiredModelMBean` does not have to be aware of the specifics of the `RequiredModelMBean` implementation. There are many potential implementation differences between JMX and JVM environments, including persistence, transactional behavior, caching, performance requirements, location transparency, remotability, and so on. `RequiredModelMBean` is responsible for implementing and managing these differences internally. Keep in mind that the MBeanServer that creates `RequiredModelMBean` may be specifically designed to support a particular `RequiredModelMBean` class. In fact, if you supply your own `RequiredModelMBean` implementation and try to use it, you may run into compatibility problems.

Because the JMX implementation provides the model MBean implementation, your application does not have to implement the model MBean, but just customize and use it. Your application's instrumentation code is consistent and minimal. You get the benefit of default policy and support for event logging, data persistence, data caching, and notification handling. In your application, you initialize your model MBean and pass in your identity, management interface, and any policy overrides. You can add custom attributes to the model MBean during execution; therefore information specific to the application can be modified without interruption during runtime. The model MBean then sets the behavior interface for the MBean and does any setup necessary for event logging and handling, data persistence and caching, and monitoring for your application's model MBean instance. The model MBean default behavior and simple APIs are intended to satisfy the management needs of most applications, but they also allow more complex application management scenarios.

You should have one instance of a model MBean for each instance of a resource (application, device, and so forth) to be managed in the system. These instances define the specific characteristics of operations, invocations, event trigger rules, event types, expiration rules, event logging, persistence, and so on for a given resource managed by the MBeanServer. Each instance of a model MBean may have completely different attributes, operations, and policies because they may manage completely unrelated resources.

In the following sections we will implement the time of day (todd) server example from Chapter 1 using model MBeans and showing various approaches for doing so. This would be useful if the todd server were already implemented and deployed such that going back into the implementation and adding instrumentation would be difficult and time-consuming.

We are going to look at two styles of model MBeans we can create: static and dynamic. Static model MBeans have their `ModelMBeanInfo` set during development through the `ModelMBeanInfo` and descriptor programming APIs. Dynamic MBeans create `ModelMBeanInfo` during execution from information that is available only while a system is running—that is, an XML file or interaction with another runtime system.

4.8.1 Creating Static Model MBeans

Static model MBeans have `ModelMBeanInfo` that is known and set during development. The developer knows what the attributes, operations, and policies will be and uses the `ModelMBeanInfo` APIs to set them. This type of model MBean can be instantiated with a `new` operation or a `create` on the MBeanServer.

Here is an example of a static model MBean approach in the todd server. Here is the todd server without an MBean being implemented as part of the todd application class. The main loop and `Server` constructor have been pulled out for discussion later:

```
package jnjmx.ch4;
// Create model MBeans for Server and Session from Server main
// Create ModelMBeanInfo from program APIs
import java.util.SortedSet;
import java.util.TreeSet;
import java.lang.reflect.Constructor;
import javax.management.*;
import javax.management.modelmbean.*;

public class Server {
  private MBeanServer mbs;

  private SessionPool sessions;
  private SortedSet connectionQueue;
  private Listener listener;
  private boolean active;

  static boolean tracing = false;
```

```
private long tzero;
private int connections;
// MAIN LOOP WILL GO HERE
// SERVER CONSTRUCTOR WILL GO HERE
public void activateSession(Connection k) {
  Session s;
  synchronized (sessions) {
    while ((s = sessions.reserve()) == null) {
      try {
        sessions.wait();
      } catch (InterruptedException x) {
        // see if a session is available
      }
    }
  }
  s.activate(k);
  connections++;
}

/**
 * Connections attribute getter
 * @returns total number of connections handled
 */
public Integer getConnections() {
  return new Integer(connections);
}

/**
 * Sessions attribute getter
 * @returns number of active sessions
 */
public Integer getSessions() {
  int as = sessions.getAvailableSessions().intValue();
  int sz = sessions.getSize().intValue();
  return new Integer(sz - as);
}

/**
 * Uptime attribute getter
 * @returns number of milliseconds since the server was started
 */
public Long getUptime() {
  return new Long(System.currentTimeMillis() - tzero);
}
```

```
public boolean isActive() {
  return active;
}

/**
 * Shut down the server, killing the process and any active
 * sessions
 */
public void shutdown() {
  System.exit(0);
}
/**
 * Start a listener thread that will queue incoming connections
 */
public void start() {
  listener = new Listener(connectionQueue);
  listener.start();
}

/**
 * Stop the server's listener thread; active sessions continue
 * to handle requests
 */
public void stop() {
  listener.stopListening();
}

public Connection waitForConnection() {
  Connection k;
  synchronized (connectionQueue) {
    while (connectionQueue.isEmpty()) {
      try {
        connectionQueue.wait();
      } catch (InterruptedException x) {
        // See if the queue is still empty
      }
    }
    k = (Connection) connectionQueue.first();
    connectionQueue.remove(k);
  }
  return k;
}
```

Here is the SessionPool class without an integrated MBean:

```
package jnjmx.ch4;
import java.util.HashSet;
import java.util.Set;
public class SessionPool  {
  private static final int POOLSIZE = 8;

  private Set sessions;
  private int size;

  public SessionPool() {
    this(POOLSIZE);
  }

  public SessionPool(int size) {
    this.size = size;
    sessions = new HashSet(this.size);
    fill();
  }

  public synchronized void grow(int increment) {
    for (int i = 0; i < increment; i++) {
      Session s = new Session(this);
      sessions.add(s);
    }
    size = size + increment;
  }

  public Integer getSize() {
    return new Integer(size);
  }

  public synchronized Integer getAvailableSessions() {
    return new Integer(sessions.size());
  }

  public synchronized void release(Session session) {
    sessions.add(session);
    notify();
  }

  public synchronized Session reserve() {
    while (sessions.isEmpty()) {
      try {
```

```
        wait();
      } catch (InterruptedException x) {
        // see if the set is still empty
      }
    }
    Session s = (Session) sessions.iterator().next();
    sessions.remove(s);
    return s;
  }

  private void fill() {
    for (int i = 0; i < size; i++) {
      Session s = new Session(this);
      sessions.add(s);
    }
  }
}
```

Here's the main program loop with a model MBean added for the todd and session pool management. Note that `ModelMBeanInfo` is defined in the program and set using the `ModelMBeanInfo` APIs. To make any adjustments would require recompiling the resource. In this example the main loop is responsible for instantiating the server and its model MBean. In the next code block we will see where the server's constructor is responsible for instantiating the session pool and its model MBean:

```
public static void main(String[] args) throws Exception {
  try {

  /* management stuff */
  /** Find an MBeanServer for our MBean */
  MBeanServer mbs = MBeanServerFactory.createMBeanServer();

  /** Instantiate the todd server */
  Server server = new Server(mbs);

  /** Create a name for the MBean */
  ObjectName son = new ObjectName("todd:id=Server");

  /** Create an unconfigured RequiredModelMBean instance in the
  * MBeanServer */
    RequiredModelMBean serverMMBean = (RequiredModelMBean)
```

```
      mbs.instantiate(
          "javax.management.modelmbean.RequiredModelMBean");

    /** Set the configuration of the ModelMBean through ModelMBeanInfo
     ** This method is below */
    ModelMBeanInfo serverMMBeanInfo =
        server.createServerModelMBeanInfo(server, son);
    serverMMBean.setModelMBeanInfo(serverMMBeanInfo);

    /** Set the todd server as the managed resource
    serverMMBean.setManagedResource(server,"ObjectReference");

    /** Register the model MBean that is now ready to run with the
    * MBeanServer */
    ObjectInstance registeredServerMMBean =
      mbs.registerMBean((Object) serverMMBean, son);

    mbs.invoke(son, "start", new Object[] {}, new String[] {});
    // executes method on MBean
    System.out.println("starting connection loop");

    while (server.isActive()) {
      Connection k = server.waitForConnection();
      server.activateSession(k);
      System.out.println("*");
    }

    } catch (Exception e) {
      System.out.println("todd Server failed with " +
          e.getMessage());
    }
  }
```

Here is the Server constructor that shows how the session pool and the session pool's model Bean are instantiated:

```
public Server(MBeanServer mbs) throws Exception {
  this.mbs = mbs;
  connectionQueue = new TreeSet();
  connections = 0;
  sessions = new SessionPool();              // create session pool
  ObjectName spon = new ObjectName("todd:id=SessionPool");
  // name of mbean
  // Instantiate the model MBean
```

```
  RequiredModelMBean sessionMMBean = (RequiredModelMBean)
    mbs.instantiate
    ("javax.management.modelmbean.RequiredModelMBean");
  // Set MBeanInfo
  ModelMBeanInfo sessionMMBInfo =
       createSessionModelMBeanInfo(sessions, spon);
  sessionMMBean.setModelMBeanInfo(sessionMMBInfo);
  // Set the managed resource
  sessionMMBean.setManagedResource(sessions, "ObjectReference");
  // Register the model MBean with the MBeanServer
  ObjectInstance registeredSessionMMBean =
       mbs.registerMBean((Object) sessionMMBean,spon);
  System.out.println("created Session ModelMBean");

  active = true;
  tzero = System.currentTimeMillis();
}
```

The `Server` model MBean has operations `start()`, `stop()`, and `shutdown()`. It has attributes `Connections`, `Sessions`, and `Uptime`. Here are the routines to set `ModelMBeanInfo`:

```
// Create the ModelMBeanInfo instance for the todd server
ModelMBeanInfo createServerModelMBeanInfo(Server managedServer,
    ObjectName serverMMBeanName) {
  Class serverClass = null;
  try {
    serverClass = Class.forName("jnjmx.ch4.Server");
  } catch(Exception e) {
    System.out.println("Server Class not found");
  }

  // Set the MBean descriptor
  Descriptor mmbDescription = new DescriptorSupport(new String[] {
      ("name="+serverMMBeanName),         // server MBean name
      "descriptorType=mbean",
      "displayName=toddServerManager",
      "log=T",                            // log all notifications
      "logFile=jmxserver.log",            // in jmxmain.log
      "currencyTimeLimit=10"});           // cache all attribute
                                          // values for 10 seconds

  // Define attributes in ModelMBeanAttributeInfo instances
  ModelMBeanAttributeInfo[] mmbAttributes =
    new ModelMBeanAttributeInfo[3];
```

```
// Declare Connections attribute
Descriptor connectionsDesc = new DescriptorSupport(
    new String[] {
    "name=Connections",              // attribute name
    "descriptorType=attribute",
    "displayName=todd connections",
    "getMethod=getConnections",      // call getTime operation
                                     // for gets
    "currencyTimeLimit=-1"} );       // don't cache time value

mmbAttributes[0] = new ModelMBeanAttributeInfo(
     "Connections",
     "java.lang.Integer",            // attribute type is String
     "todd Server connections",      // description of attribute
     true,
     false,
     false,
     connectionsDesc);               // descriptor for attribute

// Declare Sessions attribute
Descriptor sessionsDesc = new DescriptorSupport(
    new String[] {
    "name=Sessions",             // attribute name
    "descriptorType=attribute",
    "displayName=todd server sessions",
    "getMethod=getSessions",     // call operation for gets
    "currencyTimeLimit=5"} );    // cache value for 20 seconds

mmbAttributes[1] = new ModelMBeanAttributeInfo(
    "Sessions",
    "java.lang.Integer",        // type for sessions is integer
    "todd Server sessions",
    true,
    false,
    false,
    sessionsDesc);              // descriptor for sessions

// Declare Uptime attribute
Descriptor uptimeDesc = new DescriptorSupport(
    new String[] {
    "name=uptime",               // attribute name
    "descriptorType=attribute",
    "displayName=todd server sessions",
    "getMethod=getUptime",       // call operation for gets
    "currencyTimeLimit=0"} );    // don't cache uptime
```

```
mmbAttributes[2] = new ModelMBeanAttributeInfo("uptime",
    "java.lang.Integer",      // type for alarm is string
    "todd Server length of time up",
    true,
    false,
    false,
    uptimeDesc);         // descriptor for uptime

// Declare constructors for managed resource
ModelMBeanConstructorInfo[] mmbConstructors =
    new ModelMBeanConstructorInfo[1];
Constructor[] myConstructors = serverClass.getConstructors();

Descriptor mmBeanDesc = new DescriptorSupport( new String[] {
    "name=ServerClass",
    "descriptorType=operation",
           "role=constructor" } );

mmbConstructors[0] = new ModelMBeanConstructorInfo(
    "Server(): Constructs a todd Server",
    myConstructors[0],
    mmBeanDesc);

// Define operations in ModelMBeanOperationInfo instances
/* Operations: start, stop, shutdown
 * getUptime, getConnections, getSessions
 */

// Declare getValue operation String getValue()
// Set parameter array
ModelMBeanOperationInfo[] mmbOperations =
    new ModelMBeanOperationInfo[6];

// Declare start() operation void start()
// Set parameter array
MBeanParameterInfo[] parms = null;

Descriptor startDesc = new DescriptorSupport(new String[] {
    "name=start",                // operation/method name
    "descriptorType=operation",
    "class=server",              // class to run operation on
    "role=operation" } );        // this is an operation

mmbOperations[0] = new ModelMBeanOperationInfo("start",  // name
    "start server",               // description
    parms ,                       // parameters for method start
```

```
    "java.lang.boolean",          // return type start value
     MBeanOperationInfo.ACTION,   // start changes state
     startDesc);                  // descriptor for start
Descriptor stopDesc = new DescriptorSupport(new String[] {
    "name=stop",                  // operation/method name
    "descriptorType=operation",
    "class=server",               // class to run operation on
    "role=operation" } );         // this is an operation

mmbOperations[1] = new ModelMBeanOperationInfo("stop",   // name
    "stop server",                // description
    parms ,                       // parameters for method
    "java.lang.boolean",          // return type
    MBeanOperationInfo.ACTION,    // stop changes state
    stopDesc);                    // descriptor for stop

Descriptor shutdownDesc = new DescriptorSupport(new String[] {
    "name=shutdown",              // operation/method name
    "descriptorType=operation",
    "class=server",               // class to run operation on
    "role=operation" } );         // this is an operation

mmbOperations[2] = new ModelMBeanOperationInfo(
    "shutdown",                   // name
    "shutdown server",            // description
    parms ,                       // parameters for method
    "java.lang.boolean",          // return type
    MBeanOperationInfo.ACTION,    // changes state
    shutdownDesc);                // descriptor

// Declare getConnections operation String getConnections()
Descriptor getConnectionsDesc =
  new DescriptorSupport(new String[] {
    "name=getConnections",
    "descriptorType=operation",
    "class=Server",               // class to run operation on
    "role=getter"} );             // this is a getter operation

MBeanParameterInfo[] noParms = null;

mmbOperations[3] =
  new ModelMBeanOperationInfo("getConnections", // name
    "get Connections attribute",    // description
    noParms,                      // null parameter list,
    "java.lang.Integer",          // return type is Integer
```

```
    MBeanOperationInfo.INFO,   // does not change state
    getConnectionsDesc);       // descriptor for getConnections

// Declare getSessions operation - void getSession()
Descriptor getSessionsDesc = new DescriptorSupport(new String[] {
    "name=getSessions",             // name
    "descriptorType=operation",
    "class=Clock",                  // target class for method
    "role=getter"});                // operation is a setter

mmbOperations[4] = new ModelMBeanOperationInfo(
    "getSessions",                  // name
    "get Sessions attribute",       // description
    noParms,                        // parameters
    "java.lang.Integer",            // no return value
    MBeanOperationInfo.INFO,        // operation changes state
    getSessionsDesc);               // setSessions descriptor

// Declare getUptime operation
Descriptor getUptimeDesc = new DescriptorSupport( new String[] {
    "name=getUptime",               // name
    "descriptorType=operation",
    "class=Server",                 // target class
    "role=getter"});                // operation is a getter

mmbOperations[5] = new ModelMBeanOperationInfo(
    "getUptime",               // name
    "get uptime attribute",    // description
    noParms,                   // no parameters (null)
    "java.lang.Integer",       // return type is String
    MBeanOperationInfo.INFO,   // operation does not change state
    getUptimeDesc);            // uptime descriptor

// Define no notifications in ModelMBeanNotificationInfo
ModelMBeanNotificationInfo[] mmbNotifications =
    new ModelMBeanNotificationInfo[0];

  // Create ModelMBeanInfo
  ModelMBeanInfo mmBeanInfo = new ModelMBeanInfoSupport(
    "Server",
    "ModelMBeanInfo for managing a todd Server",
    mmbAttributes,
    mmbConstructors,
    mmbOperations,
    mmbNotifications);
try {
```

```
    mmBeanInfo.setMBeanDescriptor(mmbDescription);
  } catch (Exception e) {
    System.out.println("CreateServerMBeanInfo failed with " +
        e.getMessage());
  }
  return mmBeanInfo;
  }
```

The Session model MBean has operation grow() and attributes availableSessions and size:

```
ModelMBeanInfo createSessionModelMBeanInfo(SessionPool
        mmBResource, ObjectName mmbName) {
  // Create the ModelMBeanInfo instance for the session pool

  Class targetClass = null;
  try {
    targetClass = Class.forName("jnjmx.ch4.SessionPool");
  } catch(Exception e) {
    System.out.println("Server Class not found");
  }

  // Set the MBean descriptor
  Descriptor mmbDescription = new DescriptorSupport(new String[] {
      ("name="+mmbName),              // MBean name
      "descriptorType=mbean",
      ("displayName=Session Pool Manager"),
      "log=T",                        // log all notifications
      "logfile=jmxsession.log",       // in jmxmain.log
      "currencyTimeLimit=10"});       // cache all attribute values
                                      // for 10 seconds

  ModelMBeanAttributeInfo[] mmbAttributes =
      new ModelMBeanAttributeInfo[2];
  // Declare Connections attribute
  Descriptor sizeDesc = new DescriptorSupport(new String[] {
      "name=Size",            // attribute name
      "descriptorType=attribute",
      "displayName=todd size",
      "getMethod=getSize" } );

  mmbAttributes[0] = new ModelMBeanAttributeInfo("Size",
       "java.lang.Integer",      // attribute type is String
       "todd Server size",       // description of attribute
       true,
```

```
        false,
        false,
        sizeDesc);        // descriptor for attribute

// Declare availSessions attribute
Descriptor availSessionsDesc =
  new DescriptorSupport(new String[] {
    "name=AvailableSessions",         // attribute name
    "descriptorType=attribute",
    "displayName=todd server available sessions",
    "getMethod=getAvailableSessions", // call operation for gets
    "currencyTimeLimit=5"} );

mmbAttributes[1] = new ModelMBeanAttributeInfo("Sessions",
    "java.lang.Integer",      // type for sessions is integer
    "todd Server available sessions",
    true,
    false,
    false,
    availSessionsDesc);      // descriptor for sessions

// Declare constructors for MBean
Constructor[] constructors = targetClass.getConstructors();
ModelMBeanConstructorInfo[] mmbConstructors =
  new ModelMBeanConstructorInfo[1];
Descriptor mmBeanDesc = new DescriptorSupport( new String[] {
    "name=SessionClass",
    "descriptorType=operation",
    "role=constructor" } );

mmbConstructors[0] = new ModelMBeanConstructorInfo(
    "SessionPool(): Constructs a todd Server",
    constructors[0],
    mmBeanDesc);

ModelMBeanOperationInfo[] mmbOperations = new
    ModelMBeanOperationInfo[3];

// Declare grow() operation void grow()
// Set parameter array
MBeanParameterInfo[] noParms = null;

Descriptor growDesc = new DescriptorSupport(new String[] {
    "name=grow",                 // operation/method name
    "descriptorType=operation",
```

```
    "class=server",          // class to run operation on
    "role=operation" } );    // this is an operation


mmbOperations[0] = new ModelMBeanOperationInfo("grow", // name
    "grow session pool",       // description
    noParms ,
    "java.lang.boolean",
    MBeanOperationInfo.ACTION,  // changes state
    growDesc);                  // descriptor for enable


// Declare getSize operation - String getSize()
Descriptor getSizeDesc = new DescriptorSupport(new String[] {
    "name=getSize",
    "descriptorType=operation",
    "class=Sessions",       // class to run operation on
    "role=getter"} );       // this is a getter operation

mmbOperations[1] = new ModelMBeanOperationInfo(
    "getSize", // name
    "get Size attribute",      // description
    noParms,                   // null parameter list,
    "java.lang.Integer",       // return type is Integer
    MBeanOperationInfo.INFO,   // does not change state
    getSizeDesc);              // descriptor for getConnections

// Declare getAvailableSessions operation - void getSession()
Descriptor getAvailableSessionsDesc =
  new DescriptorSupport(new String[] {
    "name=getAvailableSessions",    // name
    "descriptorType=operation",
    "class=Sessions",               // target class for method
    "role=getter"});                // operation is a setter

mmbOperations[2] = new ModelMBeanOperationInfo(
    "getSessions",               // name
    "get Sessions attribute",    // description
    noParms,                     // parameters
    "java.lang.Integer",         // no return value
    MBeanOperationInfo.INFO,     // does not change state
    getAvailableSessionsDesc);   // setAvailableSessions
                                 // descriptor

ModelMBeanNotificationInfo[] mmbNotifications =
  new ModelMBeanNotificationInfo[0];
```

```
// Create ModelMBeanInfo
ModelMBeanInfo mmBeanInfo = new ModelMBeanInfoSupport("Session",
     "ModelMBeanInfo for managing todd Sessions",
     mmbAttributes,
     mmbConstructors,
     mmbOperations,
     mmbNotifications);
try {
   mmBeanInfo.setMBeanDescriptor(mmbDescription);
} catch (Exception e) {
   System.out.println("CreateServerMBeanInfo failed with " +
     e.getMessage());
}
return mmBeanInfo;
}
```

4.8.2 Creating Dynamic Model MBeans

Dynamic model MBeans have `ModelMBeanInfo` that is known and set during the runtime. Either introspection or external files are used to set this `ModelMBeanInfo`. The developer may use a service to create a `ModelMBeanInfo` instance. One thing to keep in mind is that `ModelMBeanInfo` for a newly instantiated model MBean includes all the methods on the model MBean. You will need to override this `ModelMBeanInfo` to remove methods you do not want adapters to have, like `setManagedResource()`.

The example that follows is of a dynamic model MBean approach using an XML to `MBeanInfo` service as described earlier. Basically the main loop from the previous example uses the XML service to populate `ModelMBeanInfo`. Now we can change the management interface by changing the XML file and and without having to recompile the source. This is a more flexible and dynamic model.

Here's the main program loop and `Server` constructor with a model MBean added for the todd and session pool management primed by the XML service:

```
private static XMLService XMLPrimer;
public static void main(String[] args) throws Exception {
  /* management stuff */
  /** Find an MBeanServer for our MBean */
  MBeanServer mbs = MBeanServerFactory.createMBeanServer();
  // Instantiate the XML service
  ObjectName sn = new ObjectName("todd:id=XMLPrimer");
  XMLPrimer = new XMLService(sn);
  String serverMBeanInfoFile = "ServerMBean.xml";
```

```
/** Instantiate the todd server */
Server server = new Server(mbs);

/** Create a name for the MBean */
ObjectName son = new ObjectName("todd:id=Server");

/** Set the configuration of the model MBean through the
   * XMLPrimer service, which sets ModelMBeanInfo from an
   * XML file
  ** */

RequiredModelMBean serverMMBean = (RequiredModelMBean)
  XMLPrimer.createMBeanFromXMLFile(serverMBeanInfoFile, son);
/** Create an unconfigured RequiredModelMBean instance in the
    MBeanServer */
/** Set the todd server as the managed resource
serverMMBean.setManagedResource(server,"ObjectReference");

/** Register the model MBean that is now ready to run with the
 * MBeanServer */
ObjectInstance registeredServerMMBean =
  mbs.registerMBean((Object) serverMMBean, son);

/* server stuff */
mbs.invoke(son, "start", new Object[] {}, new String[] {});

while (server.isActive()) {
  Connection k = server.waitForConnection();
  server.activateSession(k);
}

} catch (Exception e) {
  System.out.println("todd Server failed with " +
    e.getMessage());
}
}

public Server(MBeanServer mbs) throws Exception {
  this.mbs = mbs;

  connectionQueue = new TreeSet();
  connections = 0;

  sessions = new SessionPool();
  ObjectName spon = new ObjectName("todd:id=SessionPool");
```

```
  String sessionMBeanInfoFile = "SessionMBean.xml";
  RequiredModelMBean sessionMMBean = (RequiredModelMBean)
    XMLPrimer.createMBeanFromXMLFile(sessionMBeanInfoFile, spon);
    sessionMMBean.setManagedResource(sessions, "ObjectReference");
     ObjectInstance registeredSessionMMBean =
        mbs.registerMBean((Object) sessionMMBean,spon);

  active = true;
  tzero = System.currentTimeMillis();
}
```

4.8.2.1 Creating Model MBeans from the Managed Resource

Model MBeans may be instantiated, customized, and registered by the managed resources themselves. This will usually be done during initialization of the managed resource. The managed resource then updates the data in the model MBean whenever an update is necessary. In this case `manage-dResource` will be set to `this()` so that all the operations are delegated back to the object that is creating the model MBean. Here is an example of a self-managing service—the `Server` class that creates its own model MBean:

```
package jnjmx.ch4;
import java.util.SortedSet;
import java.util.TreeSet;
import java.lang.reflect.Constructor;
import javax.management.*;
import javax.management.modelmbean.*;

// Managed server creates model MBeans and ModelMBeanInfo using
// XML files
// In this example we show how to create the same model MBeans
// using an XML service to create ModelMBeanInfo

// Once again, the main loop of the Server (4) instantiates the
// server
// The server's constructor instantiates the session pool and the
// server's model MBean
// SessionPool's constructor instantiates SessionPool's model MBean


public class Server {
  private MBeanServer mbs;
```

```
private SessionPool sessions;
private SortedSet connectionQueue;
private Listener listener;
private boolean active;
static boolean tracing = false;
private long tzero;
private int connections;

private static XMLService XMLPrimer;
  public static void main(String[] args) throws Exception {
    /* server stuff */
  Server server = new Server();
  server.start();
  while (server.isActive()) {
    Connection k = server.waitForConnection();
    server.activateSession(k);
  }

  } catch (Exception e) {
    System.out.println("todd Server failed with " +
         e.getMessage());
  }
 }

public Server() throws Exception {
  /** Find an MBeanServer for our MBean */
  MBeanServer mbs = MBeanServerFactory.createMBeanServer();

  // Instantiate the XML service
  ObjectName sn = new ObjectName("todd:id=XMLPrimer");
  XMLPrimer = new XMLService(sn);
  ObjectInstance registeredXMLService =
       mbs.registerMBean((Object) XMLPrimer, sn);

  connectionQueue = new TreeSet();
  connections = 0;

  sessions = new SessionPool();

  active = true;
  tzero = System.currentTimeMillis();

  /** Create a name for the MBean */
  ObjectName son = new ObjectName("todd:id=Server");
```

```
/** Set the configuration of the model MBean through the
 * XMLPrimer service, which sets ModelMBeanInfo from an
 * XML file
** */

    String serverMBeanInfoFile = "jnjmx.ch4/ServerInfo.xml";
      ModelMBean serverMMBean = (ModelMBean)
      XMLPrimer.createMBeanFromXMLFile(
           serverMBeanInfoFile,
           "Server" , this);

    /** Register the model MBean that is now ready to run with
    * the MBeanServer */
    ObjectInstance registeredServerMMBean =
        mbs.registerMBean(serverMMBean, son);
  }

  // The rest of the methods are the same as in previous examples
  }
```

Here is the session class with an integrated model MBean:

```
package jnjmx.ch4;
import java.util.HashSet;
import java.util.Set;
import java.util.ArrayList;
import javax.management.*;
import javax.management.modelmbean.*;

public class SessionPool  {
  private static final int POOLSIZE = 8;
  private Set sessions;
  private int size;
  private MBeanServer mbs;

  public SessionPool() {
    this(POOLSIZE);
  }

  public SessionPool(int size) {
    this.size = size;
    sessions = new HashSet(this.size);
    fill();
    createSessionPoolMBean();
  }
```

```
private void createSessionPoolMBean() {
  try {
  // Change to use existing MBeanServer and existing XMLService
  // through the MBeanServer
  ArrayList mbsList = MBeanServerFactory.findMBeanServer(null);
  if ((!mbsList.isEmpty() && (mbsList.get(0) != null)))
    mbs = (MBeanServer) mbsList.get(0); // use first MBeanServer
  else {
    System.out.println("SessionPool can't find an MBeanServer");
    System.exit(0);
  }

  ObjectName xmlServiceName = new
      ObjectName("todd:id=XMLPrimer");
  XMLService XMLPrimer = new XMLService(xmlServiceName);

  ObjectName spon = new ObjectName("todd:id=SessionPool");
     String sessionXMLFile = "jnjmx.ch4/SessionInfo.xml";

     // using the XMLService MBean created by Server to load
     // ModelMBeanInfo
    ModelMBean sessionMMBean = (ModelMBean) mbs.invoke(
       xmlServiceName,
       "createMBeanFromXMLFile",
       new Object[] { sessionXMLFile,
             "SessionPool", (Object) this},
       new String[] {  "java.lang.String",
             "java.lang.String",
             "java.lang.Object"} );
     ObjectInstance registeredSessionMMBean =
       mbs.registerMBean((Object) sessionMMBean,spon);
   }
   catch (Exception e) {
    System.out.println("SessionPool MBean creation failed with "
      + e.getMessage());
   }
 }
// The rest of the methods are the same as in the previous example
// of SessionPool
}
```

4.8.2.2 Creating Model MBeans by an External Force: Assigning a Managed Resource

An application can create model MBeans to manage a completely separate resource. The program must have a reference to the managed resource for the model MBean that it can set in the `managedResource` attribute. The program is also responsible for inspecting the managed resource or another configuration file and creating the attributes, operations, and notifications. A program may instantiate model MBeans for lots of managed resources in the system. Usually this is done when a system is initialized or a management system is initialized. Another common scenario is that this program is a connector between an existing proprietary management system and a JMX-based management system. The Apache manager examples at the beginning of this chapter are excellent examples of a program creating model MBeans for external managed resources.

4.8.3 Adding Custom Descriptors

Applications using model MBeans and adapter MBeans can add their own descriptor fields to the model MBean descriptor. When would this be useful?

Applications using model MBeans could add their own management metadata that was unique to their own custom, specific management system, such as display information or roles. One interesting bit of metadata that we suggest all developers should consider adding to their attribute descriptors is an attribute classification, much like the operation role. Attributes should be classified as descriptive, configuration, capability, state, or metric. This classification of attributes is consistent with the one defined by the CIM Model.[21]

Taking the earlier `TotalAccesses` attribute as an example, we classify this attribute as a metric:

```
// Custom descriptor example
Descriptor totalAccessesCustomDesc = new DescriptorSupport();
totalAccessesCustomDesc.setField("name","TotalAccesses");
totalAccessesCustomDesc.setField("descriptorType","attribute");
totalAccessesCustomDesc.setField("displayName","NumberChanges");
totalAccessesCustomDesc.setField("getMethod","getTotalAccesses");
totalAccessesCustomDesc.setField("setMethod","setTotalAccesses");
totalAccessesCustomDesc.setField("classification","metric");
// custom descriptor
```

Adapter MBeans that translate model MBeans to represent resources into their own management systems may cache hints to help with this translation in the descriptor. For example, they may add the SNMP OID to the descriptor or the CIM name for the resource. Or they may add a business domain (e.g., for Accounting Department) or application domain (e.g., for WebSphere) to assist with context and scope.

4.8.4 Overriding the RequiredModelMBean Class

Because the `RequiredModelMBean` class is an implementation of the model MBean that is provided with every JMX implementation, it is reasonably safe to extend the `RequiredModelMBean` class and add or override behavior. For example, if you wanted to persist your `RequiredModelMBean` data to an XML file database rather than to a serialized object file, you would need to override the `load()` and `store()` methods of `RequiredModelMBean`. Here is an example of how you could do this:

```
package jnjmx.ch4;
import javax.management.*;
import javax.management.modelmbean.*;

public class XMLModelMBean extends RequiredModelMBean {


/**
   * Constructor for XMLModelMBean
   * @throws MBeanException
   * @throws RuntimeOperationsException
   */

  public XMLModelMBean() throws MBeanException,
    RuntimeOperationsException {
      super();
  }

  public XMLModelMBean(String filename, String mbeanName)
    throws MBeanException, RuntimeOperationsException {
    super();
    try {
      load(filename, mbeanName);
```

```
    } catch (Exception e) {
      // didn't find the file with primer data; that's OK
    }
  }


  /**
   * Constructor for XMLModelMBean
   * @param arg0
   * @throws MBeanException
   * @throws RuntimeOperationsException
   */

  public XMLModelMBean(ModelMBeanInfo arg0)
    throws MBeanException, RuntimeOperationsException {
    super(arg0);
    try {
      load();
    } catch (Exception e) {
      // didn't find the file with primer data; that's OK
    }
  }

  /**
   * @see javax.management.DynamicMBean#getAttribute(String)
   */

  public Object getAttribute(String arg0)
    throws AttributeNotFoundException, MBeanException,
      ReflectionException {
        return super.getAttribute(arg0);
  }


  /**
   * @see javax.management.DynamicMBean#getAttributes(String[])
   */


  public AttributeList getAttributes(String[] arg0) {
    return super.getAttributes(arg0);
  }
```

```
/**
 * @see javax.management.DynamicMBean#invoke(String, Object[],
 * String[])
 */

public Object invoke(String arg0, Object[] arg1, String[] arg2)
  throws MBeanException, ReflectionException {
  return super.invoke(arg0, arg1, arg2);
}

/**
 * @see javax.management.DynamicMBean#setAttributes(AttributeList)
 */
public AttributeList setAttributes(AttributeList arg0) {
  return super.setAttributes(arg0);
}

/**
 * This version of load() expects a file name and an MBean name
 * in the file in the format required by the Jakarta Modeler
 */

public void load(String filename, String name)
  throws MBeanException, RuntimeOperationsException,
  InstanceNotFoundException
{
  try
  { // Look for file of that name
    XMLService XMLPrimer = new XMLService();
    ModelMBeanInfo newInfo = (ModelMBeanInfo)
      XMLPrimer.createMBeanInfoFromXMLFile(filename, name);
    setModelMBeanInfo(newInfo);
  } catch (Exception e)
  {
    System.out.println(
      "load(): Persistent MBean XML file was not found");
  }
}

public void load()
throws MBeanException, RuntimeOperationsException,
   InstanceNotFoundException
{
  Descriptor mmbDesc = ((ModelMBeanInfo)
    getMBeanInfo()).getMBeanDescriptor();
```

```
    // We will use persistLocation to be the directory for the
    // XML file
    // We will use persistName to be the file to save the XML data
    // for the MBean to
    String persistDir = (String)
      mmbDesc.getFieldValue("persistLocation");
    String persistFile = (String)
      mmbDesc.getFieldValue("persistName");

    String currName = (String) mmbDesc.getFieldValue("name");

    if ((persistDir == null) || (persistFile == null))
    {  // Persistence not supported for this MBean; return
       // without error
      return;
    }

    String loadTarget = persistDir.concat("/" + persistFile);
    load(loadTarget, currName);
  }

public void store()
  throws MBeanException, RuntimeOperationsException,
     InstanceNotFoundException
  {

    /* Store in a file with name = MBean name in directory */
    /* For this example, we always persist the MBean; in a real
    * override of this method, you need to honor the persistence
    * policy descriptors:  */

    /* persist policy:
       persist if persistPolicy != never ||
       persistPolicy == always ||
       persistPolicy == onTimer && now > lastPersistTime +
         persistPeriod ||
      persistPolicy == NoMoreOftenThan && now > lastPersistTime +
         persistPeriod
       don't persist if persistPolicy == never ||
       persistPolicy == onUpdate ||
       persistPolicy = onTimer && now < lastPersistTime +
         persistPeriod
    */
```

```
    /* You should also remember to */
    /* set the lastPersistTime on attribute */

    /* Check to see if should be persisted */

    boolean MBeanPersistItNow = true; // always persist
    if (getMBeanInfo() == null)
    {
      throw new RuntimeOperationsException(new
        IllegalArgumentException("ModelMBeanInfo must not be " +
            "null"),
        ("Exception occured trying to set the store data for " +
         "the RequiredModelMBean"));
    }
    Descriptor mmbDesc = ((ModelMBeanInfo)
      getMBeanInfo()).getMBeanDescriptor();

    if (MBeanPersistItNow == true)
    {
      try
      {
        // Get directory
        String persistDir = (String)
          mmbDesc.getFieldValue("persistLocation");
        String persistFile = (String)
          mmbDesc.getFieldValue("persistName");
        String persistTarget = persistDir.concat("/" +
          persistFile);
       // Call another method in this app to write MBeanInfo as a
        // database record
        XMLService XMLPrimer = new XMLService();
        XMLPrimer.writeXMLFile(this, persistTarget);
      } catch (Exception e)
      {
        System.out.println("store(): Exception storing MBean " +
            "into file for RequiredModelMBean " +
            e.getClass() + ":" + e.getMessage());
        e.printStackTrace();
      }
    }
}
}
```

If you can put the XMLModelMBean class in the class path of the MBeanServer, then when you instantiate or create the new model MBean, it will look like this (snipped from the earlier integrated model MBean example):

```
...
  public XMLServer(MBeanServer mbs) throws Exception {
    this.mbs = mbs;

    connectionQueue = new TreeSet();
    connections = 0;

    sessions = new SessionPool();
    ObjectName spon = new ObjectName("todd:id=SessionPool");

    XMLModelMBean sessionMMBean = (XMLModelMBean)
      mbs.instantiate("jnjmx.ch4.XMLModelMBean",
      new Object [] {"jnjmx.ch4/SessionInfo.xml", "SessionPool"},
      new String[] {"java.lang.String", "java.lang.String"});
      sessionMMBean.store();
    sessionMMBean.setManagedResource(sessions, "ObjectReference");
    ObjectInstance registeredSessionMMBean =
    mbs.registerMBean((Object) sessionMMBean,spon);

    active = true;
    tzero = System.currentTimeMillis();
  }
...
```

Or you can use the create operation:

```
public XMLServer(MBeanServer mbs) throws Exception {
  this.mbs = mbs;

  connectionQueue = new TreeSet();
  connections = 0;

  sessions = new SessionPool();
  ObjectName spon = new ObjectName("todd:id=SessionPool");

  XMLModelMBean sessionMMBean = (XMLModelMBean)
    mbs.createMBean("jnjmx.ch4.XMLModelMBean",
```

```
        new Object [] {"jnjmx.ch4/SessionInfo.xml",
"SessionPool"},
        new String[] {"java.lang.String", "java.lang.String"});
  sessionMMBean.setManagedResource(sessions, "ObjectReference");
  ObjectInstance registeredSessionMMBean =
     mbs.registerMBean((Object) sessionMMBean,spon);

  active = true;
  tzero = System.currentTimeMillis();
}
```

If you can't update the class path of the MBeanServer, you will have to instantiate `XMLModelMBean` with a `new` operation in the scope of your application and then register it with the MBeanServer like this:

```
XMLModelMBean myMMB = new XMLModelMBean();
mbs.register(myMMB);
```

4.9 Common Mistakes with Model MBeans

1. **Trying to set descriptors used by the model MBean code.** The model MBean implementation uses some of the descriptor values to manage the logic of value caching. You should never manually set the following descriptor fields:
   - **Attribute descriptor:** `lastUpdatedTimeStamp`
   - **Operation descriptor:** `lastReturnedValue`, `lastUpdatedTimeStamp`

   Note that the `value` field of the attribute descriptor is where the cached value of the attribute is maintained by the model MBean. If you set the `value` field and the `getMethod` field, then the value in the `value` field will be replaced according to the caching policy. You must turn caching off entirely to retain the value you place there. It is perfectly valid to put an initial value there, but it might be more appropriate to put that value in the `defaultValue` field.
2. **Getting the attribute type wrong.** The attribute type fields must contain the *fully* qualified class name, not the relative class name.
3. **Class loader problems.** Remember that if you are using the `instantiate()` or `create()` method to create the model MBean, then the class loader of the MBeanServer is being used.

4.10 Caveats

4.10.1 Transactionality

If a model MBean implementation is executing in an environment where management operations are transactional, then the model MBean should shield the application from this knowledge. If the application must be aware of the transaction, the application will depend on a certain version of the JMX agent and model MBean to be accessible. The application's investment in the JMX instrumentation is no longer portable and protected.

4.10.2 Remoteness

If the JMX agent is remotable, then the application and/or adapters may be accessing model MBeans that are not co-residing in the same JVM. The model MBean and JMX agent must be implemented so that the applications and adapters are not aware that the model MBean is local or remote. In other words, the model MBean must support location transparency. The JMX agent does not have to provide for remotabilty for *both* the applications and the adapters; it may be remotable to just one of these.

4.11 Summary

In this chapter we have thoroughly examined the model MBean specification and examples to illustrate the use of the `RequiredModelMBean` class. You should now understand the role that descriptors play in model MBeans, their impact on model MBean behavior, and how to customize and augment them. We have also provided you with some common patterns for using model MBeans: loading from XML files, static model MBeans, and dynamic model MBeans. We also reviewed choices in the model MBean lifecycle: being created by the managed resource or by an outside program. More patterns and usage tips are provided in Chapter 9 (Designing with JMX).

Now that we understand every variation of management beans—the components that represent all of our management data—the next chapter will explain the container for these MBeans, the MBeanServer. The MBeanServer functions as a management agent role in your management architecture. Then we will turn our attention to security and how to use JMX to do the actual distributed management: monitoring and notification.

4.12 XML File Example

```
File: apachembeans.xml

<?xml version="1.0"?>
<!DOCTYPE mbeans-descriptors PUBLIC
     "-//Apache Software Foundation//DTD Model MBeans Configuration File"
     "http://jakarta.apache.org/commons/dtds/mbeans-descriptors.dtd">
<mbeans-descriptors>
<mbean
     name="ApacheServer"
     description="ModelMBean for managing an Apache Web Server"
     type="jnjmx.ch4.ApacheServer"
     >
<attribute
     name="BusyWorkers"
     description="Apache Server Busy Workers"
     type="int"
     readable="true"
     writeable="false"
     is="false"
     getMethod="getBusyWorkers"
     displayName="Apache BusyWorkers"
     >
     <descriptor>
         <field name="displayName" value="Apache BusyWorkers"/>
         <field name="currencyTimeLimit" value="3"/>
         <field name="name" value="BusyWorkers"/>
         <field name="getMethod" value="getBusyWorkers"/>
         <field name="descriptorType" value="attribute"/>
     </descriptor>
</attribute>
<attribute
     name="BytesPerSec"
     description="Apache Server Bytes Per Sec"
     type="int"
     readable="true"
     writeable="false"
     is="false"
     getMethod="getBytesPerSec"
     displayName="Apache BytesPerSec"
     >
     <descriptor>
         <field name="displayName" value="Apache BytesPerSec"/>
         <field name="currencyTimeLimit" value="10"/>
```

```
            <field name="name" value="BytesPerSec"/>
            <field name="getMethod" value="getBytesPerSec"/>
            <field name="descriptorType" value="attribute"/>
        </descriptor>
</attribute>
<attribute
        name="BytesPerReq"
        description="Apache Server Bytes Per Request"
        type="int"
        readable="true"
        writeable="false"
        is="false"
        getMethod="getBytesPerReq"
        displayName="Apache BytesPerReq"
        >
        <descriptor>
            <field name="displayName" value="Apache BytesPerReq"/>
            <field name="currencyTimeLimit" value="10"/>
            <field name="name" value="BytesPerReq"/>
            <field name="getMethod" value="getBytesPerReq"/>
            <field name="descriptorType" value="attribute"/>
        </descriptor>
</attribute>
<attribute
        name="IdleWorkers"
        description="Apache Server Idle Workers"
        type="int"
        readable="true"
        writeable="false"
        is="false"
        getMethod="getIdleWorkers"
        displayName="Apache IdleWorkers"
        >
        <descriptor>
            <field name="displayName" value="Apache IdleWorkers"/>
            <field name="currencyTimeLimit" value="10"/>
            <field name="name" value="IdleWorkers"/>
            <field name="getMethod" value="getIdleWorkers"/>
            <field name="descriptorType" value="attribute"/>
        </descriptor>
</attribute>
<attribute
        name="ReqPerSec"
        description="Apache Server Requests Per Second"
        type="float"
```

```
    readable="true"
    writeable="false"
    is="false"
    getMethod="getReqPerSec"
    displayName="Apache ReqPerSec"
    >
    <descriptor>
        <field name="displayName" value="Apache ReqPerSec"/>
        <field name="currencyTimeLimit" value="5"/>
        <field name="name" value="ReqPerSec"/>
        <field name="getMethod" value="getReqPerSec"/>
        <field name="descriptorType" value="attribute"/>
    </descriptor>
</attribute>
<attribute
    name="Scoreboard"
    description="Apache Server Scoreboard"
    type="java.lang.String"
    readable="true"
    writeable="false"
    is="false"
    getMethod="getScoreboard"
    displayName="Apache Scoreboard"
    >
    <descriptor>
        <field name="displayName" value="Apache Scoreboard"/>
        <field name="currencyTimeLimit" value="10"/>
        <field name="name" value="Scoreboard"/>
        <field name="getMethod" value="getScoreboard"/>
        <field name="descriptorType" value="attribute"/>
    </descriptor>
</attribute>
<attribute
    name="TotalAccesses"
    description="Apache Server total accesses"
    type="int"
    readable="true"
    writeable="false"
    is="false"
    getMethod="getTotalAccesses"
    displayName="Apache TotalAccesses"
    >
    <descriptor>
        <field name="displayName" value="Apache TotalAccesses"/>
        <field name="currencyTimeLimit" value="-1"/>
```

```
            <field name="name" value="TotalAccesses"/>
            <field name="getMethod" value="getTotalAccesses"/>
            <field name="descriptorType" value="attribute"/>
        </descriptor>
</attribute>
<attribute
        name="TotalKBytes"
        description="Apache Server total KiloBytes"
        type="long"
        readable="true"
        writeable="false"
        is="false"
        getMethod="getTotalKBytes"
        displayName="Apache TotalKBytes"
        >
        <descriptor>
            <field name="displayName" value="Apache TotalKBytes"/>
            <field name="currencyTimeLimit" value="-1"/>
            <field name="name" value="TotalKBytes"/>
            <field name="getMethod" value="getTotalKBytes"/>
            <field name="descriptorType" value="attribute"/>
        </descriptor>
</attribute>
<attribute
        name="Uptime"
        description="Apache Server Up Time"
        type="long"
        readable="true"
        writeable="false"
        is="false"
        getMethod="getUptime"
        displayName="Apache Uptime"
        >
        <descriptor>
            <field name="displayName" value="Apache Uptime"/>
            <field name="currencyTimeLimit" value="10"/>
            <field name="name" value="Uptime"/>
            <field name="getMethod" value="getUptime"/>
            <field name="descriptorType" value="attribute"/>
        </descriptor>
</attribute>
<attribute
        name="CpuLoad"
        description="Apache Server CPU Load"
        type="float"
```

```
    readable="true"
    writeable="false"
    is="false"
    getMethod="getCpuLoad"
    displayName="Apache Uptime"
    >
    <descriptor>
        <field name="displayName" value="Apache Uptime"/>
        <field name="currencyTimeLimit" value="10"/>
        <field name="name" value="CpuLoad"/>
        <field name="getMethod" value="getCpuLoad"/>
        <field name="descriptorType" value="attribute"/>
    </descriptor>
</attribute>
<attribute
    name="State"
    description="Apache Server state"
    type="java.lang.String"
    readable="true"
    writeable="false"
    is="false"
    getMethod="getState"
    displayName="Apache State"
    >
    <descriptor>
        <field name="displayName" value="Apache State"/>
        <field name="currencyTimeLimit" value="10"/>
        <field name="name" value="State"/>
        <field name="getMethod" value="getState"/>
        <field name="descriptorType" value="attribute"/>
    </descriptor>
</attribute>
<attribute
    name="Server"
    description="Apache Server Busy Workers"
    type="java.lang.String"
    readable="true"
    writeable="true"
    is="false"
    getMethod="getServer"
    setMethod="setServer"
    displayName="Apache Server URL"
    >
    <descriptor>
        <field name="setMethod" value="setServer"/>
```

```
        <field name="displayName" value="Apache Server URL"/>
        <field name="currencyTimeLimit" value="10"/>
        <field name="name" value="Server"/>
        <field name="getMethod" value="getServer"/>
        <field name="descriptorType" value="attribute"/>
    </descriptor>
</attribute>
<constructor
    name="jnjmx.ch4.ApacheServer"
    >
    <parameter name="apacheURL"
        description="URL of Apache Server to Manage"
        type="java.lang.String"/>
    <descriptor>
        <field name="name" value="jnjmx.ch4.ApacheServer"/>
        <field name="descriptorType" value="operation"/>
        <field name="role" value="constructor"/>
    </descriptor>
</constructor>

<notification
    name="jmx.ModelMBean.General"
    description="Apache Server Down"
    >
    <notification-type>
    jmx.ModelMBean.General.Apache.Down
    </notification-type>
    <descriptor>
        <field name="name" value="jmx.ModelMBean.General"/>
        <field name="severity" value="6"/>
        <field name="descriptorType" value="notification"/>
    </descriptor>
</notification>

<operation
    name="getValue"
    description="getValue(): get an apache status field"
    returnType="java.lang.String"
    impact="2"
    >
    <parameter name="FieldName"
        description="Apache status field name"
        type="java.lang.String"/>
    <descriptor>
        <field name="name" value="getValue"/>
```

```
            <field name="class" value="ApacheServer"/>
            <field name="descriptorType" value="operation"/>
            <field name="role" value="operation"/>
        </descriptor>
</operation>
<operation
        name="getState"
        description="getState(): current status of apache server"
        returnType="java.lang.String"
        impact="2"
        >
        <descriptor>
            <field name="name" value="getState"/>
            <field name="class" value="ApacheServer"/>
            <field name="descriptorType" value="operation"/>
            <field name="role" value="operation"/>
        </descriptor>
</operation>
<operation
        name="getServer"
        description="getServer(): URL of apache server"
        returnType="java.lang.Integer"
        impact="2"
        >
        <descriptor>
            <field name="name" value="getServer"/>
            <field name="class" value="ApacheServer"/>
            <field name="descriptorType" value="operation"/>
            <field name="role" value="operation"/>
        </descriptor>
</operation>
<operation
        name="setServer"
        description="getServer(): URL of apache server"
        returnType="java.lang.String"
        impact="1"
        >
        <parameter name="url" description="Apache Server URL"
            type="java.lang.String"/>
        <descriptor>
            <field name="name" value="setServer"/>
            <field name="descriptorType" value="operation"/>
            <field name="class" value="ApacheServer"/>
            <field name="role" value="operation"/>
        </descriptor>
</operation>
```

```
<operation
     name="start"
     description="start(): start apache server"
     returnType="java.lang.Integer"
     impact="1"
     >
     <descriptor>
         <field name="name" value="start"/>
         <field name="class" value="ApacheServer"/>
         <field name="descriptorType" value="operation"/>
         <field name="role" value="operation"/>
     </descriptor>
</operation>
<operation
     name="stop"
     description="stop(): start apache server"
     returnType="java.lang.Integer"
     impact="1"
     >
     <descriptor>
         <field name="name" value="stop"/>
         <field name="class" value="ApacheServer"/>
         <field name="descriptorType" value="operation"/>
         <field name="role" value="operation"/>
     </descriptor>
</operation>
<operation
     name="getBusyWorkers"
     description="number of busy threads"
     returnType="int"
     impact="2"
     >
     <descriptor>
         <field name="name" value="getBusyWorkers"/>
         <field name="class" value="ApacheServer"/>
         <field name="descriptorType" value="operation"/>
         <field name="role" value="operation"/>
     </descriptor>
</operation>
<operation
     name="getBytesPerSec"
     description="number of bytes per second processed"
     returnType="int"
     impact="2"
     >
     <descriptor>
```

```
            <field name="name" value="getBytesPerSec"/>
            <field name="class" value="ApacheServer"/>
            <field name="descriptorType" value="operation"/>
            <field name="role" value="operation"/>
        </descriptor>
</operation>
<operation
        name="getBytesPerReq"
        description="number of bytes per request processed"
        returnType="int"
        impact="2"
        >
        <descriptor>
            <field name="name" value="getBytesPerReq"/>
            <field name="class" value="ApacheServer"/>
            <field name="descriptorType" value="operation"/>
            <field name="role" value="operation"/>
        </descriptor>
</operation>
<operation
        name="getCpuLoad"
        description="current load of cpu"
        returnType="float"
        impact="2"
        >
        <descriptor>
            <field name="name" value="getCpuLoad"/>
            <field name="class" value="ApacheServer"/>
            <field name="descriptorType" value="operation"/>
            <field name="role" value="operation"/>
        </descriptor>
</operation>
<operation
        name="getIdleWorkers"
        description="number of idle threads"
        returnType="int"
        impact="2"
        >
        <descriptor>
            <field name="name" value="getIdleWorkers"/>
            <field name="class" value="ApacheServer"/>
            <field name="descriptorType" value="operation"/>
            <field name="role" value="operation"/>
        </descriptor>
</operation>
<operation
```

```
    name="getReqPerSec"
    description="number of bytes per second processed"
    returnType="int"
    impact="2"
    >
    <descriptor>
        <field name="name" value="getReqPerSec"/>
        <field name="descriptorType" value="operation"/>
         <field name="class" value="ApacheServer"/>
        <field name="role" value="operation"/>
    </descriptor>
</operation>
<operation
    name="getScoreboard"
    description="gets apache scoreboard "
    returnType="java.lang.String"
    impact="2"
    >
    <descriptor>
        <field name="name" value="getScoreboard"/>
        <field name="class" value="ApacheServer"/>
        <field name="descriptorType" value="operation"/>
        <field name="role" value="operation"/>
    </descriptor>
</operation>
<operation
    name="getTotalAccesses"
    description="number of bytes per second processed"
    returnType="int"
    impact="2"
    >
    <descriptor>
        <field name="name" value="getTotalAccesses"/>
        <field name="class" value="ApacheServer"/>
        <field name="descriptorType" value="operation"/>
        <field name="role" value="operation"/>
    </descriptor>
</operation>
<operation
    name="getTotalKBytes"
    description="number of Kilo bytes processed"
    returnType="long"
    impact="2"
    >
```

```
    <descriptor>
        <field name="name" value="getTotalKBytes"/>
        <field name="class" value="ApacheServer"/>
        <field name="descriptorType" value="operation"/>
        <field name="role" value="operation"/>
    </descriptor>
</operation>
<operation
    name="getUptime"
    description="number of bytes per second processed"
    returnType="long"
    impact="2"
    >
    <descriptor>
        <field name="name" value="getUptime"/>
        <field name="class" value="ApacheServer"/>
        <field name="descriptorType" value="operation"/>
        <field name="role" value="operation"/>
    </descriptor>
</operation>
<operation
    name="getCpuLoad"
    description="number CPU Load"
    returnType="float"
    impact="2"
    >
    <descriptor>
        <field name="name" value="getCpuLoad"/>
        <field name="class" value="ApacheServer"/>
        <field name="descriptorType" value="operation"/>
        <field name="role" value="operation"/>
    </descriptor>
</operation>
<descriptor>
  <field name="descriptorType" value="mbean"/>
  <field name="logfile" value="jmxmain.log"/>
  <field name="name" value="ApacheServer"/>
  <field name="visibility" value="1"/>
  <field name="log" value="true"/>
  <field name="currencyTimeLimit" value="10"/>
  <field name="type" value="jnjmx.ch4.Apacheerver"/>
  <field name="export" value="false"/>
  <field name="displayName" value="ApacheServerManager"/>
  <field name="persistPolicy" value="Never"/>
</descriptor>
```

4.13 Notes

1. "Java Management Extensions (JMX) Specification," JSR 3, http://www.jcp.org/jsr/detail/3.jsp, which was led by Sun Microsystems to create a management API for Java resources.

2. XML stands for eXtensible Markup Language. XML standards are developed by the Internet Engineering Task Force (IETF, at http://www.ietf.org) and the World Wide Web Consortium (W3C, at http://www.w3.org).

3. J2SE stands for Java 2 Platform, Standard Edition, which is Sun Microsystems' Java platform. More information is available at http://java.sun.com/j2se. Java and all Java-based marks are trademarks of Sun Microsystems, Inc., in the United States and other countries.

4. J2EE stands for Java 2 Platform, Enterprise Edition, which is Sun Microsystems' Java platform. J2EE application servers are vendor products that support the J2EE specification. More information is available at http://java.sun.com/j2ee. Java and all Java-based marks are trademarks of Sun Microsystems, Inc., in the United States and other countries.

5. J2ME stands for Java 2 Platform, Micro Edition, from Sun Microsystems. More information is available at http://java.sun.com/j2me. Java and all Java-based marks are trademarks of Sun Microsystems, Inc., in the United States and other countries.

6. JDBC (Java Database Connectivity) is an API that isolates database clients from database vendors. It is a Sun Microsystems technology.

7. EJB stands for Enterprise JavaBeans, which is a component model core to the J2EE specification. More information is available at http://java.sun.com/j2ee.

8. LDAP stands for Lightweight Directory Access Protocol, a protocol designed to provide access to the X.500 directory while not incurring the resource requirements of the Directory Access Protocol (DAP). More information is available in RFC 1777 (http://www.ietf.org/rfc/rfc1777.txt).

9. DB2 stands for Database 2, a relational database management system designed by IBM for large computers. More information is available http://www-3.ibm.com/software/data/db2.

10. NFS stands for Network File System, which allows a remote user to read and update a computer file system (see http://searchwin2000.techtarget.com/sDefinition/0,,sid1_gci214121,00.html). NFS version 4 is currently under development by the IETF (see http://www.ietf.org/html.charters/nfsv4-charter.html).

11. IDL stands for Interface Definition Language, which defined a language agnostic mechanism to define the interface of a CORBA component. More information is available at http://www.omg.org.

12. MOF stands for Managed Object Format. This format is used to describe CIM information and is defined by the DMTF (Distributed Management Task Force) in the CIM specification. More information is available at http://www.dmtf.org/standards/cim_schema_v23.php.

13. JMX Instrumentation and Agent Specification 1.1, a maintenance release of the JMX specification, reference implementation, and TCK by Sun Microsystems. See note 1.

14. IETF stands for Internet Engineering Task Force (http://www.ietf.org).

15. IETF Web Server MIB, an SNMP MIB defined to help manage and represent Web servers (HTTP servers). More information is available in IETF RFC 2594 (http://www.ietf.org/rfc/rfc2594.txt).

16. SNMP stands for Simple Network Management Protocol, which is an IETF standard. More information on SNMP is available at http://www.ietf.org.

17. HTTP MIB, an SNMP MIB defined to help manage and represent Web servers (HTTP servers). More information is available in IETF RFC 2594 (http://www.ietf.org/rfc/rfc2594.txt).

18. CIM object property, a property or attribute of a CIM class or object, as defined by the DTMF CIM model specification (http://www.dmtf.org/standards/cim_schema_v23.php).

19. The CIM DTD is part of the CIM/WBEM standard (Common Information Model/Web-Based Enterprise Management). It is defined by the DMTF. More information is available at http://www.dmtf.org/download/spec/xmls/CIM_XML_Mapping20.php.

20. Common Information Model Schema version 2.6 available from http://www.dmtf.org.

21. Jakarta Commons Modeler is an open-source tool to instantiate JMX model MBeans from XML files. More information is available at http://jakarta.apache.org/commons/modeler.html.

CHAPTER 5

The MBeanServer

This chapter describes the MBeanServer, the heart of the JMX agent layer. The MBeanServer's primary responsibility is to provide a *registry*, with a common naming model, for the MBeans that management applications used to monitor and control JMX manageable resources. It also provides a symmetric interface to management resources: Management applications interact with MBeans, and MBeans interact with other MBeans, getting and setting MBean attributes and invoking MBean operations via the MBeanServer.

Because MBean access is mediated by the MBeanServer, a resource's *management lifecycle* revolves around the MBeanServer; the resource becomes manageable when the MBean that represents it is registered with the MBeanServer, the resource remains manageable while it is registered with the MBeanServer, and the resource finally ceases to be manageable when it is unregistered. The MBeanServer also provides the *notification bus* that routes the notifications emitted by active MBeans to their respective listeners.

At the time of this writing, no standard mechanism exists for remote access to an MBeanServer. As part of the Java Community Process, a group of JMX experts is working on Java Specification Request (JSR) 160, which will define a standard remote API for the MBeanServer.

5.1 The MBeanServerFactory Class

One of the first things a developer looking at the Javadoc for the MBeanServer will notice is that it is an interface, not a class. This observation immediately raises the question, How do I instantiate an MBeanServer? And the answer is, you use one of the methods provided by the `MBeanServerFactory` class. `MBeanServerFactory` provides four methods for creating MBeanServers:

```
static MBeanServer createMBeanServer()
static MBeanServer createMBeanServer(String domain)
static MBeanServer newMBeanServer()
static MBeanServer newMBeanServer(String domain)
```

The *create* versions keep a reference to the MBeanServer that the factory creates so that they can be accessed later via the `findMBeanServer()` method. No internal reference is kept to MBeanServers returned by the `newMBeanServer()` methods.

Every MBeanServer has a *default domain* for its object names. We'll discuss object naming in detail in a moment; for now just think of the domain as a kind of namespace. A programmer can specify the default domain string by calling the version of `createMBeanServer()` or `newMBeanServer()` that takes a `String` parameter; otherwise the default value specified by the JMX implementation will be used.

To get a reference to a specific MBeanServer, or to all MBeanServers, in a JVM, `MBeanServerFactory` provides the `findMBeanServer()` method. Its signature is

```
static ArrayList findMBeanServer(String id)
```

The `id` parameter may be either the MBeanServer ID of the desired MBeanServer, or `null`. Passing `null` to `findMBeanServer()` causes it to populate the returned `ArrayList` object with references to all of the MBeanServers in the JVM that were created via one of the `MBeanServerFactory createMBeanServer()` methods.

The `MBeanServerDelegate` MBean provides a management interface for the MBeanServer itself and serves as the source of notifications that emanate from the MBeanServer. `MBeanServerDelegate` will be discussed in detail in Section 5.4. To get an MBeanServer's ID, you call `getMBeanServerId()` on its associated `MBeanServerDelegate` MBean.

The final MBeanServerFactory method is releaseMBeanServer():

```
static void releaseMBeanServer(MBeanServer server)
```

This method drops MBeanServerFactory's internal reference to the given MBeanServer so that it can be garbage-collected by the JVM once all other references to the MBeanServer are gone. If the given MBeanServer doesn't exist—that is, MBeanServerFactory has no internal reference to it, as would be the case for an MBeanServer created via one of MBeanServerFactory's newMBeanServer() methods, releaseMBeanServer() throws an IllegalArgumentException.

Now that we know how to create MBeanServers, the next questions are, How many should we create, and which MBeanServerFactory method should we use to create them? In general, a managed application—for example, an HTTP daemon—will need only a single MBeanServer. Creating the MBeanServer via a createMBeanServer() method allows manageable components loaded by the application to locate the MBeanServer using findMBeanServer() and then register their MBeans.

When would it make sense to create an MBeanServer via one of the newMBeanServer() methods? Consider the following scenario: A developer wants to create a "self-managing" component that can be used by applications without regard to an application's particular choice, or lack thereof, of management mechanism. Such a component could be composed of a set of MBeans registered with an MBeanServer created by the component itself. The component's management policy could be specified via a .properties file or an LDAP profile. If the component uses one of the createMBeanServer() methods to generate its internal MBeanServer, then that MBeanServer will be accessible to any other JMX-aware code running in the same JVM as the component. Such accessibility may be neither useful to external management agents, nor desirable from the component developer's perspective. In this case using newMBeanServer() better meets the component developer's requirements.

5.2 Object Naming

The MBeanServer uses *object names* to refer to the MBeans it manages. Using an object name rather than a direct object reference to an MBean creates a level of indirection that allows the MBeanServer to help manage the MBean's lifecycle, control access to it, and associate additional information with the MBean.

An object name is associated with an MBean when it is created by or registered with the MBeanServer. All future interactions with that MBean via the MBeanServer use that object name. Management applications never get a direct reference to the MBean. Thus the resource represented by the MBean is manageable only for the duration of its MBeanServer registration. This sort of control is important when an MBean's resource is unavailable periodically, perhaps because of an upgrade or reconfiguration. In addition, using names rather than references prevents the management application from using additional knowledge it might have about an MBean—for example, the actual class that implements the MBean's interface—to call methods or access properties outside the MBean's defined management interface.

So what do these object names look like? Here's an example:

```
book/examples:name=ExampleName,chapter=5.
```

Every object name has two parts: the *domain*, which is to the left of the colon, and the *key properties* to the right.

5.2.1 Object Name Domains

According to the JMX specification, the *domain* part of an object name is a case-sensitive string: "It provides a structure for the naming space within a JMX agent or within a global management solution." A JMX agent might play host to hundreds of MBeans. Selecting an MBean or set of MBeans from a single large MBean pool is tedious, error prone, and possibly computationally expensive. Domains help reduce that complexity by imposing some order on the agent's collection of MBeans—for example, organizing MBeans by location, associated application, or logical application.

For example, consider a generic service container that hosts various network service components. The container itself would be instrumented by one set of MBeans, and each hosted service would introduce its own set of MBeans. We could use the domain part of the object name to organize this collection of MBeans into the hierarchy illustrated in Figure 5.1.

How the structure of domain is expressed is up to the application developer. In the example in Figure 5.1 we used slashes to separate domain components à la the UNIX file system. But we might have used a period as a separator instead. The only restriction JMX puts on the domain name is that it not contain any of these five characters:

```
:    ,    =    *    ?
```

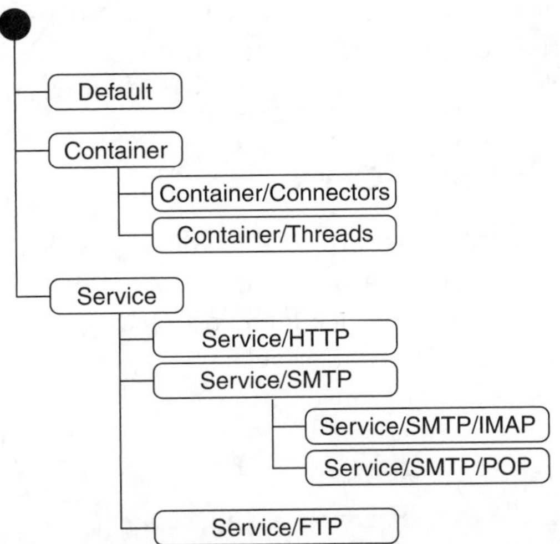

Figure 5.1 MBean Naming Hierarchy

5.2.2 Object Name Key Properties

The *key properties* component of an object name is used to uniquely identify an MBean within its domain. Key properties are a set of name/value pairs that express an MBean's identity. Suppose that we have multiple components from vendor A to manage; we can use the key properties `name` and `owner` to tell them apart:

```
Component/VendorA:name=goldQueue,owner=HttpService
Component/VendorA:name=silverQueue,owner=HttpService
Component/VendorA:name=bronzeQueue,owner=HttpService
```

In addition to expressing an MBean's identity, key properties provide a way to pass configuration information to an MBean. For example, adding a `priority` property to our `ServiceQueue` object names, like this:

```
Component/VendorA:name=silverQueue,priority=6,owner=HttpService
```

provides a means of setting `ServiceQueue`'s priority without resorting to `.property` files. When we discuss MBean creation in Section 5.3.1, we'll explain how an MBean gets access to these configuration properties.

We have been writing object names in *canonical form*—that is, as strings with the names of the key properties sorted in lexical order. In practice, the key properties can appear in any order in the string representation.

5.2.3 The ObjectName Class

Instances of the ObjectName class are used to identify MBeans registered with the MBeanServer and to specify a pattern in the context of an MBeanServer query. We'll look at the query service later in this chapter; here we examine the essential methods of the ObjectName class.

There are three ObjectName constructors:

```
ObjectName(String name)
ObjectName(String domain, Hashtable keyproperties)
ObjectName(String domain, String key, String property)
```

The first version takes the string representation of an object name, in canonical form or not, and creates the corresponding ObjectName instance. The last two are variations on a theme: create instance of ObjectName, given a domain string and a set of key properties. The second and third constructors differ only in the way the set of key properties is expressed; in the Hashtable version, a set of *N* key properties is provided via Hashtable, and in the final version a single key property is passed in as separate strings. Each of the constructors throws the MalformedObjectNameException if any of its parameters are not formatted correctly—for example, if the domain part contains an illegal character.

The following code illustrates the construction of three different object names:

```
ObjectName goldq = new ObjectName(
    "Component/VendorA:name=goldQueue,owner=HttpService");

Hashtable sqprops = new Hashtable();
sqprops.put("name", "silverQueue");
sqprops.put("priority", "6");
sqprops.put("owner", "HttpService");
ObjectName silverq = new ObjectName("Component/VendorA", sqprops);

ObjectName bronzeq = new ObjectName(
    "Component/VendorA", "name", "bronzeQueue");
```

The rest of the ObjectName methods are getters that retrieve ObjectName's domain and key property attributes in various forms:

```
String getDomain()
String getKeyProperty(String key)
Hashtable getKeyPropertyList()
String getKeyPropertyListString()
String getCanonicalName()
String getCanonicalKeyPropertyListString()
```

Note that object names are immutable. Therefore, adding additional entries to the hash table returned by getKeyPropertyList() has no effect on the object name itself.

Well-structured names can facilitate finding MBeans and grouping MBeans for a management application. We recommend that key properties contain at least one name or id property and a type property that indicates the managed resource type—for example, httpd, printer, or jvm.

5.2.4 The ObjectInstance Class

The ObjectInstance class maps an MBean's object name to the actual Java class that implements the MBean's management interface. All of the MBean creation mechanisms, as well as registerMBean() and the various flavors of createMBean() that we'll discuss in Section 5.3, return an instance of ObjectInstance. In addition, given an ObjectName instance, the MBeanServer's getObjectInstance() method returns the corresponding instance of ObjectInstance.

Why would a developer using JMX ever be interested in such a mapping? Regardless of which Java class implements a given MBean interface, the attributes and methods exposed by that interface are the only things available to a management application. Given that reality, what difference does the implementing class make? Suppose we have an MBean associated with a particular resource—say, a router—and we want to create another one just like it to represent a new router that we've added to our network. The MBeanServer doesn't provide a cloneMBean() method, so we'll have to implement something similar ourselves using methods like createMBean() that the MBeanServer does provide. The problem is that the MBeanServer's createMBean() methods all require a Java class name. That's where ObjectInstance comes in. We can take our existing MBean's ObjectName, turn it into an ObjectInstance via getObjectInstance(), and then extract the required class name from ObjectInstance using ObjectInstance's getClassName() method as illustrated here:

```
public void cloneMBean(MBeanServer mbs,
                       ObjectName prototype,
                       ObjectName clone) {
  ObjectInstance oi = mbs.getObjectInstance(prototype);
  String cn = oi.getClassName();
  mbs.createMBean(cn, clone);
}
```

The ObjectInstance class provides two constructors:

```
ObjectInstance(ObjectName objname, String clazz)
ObjectInstance(String objname, String clazz)
```

In practice they are seldom used because all of the MBeanServer methods take instances of ObjectName as parameters. The accessor methods that the ObjectInstance class supports are

```
String getClassName()
ObjectName getObjectName()
```

These methods are typically used to retrieve the underlying Java class or object name from an instance of ObjectInstance returned by one of the MBeanServer's create methods.

5.3 The MBeanServer Interface

Now that we know how to create an MBeanServer and how to name MBeans, it's time to explore the functionality provided by the MBeanServer itself. In this section we'll examine the core of the MBeanServer interface: the methods it provides for creating and manipulating MBeans, and the methods it provides for retrieving information about itself. Subsequent sections will discuss the MBeanServer's query methods and the notification facility.

As we mentioned earlier, an MBeanServer's primary responsibility is to maintain a registry of MBeans. The registry provides a common naming model, based on object names, across all management applications and makes its MBeans, and the manageable resources they represent, available to multiple management applications. MBeans become available to JMX management applications when they are added to an MBeanServer's registry, and when an MBean is removed from the registry it is no longer available to those applications. An MBean is registered with an MBeanServer, and the attributes and methods in its management interface are accessible via MBeanServer methods.

5.3.1 MBean Lifecycle Methods

The MBeanServer provides a set of *lifecycle methods*. These methods provide the mechanism for adding MBeans to the MBeanServer's registry and removing MBeans from that registry. In addition, there are methods that allow management applications to instantiate new MBeans via the MBeanServer.

5.3.1.1 Instantiation

At the beginning of this chapter we said that an MBean's management lifecycle begins when it is registered with an MBeanServer. Of course an MBean has to exist before it can be registered. One obvious way to instantiate an MBean is to call one of its constructors directly. The MBeanServer also provides a suite of methods that management applications can use to create new MBeans without directly invoking a constructor:

```
public Object instantiate(String classname)
public Object instantiate(String classname,
                          Object[] params,
                          String[] signature)
public Object instantiate(String classname, ObjectName loader)
public Object instantiate(String classname,
                          ObjectName loader,
                          Object[] params,
                          String[] signature)
```

If the class named in the first argument has a no-args constructor, no additional arguments are required; the designated class will be loaded and the no-args constructor invoked to create a new instance. If the class doesn't provide a no-args constructor, or if the management application needs to use a different constructor, we can implicitly specify one by providing a signature and the actual arguments to the constructor in the `signature` and `params` arguments. After the class is loaded, the constructor with the specified signature will be invoked with the values given in the `params` array to generate a new instance of the class.

What about the `loader` parameter? The `loader` parameter indicates the object name of the MLet (management applet) that should be used to load the specified class. (See Chapter 7 for the details on MLets, or for now, just think of them as a form of class loader.) When a loader's object name is specified, we use the MLet referred to by that name to load the class. What about when no loader is specified? In that case the MBeanServer turns to `DefaultLoaderRepository`. `DefaultLoaderRepository` is the collection of loaders that includes the class loader that loaded the MBeanServer and all of the MLets registered with the MBeanServer. When no loader is specified, the MBeanServer iterates over `DefaultLoaderRepository`'s collection of loaders looking for one that can load the specified class. If it finds one, the class instance is created as described already; if not, an instance of `ReflectionException` that wraps `java.lang.ClassNotFoundException` is thrown.

This is all well and good, but why bother with `instantiate()`? Why not just use the class's constructor without all this indirection? The reason is that the management application's class loader may not have access to the desired class. We won't go into all the details here, but the bottom line is that the MLet mechanism allows us to specify additional code sources that the MBeanServer's `instantiate()` and `createMBean()` methods can use to load classes. So in some cases even though the application's class loader may not know how to load a given class, the MBeanServer does have the necessary information and the application can use its `instantiate()` method to create instances of that class.

5.3.1.2 Registration

Once we have a reference to an instance of an MBean, it can be registered through this statement:

```
ObjectInstance registerMBean(Object mbean, ObjectName objname)
```

The `registerMBean()` method takes MBean's object reference and an `ObjectName` instance as parameters, creates an entry associating the two in the MBeanServer's registry, and returns an instance of `ObjectInstance` that maps `ObjectName` to the underlying Java class, as discussed earlier.

5.3.1.3 Creation

The "instantiate, then register" approach just described is a natural one for Java programmers used to working with `Collection` classes and the like, but it has the disadvantage of leaving a "live" reference to the MBean in the management application. JMX solves this problem by providing MBeanServer methods that, from a management application's perspective, automatically instantiate and register an instance of an MBean. The signatures for these methods are shown here:

```
ObjectInstance createMBean(String mbeancls,
                           ObjectName objname);
ObjectInstance createMBean(String mbeancls,
                           ObjectName objname,
                           Object[] params,
                           String[] sig);
ObjectInstance createMBean(String mbeancls,
                           ObjectName objname,
                           ObjectName loader);
ObjectInstance createMBean(String mbeancls,
                           ObjectName objname,
                           ObjectName loader,
                           Object[] params,
                           String[] sig);
```

The `mbeancls` and `objname` parameters that are common to all of these methods specify the fully qualified class name for the MBean and the object name under which an instance of that class is to be registered, respectively. As in the `instantiate()` methods, the `loader` parameter is used to indicate the object name of the MLet that should be used to load the MBean's class.

When the `params` and `sig` array pairs are not present, `createMBean()` uses Java reflection to invoke the no-args constructor on the specified class and registers the resulting instance under the given `ObjectName` instance. When the `params` and `sig` parameters are present, the `mbeancls` constructor whose parameter types match the class name strings in the `sig` array is invoked, again via Java reflection, with the parameters provided by the `params` array. Note that the class name strings in the `sig` array must be the *fully qualified* class names for the parameters; for example, if there is a `String` parameter in the `params` array, the corresponding element in the `sig` array must be "java.lang.String".

For example, consider the following simple MBean interface:

```
public interface SimpleSwitchMBean {
  public void flip();
  public int getState();
}
```

and the `SimpleSwitch` class that implements it:

```
public class SimpleSwitch implements SimpleSwitchMBean {
  private int state;

  public SimpleSwitch() { this(0); }
  public SimpleSwitch(int state) { this.state = state; }

  public void flip() { state = (state == 0) ? 1 : 0; }
  public int getState() { return state; }
}
```

The following code registers three separate `SimpleSwitch` MBeans with an MBeanServer:

```
MBeanServer mbs = MBeanServerFactory.createMBeanServer();

// Instantiate and register
ObjectName sone = new ObjectName("book:name=SwitchOne");
mbs.registerMBean(new SimpleSwitch(), sone);

// Create via no-args constructor
ObjectName stwo = new ObjectName("book:name=SwitchTwo");
mbs.createMBean("SimpleSwitch", stwo);

// Create via specific constructor
ObjectName sthree = new ObjectName("book:name=SwitchThree");
Object[] params = { new Integer(1) };
String[] sig = { "java.lang.Integer" };
mbs.createMBean("SimpleSwitch", sthree, params, sig);
```

Even though the calls are relatively simple, what's going on under the covers is complex, and lots of things can go wrong. When something does go wrong, an exception is thrown to indicate there is a problem. All told, `createMBean()` has six possible exceptions in its `throws` clause, and `registerMBean()` has four. By far the most common are

- `ReflectionException`, which wraps an exception that occurred while `createMBean()` was trying to invoke the MBean's constructor. Usually the wrapped exception is an instance of `java.lang.ClassNotFoundException`. `ReflectionException` provides a `getTargetException()` method that returns the wrapped exception.

- `MBeanException`, which indicates that the MBean's constructor threw an exception. `MBeanException` also provides a `getTargetException()` method that returns the exception thrown by the constructor.
- `RuntimeOperationsException`, which generally wraps an instance of `IllegalArgumentException` and indicates that one of the parameters of `createMBean()` or `registerMBean()` was bogus.

5.3.1.4 The MBeanRegistration Interface

Once a JMX developer has a handle on creating MBeans and adding them to an MBeanServer, he inevitably confronts one or more of the following questions:

- How do I know when my MBean is (de)registered?
- How does my MBean get access to the MBeanServer it's registered with?
- How does my MBean know its name?
- How can I prevent my MBean from being registered with an MBeanServer?
- How can I specify an action for my MBean to take immediately after it is (de)registered?

Although these questions could be answered in a variety of ad hoc ways, the JMX specification defines the `MBeanRegistration` interface to address each of them in a simple, flexible, and consistent manner. The `MBeanRegistration` interface is composed of four methods:

```
ObjectName preRegister(MBeanServer mbserver, ObjectName objname);
void postRegister(Boolean registered);
void preDeregister();
void postDeregister();
```

As the names suggest, these methods are invoked before and after registration and before and after deregistration, respectively. The state chart in Figure 5.2 illustrates the invocation of each of these methods as an MBean moves through its lifecycle.

When an MBean is registered, the MBeanServer inspects it to see if it implements the `MBeanRegistration` interface. If it does, the MBean's `preRegister()` method is called with a reference to the MBeanServer it is being registered with and a proposed object name. The `ObjectName` instance is the parameter passed to the `createMBean()` or `registerMBean()` method that started the registration process. If that `ObjectName` instance is `null`, then the MBean must provide its own object name; otherwise the proposed name may be accepted unchanged or augmented by the MBean—for example, by the addition of other key properties. In either case the name that is ultimately

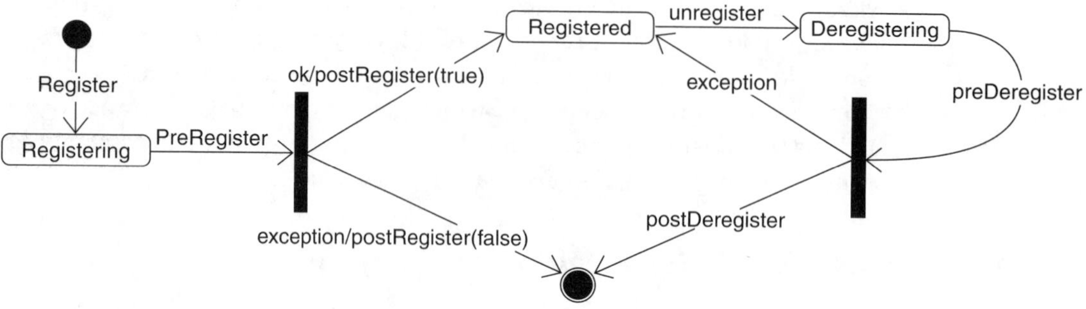

Figure 5.2 MBean Registration States and Actions

chosen and returned by `preRegister()` is the name under which the MBean is registered. If the MBean will need access to the MBeanServer—for example, to inspect the attributes or invoke the methods of other MBeans—it should save the reference provided for that purpose.

The MBeanServer catches any exception thrown by the `preRegister()` method. If the exception is an instance of `MBeanRegistrationException`, it is simply rethrown. Otherwise the actual exception is wrapped in `MBeanRegistrationException`, which is then thrown by the MBeanServer. When `preRegister()` throws an exception, the MBean is not registered with the MBeanServer.

The `postRegister()` method is invoked immediately after registration. If the registration succeeded, `postRegister()`'s `registered` parameter is `true`. If the registration failed—for example, if `preRegister()` threw an exception—`registered` is `false`. MBeans should use `postRegister()` to perform additional setup and configuration actions: adding notification listeners, creating additional MBeans, allocating resources, and so on.

The `preDeregister()` and `postDeregister()` methods are the deregistration analogs of `preRegister()` and `postRegister()`, respectively. The MBeanServer invokes `preDeregister()` prior to removing an MBean from its registry, and `postDeregister()` immediately after an MBean is deregistered. Exceptions thrown by `preDeregister()`, like those thrown by `preRegister()`, are caught by the MBeanServer, wrapped in `MBeanRegistrationException` and rethrown. If an exception is thrown by `preDeregister()`, the MBean is not deregistered and `postDeregister()` is not invoked.

Note that throwing an exception in `preRegister()` prevents the MBean from being *registered*, whereas throwing an exception in `preDeregister()` prevents the MBean from being *deregistered*. The former behavior can be useful when the MBean's environmental requirements aren't satisfied—for example, when the database it needs to connect to isn't up, or a license for the MBean can't be obtained from a license server. The latter behavior can be used to prevent an active MBean from being deregistered until either all outstanding requests have been serviced or the service that the MBean manages has been shut down.

5.3.1.5 Deregistration

MBeans are removed from the MBeanServer's registry with the following statement:

```
void unregisterMBean(ObjectName objname);
```

Deregistering an MBean makes it inaccessible through the `MBeanServer` interface. From a JMX perspective the resource represented by the MBean is no longer manageable. Of course, if the MBean was instantiated outside the MBeanServer and then registered, any reference to it retained by the application is still valid. MBeans created by a call to one of the `createMBean()` methods become candidates for garbage collection.

5.3.2 MBean Access Methods

The MBeanServer provides a common interface to the MBeans in its registry. That interface consists of six methods:

```
Object getAttribute(ObjectName objname, String attr);
AttributeList getAttributes(ObjectName objname, String[] attrs);
void setAttribute(ObjectName objname, Attribute attr);
AttributeList setAttributes(ObjectName objname,
    Attribute[] attrs);
Object invoke(ObjectName objname,
              String method,
              Object[] params,
              String[] sig);
MBeanInfo getMBeanInfo(ObjectName objname);
```

The `ObjectName` parameters in these APIs refer to MBeans registered with the MBeanServer. The `getAttribute()` and `getAttributes()` methods return the values of the specified MBean's attributes, `setAttribute()` and `setAttributes()` set the values of the specified MBean's attributes, and `invoke()` executes an operation on the specified MBean.

Three additional convenience methods exist to simplify common management application tasks:

```
ObjectInstance getObjectInstance(ObjectName objname);
boolean isInstanceOf(ObjectName objname, String cls);
boolean isRegistered(ObjectName objname);
```

The `getObjectInstance()` method returns the `ObjectInstance` for the specified object name or throws an `InstanceNotFoundException` if an MBean is not registered under that name. As we discussed earlier, `ObjectInstance` provides a mapping between an MBean's object name and the MBean's underlying Java class. Given an arbitrary MBean's object name, a management application can get the name of the Java class that implements it as follows:

```
String cls = mbs.getObjectInstance(objname).getClassName();
```

where `mbs` is a reference to an MBeanServer and `objname` is the object name of the MBean whose implementation class we are interested in.

The `isInstanceOf()` method answers the question, Is the MBean associated with this object name implemented by the specified class? Like `getObjectInstance()`, `isInstanceOf()` throws an `InstanceNotFoundException` if an MBean is not registered under the given object name.

Finally, `isRegistered()` gives us a way to check whether an MBean is registered with the specified object name before invoking `getObjectInstance()` or `isInstanceOf()`.

5.3.3 MBeanServer Methods

The MBeanServer also provides a couple of convenience methods that provide access to information about the MBeanServer itself:

```
public String getDefaultDomain()
public Integer getMBeanCount()
```

These methods do what their names imply. The `getDefaultDomain()` method returns the MBeanServer's default domain string, and `getMBeanCount()` returns the number of MBeans currently registered with the MBeanServer. Both methods tend to be used in JMX "console" applications that provide an MBeanServer GUI.

5.4 The MBeanServerDelegate MBean

Every MBeanServer implementation defines a domain named `JMImplementation`. This domain is reserved for use by JMX implementations and is guaranteed to contain at least one MBean of class `javax.management.MBeanServerDelegate`. In every JMX implementation this MBean, `MBeanServerDelegate`, has the same object name:

```
JMImplementation:type=MBeanServerDelegate
```

The `MBeanServerDelegate` MBean servers two purposes:

1. It provides information about the MBeanServer implementation.
2. It serves as a source of MBeanServer notifications.

The MBeanServer information is expressed as a set of `String`-valued attributes, which are listed in Table 5.1. The most significant of these attributes is `MBeanServerId` because this is the value used in `MBeanServerFactory`'s `findMBeanServer()` method.

The `MBeanServerDelegate` MBean's other purpose is to emit MBeanServer notifications when MBeans are registered with the MBeanServer and unregistered from the MBeanServer. The `MBeanServerNotification` class extends the base JMX `Notification` class with a method, `getMBeanName()`, that returns the object name of the MBean being registered or unregistered. The notification types `jmx.mbean.registered` and `jmx.mbean.unregistered` indicate whether the MBean named in `MBeanServerNotification` was registered or unregistered, respectively.

What does this feature mean for management applications? It gives them an opportunity to be much more dynamic than might otherwise be possible. Suppose, for example, we have an application that manages resources of type X. An essential aspect of that application would be setting up a standard monitoring configuration for all resources of type X in a system. If the system's type X resources are static and known a priori, then we can code that information into our application. Reality, however, especially in management applications, is seldom that convenient; we need to be able to deal with systems that contain varying numbers of resources of type X and in which those resources come and go over time. If we add a listener for `MBeanServerDelegateMBean`'s MBeanServer notifications, our application can react appropriately when MBeans that represent resources of type X are added to or removed from the MBeanServer.

Table 5.1 Attributes That Express MBeanServer Information

Attribute	Type	Description
`MBeanServerId`	Read-only	A unique ID for the MBeanServer. The JMX specification does not specify a format for this string, so different implementations can and do use different formats—for example, host name, time stamp, GUID. The only requirement is that the value be unique in a given JVM.
`SpecificationName`	Read-only	The full name of the specification on which the MBeanServer implementation is based. The value of this attribute must be `Java Management Extensions`.
`SpecificationVersion`	Read-only	The version of the JMX specification on which the MBeanServer implementation is based. As of this writing, the most recent specification is `1.1 Final Release`.
`SpecificationVendor`	Read-only	The name of the vendor of the JMX specification on which the MBeanServer implementation is based. The value of this attribute must be `Sun Microsystems`.
`ImplementationName`	Read-only	The implementation name of the MBeanServer—for example, `Sun RI` or `TMX4J`.
`ImplementationVersion`	Read-only	The implementation version of the MBeanServer.
`ImplementationVendor`	Read-only	The vendor name of the MBeanServer implementation—for example, `Tivoli Software` or `Sun Microsystems`.

5.5 Finding MBeans

A management application will operate on at most a subset of the MBeanServer's MBeans. Very simple management applications may require only a static set of MBeans; the object names for that set may even be hard-coded. The majority of management applications, however, must deal with a dynamic set of MBeans whose identity is not known a priori. Therefore we have to answer the question, How does a management application select the MBeans it needs from the MBeanServer?

The MBeanServer provides a simple *query service* as part of its public API that allows management applications to select a set of registered MBeans on the basis of their names and the values of one or more of their attributes.

5.5.1 Query Expressions

The `javax.management.QueryExp` interface is the fundamental building block of the MBeanServer's query service. `QueryExp` defines two methods:

```
void setMBeanServer(MBeanServer mbserver);
boolean apply(ObjectName objname);
```

The `apply()` method evaluates a `QueryExp` instance against the MBean specified by `objname`. The `setMBeanServer()` method specifies the MBeanServer that `apply()` will use to look up `objname`.

`QueryExp` represents an expression in a simple constraint language. The language expresses constraints on the values taken by an MBean's attributes. For example, suppose we have a `JobQueue` MBean with attributes `Priority`, `PendingJobs`, `AvgWaitTime`, and `MaxServiceTime`; we might be interested in `JobQueue` instances with

```
Priority > 10 and AvgWaitTime > 100
```

or for which

```
PendingJobs * AvgWaitTime > MaxServiceTime
```

The expressions represented by `QueryExp` in the query service constraint language are built up by the static methods of the `javax.management.Query` class.

The constraint language's primitive data are instances of type `javax.management.ValueExp`. `ValueExp` represents the Java primitive numeric types (`boolean`, `int`, `long`, `float`, and `double`) and Java numbers—for example, `Integer`, `Long`, `BigInteger`. The class `javax.management.StringValueExp` represents Java strings, and the class `javax.management.AttributeValueExp` represents the value of an MBean attribute. Instances of `ValueExp`, `StringValueExp`, and `AttributeValueExp` are created by the `Query` methods:

```
static AttributeValueExp attr(String attrname);
static AttributeValueExp attr(String attrcls, String attrname);
static AttributeValueExp classattr();
static StringValueExp value(String val);
static ValueExp value(boolean val);
static ValueExp value(double val);
static ValueExp value(float val);
static ValueExp value(int val);
static ValueExp value(long val);
static ValueExp value(Number val);
```

You can perform simple math on numeric instances of `ValueExp` using the `Query` methods:

```
static ValueExp plus(ValueExp v1, ValueExp v2);
static ValueExp minus(ValueExp v1, ValueExp v2);
static ValueExp times(ValueExp v1, ValueExp v2);
static ValueExp div(ValueExp v1, ValueExp v2);
```

Instances of `QueryExp` are built up by the application of one or more of the `Query` class's relational, logical, set, and regular expression methods to appropriate `ValueExp` instances. The signatures for those methods are

```
// Query relational methods
static QueryExp eq(ValueExp v1, ValueExp v2);
static QueryExp geq(ValueExp v1, ValueExp v2);
static QueryExp leq(ValueExp v1, ValueExp v2);
static QueryExp gt(ValueExp v1, ValueExp v2);
static QueryExp lt(ValueExp v1, ValueExp v2);
static QueryExp between(ValueExp val, ValueExp min, ValueExp max);

// Query logical methods
static QueryExp and(QueryExp q1, QueryExp q2);
static QueryExp or(QueryExp q1, QueryExp q2);
static QueryExp not(QueryExp query);

// Query set methods
static QueryExp in(ValueExp val, ValueExp[] valset);

// Query regular expression methods
static QueryExp initialSubString(AttributeValueExp attrval,
                                 StringValueExp prefix);
```

```
static QueryExp finalSubString(AttributeValueExp attrval,
    StringValueExp suffix);
static QueryExp anySubString(AttributeValueExp attrval,
    StringValueExp substr);
static QueryExp match(AttributeValueExp attrval,
    StringValueExp pattern);
```

Whereas the relational and logical operations have standard programming language semantics, the set and regular expression methods require a little explanation. The `Query.in()` method compares the values represented by the `ValueExp` instances, not the object references of those instances, as in this example:

```
ValueExp[] velist = { Query.value(2), Query.value(4),
    Query.value(6), Query.value(8) };
QueryExp q = Query.in(Query.value(4), velist);
```

Applying `q` to an arbitrary `ObjectName` instance yields `true`, even though the object references for the two `4` values may be different:

```
q.apply(new ObjectName("examples:name=setquery"));  // evaluates
                                                    // to true
```

The `*SubString()` methods test their second argument against the value of the attribute specified by their first argument:

```
// Evaluates to true if the value of the Status attribute begins
// with "SUCCESS"
QueryExp q1 = Query.initialSubString(Query.attr("Status"),
    Query.value("SUCCESS"));

// Evaluates to true if the value of the URL attribute ends
// with "html"
QueryExp q2 = Query.finalSubString(Query.attr("URL"),
    Query.value("html"));

// Evaluates to true if the value of the Response attribute
// contains "failed"
QueryExp q3 = Query.anySubString(Query.attr("Response"),
    Query.value("failed"));
```

Finally, the `match()` method tests simple regular expressions specified by its second argument against the value of the attribute specified by the first argument. The regular expressions are a combination of wildcards (*, which matches zero or more characters; and ?, which matches a single character), character sets (specified by the characters in the set being enclosed in square brackets, as in `[AaEeIiOoUu]`), and character ranges (specified by a hyphen [-] placed between the first character in the range and the final character in the range, as in `[0-9]`). To negate a regular expression, add an exclamation point as a prefix—for example, `![AaEeIiOoUu]` specifies the set of all upper- and lowercase consonants:

```
// Evaluates to true if the value of the Id attribute consists of
// a two-digit number that begins with a 7
QueryExp qm = Query.match(Query.attr("Id"), Query.value("7[0-9]"));
```

Now let's see how the `JobQueue` queries from the beginning of this section look expressed in terms of `Query` methods:

```
QueryExp q1 = Query.and(Query.gt(Query.attr("Priority"),
        Query.value(10)),
        Query.gt(Query.attr("AvgWaitTime"), Query.value(100)));

QueryExp q2 = Query.gt(Query.times(Query.attr("PendingJobs"),
        Query.attr("AvgWaitTime")),
        Query.attr("MaxServiceTime"));
```

To evaluate one of these queries, we first specify the MBeanServer to use as a context and then apply the query to an `ObjectName` instance:

```
q1.setMBeanServer(mbs);
boolean excessiveAvgWait =
    q1.apply(new ObjectName("examples:name=MyJobQueue"));
```

5.5.2 Query Scope and Pattern Matching

The `QueryExp apply()` method is useful if we know the object name of the MBean we want to evaluate the expression against. What if we don't know the object name a priori, in which case we can't hard-code it into the application or supply it via a `.properties` file, and the management application runs unattended, so that the object name can't be supplied by the user at runtime? What if there is a set of MBeans we want the expression evaluated against? How do we determine which object names to apply to the expression in these rather common situations?

JMX provides `ObjectName` *patterns* that allow you to specify a subset of the object names in the MBeanServer's registry. An `ObjectName` pattern is an object name whose domain and key properties components may contain wildcard characters. An asterisk (*) in the domain component matches zero or more characters. A question mark (?) in the domain component matches a single character. An asterisk in the key properties component matches zero or more name/value pairs. The set of object names that match a pattern is called the *query scope*.

For example, assume we have the following object names in the registry:

```
http:name=H001, pool=Primary
http:name=H002, pool=Reserved
https:name=H003, pool=Primary
smtp:name=H011, pool=Primary
smtp:name=H012, pool=Primary
ftp:name=H101, pool=Primary
queues/http:id=FF01, servicelevel=Gold
queues/http:id=FF02, servicelevel=Silver
queues/smtp:id=FF11, servicelevel=Gold
logs/http:filename=access.log, ownerid=FF01
logs/http:filename=error.log, ownerid=FF01
```

Here are some valid patterns and their associated query scopes:

```
queues/*:*
  // all the queues
  queues/http:id=FF01, servicelevel=Gold
  queues/http:id=FF02, servicelevel=Silver
  queues/smtp:id=FF11, servicelevel=Gold

*:filename=error.log
  // all the object names with just the filename=error.log key
  // property
  no matching ObjectNames

*:filename=error.log, *
  // all the object names with a filename=error.log key property
  logs/http:filename=error.log, ownerid=FF01
```

```
http*:*, pool=Primary
  // all the "http"-related object names with a Primary pool key
  // property
  http:name=H001, pool=Primary
  https:name=H003, pool=Primary

queues/*:servicelevel=Gold, *
  // all the queues with a Gold service level
  queues/http:id=FF01, servicelevel=Gold
  queues/smtp:id=FF11, servicelevel=Gold

logs/*:*, ownerid=FF01
  // all the logs owned by FF01
  logs/http:filename=access.log, ownerid=FF01
  logs/http:filename=error.log, ownerid=FF01
```

The patterns `*:*` and `""` (the empty string), are equivalent and match all the object names in the MBeanServer's registry. To specify a pattern on the MBeanServer's default domain, omit the domain component of the object name; for example, `:*` selects all object names in the MBeanServer's default domain.

5.5.3 MBeanServer Query Methods

The MBeanServer's two query methods bring together query scopes (specified by `ObjectName` patterns) and query expressions (specified by instances of `QueryExp`). Here are the signatures for those methods:

```
Set queryMBeans(ObjectName pattern, QueryExp constraint);
Set queryNames(ObjectName pattern, QueryExp constraint);
```

Both versions select the set of object names matching the `pattern` parameter from the MBeanServer's registry. Both versions then apply the `constraint` parameter to the MBeans associated with the selected object names. The `queryNames()` method returns the set of object names for which the `constraint` parameter was `true`. The `queryMBeans()` method returns the equivalent set of `ObjectInstance` instances.

For example, suppose we're interested in obtaining the object names of all of the queues with a `Gold` service level that are experiencing excessive average wait times. Here's a call to `queryNames()` that returns the object names we're interested in:

```
ObjectName gq = new ObjectName("queues/*:servicelevel=Gold, *");
QueryExp eaw = Query.gt(Query.times(Query.attr("PendingJobs"),
                                    Query.attr("AvgWaitTime")),
                                    Query.attr("MaxServiceTime"));
Set badgq = mbs.queryNames(gq, eaw);
```

The `queryNames()` method first uses `gq` to select the set of queues with a `Gold` service level. It then applies the `eaw` query expression to each of them and returns the set of queue `ObjectName` instances for which the `QueryExp` `eaw` was `true`.

5.6 Notifications

In Chapter 3 we described the JMX notification model from an MBean perspective. In particular we showed how to "activate" an MBean by implementing the `NotificationBroadcaster` interface. Now it's time to look at notifications from the MBeanServer perspective. There are four MBeanServer methods that deal with notifications:

```
public void addNotificationListener(ObjectName name,
                                    NotificationListener listener,
                                    NotificationFilter filter,
                                    Object handback)
public void addNotificationListener(ObjectName name,
                                    ObjectName listener,
                                    NotificationFilter filter,
                                    Object handback)
public void removeNotificationListener(ObjectName name,
    NotificationListener listener)
public void removeNotificationListener(ObjectName name,
    ObjectName listener)
```

The first two methods add notification listeners to the MBean designated by the first parameter. The only difference between the two methods is whether the listener is a Java object that implements the `NotificationListener` interface or the object name of an MBean that implements the `NotificationListener` interface in addition to its management interface. As explained in Chapter 3, the `NotificationFilter` interface determines whether or not the listener receives a given notification.

The `handback` parameter is a reference to a Java object that is delivered to the listener's `handleNotification()` method by `NotificationBroadcaster`.

Handbacks make it possible to reuse a `NotificationListener` instance; the same listener can be added multiple times, each time with a different handback object, to a given MBean. When the MBean sends a notification, the listener's `handleNotification()` method will be invoked, with the appropriate handback—once for each time it was added.

The `removeNotificationListener()` methods remove a listener, identified by its object reference or object name, from the set of listeners associated with the MBean designated by the object name in the first parameter. Note that neither of the `removeNotificationListener()` methods takes a handback object. This is an unfortunate asymmetry in the 1.0 version of the JMX specification. It is unfortunate because it means that when a listener has been added multiple times, the MBeanServer has no way to distinguish which of the additions is being removed, so *it removes all of them*.

5.7 Summary

The MBeanServer is the core of any JMX-based management application. The `MBeanServerFactory` class allows us to create, look up, and release individual MBeanServers. Using the MBeanServer, we can create and register new MBeans, retrieve their attributes and invoke operations on them, and add listeners that react to the notifications they generate. The MBeanServer also provides a simple but useful query mechanism that allows us to select sets of MBeans on the basis of their attribute values.

CHAPTER 6

Monitors and Monitoring

Monitoring is an essential activity for a management application. Instrumentation provides raw information about the status of an application or device. Administrators specify acceptable values, or ranges of values, for the status information the instrumentation provides. In many cases the administrator would also like to specify an action to take if the status information indicates a problem. For example, an important aspect of managing a database is ensuring that the file system that holds the database's tables has sufficient space; if the file system begins to fill up, an e-mail or a page needs to be sent to the administrator so that the appropriate action—for example, extending the file system or archiving data—can be taken.

Management applications use monitors to automate administration; they configure their monitors to check an application's status information periodically and send notifications if the values don't meet the administrator's specifications. The management application reacts to those notifications, perhaps by taking some prearranged corrective action or by sending e-mail to, or even paging, a human administrator.

Because monitoring plays such a central role in management applications, JMX provides a set of monitor services that simplify the task of building sophisticated management applications.

6.1 The JMX Monitor Service

The `javax.management.monitor` package provides a set of *monitoring services* that JMX-based management applications can use to monitor MBeans registered with the MBeanServer. Each of these services is packaged as an MBean. Management applications create and manipulate monitors via the MBeanServer just like they do other MBeans.

6.1.1 The Monitoring Package Structure

The monitoring package is composed of four interfaces and five classes. Figure 6.1 illustrates their interrelationships.

The abstract `Monitor` class is the core of the package. It extends `NotificationBroadcasterSupport` so that its instances can send JMX notifications when they detect conditions of interest to management applications. Because each of its concrete subclasses will be MBeans, `Monitor` also implements the `MonitorMBean` interface, which captures the common aspects of a monitor's management interface. Finally, `Monitor` implements `MBeanRegistration`, which provides a means for the concrete `Monitor` subclass instances to get a reference to their MBeanServer.

The `javax.management.monitor` package defines three concrete monitor types: `StringMonitor`, `CounterMonitor`, and `GaugeMonitor`. Each of these monitor types extends `Monitor`, reusing the common behavior it defines, and defining a distinct MBean type by implementing its own management interface. We will treat each of these concrete monitor types in detail later in this chapter.

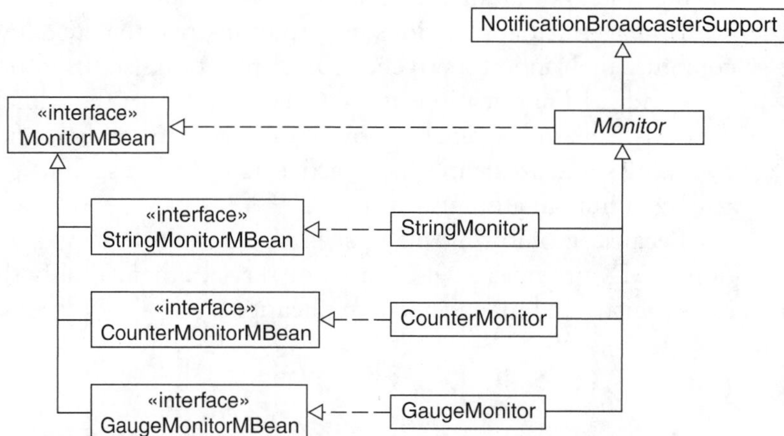

Figure 6.1 Static Structure of the `javax.management.monitor` Package

The MonitorNotification class extends the base JMX Notification class with additional monitor-related information.

6.1.2 The Monitor MBean

The Monitor MBean defines three read/write attributes, one read-only attribute, and two operations that are shared by all of the JMX monitor MBeans. Tables 6.1 and 6.2 describe these aspects of the Monitor MBean.

The GranularityPeriod attribute defaults to 10 seconds, 10,000 milliseconds. Attempting to set it to a value less than or equal to zero results in an IllegalArgumentException.

Both ObservedAttribute and ObservedObject default to null. The monitor does not attempt to validate either of these values until its start() method is invoked. If either value is invalid—for example, null, meaning nonexistent MBean or attribute—the monitor sends a MonitorNotification

Table 6.1 Common Monitor Management Interface Attributes

Attribute	Type	Description
GranularityPeriod	Read/write	A long value that indicates the number of milliseconds between observations
ObservedAttribute	Read/write	The String name of the attribute that the monitor is observing
ObservedObject	Read/write	The object name of the MBean whose attribute is being observed
Active	Read-only	A boolean value indicating whether or not the monitor is active

Table 6.2 Common Monitor Management Interface Operations

Operation	Description
start	Tells the monitor to start observing the observed attribute on the observed object.
stop	Stops further observations.

instance whose type indicates the nature of the error. We'll say more about MonitorNotification in a moment.

Each JMX monitor also provides a *derived gauge* attribute. It doesn't show up in the MonitorMBean interface because its type is not the same in each of the monitors. The concept, however, is the same in each case. A monitor's derived gauge is the value that the monitor derives from the value of ObservedAttribute. The value may be either the exact value of ObservedAttribute or the difference between two successive ObservedAttribute values.

The start() and stop() operations are idempotent. That is, invoking start() on an active monitor has no effect, and the same is true for invocations of stop() on an inactive monitor.

6.1.3 MonitorNotification

Monitors are responsible for alerting the management applications that use them to specific conditions. In JMX the obvious mechanism to use for that purpose is a *notification*; that is, the monitor sends a JMX notification when the derived gauge for an observed attribute satisfies the condition. Rather than sending an instance of the standard JMX Notification class, the javax.management.monitor package provides the MonitorNotification class, which extends Notification. In addition to the information provided by Notification, MonitorNotification includes four other values:

1. The value of the derived gauge, which is returned by the getDerivedGauge() method
2. The name of the observed attribute, which is returned by the getObservedAttribute() method
3. The object name of the observed MBean, which is returned by the getObservedObject() method
4. The string that triggered the notification, by a StringMonitor instance, which is returned by getTrigger()

The monitoring services also define a set of notification types that are associated with the monitor notifications they send. Figure 6.2 shows the MonitorNotification type hierarchy.

The "error" types are common to all monitors, so we will describe them here (see Table 6.3). The other types will be covered in our discussions of the monitors that send them.

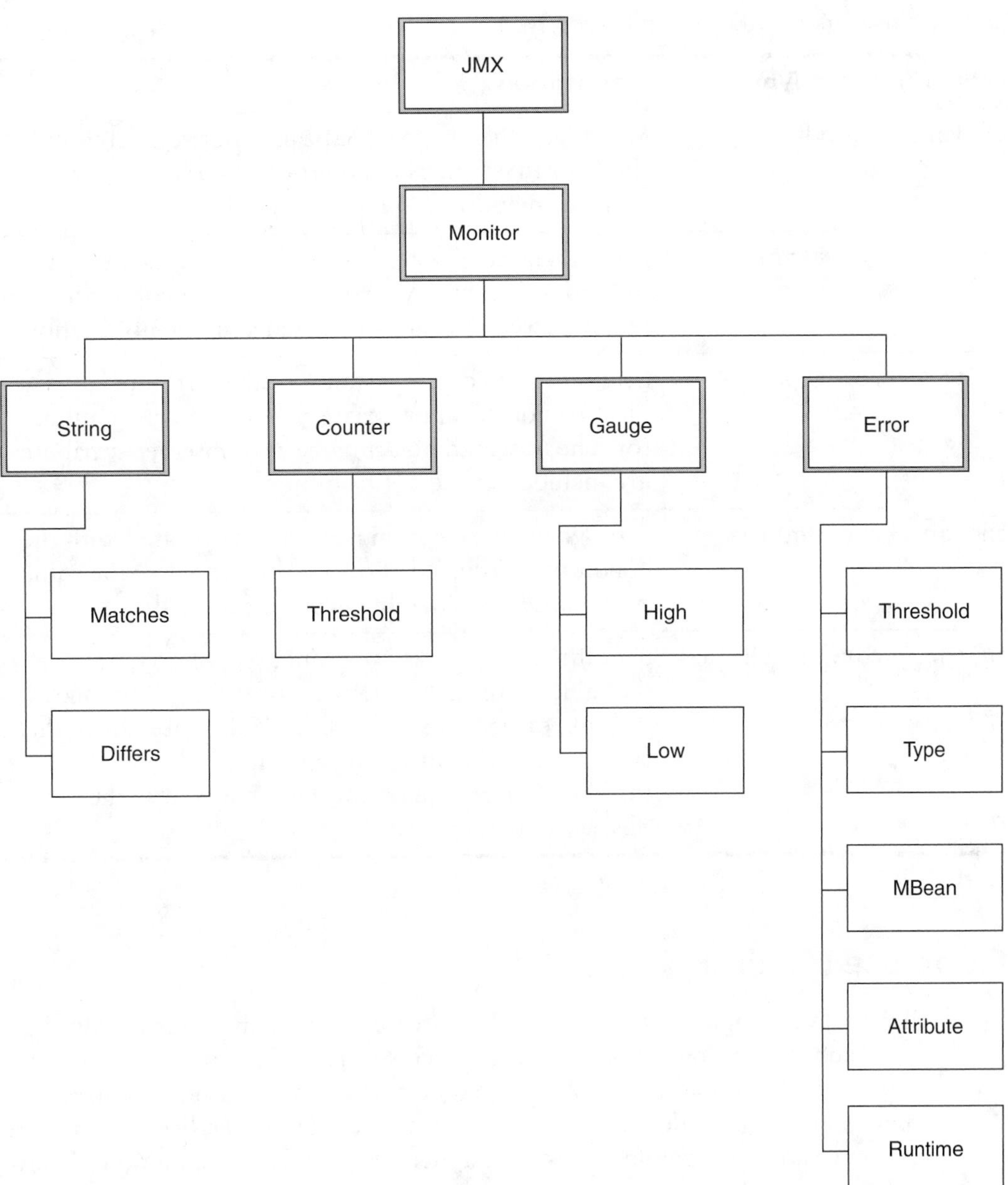

Figure 6.2 The Hierarchy of `MonitorNotification` Types

Table 6.3 Common Monitor Error Notification Types

MonitorNotification Type	Description
jmx.monitor.error.mbean	Sent when the observed MBean is not registered in the MBeanServer. The monitor's observed object name is included in the notification.
jmx.monitor.error.attribute	Sent when the observed attribute does not exist in the monitor's observed MBean. The observed object name and observed attribute are included in the notification.
jmx.monitor.error.type	Sent when the object instance of the attribute value is null or not the appropriate type for the given monitor. The observed object name and observed attribute are included in the notification.
jmx.monitor.error.runtime	Sent when an exception (save one associated with the conditions discussed above) is thrown while the value of the observed attribute is being accessed.
jmx.monitor.error.threshold	Sent if the monitor is misconfigured—for example, the values of the CounterMonitor attributes Threshold, Offset, or Modulus (see Section 6.2.4) are not of the same type as the observed attribute, and low- or high-threshold values are not of the same type as the observed attribute.

6.2 Concrete Monitors

Every JMX implementation provides three concrete subclasses of Monitor: StringMonitor, CounterMonitor, and GaugeMonitor. Each of them is designed for a specific monitoring task that requires attributes and notification types beyond those provided by the Monitor base class. However, because they are all extensions of a common base class, their usage follows a common pattern. This section describes that usage pattern and then explores the additional attributes and behavior specific to each of the concrete monitors.

6.2.1 Monitoring Apache's Status

In order to demonstrate monitors, we need something to monitor. Rather than making up a toy example, we'll use the Apache MBean we developed in

Chapter 3. Not only does it have a rich set of attributes to monitor, but given the ubiquity of Apache-based Web sites, our code could have immediate application in the real world of systems management.

6.2.1.1 Apache MBean Refresher

Recall that the Apache MBean leverages Apache's `mod_status` module to retrieve diagnostic information about an Apache instance. When we do an HTTP `GET` on URLs of the form

```
http://<hostname>/server-status?auto
```

an Apache instance with the `mod_status` module enabled will return a machine-readable page of diagnostic information. Here is the `ApacheMBean` interface from Chapter 3:

```
package net.jnjmx.ch3;

public interface ApacheMBean {
  public String DOWN = "OWN";
  public String NOT_RESPONDING = "NOT_RESPONDING";
  public String RUNNING = "RUNNING";
  public String UNKNOWN = "UNKNOWN";

  public int getBusyWorkers() throws ApacheMBeanException;
  public int getBytesPerSec()throws ApacheMBeanException;
  public float getBytesPerReq()throws ApacheMBeanException;
  public long getCacheLifetime();
  public float getCpuLoad()throws ApacheMBeanException;
  public int getIdleWorkers()throws ApacheMBeanException;
  public float getReqPerSec()throws ApacheMBeanException;
  public String getScoreboard()throws ApacheMBeanException;
  public String getServer();
  public String getState();
  public int getTotalAccesses()throws ApacheMBeanException;
  public long getTotalKBytes()throws ApacheMBeanException;
  public long getUptime(throws ApacheMBeanException);
  public boolean isCaching();
  public void setCacheLifetime(long lifetime);
  public void setCaching(boolean caching);
  public void setServer(String url) throws MalformedURLException,
    IllegalArgumentException;
  public int start()throws ApacheMBeanException;
```

```
  public int stop()throws ApacheMBeanException;
}
```

After we describe the common aspects of JMX monitor programming, we'll use the attributes defined in this interface to explore the use of the various JMX monitors.

6.2.2 Canonical Usage Pattern

Using a monitor follows a general pattern regardless of the monitor's type. Once the MBean we're interested in has been created, we instantiate the monitor, configure it, set up the appropriate notification listeners, and start the monitor.

6.2.2.1 *Creating and Configuring the Monitor*

Because each of the concrete monitors provides a no-args constructor, it's simple to create instances via the MBeanServer's `createMBean()` method. Once the monitor has been created, we have to set its various attributes; the most efficient way to do that is with the MBeanServer's `setAttributes()` method, which lets us set multiple attributes in a single invocation:

```
package net.jnjmx.ch6;

import javax.management.*;
import javax.management.monitor.*;

import net.jnjmx.ch3.Apache;
import net.jnjmx.ch3.ApacheMBean;

public class ApacheMonitor {
...
  public ObjectName setupStateMonitor(MBeanServer mbs,
       ObjectName server) throws Exception {
    /* Assume ApacheStatus object names are of the form:
     *    <domain>:type=ApacheStatus,url=<URL of the server we're
     *    interested in>
     */
    String url = server.getKeyProperty("url");
    ObjectName mon = new ObjectName(
        "monitors:type=String,attr=State,url=" + url);
    mbs.createMBean("javax.management.monitor.StringMonitor", mon);
```

```
        AttributeList al = new AttributeList();
        al.add(new Attribute("ObservedObject", server));
        al.add(new Attribute("ObservedAttribute", "State");
        al.add(new Attribute("GranularityPeriod", 60000);
        // Add additional StringMonitor-specific attributes

        AttributeList sl = mbs.setAttributes(mon, al);
        // Check to make sure all of the attributes were set

        return mon;
    }
...
}
```

The `setupStateMonitor()` method illustrates this process. The `State` attribute values are strings, so we need a `StringMonitor` instance. The caller passes in the object name of the `ApacheStatus` MBean that is to be monitored; we use the `url` key property of that `ObjectName` instance to create a unique object name for our `StringMonitor` object. After we create the `StringMonitor` instance via `createMBean()`, we populate an `AttributeList` instance with the attributes we want to set *on* `StringMonitor`. The call to `setAttributes()` sets the specified attributes; after checking to make sure that they were in fact set—that is, that the instance of `AttributeList` returned by `setAttributes()` contains an entry for each attribute successfully set—we return the `StringMonitor` object name.

Note that this example illustrated the pattern with `StringMonitor`, but the pattern is the same regardless of the monitor's concrete type. The only difference is in the attributes we use to configure the monitor.

6.2.2.2 Listening for Notifications

Once a monitor is set up, a management application can listen for and react to the notifications it sends:

```
package net.jnjmx.ch6;

import javax.management.*;
import javax.management.monitor.*;

import net.jnjmx.ch3.Apache;
import net.jnjmx.ch3.ApacheMBean;
```

```
public class ApacheMonitor {
  public static class StateNotificationListener implements
      NotificationListener {
    public void handleNotification(Notification notification,
        Object handback) {
      // Take some action when a notification is received from the
      // State attribute monitor
    }

  public static void main(String[] args) throws Exception {
    // Create the MBean to be monitored
    MBeanServer mbs = MBeanServerFactory.createMBeanServer();
    ObjectName server = new ObjectName(
        "resources.http:type=ApacheStatus,url=www.jnjmx.net");
    mbs.createMBean("net.jnjmx.ch3.Apache",
                    server,
                    new Object[] { "www.jnjmx.net" },
                    new String[] { "java.lang.String" });

    // Create a monitor for the MBean's State attribute
    ApacheMonitor am = new ApacheMonitor();
    ObjectName monitor = am.setupStateMonitor(mbs, server);

    // Add a listener for notifications from the State monitor
    mbs.addNotificationListener(monitor,
                   new ApacheMonitor.StateNotificationListener(),
                   null,
                   new Object());

    // Start the State monitor
    mbs.invoke(monitor, "start", new Object[] {}, new String[] {});

    // remainder of the ApacheMonitor application
    ...
  }
...
}
```

Once the `State` attribute monitor is set up, we add a notification listener to that monitor. That listener is responsible for taking appropriate action when it receives a notification from the monitor. For example, if the server is not responding, there is no point in attempting to monitor its other attributes; so when the value of the `State` attribute is `ApacheStatusMBean.NOT_RESPONDING`, we could stop any other monitors configured for that server. Of course, if we stop the monitors when the server is not responding, we should start them again when it is responding. In the next section we'll see how to use `StringMonitor`'s attributes to arrange for that behavior.

6.2.3 StringMonitor

`StringMonitor` observes an attribute of type `String` and can detect two conditions:

1. If the observed attribute's value matches a specific string
2. If the observed attribute's value differs from the specified string

The `StringMonitorMBean` interface adds five attributes to the management interface defined by `MonitorMBean`. These attributes are described in Table 6.4.

There are also two `MonitorNotification` types specific to `StringMonitor` (see Table 6.5).

Table 6.4 `StringMonitor`-Specific Attributes

Attribute	Type	Description
`DerivedGauge`	Read-only	The most recently observed value of the observed attribute.
`DerivedGaugeTimeStamp`	Read-only	The time, in milliseconds, from midnight January 1, 1970, UTC, at which time the last observation was made.
`NotifyDiffer`	Read/write	A `boolean`-valued attribute that determines whether a `MonitorNotification` instance is sent when the derived gauge differs from the string to compare.
`NotifyMatch`	Read/write	A `boolean`-valued attribute that determines whether a `MonitorNotification` instance is sent when the derived gauge matches the string to compare.
`StringToCompare`	Read/write	A `String`-valued attribute containing the string to which the observed MBean's derived gauge is to be compared.

Table 6.5 StringMonitor-Specific Notification Types

Notification Type	Description
jmx.monitor.string.matches	Sent when StringMonitor's StringToCompare attribute matches the value of the observed MBean's observed attribute.
jmx.monitor.string.differs	Sent when StringMonitor's StringToCompare attribute differs from the value of the observed MBean's observed attribute.

As a convenience, the MonitorNotification class defines static final fields representing both of these types. The field identifiers are

```
MonitorNotification.STRING_TO_COMPARE_VALUE_MATCHED
// for jmx.monitor.string.matches
MonitorNotification.STRING_TO_COMPARE_VALUE_DIFFERED
// for jmx.monitor.string.differs
```

At the beginning of each granularity period, a StringMonitor instance retrieves the value of the observed attribute from the MBean it is observing. That value is saved in the monitor's DerivedGauge attribute, and the time of the observation is saved in the DerivedGaugeTimeStamp attribute. The new value of the DerivedGauge attribute is then compared to the value of the StringToCompare attribute. This comparison has two possible outcomes: match, no match. If the outcome is the same as that of the comparison that occurred at the beginning of the previous granularity period—that is, there was a match before and there's still a match, or the two values didn't match before and they still don't match—then nothing happens. Otherwise, if the values used to be different and now they match *and* the value of the monitor's NotifyMatch attribute is true, a MonitorNotification instance of type jmx.monitor.string.matches is sent. Similarly, if the values used to match and now they don't *and* the value of the monitor's NotifyDiffer attribute is true, a MonitorNotification instance of type jmx.monitor.string.differs is sent.

Note that it is perfectly legal to make the monitor's NotifyMatch and NotifyDiffer attributes true *simultaneously*. Doing so will result in a notification whenever the relationship between the StringToCompare attribute and the observed attribute changes.

6.2.3.1 Using StringMonitor

Now we have enough information to complete ApacheMonitor's setupStateMonitor() method we sketched in Section 6.2.2.1. Let's say we want to monitor ApacheStatusMBean's State attribute so that we can start monitoring the server whenever it is running and stop monitoring it when it stops responding or goes down. The brute-force approach would be to use three StringMonitor instances—one for each of the possible values of ApacheStatusMBean's State attribute. That approach would work and have the advantage of being simple to code and easy to understand for any future developer maintaining the code. The downside is that each of those monitors has an associated overhead. Although it is generally a bad idea to indulge in gratuitous optimizations, in this case we can use the technique mentioned in the previous section to meet the management application's requirements with a single instance of StringMonitor.

All we want to know is when the value of ApacheStatusMBean's State attribute goes from ApacheStatusMBean.RUNNING to another value and back again. Setting the monitor's StringToCompare attribute to ApacheStatusMBean.RUNNING and *both* its NotifyMatch *and* NotifyDiffer attributes to true provides the desired behavior.

The first time the State attribute and the value of the StringToCompare attribute (ApacheStatusMBean.RUNNING) match, a MonitorNotification instance of type jmx.monitor.string.matches is sent. No further notifications are sent until the State attribute no longer matches ApacheStatusMBean.RUNNING; then a MonitorNotification instance of type jmx.monitor.string.differs is sent. Monitor notifications of the appropriate type continue to be sent as the value of the State attribute changes. It's now up to the management application listening for those notifications to react so as to provide the desired behavior. The expanded version of ApacheMonitor that follows demonstrates how to configure the State monitor and handle the subsequent notifications:

```
package net.jnjmx.ch6;

import javax.management.*;
import javax.management.monitor.*;

import net.jnjmx.ch3.Apache;
import net.jnjmx.ch3.ApacheMBean;

public ApacheMonitor {
  public static class StateNotificationListener implements
    NotificationListener {
```

```
    public void handleNotification(Notification notification,
        Object handback) {
      String type = notification.getType();
      if (type.compareTo(
            MonitorNotification.STRING_TO_COMPARE_VALUE_MATCHED)
            == 0) {
        Iterator i = monitors.iterator();
        while (i.hasNext()) {
          ObjectName on = (ObjectName) i.next();
          ((MBeanServer) handback).invoke(on, "start",
            new Object[] {}, new String[] {});
        }
      } else if (type.compareTo(
            MonitorNotification.STRING_TO_COMPARE_VALUE_DIFFERED)
            == 0) {
        Iterator i = monitors.iterator();
        while (i.hasNext()) {
          ObjectName on = (ObjectName) i.next();
          ((MBeanServer) handback).invoke(on, "stop", new
              Object[] {}, new String[] {});
        }
      }
    }

  private static List monitors;

  public static void main(String[] args) throws Exception {
    // Create the MBean to be monitored
    MBeanServer mbs = MBeanServerFactory.createMBeanServer();
    ObjectName server = new ObjectName(
        "resources.http:type=ApacheStatus,url=www.jnjmx.net");
    mbs.createMBean("net.jnjmx.ch3.Apache", server);

    // Create a monitor for the MBean's State attribute
    ObjectName monitor = setupStateMonitor(mbs, server);

    // Add a listener for notifications from the State monitor
    mbs.addNotificationListener(monitor,
                new ApacheMonitor.StateNotificationListener(),
                null,
                mbs);

    // Start the State monitor
    mbs.invoke(monitor, "start", new Object[] {}, new String[] {});
```

```
    monitors = new ArrayList();
    // Create the rest of the application's monitors and add them
    // to the monitor list so that we can access them in
    // NotificationListener

    // remainder of the ApacheMonitor application
    ...
  }
...
  public ObjectName setupStateMonitor(MBeanServer mbs,
      ObjectName server) throws Exception {
    /* Assume ApacheStatus object names are of the form:
     *    <domain>:type=ApacheStatus,url=<URL of the server we're
     *    interested in>
     */
    String url = server.getKeyProperty("url");
    ObjectName mon = new ObjectName(
       "monitors:type=String,attr=State,url=" + url);
    mbs.createMBean("javax.management.monitor.StringMonitor",
       mon);

    AttributeList al = new AttributeList();
    al.add(new Attribute("ObservedObject", server));
    al.add(new Attribute("ObservedAttribute", "State");
    al.add(new Attribute("GranularityPeriod", 60000);
    al.add(new Attribute("StringToCompare", ApacheMBean.RUNNING);
    al.add(new Attribute("NotifyMatch", new Boolean(true));
    al.add(new Attribute("NotifyDiffer", new Boolean(true));
    AttributeList sl = mbs.setAttributes(mon, al);
    // Check to make sure all of the attributes were set

    return mon;
  }
...
}
```

We add three StringMonitor-specific attributes to the attribute list in setupStateMonitor. When the main() method creates the remaining monitors, it adds them to a list that NotificationListener's handleNotification() method uses. Finally, note that the application need not start the other monitors; NotificationListener will take care of that as soon as it notices that the server is running.

6.2.4 CounterMonitor

Counters are attributes whose numeric values increase monotonically over time. The number of requests a Web server has handled, the number of packets a router has forwarded, the number of orders a system has processed, and so on are all example of counters. Management applications often need to initiate an action when counters reach a threshold value—taking the system offline for scheduled maintenance, paging the administrator, and so on.

JMX-based management applications use instances of `CounterMonitor` to observe counter attributes and send notifications when threshold values are reached. Table 6.6 describes the attributes that the `CounterMonitorMBean` interface adds to the common `MonitorMBean` interface.

Table 6.6 `CounterMonitor`-Specific Attributes

Attribute	Type	Description
`DerivedGauge`	Read-only	The actual value of the observed attribute at a particular instant in time.
`DerivedGaugeTimeStamp`	Read-only	The time, in milliseconds, from midnight January 1, 1970, UTC, at which time the last observation was made.
`DifferenceMode`	Read/write	A `boolean`-valued attribute. If it is `true`, the derived gauge is the difference between the value of the observed attribute in the current observation and the observation immediately preceding it. If it is `false`, the derived gauge is simply the value of the observed attribute in the current observation.
`Modulus`	Read/write	The counter's maximum value after which it will "roll over" and start again at zero.
`Notify`	Read/write	A `boolean`-valued attribute that indicates whether or not the monitor should send notifications when its threshold is exceeded.
`Offset`	Read/write	The value to be added to the monitor's threshold after the observed attribute exceeds the current threshold value

Attribute	Type	Description
`Threshold`	Read/write	A value to which the value of the observed attribute is compared. If the observed attribute's value exceeds the threshold, a notification is sent if the value of the counter's `Notify` attribute is `true`.

`CounterMonitor` adds a single new `MonitorNotification` type. A `MonitorNotification` instance of type `jmx.monitor.counter.threshold` is sent whenever the monitor's threshold is exceeded and the value of the monitor's `Notify` attribute is `true`. The `MonitorNotification` field that corresponds to this type is

```
MonitorNotification.THRESHOLD_VALUE_EXCEEDED
// for jmx.monitor.counter.threshold
```

`CounterMonitor` enforces the following constraints on the values of its attributes:

- Values for the `Threshold`, `Offset`, and `Modulus` attributes must all be of an integer type—that is, `Byte`, `Integer`, `Short`, or `Long`.
- The integer type of the `Threshold`, `Offset`, and `Modulus` attribute values must match that of the observed attribute.

Violating either of these constraints will cause a `MonitorNotification` instance of type `jmx.monitor.error.threshold` to be sent when `CounterMonitor` is started.

The logical model for `CounterMonitor` is simple: The monitor makes periodic observations of the counter attribute's value, and the first time that value exceeds the value of the monitor's `Threshold` attribute, a `MonitorNotification` instance of type `jmx.monitor.counter.threshold` is sent. In practice, several issues arise that make the actual implementation more complex:

- What happens after the threshold is exceeded and the appropriate notification sent? If the monitor is going to generate any further notifications, the value of its `Threshold` attribute will have to be increased. Who is responsible for increasing it?

- Because they are represented in computer memory, most counters have a finite range of values; for example, a counter stored in a Java `byte` can take on positive values between 0 and 127. When the value of a counter is incremented past its upper bound, it "rolls over" and becomes 0 again. How does `CounterMonitor` handle this behavior?

Whereas the management application could take responsibility for increasing `CounterMonitor`'s `Threshold` attribute when it receives a `jmx.monitor.counter.threshold` notification, `CounterMonitor` provides its own mechanism for addressing this issue. Whenever the value of the observed attribute exceeds the value of `CounterMonitor`'s `Threshold` attribute, the monitor sends the appropriate notification and then computes a new value for its `Threshold` attribute by adding the value of its `Offset` attribute to the current `Threshold` attribute value:

```
Threshold_new = Threshold_current + Offset
```

Now we will be notified the first time the value of the observed counter attribute exceeds this new threshold. This behavior allows management applications to receive periodic notifications based on the value of a counter attribute—for example, every hundred requests.

`CounterMonitor`'s `Modulus` attribute addresses the second issue. When the monitor is configured, its `Modulus` attribute should be set to the observed attribute's maximum value. The `Modulus` value is then used in the computation of the new `Threshold` value. The pseudocode that follows illustrates this computation:

```
if (Threshold_current + Offset > Modulus) then
  Threshold_new = Threshold_original
else
  Threshold_new = Threshold_current + Offset
```

For example, assume that the maximum value of the observed attribute is `64`. Suppose we configure a `CounterMonitor` instance for this attribute with an initial `Threshold` value of `16` and an `Offset` value of `16`. This configuration will work fine until the observed attribute rolls over at 64 while the `Threshold` value is increased to 80. Setting the `Modulus` value to 64 allows us to avoid this unfortunate situation.

Finally, `CounterMonitor` has two modes of operation. The first, raw mode, is the default; in *raw mode* the monitor's derived gauge is the raw value of the observed attribute. In *difference mode*, which we enable by setting the value of the monitor's `DifferenceMode` attribute to `true`, the derived gauge is the difference between the current value of the observed attribute and its previous value. If the difference is negative, because of a rollover between observations, `Modulus` is added to the difference. In `DifferenceMode`, `CounterMonitor` measures a *rate*; so, for example, if the observed attribute is `TotalRequests` and the monitor's `GranularityPeriod` is one minute, by using `DifferenceMode` we can monitor the number of requests per minute without adding any additional instrumentation to the observed MBean.

6.2.4.1 Using CounterMonitor

Let's use the `DifferenceMode` technique to monitor an Apache server for traffic spikes. `ApacheStatusMBean` has two counter attributes: `TotalAccesses` and `TotalKBytes`; we are interested in the latter. The `setupTrafficRate-Monitor()` method creates and configures an instance of `CounterMonitor` that will do the job.

```
package net.jnjmx.ch6;

import javax.management.*;
import javax.management.monitor.*;

import net.jnjmx.ch3.Apache;
import net.jnjmx.ch3.ApacheMBean;

public class ApacheMonitor {
...
public ObjectName setupTraffidRateMonitor(MBeanServer mbs,
    ObjectName server) throws Exception {
  /* Assume ApacheStatus object names are of the form:
   *     <domain>:type=ApacheStatus,url=<URL of the server we're
   *     interested in>
   */
  String url = server.getKeyProperty("url");
  ObjectName mon = new ObjectName(
    "monitors:type=Counter,attr=TotalTraffic,url=" + url);
  mbs.createMBean("javax.management.monitor.CounterMonitor",
    mon);

  AttributeList al = new AttributeList();
  al.add(new Attribute("ObservedObject", server));
  al.add(new Attribute("ObservedAttribute", "TotalKBytes");
```

```
    al.add(new Attribute("GranularityPeriod", 60000);
    al.add(new Attribute("Modulus", new Long(4294967295));
    al.add(new Attribute("DifferenceMode", new Boolean(true));
    al.add(new Attribute("Threshold", new Long(7500));
    AttributeList sl = mbs.setAttributes(mon, al);
    // Check to make sure all of the attributes were set

    return mon;
  }
  ...
}
```

The only mysterious part of the configuration is the `Modulus` setting. Where did we get the number 4294967295? A quick look at the source to Apache's `mod_status` module reveals that an unsigned `long` value is used to hold the `TotalKBytes` value. In C, the largest number an unsigned `long` value can represent is 4294967295—hence the `Modulus` setting.

Once the traffic rate monitor is configured, the management application can add a notification listener that takes the appropriate action when a traffic spike is detected by the monitor.

6.2.5 GaugeMonitor

A *gauge*, like a counter, is a numeric attribute. Unlike a counter, the value of a gauge may increase and decrease over time. Transfer rate, hit rate, average wait time, and so forth are all examples of gauges. In the management interface presented by `ApacheStatus`, the `ReqPerSec` attribute is a gauge.

Management applications that monitor gauge attributes usually do so to see that their values fall into a range of "acceptable" values—neither too high nor too low. When a gauge's value falls outside the range of acceptable values, the management application needs to be notified so that it can take the appropriate action. Management applications may also want to be notified when the gauge's value falls back into the acceptable range so that corrective actions—for example, blocking new connection requests—can be terminated.

The `GaugeMonitorMBean` interface adds seven attributes to the management interface defined by `MonitorMBean`. These attributes are listed in Table 6.7.

Unlike `StringMonitor` and `CounterMonitor`, `GaugeMonitor` also defines an operation:

```
public void setThresholds(Number high, Number low)
```

Table 6.7 GaugeMonitor-Specific Attributes

Attribute	Type	Description
DerivedGauge	Read-only	The most recently observed value of the observed attribute.
DerivedGaugeTimeStamp	Read-only	The time, in milliseconds, from midnight January 1, 1970, UTC, at which time the last observation was made.
DifferenceMode	Read/write	A boolean-valued attribute. If it is true, the derived gauge is the difference between the value of the observed attribute in the current observation and that of the observation immediately preceding it. If it is false, the derived gauge is simply the value of the observed attribute in the current observation.
HighThreshold	Read-only	A number that the value of the observed attribute should not exceed.
LowThreshold	Read-only	A number that the value of the observed attribute should always exceed.
NotifyHigh	Read/write	A boolean-valued attribute that indicates whether or not the monitor should send notifications when HighThreshold is exceeded.
NotifyLow	Read/write	A boolean-valued attribute that indicates whether or not the monitor should send notifications when LowThreshold is not exceeded.

The somewhat unfortunately named setThresholds() method (the *set* name makes it easy to mistake it for an attribute) establishes values for GaugeMonitor's HighThreshold and LowThreshold attributes in a single call. Why not make these two attributes read/write—that is, provide independent setters for each of them—and avoid the confusion? At first blush that seems like a reasonable approach; it turns out, however, that GaugeMonitor's behavior depends on having meaningful values for *both* of these attributes. If their values were established independently, there would be no way to guarantee that both values got set, and it's not possible to come up with an appropriate default value for one threshold based on the value of the other.

Two additional MonitorNotification types, listed in Table 6.8, are associated with GaugeMonitor.

As a convenience, the MonitorNotification class defines static final fields representing both of these types. The field identifiers are

```
MonitorNotification.THRESHOLD_HIGH_VALUE_EXCEEDED
// for jmx.monitor.gauge.high
MonitorNotification.THRESHOLD_LOW_VALUE_EXCEEDED
// for jmx.monitor.gauge.low
```

GaugeMonitor enforces the following constraints on its attributes:

- The types of the values specified for the HighThreshold and LowThreshold attributes must match the type of the observed attribute.
- The value of the HighThreshold attribute must be greater than or equal to the value of LowThreshold.

Violating either of these constraints will cause a MonitorNotification instance of type jmx.monitor.error.threshold to be sent when GaugeMonitor is started.

When the value of the observed attribute is increasing and exceeds the value of GaugeMonitor's HighThreshold attribute and GaugeMonitor's NotifyHigh attribute is true, a MonitorNotification instance of type jmx.monitor.gauge.high will be sent. Likewise, when the value of the observed attribute is decreasing and it becomes less than the value of GaugeMonitor's LowThreshold attribute and GaugeMonitor's NotifyLow attribute is true, a MonitorNotification instance of type jmx.monitor.gauge.low

Table 6.8 GaugeMonitor-Specific Notification Types

Notification Type	Description
jmx.monitor.gauge.high	Sent when the value of the observed attribute exceeds the value of GaugeMonitor's HighThreshold attribute.
jmx.monitor.gauge.low	Sent when the value of the observed attribute is less than the value of GaugeMonitor's LowThreshold attribute.

will be sent. In both of these cases, after a notification has been sent, no further notifications will be sent until the observed attribute's value crosses the opposite threshold—for example, after the observed attribute's value exceeds the monitor's `HighThreshold` value, which generates a `jmx.monitor.gauge.high` notification—no further `jmx.monitor.gauge.high` notifications will be sent until the observed attribute's value goes below the monitor's `LowThreshold`.

There are two things to note about the behavior just described. The first is that if the observed attribute's value oscillates across either of the threshold values, only the first threshold crossing will generate a notification. The second is that when an observed attribute's value exceeds `HighThreshold`, a notification is sent only if the value is *increasing*; similarly, when an observed attribute's value is less than `LowThreshold`, a notification is sent only if the value is *decreasing*. This behavior has two implications. First, at least two observations are required before a notification can be sent from `GaugeMonitor`. Second, when `GaugeMonitor` is started, the monitor may see a sequence of values that are all above `HighThreshold`, or below `LowThreshold`, and not send a notification because the values are always decreasing, or increasing, respectively.

Finally, like `CounterMonitor`, `GaugeMonitor` operates in one of two modes: *raw mode*, the default, which uses the actual values of the observed attribute in its comparisons; or *difference mode*, which uses the difference between the current observation and the previous one as the basis for comparison. We enable difference mode by setting the monitor's `DifferenceMode` attribute to `true`.

6.2.5.1 Using GaugeMonitor

Management applications usually create an instance of `GaugeMonitor` for each "boundary" in an attribute's range of acceptable values. So in the general case where there was an upper and a lower bound on the range of acceptable values, a management application would create a `GaugeMonitor` instance for the upper bound and another for the lower bound. Why two? Why not a single `GaugeMonitor` instance with the `HighThreshold` value set to the upper bound and the `LowThreshold` value set to the lower bound? An administrator or a management application needs to know when normal operations have been restored, not just when something has gone wrong. If we use a single monitor, we'll get a notification when the attribute's value goes below the lower bound; that's fine. However, we won't get any more notifications until the attribute's value exceeds the upper bound; that's not fine. If we take some action to bring the attribute's value up, we want to know as soon as the value is acceptable again, not when it becomes unacceptable on the other side of the range.

How does all this apply to our ApacheMonitor management application? The Apache MBean's management interface includes several gauge attributes. Let's pick one and monitor it. The ReqPerSec attribute is one of the Apache MBean gauges; how we monitor it depends on our site. For example, if this is a product support site, we are probably concerned only about the site being inundated with requests; lack of traffic isn't an issue (if the site is not getting any requests, our product must be so wonderful that customers don't need support). On the other hand, if we're running a commercial site, we're still concerned about too many requests but we also want to know if we're not at least receiving some minimum level of traffic.

For the sake of simplicity, let's assume that this is a product support site and all we're concerned about is receiving more requests than we can handle—say, 100 requests per second. In that case we'll create a single instance of GaugeMonitor with a HighThreshold value of 100 and a LowThreshold value of 95. The code in the setupRPSMonitor() method presented here does the job:

```
package net.jnjmx.ch6;

import javax.management.*;
import javax.management.monitor.*;

import net.jnjmx.ch3.Apache;
import net.jnjmx.ch3.ApacheMBean;

public class ApacheMonitor {
...
  public ObjectName setupRPSMonitor(MBeanServer mbs,
      ObjectName server) throws Exception {
    /* Assume ApacheStatus object names are of the form:
     *    <domain>:type=ApacheStatus,url=<URL of the server we're
     *    interested in>
     */
    String url = server.getKeyProperty("url");
    ObjectName mon = new ObjectName(
      "monitors:type=Gauge,attr=RequestsPerSecond,url=" +
      url);
   mbs.createMBean("javax.management.monitor.GaugeMonitor", mon);

    AttributeList al = new AttributeList();
    al.add(new Attribute("ObservedObject", server));
    al.add(new Attribute("ObservedAttribute", "ReqPerSec");
    al.add(new Attribute("GranularityPeriod", new Long(60000));
```

```
        al.add(new Attribute("NotifyHigh", new Boolean(true));
        al.add(new Attribute("NotifyLow", new Boolean(true));
        AttributeList sl = mbs.setAttributes(mon, al);
        // Check to make sure all of the attributes were set

        mbs.invoke(mon,
                   "setThresholds",
                   new Object[] { new Float(100.0), new Float(95.0) },
                   new String[] { "float", "float" });

        return mon;
    }
...
}
```

Now we can add a notification listener to this instance of `GaugeMonitor` and perhaps react to `MonitorNotification` instances of type `jmx.monitor.gauge.high` by instructing the server to return a "busy" page when new requests arrive and then restore service when we get a subsequent `MonitorNotification` instance of type `jmx.monitor.gauge.low`.

6.3 Summary

Monitors autonomously observe the values of MBean's attributes. They help automate an essential aspect of every management application. This chapter has explored the features and usage patterns common to all the standard JMX monitors. We have also looked at each of the separate types of monitors in detail. Although they are essential, monitors aren't the only service component that JMX offers. In the next chapter we'll examine the others—the services that JMX provides to handle simple scheduling tasks, dynamic configuration of the MBeanServer, and management of inter-MBean relationships.

CHAPTER 7

JMX Agent Services

Agent services are MBeans that are distinguished from other MBeans that represent managed resources by the roles they play and functions they provide rather than by the interfaces they support. A service's role may be management oriented; for example, monitoring attribute values is an obvious management-oriented service that is supported in JMX by the monitor agent services described in Chapter 6. Another management-oriented service is a *status aggregator* that examines the status of a set of related MBeans to determine the status of a higher-level MBean in an application. Alternatively, an agent service may play a more utilitarian role, like the XML service described in Chapter 4 that supports management applications by instantiating model MBeans from an XML file and persisting model MBeans to an XML file. In this chapter we describe the JMX agent services that must be provided by every JMX implementation: the timer service, the MLet service, and the relation service. We also discuss the connector services that provide remote access to an otherwise local MBeanServer.

7.1 Timer Service

Many management tasks are schedule driven. Incremental workstation backups are scheduled to take place every morning at 2:00 A.M. Web server logs are collected and aggregated every hour. New content or a new service is scheduled to go online at midnight. The list goes on and on. To help developers and administrators handle scheduled activities, JMX provides a basic timer service.

Instances of the timer service send JMX notifications at specified dates and times. The notifications may be scheduled to occur just once or to recur with a given frequency. The number of times a recurring notification is sent may be specified beforehand, or the notification may continue to recur indefinitely. Management applications react to timer service notifications by listening for them with notification listeners.

The code in Listing 7.1 illustrates the basics of timer service use.

Listing 7.1 A Service That Uses Timer Service to Restart

```
RestartingServiceMBean.java
package net.jnjmx.ch7;

public interface RestartingServiceMBean {
  void start();
  void stop();
}

RestartingService.java
package net.jnjmx.ch7;

import java.util.Date;

import javax.management.MBeanServer;
import javax.management.MBeanServerFactory;
import javax.management.Notification;
import javax.management.NotificationListener;
import javax.management.ObjectName;
import javax.management.timer.Timer;

public class RestartingService implements RestartingServiceMBean,
    NotificationListener {
  private long tzero = -1;

  public RestartingService() {}

  /** Start the service and remember the start time
   */
  public void start() {
    if (tzero < 0) {
      tzero = System.currentTimeMillis();
```

```
      System.out.println("Restarted at: " + tzero);
    }
  }

  /** Stop the service if it is running
   */
  public void stop() {
    if (tzero > 0)
      tzero = -1;
  }

  /** Restart the service
   */
  public void handleNotification(Notification notification, Object hb) {
    stop();
    start();
  }

  public static void main(String[] args) throws Exception {
    MBeanServer mbs = MBeanServerFactory.createMBeanServer();

    // Create a timer service instance and start it
    ObjectName ton = new ObjectName("examples:id=RestartTimer");
    mbs.createMBean("javax.management.timer.Timer", ton);
    mbs.invoke(ton, "start", new Object[] {}, new String[] {});

    // Schedule a jnjmx.examples.restart notification every 24 hours
    Integer nid = (Integer) mbs.invoke(ton,
                                   "addNotification",
                                   new Object[] {"jnjmx.examples.restart",
                                                 "restart",
                                                 null,
                                                 tomorrow(),
                                                 new Long(Timer.ONE_DAY) },
                                   new String[] {"java.lang.String",
                                                 "java.lang.String",
                                                 "java.lang.Object",
                                                 "java.util.Date",
                                                 "long" });

    // Listen for restart notifications
    mbs.addNotificationListener(ton,
                                new RestartingService(),
                                null,
                                new Object());
```

```
      // If you have something useful to do, do it here ...
      Thread.sleep(Timer.ONE_DAY + 7);
    }

    /** Compute 24 hours from now in milliseconds
     */
    private static Date tomorrow() {
      return new Date(System.currentTimeMillis() + Timer.ONE_DAY);
    }
}
```

To use the timer service we need an instance of it, so we use the MBean-Server's `createMBean()` method to create and register one. Now we can schedule a notification. We always have to specify the notification type, associated message, user data, and date. The type, message, and user data will be included in the notification that is delivered to listeners at the appointed date. The notification *period* (the number of milliseconds to delay between recurring notifications) and the number of times the notification is to be sent may be specified as well; if we don't specify how many times to send the notification, it will be sent indefinitely. Finally, each notification is identified by an ID, an integer that uniquely identifies the notification in the context of a given timer service instance.

To listen for the notification we scheduled, we attach an instance of `NotificationListener` to the timer service instance. When the notification is sent, the listener's `handleNotification()` method will be invoked with an instance of `TimerNotification` that encapsulates all of the information associated with the notification when it was scheduled.

7.1.1 The Notification Queue

The JMX timer service is organized around a priority *queue* of scheduled notifications. Each entry in the queue is an ordered pair consisting of a date and a *set* of notifications. The queue is prioritized by date so that the earliest—that is, next chronological—date is at the head of the queue. Entries are added to the queue via one of the timer service's `addNotification()` methods. Entries are removed from the queue either by the timer service itself after the notification has been sent the specified number of times, or via one of its `removeNotification()` methods.

Figure 7.1 illustrates the timer service's use of its notification queue.

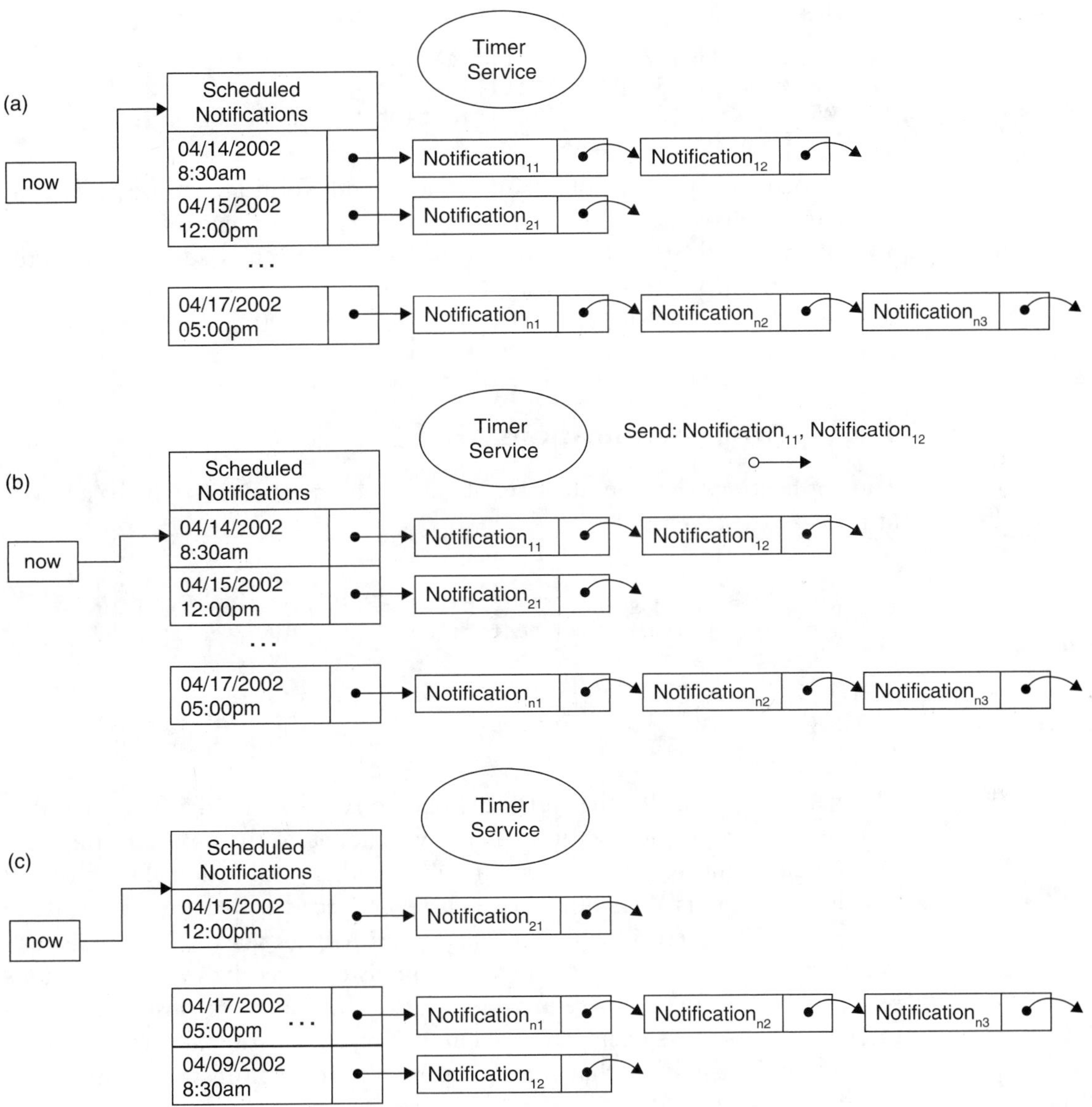

Figure 7.1 Notification Queues at Three Points in Time. (a) The notification queue prior to 8:30 A.M., April 14, 2002. (b) At 8:30 A.M., April 14, 2002, Notification$_{11}$ and Notification$_{12}$ are sent to all of this timer service's listeners. (c) The notification queue prior to 12:00 A.M., April 15, 2002.

The queue in Figure 7.1 contains three entries:

```
1.(08:30am 04/14/2002, {Notification_11, Notification_12})
2.(12:00am 04/15/2002, {Notification_21})
3.(05:00pm 04/17/2002, {Notification_n1, Notification_n2,
  Notification_n3})
```

At 8:30 A.M. on April 14, 2002, Notification_{11} and Notification_{12} are sent to any listeners that have been added to this timer service instance. Notification_{12} is a recurring notification with a period of five days, so it is added back to the queue in the entry `(8:30am 04/19/2002, {Notification_12})`. Now the timer service will wait until 12:00 A.M. on April 15, 2002, when it will send Notification_{21}.

7.1.2 Timer Notifications

The notifications that the timer service sends are a subclass of the basic JMX `Notification` class:

```
public class TimerNotification extends Notification {
  // package private constructor; only the timer service may
  // create instances
  public Integer getNotificationID() { … }
}
```

The value returned by the `getNotificationID()` method is the identifier associated with this notification when it was added to the notification queue.

Management applications commonly use this notification ID to control which notifications their notification listeners receive. Recall that when we add a `NotificationListener` instance to an MBean via the MBeanServer's `addNotificationListener()` method, our listener receives *all* notifications sent by that MBean unless we provide a `NotificationFilter` instance to indicate which ones we're really interested in. Listing 7.2 is a simple `NotificationFilter` implementation that filters `TimerNotification` instances according to their notification IDs.

Listing 7.2 A Notification ID–Based Instance of `NotificationFilter`

```
import java.util.HashSet;

import javax.management.Notification;
import javax.management.NotificationFilter;
```

```
import javax.management.timer.TimerNotification;

public class TimerFilter implements NotificationFilter {
  private final HashSet idset;

  /**
   * Create a new TimerFilter instance with no notification IDs enabled
   */
  public TimerFilter() {
    this(new HashSet());
  }

  /**
   * Create a new TimerFilter instance with the specified notification IDs
   * enabled
   * @param idset - the set of enabled notification IDs
   */
  public TimerFilter(Collection ids) {
    this.idset = new HashSet(ids);
  }

  /**
   * Determine whether or not the given notification is enabled
   * @param notification - the notification in question
   * @return true if notification is an enabled TimerNotification instance
   */
  public boolean isNotificationEnabled(Notification notification) {
    if !(notification instanceof TimerNotification) {
      return false;
    }
    return idset.contains(notification.getNotificationID());
  }

  /**
   * Add a notification ID to the enabled set
   * @param id - notification ID to enable
   */
  public void enableNotificationID(Integer id) {
    idset.add(id);
  }

  /**
   * Remove a notification ID from the enabled set
   * @param id - notification ID to disable
   */
```

```
  public void disableNotificationID(Integer id) {
    id.remove(id);
  }
}
```

If a management application were interested in only notifications with IDs in the set {7, 11, 13}, it would create an instance of `TimerFilter`, enable those IDs, and then call `addNotificationListener()` with a listener and the `TimerFilter` instance it just configured:

```
...
TimerFilter tf = new TimerFilter();
tf.enableNotificationID(new Integer(7));
tf.enableNotificationID(new Integer(11));
tf.enableNotificationID(new Integer(13));
mbs.addNotificationListener(objname, listener, tf, new Object());
```

If the application loses interest in the notification with ID 11, it simply disables that notification via `TimerFilter`:

```
...
tf.disableNotificationID(new Integer(11));
```

Now invocations of `handleNotification()` will be limited to notifications 7 and 13.

7.1.3 The Timer Class

The `Timer` class implements the management interface defined by the `TimerMBean` interface. That interface is composed of a set of attributes that provide information about the notification queue controlled by the timer and a set of operations that allow you to start and stop the timer itself, add notifications to and remove notifications from the notification queue, and get information about a specific notification on the notification queue.

7.1.3.1 TimerMBean Attributes

The `TimerMBean` interface defines the five attributes listed in Table 7.1.

Table 7.1 TimerMBean Attributes

Attribute	Type	Description
AllNotificationIDs	Read-only	A Vector-valued attribute containing the notification ID for each notification currently on the notification queue
NbNotifications	Read-only	An int-valued attribute indicating the number of notifications currently on the notification queue
SendPastNotifications	Read/write	A boolean-valued attribute that indicates whether or not the timer should send notifications whose scheduled date and time have passed
Active	Read-only	A boolean-valued attribute that indicates whether or not the timer has been started
Empty	Read-only	A boolean-valued attribute that indicates whether or not the timer's notification queue contains any entries

7.1.3.2 Timer Notification Operations

The TimerMBean interface defines a suite of addNotification() and removeNotification() operations that management applications and MBeans use to schedule their notifications:

```
public Integer addNotification(String type,
                               String message,
                               Object userdata,
                               Date date)
public Integer addNotification(String type,
                               String message,
                               Object userdata,
                               Date date,
                               long period)
public Integer addNotification(String type,
                               String message,
                               Object userdata,
```

```
                          Date date,
                          long period,
                          long nbOccurences)
```

All of the addNotification() operations construct a TimerNotification object, place it on the notification queue, and return an Integer ID for the notification rather than a reference to the notification itself. The only difference among the three versions is whether the new notification's period and number of occurrences are specified. Table 7.2 describes the notification's scheduling behavior in each possible case.

The timer service doesn't support scheduling notifications in the past; that is, the value of the date parameter can't be earlier than the current date and time. If it is, all of the addNotification() methods throw an IllegalArgumentException.

We can remove notifications en masse, or all notifications of a specified type, by calling removeAllNotifications(), or we can remove just the notification with a specific notification ID using removeNotification():

```
public void removeAllNotifications()
public void removeNotifications(String type)
public void removeNotification(Integer id)
```

Table 7.2 Timer Notification Scheduling Behaviors

period and nbOccurence Values	**Scheduling Behavior**
None	The notification is a one-shot notification. It will be sent once and not rescheduled.
period	The notification is a recurring notification. It will be sent at its scheduled date and time and then rescheduled to occur in period milliseconds. It will continue to be rescheduled until it is removed from the notification queue.
period and nbOccurence	The notification is a recurring notification. It will be sent at its scheduled date and time and then rescheduled to occur in period milliseconds. It will be rescheduled until it has occurred nbOccurence times.

Finally, the `TimerMBean` interface supplies methods that access the information about scheduled notifications:

```
public Vector getNotificationIDs(String type)
public String getNotificationMessage(Integer id)
public Object getNotificationUserData(Integer id)
public Long getNbOccurences(Integer id)
public Long getPeriod(Integer id)
public Date getDate(Integer id)
```

Use `getNotificationIDs()` to obtain a vector containing the notification IDs for all scheduled notifications of a specified type. Except for `getPeriod()` and `getNbOccurences()` (yes, *occurrences* is misspelled in the method name), each of the other five methods does just what its name implies: returns the value of the notification field indicated by its name. The `getPeriod()` method returns the specified notification's period unless the notification is a one-time occurrence, in which case `getPeriod()` returns `null`. The `getNbOccurences()` method returns the number of occurrences *remaining* on the specified notification's schedule; if the notification recurs indefinitely, a `null` value is returned.

7.1.3.3 Starting and Stopping

The final timer methods are responsible for controlling the service's execution:

```
public void start()
public void stop()
```

When `start()` is called, the `Timer` instance begins processing its notification queue and sending notifications at the appointed dates and times. Calling `stop()` halts the timer's processing of the notification queue. Of course nothing is ever that simple. What happens if a notification's appointed date and time come and go before the timer is started? It depends on the value of the `SendPastNotifications` attribute. `SendPastNotifications` is a `boolean`-valued attribute, so there are only two possibilities. Table 7.3 explains what happens in each.

Setting `SendPastNotifications` to `true` will ensure that no scheduled notifications are "lost" as the result of a delay in starting the timer service. The downside is that a "notification storm" may occur when the timer service is started. In a notification storm, tens or hundreds of notifications arrive simultaneously and are dispatched to handlers, which then take some action

Table 7.3 The Effect of `SendPastNotifications` on Timer Service Startup

`SendPastNotifications` Value	Timer Service Behavior
`True`	Any one-shot notifications whose scheduled times have passed are sent. Any recurring notifications are sent as many times as they should have occurred before the timer was started.
`False`	Any one-shot notifications whose scheduled times have passed are ignored. The notification schedules for any recurring notifications are updated, but no notifications are sent.

in response. At the very least there will be a CPU spike as the notifications are dispatched and handled; the CPU spike may trigger other notifications, which will compound the problem, possibly snowballing into a system crash.

7.2 Dynamic MBean Loading Service

One of Java's great strengths as a software platform is its ability to dynamically load new classes. The ability to load secure, platform-independent code over the network at both the client (applets) and the server (servlets) has played a major role in the Java success story. It should come as no surprise, then, that JMX takes advantage of this same capability in the management domain; nor should it be hard to guess what the mechanism is called: MLets.

7.2.1 The MLET Tag

The MLet service is responsible for dynamically loading new MBeans into the MBeanServer. How does it know which MBeans to load and where to load them from? It reads one or more `MLET` tags from an MLet file. An *MLet file* is just a text file that contains a set of `MLET` tags. `MLET` *tags* are like the `APPLET` tags found in HTML documents that cause a browser to load Java applets. Here's an `MLET` tag that will cause the MLet service to load a `SessionPool` MBean:

```
sessionpool.mlet
<MLET CLASS=net.jnjmx.ch3.todd.SessionPool
```

```
        ARCHIVE="todd.jar"
        CODEBASE=http://www.jnjmx.net/
        NAME=book:id=SessionPool>
                <ARG TYPE=int VALUE=16>
</MLET>
```

The interaction diagram in Figure 7.2 illustrates the process that the MLet service uses to go from the `MLET` tag in `sessionpool.mlet` to having a `SessionPool` MBean loaded in the MBeanServer.

The MLet service reads the `MLET` tag from `sessionpool.mlet` and then loads the `net.jnjmx.ch3.todd.SessionPool` class from http://www.jmx.net/todd.jar. Once the class has been loaded, the MLet service creates an instance of the class and registers it with the MBeanServer under the name `book:id=SessionPool`.

There are a couple of things worth noting even about this simple example. The first is that the `SessionPool` MBean class file lives on a Web server,

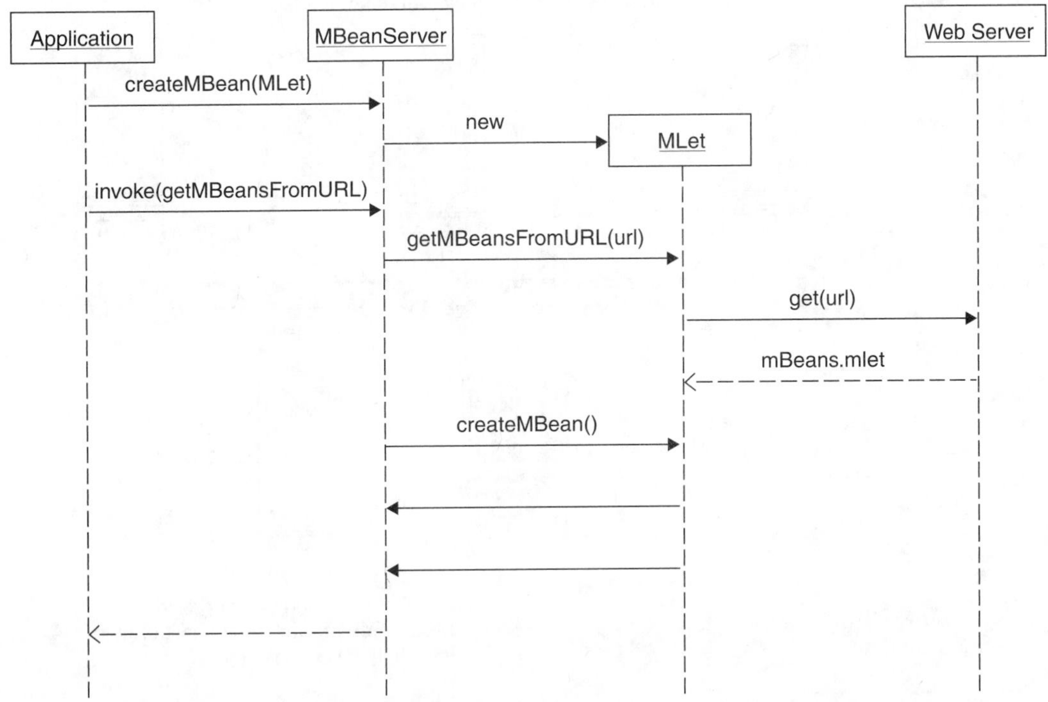

Figure 7.2 Processing an `MLET` Tag

not necessarily on the machine where the MBeanServer is running. This arrangement markedly simplifies software installation and upgrade; rather than installing `.jar` files, we just install appropriately configured `.mlet` files and use the MLet service to fetch the class files on demand. For upgrades, new `.jar` files are dropped on the Web server and the applications that use them are restarted; the application need not be restarted immediately because the applications will continue to run using the old class files. When they are eventually restarted, they will load the new ones. This allows management systems to "push down" manageability automatically, where it's needed, when it's needed.

The second thing to note is that the `sessionpool.mlet` file also does not have to be on the MBeanServer's machine. It can be read via a URL and therefore could also be remote. That means that an administrator could use a single `.mlet` file to bootstrap and configure a whole set of MBeanServers, as illustrated in Figure 7.3.

MBean's MLet services all contact the Configuration server
at startup for configuration information and MBean code.
Administrators use the console
to create and modify configuration
information.
Admin Console
config.
mlet
Configuration Server
The Configuration server provides
MBeanServers with their configuration
information via config.mlet.

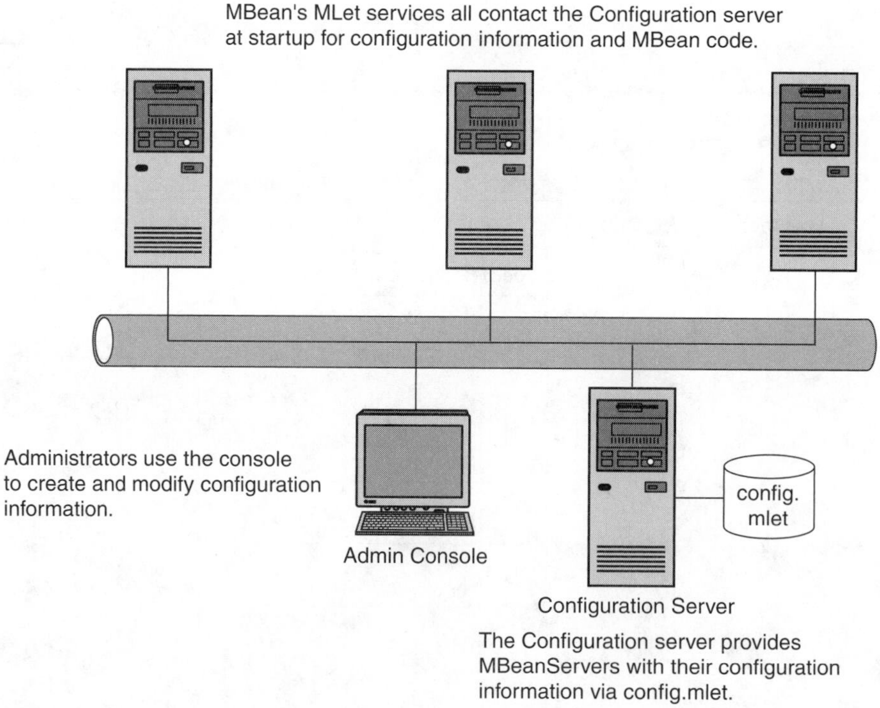

Figure 7.3 Centralized Configuration of Multiple MBeanServers Using the MLet Service

Finally, note that we can generalize this capability. As a management application discovers resources that it knows how to manage—a new device, a database instance, or a Web server, for example—it can dynamically load and configure the necessary MBeans. This approach minimizes the management application's size; it loads only the MBeans it needs, without constraining the range of resources the application can handle. This approach also allows resources that don't provide their own MBeans to be managed by management applications.

7.2.2 MLet Examples

In Chapter 6 we used the `Apache` MBean to explore the use of JMX monitors. The sample code for the `ApacheMonitor` application presented in that chapter used `createMBean()` to instantiate `Apache` MBean. In this section we will modify `ApacheMonitor` to use the MLet service to create instances of `Apache` MBean.

There are two ways to use the MLet service to create MBean instances:

1. Directly, to create MBeans specified by a set of `MLET` tags
2. Indirectly, by specifying a `loader` parameter in a call to `createMBean()`

The first approach moves the configuration of the management application's MBeanServer out of the application. To add some more MBeans to the management server, all an administrator has to do is change a text file on a Web server; no Java is required. The second approach allows developers to take advantage of Java's ability to load code dynamically from remote sources.

Let's examine the first approach first. Rather than calling `createMBean()`, the `ApacheMonitor` application will now use the MLet service's `getMBeansFromURL()` method. Here is the updated version of `ApacheMonitor`:

```
package net.jnjmx.ch7;

import javax.management.*;
import javax.management.monitor.*;

public ApacheMonitor {
  public static class StateNotificationListener implements
        NotificationListener {
    public void handleNotification(Notification notification,
        Object handback) {
      // Take some action when a notification is received from
      // the State attribute monitor
    }
```

```
    public static void main(String[] args) throws Exception {
      if (args.length < 1) {
        System.err.println(
            "Usage: java net.jnjmx.ch7.ApacheMonitor <mlet url>");
        System.exit(-1);
      }

      // Create the MBean to be monitored
      MBeanServer mbs = MBeanServerFactory.createMBeanServer();
      ObjectName loader = new ObjectName("loaders:name=Apache");
      mbs.createMBean("javax.management.loading.MLet", loader);

      // Load Apache MBean from the MLet file specified on the
      // command line
      mbs.invoke(loader,
                 "getMBeansFromURL",
                 new Object[] { args[0] },
                 new String[] { "java.lang.String" });

      // remainder of the ApacheMonitor application: set up
      // monitors, notification listeners, etc.
      ...
    }
  ...
  }
```

The first difference is the creation of the MLet service. Once we have an `MLet` instance in the MBeanServer, we can invoke its methods. That's the second difference; we call the MLet service's `getMBeansFromURL()` method via the MBeanServer and pass in a `String` object representing the URL of the `.mlet` file. That's all there is to it. The `getMBeansFromURL()` method will read the `.mlet` file, interpret the `MLET` tags it contains, and create the specified MBeans. To complete the picture, here is an `.mlet` file that specifies an `Apache` MBean:

```
apache.mlet
<MLET CLASS=net.jnjmx.ch3.Apache
      ARCHIVE="apache.jar"
      CODEBASE=http://www.jnjmx.net/jars
      NAME=resources:type=Apache,url=www.jnjmx.net>
<ARG TYPE=String VALUE=www.jnjmx.net>
</MLET>
```

Now for the `createMBean()` alternative. Recall from Chapter 5 that two of the MBeanServer's four `createMBean()` methods take `loader` parameters. It turns out that a loader is the object name of an MLet service instance, and `createMBean()` uses that MLet service to load the desired MBean's class rather than using the system `ClassLoader` class. Because `MLet` extends `URLClassLoader`, everything works out rather nicely. Here is a version of `ApacheMonitor` that uses this technique:

```
package net.jnjmx.ch7;

import javax.management.*;
import javax.management.monitor.*;

public ApacheMonitor {
  public static class StateNotificationListener implements
        NotificationListener {
    public void handleNotification(Notification notification,
        Object handback) {
      // Take some action when a notification is received from
      // the State attribute monitor
    }

  public static void main(String[] args) throws Exception {
    // Create the MBean to be monitored
    MBeanServer mbs = MBeanServerFactory.createMBeanServer();
    ObjectName loader = new ObjectName("loaders:name=Apache");
    mbs.createMBean("javax.management.loading.MLet", loader);

    // Add the URL for the ApacheMBean classes to the MLet's
    // search path
    mbs.invoke(loader,
          "addURL",
          new Object[] { "http://www.jnjmx.net/jars/apache.jar" },
          new String[] { "java.lang.String" });

    ObjectName server = new ObjectName(
        "resources.http:type=Apache,url=www.jnjmx.net");
    mbs.createMBean("net.jmx.ch3.Apache",
                    server,
                    loader,
                    new Object[] { "www.jnjmx.net" },
                    new String[] { "java.lang.String" });
```

```
    // remainder of the ApacheMonitor application: set up
    // monitors, notification listeners, etc.
    ...
  }
...
}
```

After creating the MLet instance, we invoke its addURL() method. Every MLet instance maintains an array of URLs that it will search for classes and resources during the loading process; addURL() adds an element to that array and thereby extends the search path. The invocation here adds the .jar file that contains the Apache MBean class file on the www.jnjmx.net server. Finally, we call createMBean() as before, except we include the object name of the MLet service that we just configured. Now createMBean() will use the MLet instance to load the Apache MBean class.

7.2.3 The MLet API

The MLet class implements the management interface defined by the MLetMBean interface. MLet also extends the URLClassLoader class and so is a full-fledged class loader. That is a useful fact to keep in mind if your application happens to have direct access to an MLet object reference. As usual, however, management applications that access an MLet via the MBeanServer interface may use only the attributes and operations defined by the MLetMBean interface.

7.2.3.1 MLet Constructors

There are four MLet constructors to choose from:

```
public MLet()
public MLet(URL[] urls)
public MLet(URL[] urls, ClassLoader parent)
public MLet(URL[] urls, ClassLoader parent,
    URLStreamHandlerFactory factory)
```

In each of the constructors the urls parameter specifies a set of URLs to search for classes; think of it as a classpath. So what good is the first, no-args, constructor? It turns out that because the MLetMBean interface defines addURL() methods that add URLs to the search path, even the no-args version provides some value.

The third and fourth versions allow us to specify an alternative delegation parent class loader. The final version allows us to include an instance of `URLStreamHandlerFactory`. If the array of URLs includes URLs for nonstandard protocols (e.g., a URL beginning with *https*), the `MLet` instance uses the specified `URLStreamHandlerFactory` to deal with those URLs.

What's an *alternative delegation parent class loader*, and why would you want to specify one? Recall that beginning in Java 2—that is, version 1.2—the set of class loaders in a JVM is arranged in a tree rooted at the "bootstrap," or "primordial," class loader. When asked to load a class, a class loader first delegates the task to its parent, which recursively delegates to *its* parent, and so on, until the process reaches the root of the tree. Only if the parent fails to load the class does the original class loader attempt to load it. By default, an `MLet` instance's parent class loader is the one that loaded the `MLet` class itself. Often the default is fine. There are, however, occasions when an application wants a different parent class loader—for example, if it wants to bypass the system class loader and load only classes from its own search path. On those occasions the application will use one of the `MLet` constructors that takes a `ClassLoader` parameter.

7.2.3.2 MLetBean Attributes

The `MLetMBean` interface defines two attributes, as shown in Table 7.4.

7.2.3.3 MLet Operations

The MLet operations break down into three categories: search path extension, MBean loading, and resource access. As mentioned in Section 7.2.3.1, two methods are provided to add additional URLs to `MLet`'s search path:

Table 7.4 `MLetBean` Attributes

Attribute	Type	Description
`URLs`	Read-only	A URL array–valued attribute that contains the current search path
`LibraryDirectory`	Read/write	A `String`-valued attribute that indicates where any native libraries required by classes that the MLet loads should be placed prior to loading those libraries

```
public void addURL(String url)
public void addURL(URL url)
```

The responsibility for reading an `.mlet` file, loading the MBeans specified by the `MLET` tags it contains, and registering them with the MBeanServer falls to the `getMBeansFromURL()` methods:

```
public Set getMBeansFromURL(String url)
public Set getMBeansFromURL(URL url)
```

The `url` parameter has nothing to do with the `MLet` instance's search path. Instead it tells the MLet where to find the `.mlet` file. The return value is a set of object instances, one for each of the MBeans that the call caused to be registered.

Finally, three operations provide access to resources found in `MLet`'s search path:

```
public Enumeration getResources(String name)
public URL getResource(String name)
public InputStream getResourceAsStream(String name)
```

The first two operations return URLs for the named resource, not the resource itself. The `getResources()` method returns an `Enumeration` of all the URLs for the specified resource. The `getResource()` method returns a single URL to the specified `String` resource. Unlike the `getResource()` methods, `getResourceAsStream()` returns an `InputStream` instance from which the contents of the named resource may be read.

7.3 Relation Service

MBeans seldom exist in isolation. They are usually clustered together in small groups of interrelated MBeans. For example, the MBean representing a managed device is related to the monitors that observe its attributes and perhaps to a timer service instance. A managed application provides a more complex example. In that case we have relationships between the application's managed components and between the monitors and services associated with each of those components.

Management applications need a simple, efficient way to access related sets of MBeans. One possible solution would be to use the MBeanServer's query methods to look up all the monitors for a device or to find an application's managed components. To be successful, this approach requires that every MBean consistently follow a specific object-naming convention. Defining such a convention is problematic under the best of circumstances; in the dynamic management environment supported by JMX, where MBeans and management applications from multiple vendors come together, it rapidly becomes unworkable. The JMX relation service addresses this requirement by explicitly modeling the relationships between MBeans.

The relation service implements a dynamic object model that allows management applications to define and instantiate new types of *relations*—associations between multiple MBeans in named roles—at runtime. Once a relation has been defined and one or more instances have been created, other management applications use the relation service to find related sets of MBeans. The relation service is also responsible for monitoring the consistency of each relation under its control. Finally, it is possible, with a little programming, to use relation service facilities to create and manage compound MBeans.

7.3.1 A Simple Example: The SessionPool Relation

Before we jump into the details of the relation service API, let's look at a simple example to make things more concrete.

Resource pooling is a common server-side technique for meeting performance and scalability requirements. Most application servers pool all kinds of things—threads, database connections, even whole JVMs. You may recall that the "time of day daemon," todd, developed in Chapter 2's Quick Tour section (Section 2.6) pooled todd sessions. In the managed version of todd we created the `SessionPoolMBean` interface. In this section we'll demonstrate how to use the relation service to explicitly model the relationships between the `SessionPool` class and its associated JMX components.

Every relation managed by the relation service is an instance of a particular *relation type*. A relation type describes a relation's *roles*. Each role has a name and indicates the class and multiplicity of the MBeans that satisfy that role. For this example we'll define a relation type named `SessionPool` with three roles:

1. **`gauges`** contains at least one but no more than two instances of `GaugeMonitor`; these will be the monitors that observe how many sessions are available and, optionally, the size of the pool.
2. **`timer`** contains at most one instance of the `Timer` class that `SessionPool` uses to send *epoch* notifications.
3. **`pool`** is the `SessionPoolMBean` itself.

Before we do anything else, we need to instantiate the relation service. Because it is an MBean, we can instantiate it via the MBeanServer:

```
ObjectName rson = new ObjectName("todd:id=RelationService");
mbs.createMBean("javax.management.relation.RelationService",
                rson,
                new Object[] { new Boolean(true) },
                new String[] { "boolean" });
```

The `RelationService` constructor takes a single Boolean argument that determines whether or not relations are purged from the service immediately. The alternative is to leave them in place until they are explicitly purged by a call to `purgeRelations()`. The trade-off here is similar to the trade-off between automatic garbage collection and explicit memory deallocation: The former is safer but less efficient than the latter. In this example we go with safety over efficiency.

To create our new relation type, we use the `RelationService`'s `createRelationType()` method. The `createRelationType()` method takes a name and an array of `RoleInfo` instances as arguments. Each element of the `RoleInfo` array provides a description of one of the new relation type's roles. The following code sets up the `RoleInfo` array for our `SessionPool` relation type:

```
RoleInfo[] sproles = new RoleInfo[3];
sproles[0] = new RoleInfo("pool", "net.jnjmx.ch3.todd.SessionPool");
sproles[1] = new RoleInfo("gauges",
                          "javax.management.monitor.GaugeMonitor",
                          true, false, 1, 2, null);
sproles[2] = new RoleInfo("timer",
                          "javax.management.timer.Timer",
                          true, false, 0, 1, null);
```

The `RoleInfo` constructor requires the role name and MBean class parameters. The remaining, optional, parameters are

- **`Readable`**, which indicates whether the role is readable; it defaults to `true`.
- **`Writeable`**, which indicates whether the role is writable; it defaults to `true`.
- **`MinimumDegree`**, which specifies the minimum number of MBeans that may be provided for the role; it defaults to `1`.

- **`MaximumDegree`**, which specifies the maximum number of MBeans that may be provided for the role; it defaults to `1`.
- **`Description`**, which is a text description of the role; it defaults to `null`.

Now we have the necessary raw materials to create our `SessionPool` relation type:

```
mbs.invoke(rson,
           "createRelationType",
           new Object[] { "SessionPool", sproles },
           new String[] { "java.lang.String",
               "[Ljavax.management.relation.RoleInfo)" });
```

The only tricky part in the MBeanServer invocation of `createRelationType()` is the description of the `RoleInfo[]` parameter in the signature array. You have to use a JNI-style signature string—that is, "[L<fully qualified classname>)" [http://java.sun.com/products/jdk/1.2/docs/guide/jni/spec/jniTOC.doc.html].

We instantiate the `SessionPool` relation type via the `RelationService`'s `createRelation()` method. The `createRelation()` signature is

```
public void createRelation(String id, String relname,
    RoleList roles) {}
```

The `id` parameter is a unique identifier for this instance of `RelationService`. The `relname` parameter designates the relation type being instantiated. The final parameter is a list of `Role` values that meet the relation type's `RoleInfo` specifications.

Each `Role` value consists of a role name and a list of object names that play that role in this instance of the relation type. We build up the role list by creating instances of `Role` and then adding them to `RoleList` using the `add()` method:

```
RoleList sprl = new RoleList();
ArrayList poolval = new ArrayList();
poolval.add(new ObjectName("todd:id=SessionPool"));
sprl.add(new Role("pool", poolval));
ArrayList gaugesval = new ArrayList();
gaugesval.add(new ObjectName("todd:id=SessionPoolMonitor"));
sprl.add(new Role("gauges", gaugesval));
```

Finally, we can invoke `createRelation()` to instantiate a `SessionPool` relation type:

```
mbs.invoke(rson, "createRelation",
        new Object[] { "todd.sessionpool", "SessionPool", sprl },
        new String[] { "java.lang.String",
                       "java.lang.String",
                       "javax.management.relation.RoleList" });
```

What's the payoff for all this work? The `RelationService` class has a suite of get methods that provide lots of useful information about the relations under its control. In addition, it has a couple of useful query methods. For example, `RelationService`'s `AllRelationIds` attribute holds a list of the unique IDs associated with its relations. Given a relation ID, we can retrieve the relation's `RoleList`, which we can then iterate over to get the object names of the MBeans in each of the roles. Alternatively, we can start with an object name and use the `findReferencingRelations()` method to determine which relations an MBean is part of. We'll look at the methods of `RelationService` in more detail in the next section.

In the interest of full disclosure, we should point out that using the relation service in todd is overkill. There are only a handful of MBeans in todd, so it is easy to keep track of them. We used todd here because it provided a simple, familiar environment for our sample code. In general the relation service's utility grows as the number of MBeans in a system and the number of management applications that deal with that system increase.

7.3.2 The RelationService Class

The `javax.management.relation` package contains four interfaces and a dozen classes. The `RelationService` class is the core of the package. All of the other classes and interfaces come together in the `RelationService` class, and `RelationService` is the class that users of the package interact with most. Therefore, we will describe many of the package's classes and interfaces in the context of `RelationService`.

The fact that the `RelationService` class implements the `RelationServiceMBean` interface makes it a standard MBean. This also means that from a JMX perspective, `RelationService` has a well-defined management interface consisting of constructors, attributes, operations, and notifications.

7.3.2.1 RelationService Attributes

The RelationService's management interface defines four attributes, which are listed in Table 7.5.

Because RelationService is an MBean, the values of each of these attributes can be retrieved via one of the MBeanServer's getAttribute() methods.

7.3.2.2 RelationType Operations

Two RelationService methods support the creation of new relation types:

```
public void addRelationType(RelationType reltype)
public void createRelationType(String typename, RoleInfo[] roles)
```

We used the createRelationType() method in the SessionPool example. Because the relation type it creates exists only within the confines of the relation service, it is known as an *internal* relation type. The addRelationType()

Table 7.5 RelationService Attributes

Attribute	Type	Description
AllRelationIds	Read-only	A List-valued attribute containing the unique identifier for each relation under RelationService's control.
AllRelationTypeNames	Read-only	A List-valued attribute containing the unique identifier for each relation type defined in RelationService.
PurgeFlag	Read/write	A boolean-valued attribute indicating whether or not a relation should be purged from RelationService as soon as it becomes invalid.
Active	Read-only	A boolean-valued attribute indicating whether or not the relation service is active. A RelationService instance is considered active if it is registered with the MBeanServer.

method is used to create *external* relation types—that is, relation types that exist outside the relation service itself. External relations are represented by the RelationType interface, which defines methods for accessing the relation type's name and role information.

The relation service provides a couple of methods for retrieving information about defined relation types:

```
public RoleInfo getRoleInfo(String typename, String rolename)
public List getRoleInfo(String typename)
```

The former method returns a RoleInfo instance that describes the specified role in the relation type indicated by the typename parameter. The latter method returns a java.util.List object of RoleInfo instances that describes all of the specified relation type's roles.

When a relation type is no longer needed, it can be removed by the removeRelationType() method:

```
public void removeRelationType(String typename)
```

Any relations of the relation type will be removed from the relation service when the relation type is removed.

7.3.2.3 Relation Operations

Two RelationService methods support the creation of new relations:

```
public void addRelation(ObjectName objname)
public void createRelation(String relid, String typename,
    RoleList roles)
```

Like relation types, relations may be internal or external. *Internal* relations are created via createRelation() as we saw in the SessionPool example. *External* relations are instantiated with the addRelation() method.

The RoleList class extends the java.util.ArrayList class and contains the Role values that will be used to instantiate the relation type. Each Role instance consists of a name, which must match one of the roles defined by the relation type, and a list of object names that play that role in this instance.

When a relation is no longer needed, it can be removed by the `removeRelation()` method:

```
public void removeRelation(String relid)
public void purgeRelations()
```

Removing a relation has no effect on any of the MBeans it references. When MBeans are removed from the MBeanServer, the relations they belong to may become invalid; for example, a role is no longer filled, or a cardinality constraint is no longer met. The `purgeRelations()` method checks all the data structures in the relation service and removes all relations that are no longer valid. When the value of the relation service's `PurgeFlag` attribute is `true`, `purgeRelations()` is called automatically whenever a deregistration notification is received from the `MBeanServerDelegate` MBean.

`RelationService` provides a set of three get methods that retrieve information about a particular relation:

```
public RoleResult getAllRoles(String relid)
public String getRelationTypeName(String relid)
public Integer getRoleCardinality(String relid, String rolename)
```

As the name implies, the `getRelationTypeName()` operation returns the name of the given relation ID's relation type. The remaining operations return information about the relation ID's roles. The `getAllRoles()` method returns a `RoleResult` object that contains all of the `RelationService` instance's roles.

What is a `RoleResult` object? It is an object that provides access to several roles of a relation for reading and/or writing. Here is its class skeleton:

```
public class RoleResult {
  public RoleList getRoles() {}
  public RoleUnresolvedList getRolesUnresolved() {}
  public void setRoles(RoleList roles) {}
  public void setRolesUnresolved(RoleUnresolvedList unroles) {}
}
```

In addition to getting a `RoleList` instance, via `getRoles()`, that we could iterate over to extract the object names of the MBeans in that role, we can use the `setRoles()` method to change the role's members, provided that the role in question is writable. The getRolesUnresolved() method returns a list of roles that the relation service was not able to resolve; generally roles are not resolved because either they are not readable or the referenced relation doesn't have a role with the given name. The setRolesUnresolved() method is used by code that needs to return a RoleResult object—for example, the RelationSupport class.

Finally, getRoleCardinality() returns the number of MBeans that the specified relation currently has in the specified role.

7.3.2.4 Query Operations

RelationService provides four query operations:

```
public List findRelationsOfType(String typename)
public Map getReferencedMBeans(String relid)
public Map findAssociatedMBeans(ObjectName objname, String
    typename, String rolename)
public Map findReferencingRelations(ObjectName objname, String
    typename, String rolename)
```

The first two are straightforward. The findRelationsOfType() method does just that: It finds all the relations of the specified type and returns their relation IDs in a List object. The getReferencedMBeans() method returns a Map object of the MBeans that the given relation ID currently references; the Map keys are the object names of the MBeans, and the corresponding values are lists of the names of the roles that those MBeans play.

The findAssociatedMBeans() and findReferencingRelations() methods differ only in the Map instance that they return. The former returns a Map instance whose keys are the object names of MBeans associated with the given MBean. The values that correspond to those keys are lists of the relation IDs in which the association exists. The latter returns a Map instance whose keys are the relation IDs of the relations that reference the given MBean. The values that correspond to those keys are lists of the names of the roles played in those relations.

7.4 JMX Connectors

The current JMX specification is scoped to define a management infrastructure that exists in a single JVM. The specification only hints at how remote programs can access these agent services and request that operations be performed on managed resources from outside of the agent's JVM. The mechanism described in the JMX specification is a connector object that exposes an interface similar to the `MBeanServer` interface for remote invocation and delegates requests received from remote processes to the agent's `MBeanServer` instance.

JMX connectors typically expose a subset of the whole `MBeanServer` interface to remote clients because a few of `MBeanServer`'s methods are not appropriate for invocation by remote processes. For example, the `instantiate()` methods return `java.lang.Object` references that are intended for use in the agent's JVM, not in a remote client JVM. Connectors typically do not convert the semantics of the JMX `MBeanServer` interface into a different semantic protocol. Mechanisms that provide both remote access to JMX agent functionality and translation of standard `MBeanServer` semantics to some other semantics (SNMP, for example), are commonly referred to as JMX adapters rather than connectors.

Through connectors and adapters, remote MBeanServers can be integrated with a wide variety of different management systems. Connectors for RMI and SNMP are very common. Connectors that use SOAP over different protocols are becoming more available in products. Connectors can be used to bridge JMX to telecommunication protocols, peer-to-peer protocols, Web services protocols, and messaging system protocols. By decoupling the communication channel aspect from the core management services, JMX provides a flexible and powerful architecture.

The standardization of JMX connectors is under way through the Java Community Process (JCP), in the JSR 160 ("Java Management Extensions [JMX] Remoting 1.2") effort. At the time of this writing, this JSR was just organized and getting under way. Because the definition of this standard is not far enough along at the time of this writing, we have included the basic concepts of the JMX connector in this chapter based on several implementations of products in the field.

Implementations of a JMX connector involve at least two components: an MBean registered in the MBeanServer that represents the server-side portion of the connector logic, and a remote proxy for that connector MBean that contains the client-side logic for packaging requests to be sent to and received from the server component. Figure 7.4 illustrates this relationship. The following sections examine these connector components. For some of these components we will look at some sample interfaces from IBM's WebSphere Application Server 5.0 (more information is available at http://www-3.ibm.com/software/webservers/appserv) to illustrate the concept.

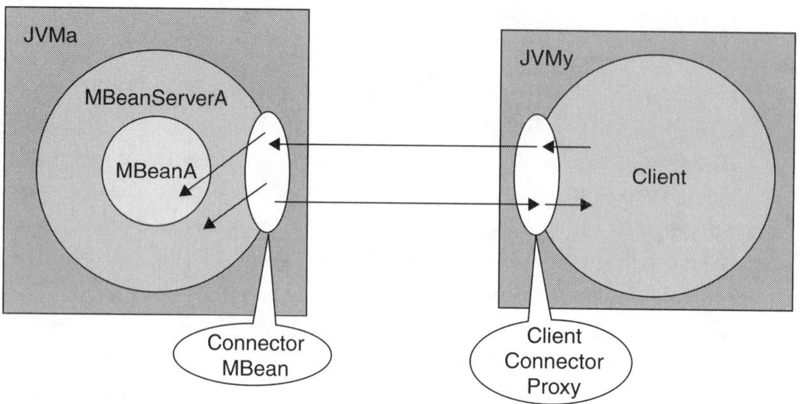

Figure 7.4 JMX Connector Structure

7.4.1 Connector MBean

The MBean that represents the server portion of a JMX connector is registered with the MBeanServer that it exposes to remote clients. The purpose of this MBean is to receive requests from remote clients over a communication protocol, unmarshall these requests, delegate the requests to the local MBeanServer, and return the result of the request to the client.

At present there is no specification for what the JMX connector MBean interface should look like. Some implementations expose an interface identical to the underlying `MBeanServer` interface; other implementations expose only a single `invoke()` method. The interface for the MBean representing the MBeanServer is not as important as the interface of the client-side proxy with which the remote management application must interact.

The important thing about the connector MBean is that it is the server-side logic for the communication channel that receives requests from outside of the JVM and hands those requests to the local MBeanServer for the real processing. In this sense, the connector MBean can also act as a request interceptor that provides additional services, such as authorization, before delegating the request to the MBeanServer. The WebSphere implementation does just this, checking that the caller is actually authorized to perform the request before passing it on to the local MBeanServer.

7.4.2 Connector Client Proxy

The client portion of the JMX connector presents an interface to the client program that is very similar to the `MBeanServer` interface. A simple implementation could present methods to the client program that expose the details of the communications protocol and the marshalling logic used to send requests to the connector MBean on the server. A more sophisticated product would anticipate supporting multiple protocols for remote access and present a common API to the client, thus hiding the details of the transport mechanism beneath this common interface.

For instance, the WebSphere 5.0 JMX connector is exposed through the `AdminClient` interface. As shown in the code example that follows, the `AdminClient` interface looks very similar to the standard `MBeanServer` interface, except that it is missing the `deserialize()`, `registerMBean()`, `createMBean()`, and `instantiate()` methods. Those methods are oriented toward operations that are to be performed by local `MBeanServer` clients.

```
package com.ibm.websphere.management;

import java.util.Set;
import javax.management.*;
import com.ibm.websphere.management.exception.ConnectorException;
import com.ibm.websphere.management.exception.ConnectorNotAvailableException;

public interface AdminClient
{

     public Set queryNames(ObjectName name, QueryExp query) throws
        ConnectorException ;

     public Integer getMBeanCount()  throws ConnectorException ;

     public String getDomainName() throws ConnectorException ;

     public String getDefaultDomain() throws ConnectorException ;

     public MBeanInfo getMBeanInfo(ObjectName name)
        throws InstanceNotFoundException,
               IntrospectionException
               ReflectionException,
               ConnectorException ;

     public boolean isInstanceOf(ObjectName name, String className)
               throws InstanceNotFoundException,
                      ConnectorException ;
```

```
    public boolean isRegistered(ObjectName name) throws
       ConnectorException ;

    public Object getAttribute(ObjectName name, String attribute)
             throws MBeanException,
                    AttributeNotFoundException,
                    InstanceNotFoundException,
                    ReflectionException,
                    ConnectorException ;

    public AttributeList getAttributes(ObjectName name,
        String[] attributes)
             throws InstanceNotFoundException,
                    ReflectionException,
                    ConnectorException ;

    public void setAttribute(ObjectName name,
        Attribute attribute)
             throws InstanceNotFoundException,
                    AttributeNotFoundException,
                    InvalidAttributeValueException,
                    MBeanException,
                    ReflectionException,
                    ConnectorException ;

    public AttributeList setAttributes( ObjectName name,
        AttributeList attributes)
             throws InstanceNotFoundException,
                    ReflectionException,
                    ConnectorException ;

    public Object invoke(ObjectName name,
                        String operationName,
                        Object params[],
                        String signature[])
             throws InstanceNotFoundException,
                    MBeanException,
                    ReflectionException,
                    ConnectorException ;

   public void addNotificationListener(ObjectName name,
       NotificationListener listener, NotificationFilter filter,
       Object handback)
             throws InstanceNotFoundException,
                    ConnectorException;
```

```
    public void addNotificationListenerExtended(ObjectName name,
        NotificationListener listener, NotificationFilter filter,
        Object handback)
               throws ConnectorException;

    public void removeNotificationListener(ObjectName name,
        NotificationListener listener)
               throws InstanceNotFoundException,
                      ListenerNotFoundException,
                      ConnectorException;

    public void removeNotificationListenerExtended(
        NotificationListener listener)
               throws ListenerNotFoundException,
                      ConnectorException;

    public String getType();

    public java.util.Properties getConnectorProperties();

    public ObjectName getServerMBean() throws ConnectorException;

    public Session isAlive() throws ConnectorException ;

}
```

Notice that in many cases the only difference between an `AdminClient` method and the corresponding `MBeanServer` method is the set of exceptions in the `throws` clause. Because it is a remote proxy for `MBeanServer`, `AdminClient` must throw exceptions that are remotable.

Some methods in the `AdminClient` interface have no analog in the standard `MBeanServer` interface. These methods (`getType()`, `getConnectorProperties()`, `getServerMBean()`, `isAlive()`) provide information about the connection to the server for the caller of the `AdminClient` interface to use to test the health of the connection to the server. Even though many JMX connector implementations do not supply such optional methods, the methods can be handy if the client supports logic for dynamic diagnosis of the connector.

7.4.2.1 Connector Client Factory

In a typical implementation, the client proxy is obtained via a factory object that abstracts the details of how to establish the connection between processes and initialize the client proxy. For instance, we obtain the WebSphere client proxy by calling the `AdminClientFactory` static method to `getAdminClient()`:

```
package com.ibm.websphere.management;

import java.util.*;
import com.ibm.websphere.management.exception.InvalidAdminClientTypeException;
import com.ibm.websphere.management.exception.ConnectorException;

public abstract class AdminClientFactory
{
    public static AdminClient createAdminClient(Properties props)
                throws ConnectorException
    {
    }
}
```

This factory allows many different protocols to be supported by JMX connectors with a common interface. Regardless of the details of the underlying protocol and communications semantics, `AdminClientFactory` always returns an object that implements the `AdminClient` interface. The values in the `Properties` object passed to the factory may specify a connector that communicates using SOAP over HTTP, RMI/IIOP, or any number of other protocols. But the client of the JMX connector is shielded from those details and has to interact only with the common connector interface.

7.4.2.2 Security

Because management channels typically represent sensitive capabilities for the managed system, it is reasonable and often desirable to protect the connectors by forcing the connector client to authenticate before proceeding with the request. Such authentication is usually limited by the constraints of the underlying communications channel. For instance, RMI/IIOP connectors are likely to offer more support for authentication than SOAP/HTTP connectors because more time has been devoted to developing RMI/IIOP security measures and authentication schemes, although this situation is changing because a lot of effort is going into Web services security. But as each new JMX connector protocol is introduced, the various authentication mechanisms (such as basic authentication, credential-based authentication, or trust association authentication) have to be ported to the new protocol before the connector can be considered complete for production environments.

Regardless of the authentication mechanism used, the authentication data identifying the user has to be passed to the connector so that the connector can use it when establishing a connection to the server. In WebSphere, the initialization properties passed to `AdminClientFactory` contain the authentication data needed by the connector client proxy. Other implementations use system properties or security property files to pass the data to the connector so that it can establish an identity with the server.

7.5 Summary

This chapter has examined all the nonmonitoring standard services defined by the JMX specification. The timer service allows us to generate scheduled notifications so that our management applications can handle recurring tasks. Using the MLet service simplifies the deployment of MBeans to MBeanServers spread across our networks. And the relation service helps management applications organize large constellations of MBeans. JMX connectors allow remote access to the MBeanServer and the resources it aggregates. Although these are certainly valuable services that you would expect any management infrastructure to provide, they are by no means the last word in JMX services. The various JMX implementations all come with their own custom services—for example, distributed services or scripting services—and of course you are encouraged to build your own services to meet your particular management requirements.

CHAPTER 8

Securing JMX

Security is a central requirement for modern networked systems. This requirement applies to the components of systems that provide essential business function and to the infrastructure and applications that monitor and manage those components. Unfortunately, security is often one of the last things considered during design and one of the first things compromised in implementation. Version 1.0 of the JMX specification followed in this unfortunate tradition by not addressing obvious security concerns; in fairness to the developers of that specification, they expected JMX to be used in an environment where a management system—for example, Tivoli's TME, or BMC's PATROL—controlled, and secured, access to the MBeanServer. Version 1.1 began to address this issue by defining a new permission to control access to `MBeanServerFactory`. Extending that work to address other JMX security issues is high on the priority list of the Java Community Process (JCP) Expert Group working on version 1.2 of the specification.

In this chapter we will examine the JMX 1.1 security model and some proposed extensions implemented in the MX4J open-source JMX project. Although what emerges in the specifications may not be identical to what is in MX4J, at the time of this writing the MX4J implementation provides the best starting point for exploring JMX security issues.

8.1 JMX Security Exposures

Security is in large part about risk management. Because it is impossible to defend against every potential threat, one of the first steps taken in any security design is to assess which attacks are most likely or most costly or both. On the basis of that threat assessment, a solution is designed to reduce to a manageable level, or optimally eliminate, the risk associated with those threats. Table 8.1 summarizes the security exposures associated with JMX.

Table 8.1 JMX Security Exposures and Consequences

Exposure	Consequence
Unauthorized `MBeanServerFactory` Access	`MBeanServerFactory` creates new MBeanServers, and it looks up and releases existing ones. Access to each of these capabilities needs to be controlled. For example, a malicious management application could look up and release a system's MBeanServer and replace it with one populated with bogus MBeans.
Untrusted MBean Registration	The MBeans that instrument new applications and devices will ship with those applications and devices. Updated instrumentation may also be made available over the Web. An obvious attack on these JMX-enabled systems is to create MBeans that "spoof" the system's actual MBeans. If the attacker's MBeans are registered instead of the legitimate MBeans, the system is compromised. Therefore we need a way to ensure that only "trusted" MBeans become registered in the MBeanServer.
Unauthorized MBean Access	MBeans represent managed resources to management applications (e.g., a Web server or a router). The management interface that an MBean presents enables those applications to get and set attributes, like the open ports on a router, or invoke operations, like starting or stopping a service or server. Clearly, administrators need the ability to control which management applications and users can perform these actions.

8.2 Permission-Based Security Fundamentals

Before we launch into a detailed discussion of the MX4J security design, we'll quickly review the fundamental concepts behind Java's permission-based access control mechanism.

8.2.1 Permissions

In the Java 2 security model a *permission* is the authority to access a particular resource or to perform a particular operation. The class `java.security.Permission` and its subclasses represent permissions at runtime. For example, in the statement

```
FilePermission fp = new FilePermission("/etc/passwd",
    "read, write");
```

`fp` represents permission to read and write the `/etc/passwd` file. In the statement

```
RuntimePermission rp = new RuntimePermission("exitVM");
```

`rp` represents permission to shut down the JVM.

`FilePermission` and `RuntimePermission` are part of the standard set of J2SE permissions. MX4J defines its own permissions to control access to JMX-based resources and operations.

8.2.2 SecurityManager

The Java `SecurityManager` class is responsible for enforcing security policy. It does so by determining whether or not the class making a given request has the necessary permission. In code these checks generally take the following form:

```
SecurityManager sm = System.getSecurityManager();
if (sm != null) {
  sm.checkPermission(new <RequiredPermission>(target, action));
}
```

If the call to `checkPermission()` succeeds, execution continues normally; otherwise a `SecurityException` is thrown. The `checkPermission()`

method succeeds if the permissions associated with the class calling it either contain or imply the permission that is passed to it as a parameter; that is, in the preceding example, `checkPermission()` succeeds if the class calling it has been granted `RequiredPermission(target, action)`.

8.2.3 Policy

Permissions are granted to classes via Java's policy mechanism. By default, policy is specified by statements in a simple policy language. For example, the policy "any class signed by `Root` may read and write `/etc/passwd`" is specified by the following statement:

```
grant signedBy Root {
  java.io.FilePermission "/etc/passwd", "read,write";
};
```

Permissions may be granted to code signed by a specific signer as just illustrated, or to code loaded from a specific URL, as here:

```
grant codeSource file:/opt/java/mx4j.jar {
  java.util.PropertyPermission "java.home", "read";
};
```

This statement allows code loaded from `/opt/java/mx4j.jar` to read the `java.home` system property.

A concrete extension of the abstract class `java.security.Policy` is responsible for reading policy statements and mapping from a class's code source and signer attributes to the corresponding permissions at runtime.

In this section we have identified only the principal aspects of the Java 2 security architecture. For a detailed treatment of the topic, see Li Gong's book *Inside Java 2 Platform Security: Architecture, API Design, and Implementation* (Addison-Wesley, 1999).

8.3 JMX Permissions

Version 1.1 of the JMX specification defines a new permission: `MBeanServerPermission`. In addition, MX4J defines two new permissions to address the security exposures described earlier. `MBeanServerPermission` and `MBeanTrustPermission` extend `java.security.BasicPermission` and represent "named" permissions that you either have or don't have. MBeanPermission, the other new MX4J permission, extends java.security.Permission and allows you to specify a target, the MBean(s) to which access is being granted, and the action (i.e., what you're allowed to do to the target MBean). Each of these permissions is described in more detail in Sections 8.3.1 through 8.3.3.

8.3.1 MBeanServerPermission

MBeanServerPermission controls access to the methods of MBeanServer-Factory. Its associated target name is the name of the method to which access is being granted. Table 8.2 describes each of MBeanServerPermission's target names.

Access to MBeanServerFactory makes it easy to attack your application's management facilities. For example, an attacker could mount a denial-of-service attack by simply finding and releasing the application's MBeanServer(s), rendering the MBeanServer(s) unmanaged and unmanageable, at least by JMX. Therefore, you should carefully control access to MBeanServerFactory.

8.3.2 MBeanTrustPermission

MBeanTrustPermission controls which MBeans can be registered with the MBeanServer. It has a single target name, "register," associated with it.

MBeanTrustPermission allows you to make policy statements like, "MBeans signed by Tivoli may be registered with the MBeanServer" or "MBeans that were loaded from /opt/ibm/mbeans may be registered with

Table 8.2 Target Names Recognized by MBeanServerPermission

Target Name	What the Permission Allows
MBeanServerFactory.createMBeanServer	Creation of an MBeanServer retaining a reference to the new MBeanServer within the factory
MBeanServerFactory.newMBeanServer	Creation of an MBeanServer
MBeanServerFactory.findMBeanServer	Lookup of one or all of the MBeanServers created by the factory
MBeanServerFactory.releaseMBeanServer	Removal of one of the MBeanServers created by the factory

the MBeanServer." Note that these statements are not saying that code signed by Tivoli or loaded from /opt/ibm/mbeans may call the MBeanServer's registerMBean() method. Instead, the statement is that we allow only MBeans signed by Tivoli or loaded from /opt/ibm/mbeans in the MBeanServer's registry.

MBeanTrustPermission addresses the "untrusted MBean registration" exposure described in Table 8.1. It allows us to be sure, for example, that the MBeans being used to manage the Cisco routers in our network are the MBeans that Cisco shipped with those routers and not some look-alike MBeans that an attacker managed to slip into our classpath ahead of the Cisco MBeans.

8.3.3 MBeanPermission

MBeanPermission controls access to MBeans. An MBeanPermission instance must specify the MBean(s) it applies to and the actions allowed on those MBeans. Any MBean that a particular instance of MBeanPermission applies to is called the permission's *target* and is specified via a string, called the *target name*, composed of the target MBean's class name, the name of one of the target MBean's attributes or operations, and an object name. For example, suppose we have an MBean whose class name is net.jnjmx.ch8.Demo, with a single attribute (Title) and the operation start. If an instance of the Demo MBean is registered under the object name jnjmx:id=FooOne,ch=8, then the MBeanPermission target name for the Title attribute is

```
net.jnjmx.ch8.Demo#Title[jnjmx:id=ExampleOne,ch=8]
```

and the MBeanPermission target name for the start operation is

```
net.jnjmx.ch8.Demo#start[jnjmx:id=ExampleOne,ch=8]
```

In general, MBeanPermission target names have the form

```
<classname>#<attribute/operation>[<objectname>]
```

The attribute/operation and objectname components are optional.

Wildcards (i.e., the asterisks) may be used in the classname and attribute/operation components of the target name (for example, see Table 8.3). ObjectName patterns may be used in the target name's object name component.

The actions supported by MBeanPermission are described in Table 8.4.

Table 8.3 Examples of Wildcards in `MBeanPermission` Target Names

Target Name	Explanation
`net.jnjmx.ch8.*#start`	Designates all the `start` operations of any MBean whose class name begins with "net.jnjmx.ch8".
`net.jnjmx.ch8.Demo#*`	Designates all of the `net.jnjmx.ch8.Demo` MBean's attributes and operations.
`net.jnjmx.ch8.*#*[jnjmx:*]`	Designates all of the attributes and operations associated with any MBean whose name begins with "net.jnjmx.ch8" and that is registered in the `jnjmx` domain.

Table 8.4 `MBeanPermission` Actions

Action	What the Action Allows
`addListener`	Addition of notification listeners, either directly (i.e., via an object reference to the MBean) or via the MBeanServer's `addNotificationListener()` method.
`getAttribute`	Retrieval of the value of an MBean's attribute.
`getMBeanInfo`	Retrieval of the MBean's metadata.
`newMBean`	Creation of a new instance of the MBean in the MBeanServer via the MBeanServer's `createMBean()` method.
`invokeOperation`	Invocation of an operation on the MBean via the MBeanServer's `invoke()` method.
`registerMBean`	Registration of an instance of the MBean via the MBeanServer's `registerMBean()` method.
`removeListener`	Removal of notification listeners, either directly (i.e., via an object reference to the MBean) or via the MBeanServer's `removeNotificationListener()` method.
`setAttribute`	Setting the value of an MBean's attribute.
`unregisterMBean`	Deregistration of an instance of the MBean via the MBeanServer's `unregisterMBean()` method.
*	All of the above.

The security exposures associated with some of these actions are obvious. For example, given the ability to unregister MBeans, an attacker's code could remove MBeans that provide vital data or control to a management application. With permission to create and register new MBeans, an attacker could "spoof" legitimate MBeans by substituting rogue versions of those MBeans. Other exposures are more subtle. How much harm can be done by adding an additional listener? Perhaps quite a bit if the JMX notifications that the new listener receives contain sensitive data. Likewise, although access to an MBean's metadata, via the `getMBeanInfo()` method, may seem innocuous, it may provide an attacker with information necessary to mount a successful attack against the system.

8.4 Using JMX Security

One of the interesting things about Java 2 Platform security is that *using* it has very little impact on your code. Application code that just wants to take advantage of the security features built into the classes it is using only needs to handle the additional failure cases—that is, instances of `SecurityException`—that may arise, and it is ready to run with Java security enabled. No messing about with permissions, security managers, and so on is required. The next time you bump into Li Gong, or one of the other Java 2 Platform security designers, shake their hand!

Of course there is no free lunch. Security is a complex business, and if the complexity doesn't show up in the application code, it must be dealt with elsewhere. Classes that provide security features manage some of that complexity by making calls to `SecurityManager` at the appropriate places. The remaining complexity is allocated to the Java 2 Platform security policy mechanism.

In this section we will demonstrate how to configure MX4J security policy. Starting with a simple application, we'll turn on security and then experiment with different security policies.

8.4.1 A Simple Process Management Application (SPMA)

Suppose that our operating system vendor of choice shipped a `ProcessManager` MBean with its operating systems. Here's a very minimal version of such an MBean:

```
public interface ProcessManagerMBean {
  int[] getPids();
```

```
    void kill(int pid);
}
```

Let's further suppose that this interface, the MBean class that implements it, and some other OS-specific MBeans are packaged in `osmbeans.jar`.

Here is the `main()` method of a simple process management application that uses the `ProcessManager` MBean:

```
public class spma {
    public static void main(String[] args) throws Exception {
        ObjectName pmname = new ObjectName("ch8:id=ProcessManager");
        MBeanServer mbs = setupProcessManager(pmname);
        char cmd;
        System.out.print("% ");
        while ((cmd = readcmd()) != 'q') {
            switch (cmd) {
                case 'l' :
                    doListCmd(mbs, pmname);
                    break;
                case 'k' :
                    doKillCmd(mbs, pmname);
                    break;
                default :
                    usage(cmd);
            }
            System.out.print("% ");
        }
    }

    ...
}
```

The `setupProcessManager()` method uses `MBeanServerFactory` to create an MBeanServer and then uses that server to create a `ProcessManager` MBean. The `doListCmd()` and `doKillCmd()` methods invoke the `ProcessManager` MBean's `getPids()` and `kill()` operations via the MBeanServer.

A user runs `spma` from the command line by typing

```
$ java net.jnjmx.ch8.spma
```

Here's a snapshot of an spma session that gets a list of pids, kills 8502, then gets a new list of pids to verify that 8502 is gone:

```
% l
pids: [9064, 8502, 2025, 2446, 4629, 1396, 4147, 7231, 6878, 922,
       9324, 7610]
% k 8502
% l
pids: [9064, 2025, 2446, 4629, 1396, 4147, 7231, 6878, 922, 9324,
       7610]
% q
```

Obviously this is not something we want an arbitrary user to be able to do. So let's look at how we can make it more secure.

8.4.2 Running with Security Enabled

By default the `java` command does not instantiate `SecurityManager` in the JVM that it creates to execute Java programs. Because `SecurityManager` is responsible for enforcing Java security, the first thing to do is to run `spma` with `SecurityManager`. To do that, we specify the `java.security.manager` and `java.security.policy` system properties on the command line:

```
$ java -Djava.security.manager -Djava.security.policy=/home/wkh/
spma.policy net.jnjmx.ch8.spma
```

If we absolutely, positively never want `spma` to run without `Security-Manager`, we can also modify its `main()` method as follows:

```
public class spma {
    public static void main(String[] args) throws Exception {
        SecurityManager sm = System.getSecurityManager();
        if (sm == null) {
            System.err.println(
                "spma must be run with a SecurityManager");
            System.exit(-1);
        }
        ...
    }
}
```

Note that rather than specify the `java.security.policy` system property on the command line, we could add an additional `policy.url` entry to the `${JRE_HOME}/lib/security/java.security` file. That is, if we add the entry

```
policy.url.3=/home/wkh/spma.policy
```

then the command line above can be shortened to

```
$ java -Djava.security.manager net.jnjmx.ch8.spma
```

8.4.3 Policy Configuration

When `spma` is run with security enabled on a standard J2SE installation with no `spma`-specific policy, it fails with an `AccessControlException`. That's actually a good thing; it indicates that `SecurityManager` is on the job, and because none of the code we're running has any JMX-specific permissions, it doesn't get to run. Of course, it would be even better to be able to use `spma` with security enabled. How do we do that?

First we have to grant the necessary permissions to MX4J itself. To do that, we add the following grant block to `spma.policy`:

```
grant codeBase "file:/opt/mx4j/*" {
  permission javax.management.MBeanServerPermission
    "createMBeanServer";
  permission mx4j.server.MBeanPermission "*",
    "getAttribute,setAttribute,invokeOperation";
};
```

The first line says that we're granting permissions to code that is loaded from `file:/opt/mx4j/`, which is where all the MX4J `.jar` files live. The permissions we're granting are indicated by the two `permission` statements. The first one grants MX4J access to all the `MBeanServerFactory` methods. The second line grants MX4J access to all MBean attributes and operations.

Next we have to give `spma` the access it needs to the MBeanServer and MBean resources. So we add another grant block to `spma.policy`:

```
grant codeBase "file:/opt/admin/spma/" {
  permission javax.management.MBeanServerPermission
    "createMBeanServer";
```

```
  permission mx4j.server.MBeanPermission
    "net.jnjmx.ch8.ProcessManager#*[ch8:*]",
    "newMBean,registerMBean,getAttribute,invokeOperation,
unregisterMBean";
}
```

This block grants code loaded from `file:/opt/admin/spma/` permission to create an MBeanServer. Then it grants permission to invoke operations on and get attributes of any MBeans in packages rooted at `net.jnjmx.ch8`.

Finally, because we want to make sure that `spma` uses only legitimate MBeans, we express "trust" in MBeans loaded from `file:/usr/lib/osmbeans.jar` by adding this grant block:

```
grant codeBase "file/usr/lib/osmbeans.jar" {
  permission mx4j.server.MBeanTrustPermission "register";
};
```

8.5 Summary

Security is vital for real-world systems. Management systems are as real-world as they come, so securing management applications is essential. Unfortunately, getting security "right" is a difficult, generally thankless, task. This chapter has covered some of the JMX security basics by examining the exposures that attackers might exploit and discussing the security features provided by MX4J. The complicated task of putting those features to work in policies that make sense for a particular application is an exercise left to the reader.

CHAPTER 9

Designing with JMX

The authors of this book have approached JMX from different points of view, with different goals, with different skills. These differences have yielded many opportunities to be exposed to a wide variety of applications, problems, and solutions. This chapter looks at how and where to deploy MBeanServers, what options are available to you when you're designing MBeans for your Java resources, and who should create and register your MBeans and when. We also describe and illustrate some of the best practices we've picked up in the course of applying JMX to management problems, including MBean granularity, application managers, management models, and federation.

9.1 MBeanServer Deployment Patterns

This section discusses three JMX *deployment models* that we have identified: daemon, component, and driver. In the *daemon* model, the MBeanServer owns its own JVM separate from the application. In the *component* model, the MBeanServer runs in the JVM owned by the application. In the *driver* model, the MBeanServer owns the JVM and the application runs within the scope of the MBeanServer.

These models can be applied in a broad spectrum of environments ranging from traditional daemon-based "agents" to pervasive device applications. It is important to be aware of this spectrum when you're thinking about products and tools that take advantage of JMX technology. In all these deployment patterns, the JMX agent, or MBeanServer, functions in the agent role of the manager-agent management architecture. This section discusses some options for deploying the MBeanServer in your application, middleware, JVM, or system.

9.1.1 Daemon

The daemon deployment model for JMX is the most familiar from a traditional manager-agent systems management model, in which a management agent runs in its own process. The manager role is generally filled by a remote console and specifies data to be collected or actions to be taken by an agent. The agent runs as a separate process, or daemon, on a managed system. The agent is responsible for monitoring and acting on the local system-level resources (devices, processes, and so on) as directed by its manager.

The JMX incarnation of this model is illustrated in Figure 9.1. A platform-specific daemon process loads a Java Virtual Machine (JVM). One or

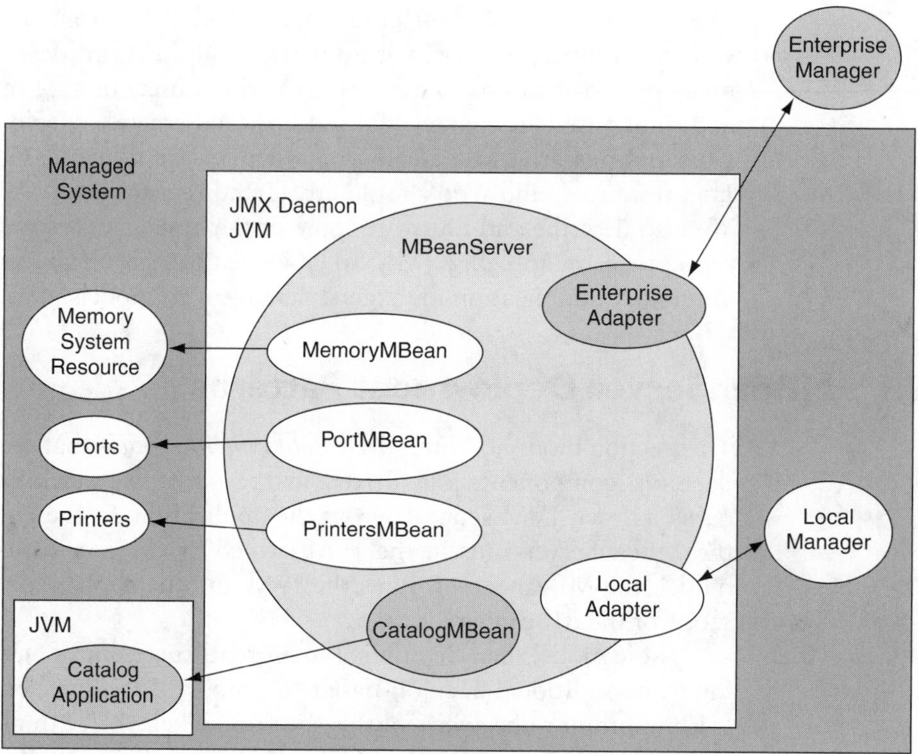

Figure 9.1 The Daemon MBeanServer

more JMX agents are then instantiated by the JVM. In the JMX specification a *JMX agent* is defined as being "composed of an MBean server, a set of MBeans representing managed resources, a minimum number for agent services implemented as MBeans, and typically at least one protocol adaptor or connector." When we talk about instantiating an MBeanServer, we assume that the services and adapters are instantiated with it. There is no net difference between a JMX agent and an MBeanServer.

In the daemon model there are MBeans responsible for monitoring and/or managing specific system-level resources. The manager connects to the MBeanServer(s) via the available adapters. In fact, the MBeanServer *must* have adapters to handle remote communications to both manager and possibly managed resources. The local MBeans that represent the remote resources may use the adapters to communicate with their resources. Managed applications must use an adapter to communicate with the MBeanServer—that is, create, update, invoke, and remove MBeans. If the application is written in Java, then an RMI adapter is most commonly used. Unfortunately, at this time the JMX adapters are not standardized and RMI adapters may have different interfaces between MBeanServers. Hopefully some common adapters for RMI and HTTP will be standardized as part of the ongoing JCP (Java Community Process) for JMX.

Advantages of a JMX daemon over traditional native daemons include portability, dynamic loading, and standardization. Because the JMX agent is written in Java, it runs unchanged on most platforms. Only the JMX daemon, a much simpler piece of code, needs to be ported. The MLet service allows MBeans for resources on the managed node to be loaded by the JMX agent as needed. In addition, local management services that act as a proxy for the remote manager can also be loaded dynamically. Finally, JMX provides a standard model for both the instrumentation MBeans and the MBeanServer they communicate with.

Having just one MBeanServer in a system, or one MBeanServer serving several JVMs and applications, can be more efficient in terms of system resources and interaction complexity. There is just one list of MBeans to get from one MBeanServer (or at least fewer MBeanServers). There is only one instance of each type of adapter. This reduction of complexity can be a big benefit because adapters that perform object model and protocol conversion sometimes have a very large footprint and resource requirement. This arrangement can be simpler for management systems as well because they have just one, or fewer, connections to the managed system to work with. Applications using external MBeanServers have a smaller footprint and use fewer system resources. The overhead of the managers interacting with the MBeanServer does not add to the resources used by the application.

Using a daemon JMX agent also means that the MBeanServer exists outside of the scope of the application and can therefore be used to control the lifecycle of the application—that is, start, stop, monitor availability, and recover.

However, using a daemon JMX agent is a bit trickier for applications. Applications in other JVMs (or not in any JVM at all) using daemon JMX agents must be able to find the MBeanServer, use the MBeanServer through an adapter, and handle remoteness issues.

9.1.1.1 Adapters

Because JMX adapters are not standardized, the application's choice of an adapter may depend on the JMX implementation it uses. The application may either use one that's already provided or install its own into the JMX agent when it is installed.

9.1.1.2 Discovery

MBeanServer and adapter discovery has also not been standardized for JMX. The JSR 160 expert group for JMX is working on this area as well. In the meantime there are several ways to find a daemon MBeanServer:

- The MBeanServer's RMI stub reference can be saved in an environment variable
- A JNDI name for finding the MBeanServer's reference can be saved in the application's configuration during installation or deployment
- A "well-known" name for looking up an MBeanServer using a directory lookup (like JNDI). Of course, this well-known name is not yet standardized either and will apply only for the application, domain, or enterprise.

9.1.1.3 Remoteness

Because the MBeanServer is remote, the managed applications must be able to deal with the failures and delays due to MBeanServer remoteness. The applications must be programmed to handle the situation in which the MBeanServer doesn't exist or is suddenly unavailable. The managed application cannot just create another one to use. It will have to store updates for later or remember its MBean's state so that it can reset it when the MBeanServer is available again. In fact, these same requirements are true for managers of the remote MBeanServer as well.

9.1.2 Component

In the JMX component deployment model the MBeanServer is embedded in the application being managed as illustrated in Figure 9.2. Here the MBeanServer is actually a component of the application and is responsible for providing the application's management interface.

Making the MBeanServer and application MBeans part of the application provides access to much finer-grained instrumentation. More extensive control of the application by the manager is also possible with this model; instead of just starting and stopping the application, the manager can tune it dynamically at runtime via the attributes and operations of the application resource MBeans registered with the MBean server. As more applications become JMX enabled, we expect this model to become more common.

One advantage of this approach is that the application is in complete control of instantiating the MBeanServer. The application can count on an MBeanServer being there when it needs it. If the MBeanServer is not there, the application can create one without concern for duplication. Containing

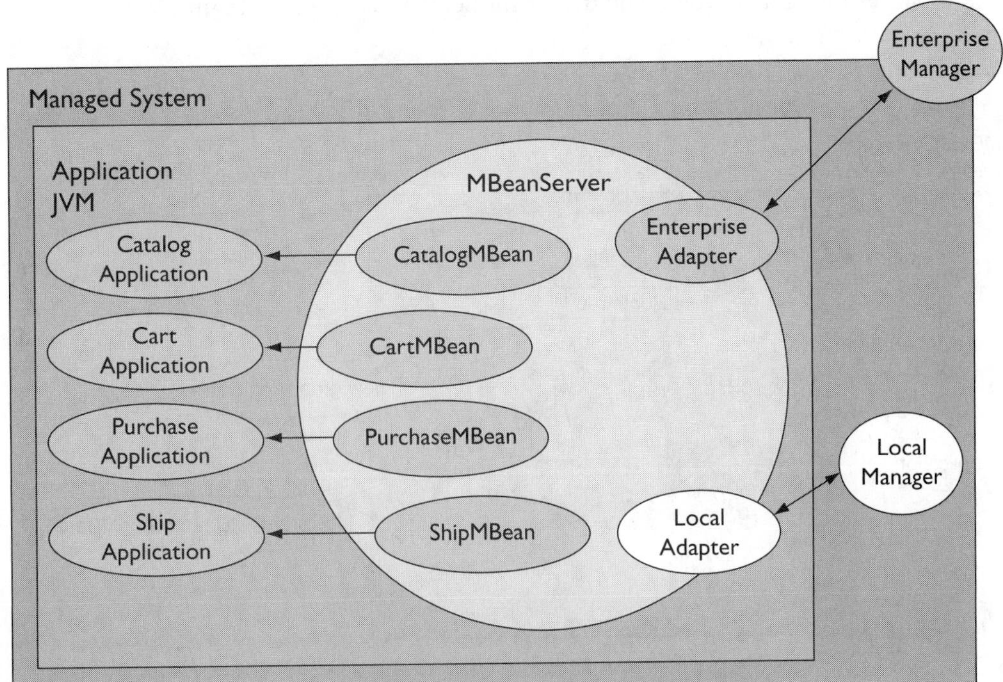

Figure 9.2 The Component MBeanServer

its own MBeanServer also means that the application is more easily portable to other systems that may or may not have a suitable MBeanServer available. These types of applications have fewer installation requirements on their target systems.

One of the challenges of supporting this model is finding a way to *federate* JMX agents. A single machine may run multiple JMX-enabled applications, each of which may have an embedded JMX agent. Those agents need to be organized—federated—in some way so that they appear as a single agent in a management console. We will look at ways to federate JMX agents later in this chapter (see Section 9.4.5).

9.1.3 Driver

The driver deployment model for JMX is similar to the component model. In the driver case, the JMX agent becomes the core of the application rather than a component of an application. The MBeanServer is used to start and own the JVM. The application actually runs within the MBeanServer's JVM. Because the MBeanServer owns the JVM, it will always be available. Therefore, any applications running in the JVM can always count on the MBeanServer being available. The driver model is illustrated in Figure 9.3.

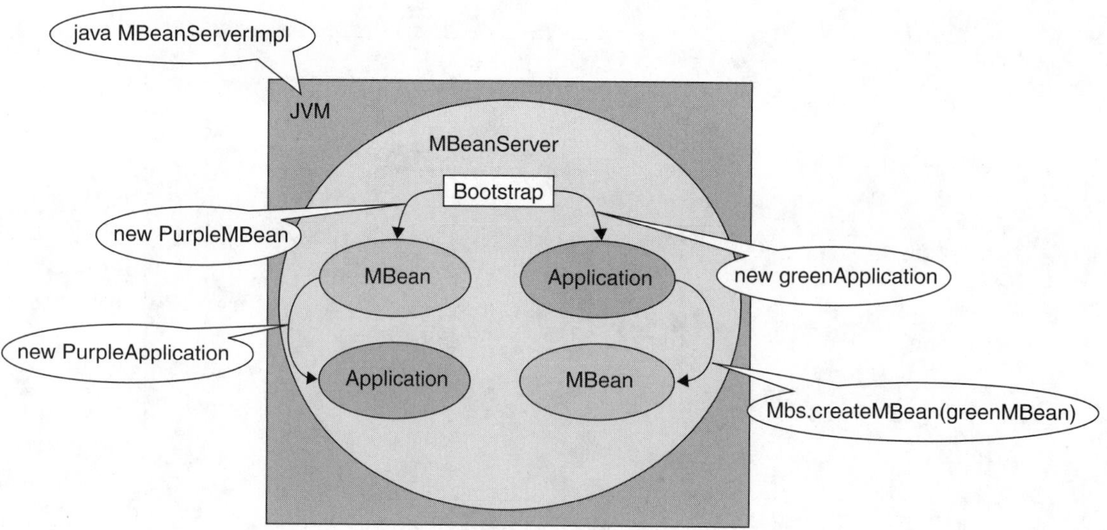

Figure 9.3 The Driver MBeanServer

The application is designed and constructed as a set of cooperating MBeans that are loaded at startup. Therefore, the MBeanServer used in the driver model must have a *bootstrap service*. This service is responsible for loading and configuring the application components when the MBeanServer is instantiated. The application's configuration information could come from a variety of sources—for example, a directory service or some device firmware. Either the bootstrap service can start the MBeans that in turn start the application they manage, or it can start the application components that in turn instantiate their MBeans.

In either case, the MBeans can be designed so that they control the lifecycle of the application they are associated with. Instantiating MBeans that start the application components is straightforward. You should create the MBean in the MBeanServer using the MBeanServer as a factory or by the MBeanServer bootstrap. If you choose to instantiate application components that create the MBeans, then you must decide if you are going to remove the MBean when the application is stopped. If you remove the MBean, you will not be able to do lifecycle control (start and stop of the application) with it. If you let the MBean continue after the application is stopped, then the application must be careful not to try to create a new one when one exists, and always interact with it through the MBeanServer. MBeans that continue to exist can be used to stop and restart applications, but another strategy must be used for the initial start of the application.

The driver style is the most reliable strategy, but the JMX support must be designed into the application from the beginning, and it is very hard, if not impossible, to use for existing applications without causing a major overhaul of the application. The component strategy has less impact on the existing application than the driver style, but the application will still require modification in order to add JMX manageability. The daemon style is a more traditional style and allows management of existing applications without requiring that the applications be recompiled. The daemon style requires that discovery and remote access be provided for, which the component and driver styles do not do. However, the daemon style can be used to manage non-Java applications and existing Java applications with less impact.

9.2 Instrumentation Patterns

Any Java resource can be managed with JMX. How it is managed can vary pretty widely. This section will discuss some of the approaches you can use when designing new applications to be manageable. We will also point out which ones are useful for enabling existing applications to be manageable.

9.2.1 Applications as MBeans

In this pattern the application is also an MBean. The time of day daemon (todd) discussed in Chapters 2 and 3 illustrates this pattern. todd is an example of a very simple application that may have some control methods as part of its interface. Applications of any complexity usually have a separate class that contains the control methods. These control methods are invoked in various ways: through a command-line interface, through a browser interface, or sometimes through a custom user application. Control classes are a good candidates to double as an MBean. All you need to do is modify the class to add "`implements classnameMBean`" and create a new Java interface class containing the signatures of the methods that you want to be part of the MBean.

Here is an example of a simple tack catalog application that is also a standard MBean. There are base interfaces and classes for the catalog that are not specific to selling tack: `Item`, `Category`, and `Catalog`. The implementations of these interfaces for the tack catalog are `TackItem`, `TackCategory`, and `TackCatalog`. In addition, a `TackCatalogMBean` interface is implemented by the `TackCatalog` class. The management system, through the adapters of course, will have access to only the methods in `catalogMBean`, and not any in the `catalog` interface. For the full sample code, see the appendix or the book's Web site (http://www.awprofessional.com/titles/0672324083):

- Interface `Item`:

```
package jnjmx.ch9;
public interface Item {
        int getCatalogNo();
        String getName();
        int getPrice();
        int getQuantity();
}
```

- Interface `Category`:

```
package jnjmx.ch9;

import java.util.List;
public interface Category {
        int getItemCount();
        List getItems();
        String getName();
}
```

- Interface `Catalog`:

```
package jnjmx.ch9;
import java.io.Serializable;
import java.util.ArrayList;
import java.io.IOException;
import java.util.List;
import java.util.Map;

public interface Catalog  {
        public Category createCategory(String name)
                throws CategoryExistsException;
        public Category getCategory(String name);
        public Map getCategories();
        public void removeCategory(Category category)
                throws NoSuchCategoryException;
        public void removeCategory(String name)
                throws NoSuchCategoryException
        public void classify(Item item, Category category);
        public void declassify(Item item, Category category);
        public void increaseInventory(Item item, int amount);
        public void decreaseInventory(Item item, int amount)
                throws InventoryUnderflowException;
        public Item createItem(String name, int price,
                int quantity) throws ItemExistsException;
        public List getItems();
        public void removeItem(Item item)
                throws NoSuchItemException;
        public void removeItem(int catalogNo)
                throws NoSuchItemException;
}
```

- Interface `TackCatalogMBean`:

```
package jnjmx.ch9;

import java.io.Serializable;
import java.io.IOException;

public interface TackCatalogMBean  {
        public Catalog load(String name)
                throws IOException, ClassNotFoundException;
        public boolean isAutoCheckpointing();
        public void setAutoCheckpoint(boolean autoCheckpoint);
```

```
        public void doCheckpoint();
        public int getNumberOfItems();
        public int getTotalSales();
        public int getAccesses();
        public int getInventorySize();
}
```

- Class TackItem:

```
package jnjmx.ch9;

import java.io.Serializable;

public class TackItem implements Item, Serializable {
          Catalog catalog;
          int catalogNo;
          String name;
          int price;
              int quantity;

        public TackItem(
            Catalog catalog,
            int catalogNo,
            String name,
            int price,
            int quantity) {
            this.catalogNo = catalogNo;
            this.catalog = catalog;
            this.name = name;
            this.price = price;
            this.quantity = quantity;
        }

        public int getCatalogNo() {
            return this.catalogNo;
        }

        public boolean equals(Object obj) {
            if (!(obj instanceof TackItem)) {
                    return false;
            }

            Item item = (TackItem) obj;
```

```
            return (this.name.compareTo(item.getName())
                == 0)&& (this.price == item.getPrice()););
        }

        public String getName() {
            return this.name;
        }

        public int getPrice() {
            return this.price;
        }

        public int getQuantity() {
            return this.quantity;
        }

        public void setQuantity(int quantity) {
            this.quantity = quantity;
    }
}
```

- Class TackCategory:

```
Package jnjmx.ch9;
import java.io.Serializable;
import java.util.List;
import java.util.ArrayList;
public class TackCategory implements Category, Serializable {
    /* Categories can be: new, old, sale,
     * saddles, bridles, girths, breastcollers,
     * saddleblankets */
    public String getCategory() {return "";} ;
    public void setCategory(String currentCategory) {};

    private Catalog catalog;
    private String name;
    private List items;

    public TackCategory(Catalog catalog, String name) {
        this.catalog = catalog;
        this.name = name;
        this.items = new ArrayList();
    }
```

```
        public boolean equals(Object obj) {
                if (!(obj instanceof TackCategory)) {
                        return false;
                }

                return this.name.compareTo(
                    ((TackCategory) obj).name) == 0;
        }

        public int getItemCount() {
                return this.items.size();
        }

        public List getItems() {
                return this.items;
        }

        public String getName() {
                return this.name;
        }

}
```

- Class TackCatalog:

```
package jnjmx.ch9;
import java.io.File;
import java.io.FileInputStream;
import java.io.FileNotFoundException;
import java.io.FileOutputStream;
import java.io.IOException;
import java.io.ObjectInputStream;
import java.io.ObjectOutputStream;
import java.io.Serializable;
import java.util.ArrayList;
import java.util.HashMap;
import java.util.Iterator;
import java.util.List;
import java.util.Map;

public class TackCatalog
    implements Catalog, Serializable, TackCatalogMBean {

        private static final String FILEEXT = ".catalog";
```

```
private final String name;
private boolean autoCheckpoint = false;
private Map categories;
private List items;
private int nextCatalogNo = 1;
private int accesses=0, sales=0, inventorySize=0;

public TackCatalog(String inName) {
        this.name = inName;
        this.categories = new HashMap();
        this.items = new ArrayList();
}
public static TackCatalog create(String inName)
    throws IOException {
        String cfn = inName + FILEEXT;
        File cf = new File(cfn);
        if (cf.exists()) {
                cf.delete();
        }

        TackCatalog catalog = new TackCatalog(inName);
        ObjectOutputStream db =
                new ObjectOutputStream(
                    new FileOutputStream(cf));
        db.writeObject(catalog);
        db.flush();
        db.close();

        return catalog;
}

// load is exposed in TackCatalogMBean

public TackCatalog load(String name)
        throws IOException, ClassNotFoundException {
        String cfn = name + FILEEXT;
        File cf = new File(cfn);
        if (cf.exists() == false) {
                throw new FileNotFoundException(cfn +
                    " doesn't exist");
        }

        ObjectInputStream db = new ObjectInputStream(
            new FileInputStream(cf));
```

```
            TackCatalog catalog = (TackCatalog)
                db.readObject();
            db.close();
            return catalog;
    }


    public synchronized Map getCategories() {
            return this.categories;
    }

    public synchronized void classify(Item item,
        Category category) {
            List items = ((TackCategory)
                category).getItems();
            if (items.contains(item) == false) {
                    items.add(item);
            }
    }

    public synchronized Category createCategory(String name)
            throws CategoryExistsException {
            TackCategory result = new
                TackCategory(this, name);
            if (this.categories.get(name) != null) {
                    throw new CategoryExistsException();
            }
            this.categories.put(name, result);
            return result;
    }

    public synchronized Item createItem(String name,
        int price, int quantity)
        throws ItemExistsException {

            TackItem result = new TackItem(this,
               nextCatalogNo++, name, price, quantity);
            if (this.items.contains(result)) {
                    throw new ItemExistsException();
            }
            this.items.add(result);
            inventorySize = inventorySize + quantity;
            return result;
    }
```

```
public synchronized void declassify(
    Item item, Category category) {
        List items = category.getItems();
        items.remove(item);
}

public synchronized void decreaseInventory(
    Item item, int amount)
        throws InventoryUnderflowException {
        inventorySize = inventorySize - amount;
        sales = sales + amount;
        int nq = item.getQuantity() - amount;
        if (nq < 0) {
            throw new InventoryUnderflowException();
        }
        ((TackItem)item).setQuantity(nq);
}

public void destroy() throws IOException {
        String cfn = this.name + FILEEXT;
        File cf = new File(cfn);
        if (cf.exists()) {
            cf.delete();
        }
}

public synchronized Category getCategory(String name) {
        Category result = (Category)
            this.categories.get(name);
        return result;
}

public synchronized void increaseInventory(
    Item item, int amount) {
        inventorySize = inventorySize + amount;
        if (amount < 0) {
            throw new IllegalArgumentException();
        }

        int nq = item.getQuantity() + amount;
        ((TackItem) item).setQuantity(nq);
}

public synchronized List getItems() {
        accesses++;
```

```
        return this.items;
    }

    public synchronized void removeCategory(
        Category category)
        throws NoSuchCategoryException {
            removeCategory(category.getName());
    }

    public synchronized void removeCategory(String name)
        throws NoSuchCategoryException {
            Category category = (Category)
                this.categories.remove(name);
            if (category == null) {
                    throw new NoSuchCategoryException();
            }
    }

    public synchronized void removeItem(Item item)
        throws NoSuchItemException {
            boolean exists = this.items.remove(item);
            if (exists == false) {
                    throw new NoSuchItemException();
            }
            inventorySize = inventorySize -
                item.getQuantity();
            removeItemFromCategories(item);
    }

    public synchronized void removeItem(int catalogNo)
        throws NoSuchItemException {
            boolean removed = false;
            Iterator i = this.items.iterator();
            while (i.hasNext()) {
                    Item item = (Item) i.next();
                    if (item.getCatalogNo() == catalogno) {
                            this.items.remove(item);
                            inventorySize = inventorySize
                                - item.getQuantity();
                            removeItemFromCategories(item);
                            removed = true;
                            break;
                    }
            }
            if (removed == false) {
```

```
                throw new NoSuchItemException();
            }
    }

    private void removeItemFromCategories(Item item) {
            Iterator i =
                this.categories.keySet().iterator();
            while (i.hasNext()) {
                String category = (String) i.next();
                declassify(item, (Category)
                    this.categories.get(category));
            }
    }

    // TackCatalogMBean methods

    public boolean isAutoCheckpointing() {
            return this.autoCheckpoint;
    }

    public synchronized void setAutoCheckpoint(
        boolean autoCheckpoint) {
            this.autoCheckpoint = autoCheckpoint;
    }

    public void doCheckpoint() {
            if (this.autoCheckpoint == true) {
                checkpoint();
            }
    }

    public synchronized void checkpoint() {
    }

    public int getNumberOfItems() {
            return items.size();
    }

    public int getInventorySize() {
            return inventorySize;
    }

    public int getTotalSales() {
            return sales;
    }
```

```
        public int getAccesses() {
                return accesses;
        }
}
```

You can see that this approach requires you to modify the base application code to accommodate JMX accessibility. Therefore, this approach works best when you are creating new applications and building in manageability. Because the changes are actually pretty minimal and not disruptive to the general flow of the application, it is possible to modify existing applications, provided that you have and own the code for JMX manageability.

The MBeanInfo instance created for this situation would look like this:

- Attributes:

```
TotalSales
NumberOfItems
TotalSales
Accesses
InventorySize
AutoCheckpoint
```

- Operations:

```
load()
doCheckpoint()
```

- Notifications: none

Each attribute has at least a getter in order for the attribute to be recognized in standard MBeans.

You can also make your application a dynamic MBean. You would have to add the DynamicMBean interface to your application. One of the benefits of this approach is that you don't have to keep your application and the MBean interface in synch. If your application is not using get/set pairs for its attributes in the JavaBean style, then you might want to use the dynamic-MBean option. In the following example (TackCatalogD) the tack catalog application is also a dynamic MBean. You can see that we no longer implement the TackCatalogMBean interface, but we do implement the DynamicMBean interface:

```
package jnjmx.ch9;

import java.io.File;
import java.io.FileInputStream;
import java.io.FileNotFoundException;
import java.io.FileOutputStream;
import java.io.IOException;
import java.io.ObjectInputStream;
import java.io.ObjectOutputStream;
import java.io.Serializable;
import java.util.ArrayList;
import java.util.HashMap;
import java.util.Iterator;
import java.util.List;
import java.util.Map;
import java.lang.reflect.*;
import javax.management.*;

public class TackCatalogD implements Catalog, Serializable, DynamicMBean {

	private static final String FILEEXT = ".catalog";
	private final String name;
	private boolean autoCheckpoint = false;
	private Map categories;
	private List items;
	private int nextCatalogNo = 1;
	private int accesses=0, sales=0, inventorySize=0;

	public TackCatalogD(String inName) {
		this.name = inName;
		this.categories = new HashMap();
		this.items = new ArrayList();
	}

public static TackCatalogD create(String inName) throws IOException {
		String cfn = inName + FILEEXT;
		File cf = new File(cfn);
		if (cf.exists()) {
			cf.delete();
		}

		TackCatalogD catalog = new TackCatalogD(inName);
		ObjectOutputStream db =
			new ObjectOutputStream(new FileOutputStream(cf));
```

```
        db.writeObject(catalog);
        db.flush();
        db.close();

        return catalog;
}

// load is exposed in TackCatalogMBean

public Catalog load(String name)
    throws IOException, ClassNotFoundException {
        String cfn = name + FILEEXT;
        File cf = new File(cfn);
        if (cf.exists() == false) {
            throw new FileNotFoundException(cfn + " doesn't exist");
        }

        ObjectInputStream db = new ObjectInputStream(
            new FileInputStream(cf));
        TackCatalogD catalog = (TackCatalogD) db.readObject();
        db.close();
        return catalog;
}


public synchronized Map getCategories() {
        return this.categories;
}


public synchronized void classify(Item item, Category category) {
        List items = ((TackCategory) category).getItems();
        if (items.contains(item) == false) {
            items.add(item);
        }
}

public synchronized Category createCategory(String name)
    throws CategoryExistsException {
        TackCategory result = new TackCategory(this, name);
        if (this.categories.get(name) != null) {
            throw new CategoryExistsException();
        }
        this.categories.put(name, result);
```

```
        return result;
    }

    public synchronized Item createItem(String name, int price, int quantity)
        throws ItemExistsException {
            TackItem result = new TackItem(this, nextCatalogNo++, name,
                price, quantity);
            if (this.items.contains(result)) {
                throw new ItemExistsException();
            }
            this.items.add(result);
            inventorySize = inventorySize + quantity;
            return result;
    }

    public synchronized void declassify(Item item, Category category) {
            List items = category.getItems();
            items.remove(item);
    }

    public synchronized void decreaseInventory(Item item, int amount)
        throws InventoryUnderflowException {
            inventorySize = inventorySize - amount;
            sales = sales + amount;
            int nq = item.getQuantity() - amount;
            if (nq < 0) {
                throw new InventoryUnderflowException();
            }
            ((TackItem)item).setQuantity(nq);
    }

    public void destroy() throws IOException {
            String cfn = this.name + FILEEXT;
            File cf = new File(cfn);
            if (cf.exists()) {
                cf.delete();
            }
    }

    public synchronized Category getCategory(String name) {
            Category result = (Category) this.categories.get(name);
            return result;
    }
```

```
public synchronized void increaseInventory(Item item, int amount) {
        inventorySize = inventorySize + amount;
        if (amount < 0) {
                throw new IllegalArgumentException();
        }

        int nq = item.getQuantity() + amount;
        ((TackItem) item).setQuantity(nq);
}



public synchronized List getItems() {
        accesses++;
        return this.items;
}

public synchronized void removeCategory(Category category)
    throws NoSuchCategoryException {
        removeCategory(category.getName());
}

public synchronized void removeCategory(String name)
    throws NoSuchCategoryException {
        Category category = (Category) this.categories.remove(name);
        if (category == null) {
                throw new NoSuchCategoryException();
        }
}

public synchronized void removeItem(Item item)
    throws NoSuchItemException {
        boolean exists = this.items.remove(item);
        if (exists == false) {
                throw new NoSuchItemException();
        }
        inventorySize = inventorySize - item.getQuantity();
        removeItemFromCategories(item);
}

public synchronized void removeItem(int catalogno)
    throws NoSuchItemException {
        boolean removed = false;
        Iterator i = this.items.iterator();
        while (i.hasNext()) {
                Item item = (Item) i.next();
```

```
                        if (item.getCatalogNo() == catalogno) {
                                this.items.remove(item);
                                inventorySize = inventorySize - item.getQuantity();
                                removeItemFromCategories(item);
                                removed = true;
                                break;
                        }
                }
                if (removed == false) {
                        throw new NoSuchItemException();
                }
        }

        private void removeItemFromCategories(Item item) {
                Iterator i = this.categories.keySet().iterator();
                while (i.hasNext()) {
                      String category = (String) i.next();
                      declassify(item, (Category) this.categories.get(category));
                }
        }

        // TackCatalogMBean methods

        public boolean isAutoCheckpointing() {
                return this.autoCheckpoint;
        }

        public void setAutoCheckpoint(boolean autoCheckpoint) {
                this.autoCheckpoint = autoCheckpoint;
        }

        public void doCheckpoint() {
                if (this.autoCheckpoint == true) {
                        checkpoint();
                }
        }

        public void checkpoint() {
        }

        /* MBean methods */
        public Object getAttribute(String attributeName)
            throws AttributeNotFoundException,
                  MBeanException,
                  ReflectionException
        {
```

```
        if ( attributeName.equals("AutoCheckpointing") )
            return new Boolean(autoCheckpoint);
        if ( attributeName.equals("NumberOfItems") )
            return new Integer(items.size());
        if ( attributeName.equals("Accesses") )
            return new Integer(accesses);
        if ( attributeName.equals("TotalSales") )
            return new Integer(sales);
        if ( attributeName.equals("InventorySize") )
            return new Integer(inventorySize);
        else throw(new AttributeNotFoundException("Attribute " +
            attributeName + " not found in " +
            this.getClass().getName()));
    }

    public AttributeList getAttributes(String[] attributes) {
        // In this simple example we always return all attributes
        // in a production example, you need to only return the
        // attributes in the list passed in
        AttributeList returnList = new AttributeList();
        if ( (attributes == null) || (attributes.length == 0) ||
             (attributes.length > 0)) {
            returnList.add(new Attribute("AutoCheckpointing",
                new Boolean(autoCheckpoint)) );
            returnList.add(new Attribute("NumberOfItems",
                new Integer(items.size())));
            returnList.add(new Attribute("Accesses",
                new Integer(accesses)) );
            returnList.add(new Attribute("TotalSales",
                new Integer(sales)) );
            returnList.add(new Attribute("InventorySize",
                new Integer(inventorySize)) );
        }
        return returnList;
    }

    public void setAttribute(Attribute newAttribute)
        throws AttributeNotFoundException,
             InvalidAttributeValueException,
             MBeanException,
             ReflectionException
    {
        String attributeName = newAttribute.getName();
        if ( attributeName.equals("Autocheckpointing") )
```

```
                autoCheckpoint =
                    ((Boolean)(newAttribute.getValue())).booleanValue();
            else if ( (attributeName.equals("NumberOfItems")) ||
                        (attributeName.equals("TotalSales" )) ||
                        (attributeName.equals("Accesses" )) ||
                        (attributeName.equals("InventorySize")) ) {
                throw(new AttributeNotFoundException("Attribute " + name +
                    " not updateable in " + this.getClass().getName()));
            } else
                throw(new AttributeNotFoundException("Attribute " + name +
                    " not found in " + this.getClass().getName()));
    }

    public AttributeList setAttributes(AttributeList newAttributes) {
            AttributeList returnList = new AttributeList();
            if ( newAttributes == null || newAttributes.isEmpty() )
                    return returnList;

            for ( Iterator I=newAttributes.iterator(); I.hasNext(); ) {
                    Attribute newAttribute= (Attribute)I.next();
                    try {
                        setAttribute(newAttribute);
                        returnList.add(new Attribute(newAttribute.getName(),
                                    newAttribute.getValue() ) );
                    } catch ( Exception e ) {
                    }

                    return returnList;
            }
            return returnList;
    }

    public Object invoke(String operationName, Object[] parms, String[] sig) {
        try {
            if ( operationName.equals("doCheckpoint") ) {
                    checkpoint();
            } else if ( operationName.equals("load") ) {
                    try {
                            return load((String)(parms[0]));
                    }
                    catch (Exception e) {
                            System.out.println("Load of TackCatalog failed");
                    }
                    return null;
```

```
        } else {
            throw new
                ReflectionException(
                new NoSuchMethodException(operationName),
                "Cannot find the operation " + operationName +
                " in TackCatalog");
        }
    }
    catch (ReflectionException e) {
        System.out.println("Load of TackCatalog failed");
    }
    return null;
}

public MBeanInfo getMBeanInfo() {
/* attributes: boolean AutoCheckpointing r/w,
int numberOfItems r/o,
int Accesses r/o,
int Sales r/o
int InventorySize r/o */
/* operations: void saveCatalog,
Catalog load,
void doCheckpoint */
/* notifications: none */
        String catDescription = "Tack Catalog Dynamic MBean";
        MBeanAttributeInfo[] catAttributes = new MBeanAttributeInfo[5];
        catAttributes[0] = new MBeanAttributeInfo("AutoCheckpointing",
                "java.lang.Boolean",
                "AutoCheckpointing: boolean value if checkpointing" +
                    " of catalog is done automatically",
                    true,true,false);

        catAttributes[1] = new MBeanAttributeInfo("NumberOfItems",
                    "java.lang.Integer",
                    "NumberOfItems: number of items in the catalog",
                    true,false,false);

        catAttributes[2] = new MBeanAttributeInfo("Accesses",
                    "java.lang.Integer",
                    "Accesses: number of time items in the catalog" +
                        " database have been listed",
                    true,false,false);
```

```
catAttributes[3] = new MBeanAttributeInfo("TotalSales",
                "java.lang.Integer",
                "Sales: number of items sold",
                true,false,false);

catAttributes[4] = new MBeanAttributeInfo("InventorySize",
                "java.lang.Integer",
                "InventorySize: Total number of all items " +
                            "currently in inventory",
                true,true,false);

MBeanConstructorInfo[] catConstructors =
    new MBeanConstructorInfo[2];

Constructor[] constructors = this.getClass().getConstructors();

catConstructors[0] = new MBeanConstructorInfo(
                "tackCatalog(dbName): Constructs a tackCatalog " +
                       "from an existing database",
                constructors[0]);

MBeanOperationInfo[] catOperations = new MBeanOperationInfo[2];

MBeanParameterInfo[] params = new MBeanParameterInfo[0];

catOperations[0] = new MBeanOperationInfo("doCheckpoint",
                "doCheckpoint(): saves the catalog to a file",
                params ,
                "void",
                 MBeanOperationInfo.ACTION);
params = new MBeanParameterInfo[] {
                (new MBeanParameterInfo("name",
                "java.lang.String",
                "Tack Catalog name"))};

catOperations[1] = new MBeanOperationInfo("load",
                "load(dbName): loads the catalog from a file",
                params ,
                "void",
                MBeanOperationInfo.ACTION);

MBeanNotificationInfo[] catNotifications =
    new MBeanNotificationInfo[0];

String className = this.getClass().getName();
```

```
        MBeanInfo catMBeanInfo = new MBeanInfo(className,
                       catDescription,
                       catAttributes,
                       catConstructors,
                       catOperations,
                       catNotifications );

        return catMBeanInfo;
    } // getMBeanInfo

}       // class
```

Note that the `getAttribute()` method doesn't delegate to the original `get` methods. We could have retained the MBean interface methods from the previous example and simply added the dynamic-MBean delegators, but we wanted to show an example of a case in which actual methods on the actual MBean may not exist.

Making an application that is also a model MBean is a little more complicated and less common. For the sake of completeness, we will discuss it. One way to do this is to have your application inherit from the model MBean implementation that accompanies the MBeanServer. Another way is to have your application implement the model MBean interfaces. However, we don't recommend the latter approach. Because Model MBeans may be specific to a particular MBeanServer, you may have some functional mismatch between your model MBean and the MBeanServer. If you ever need to extend or override the behavior of a model MBean, you should inherit from the one provided with the MBeanServer rather than implement one from scratch. Model MBeans are much better suited to remaining separate from the applications, as we will see in the next section.

9.2.2 MBeans on Behalf of Applications

Sometimes it is not appropriate to have the application code serve the dual purpose of application and MBean. In such cases you will have a separate MBean that manages the application. This MBean can be created and registered by the application itself, another class, or an adapter. These options are discussed in Section 9.2.3.

MBeans that manage separate applications should be fully implemented and can delegate some of the methods to the application itself. This delegation can be very useful when the management methods of the application are dispersed among multiple classes or distributed components. The methods in the MBean could also do out-of-band work like reading logs or interacting with system APIs, JVM APIs, or other management systems.

Standard MBeans are easy to create for this design. Standard MBeans can be used when the management interface, `MBeanInfo`, is stable and completely known at runtime. The standard MBean method implementations would invoke the appropriate methods on your application.

The standard MBean in the following example has a method that invokes methods on the application and methods that perform functions in their own right. We saw this application of MBeans for the Apache examples in Chapters 2 and 3. We are going to refactor the `TackCatalog` example into the following `TackCatalogSS` example, but now there are two classes: `TackCatalogSS` and `CatalogManager`, an MBean that has an MBean interface `CatalogManagerMBean`. Notice that we had to add a method—`getStats()`—and expose the existing `load()` and the `AutoCheckpointing` methods to `TackCatalogSS` so that `CatalogManager` would have the same functionality as when the two were part of the same class. We consolidated `getAccesses()`, `getTotalSales()`, `getInventorySize()`, and `getNumberOfItems()` into one method. This example is somewhat contrived because it would be better programming practice to have a get method for each as we did in the original `TackCatalog`, but we did this to make sure you see that there does not have to be one-to-one correspondence between the managed resource (`TackCatalogSS`) and the standard MBean (`CatalogManager`).

```
package jnjmx.ch9;

import java.io.File;
import java.io.FileInputStream;
import java.io.FileNotFoundException;
import java.io.FileOutputStream;
import java.io.IOException;
import java.io.ObjectInputStream;
import java.io.ObjectOutputStream;
import java.io.Serializable;
import java.util.ArrayList;
import java.util.HashMap;
import java.util.Iterator;
import java.util.List;
import java.util.Map;

// Separate Standard MBean Tack Catalog Example

public class TackCatalogSS implements Catalog, Serializable {
```

```
private static final String FILEEXT = ".catalog";
private final String name;
private boolean autoCheckpoint = false;
private Map categories;
private List items;
private int nextCatalogNo = 1;
private int accesses=0, sales=0, inventorySize=0;

public TackCatalogSS(String inName) {
        this.name = inName;
        this.categories = new HashMap();
        this.items = new ArrayList();
}

public static TackCatalogSS create(String inName) throws IOException {
        String cfn = inName + FILEEXT;
        File cf = new File(cfn);
        if (cf.exists()) {
                cf.delete();
        }

        TackCatalogSS catalog = new TackCatalogSS(inName);
        ObjectOutputStream db =
                new ObjectOutputStream(new FileOutputStream(cf));
        db.writeObject(catalog);
        db.flush();
        db.close();
        return catalog;
}

// Load is exposed in TackCatalogMBean

public TackCatalogSS load(String name)
    throws IOException, ClassNotFoundException {
        String cfn = name + FILEEXT;
        File cf = new File(cfn);
        if (cf.exists() == false) {
                throw new FileNotFoundException(cfn + " doesn't exist");
        }

        ObjectInputStream db = new ObjectInputStream(
             new FileInputStream(cf));
        TackCatalogSS catalog = (TackCatalogSS) db.readObject();
```

```
        db.close();
        return catalog;
}

public synchronized Map getCategories() {
        return this.categories;
}


public synchronized void classify(Item item, Category category) {
        List items = ((TackCategory) category).getItems();
        if (items.contains(item) == false) {
                items.add(item);
        }
}

public synchronized Category createCategory(String name)
    throws CategoryExistsException {
        TackCategory result = new TackCategory(this, name);
        if (this.categories.get(name) != null) {
                throw new CategoryExistsException();
        }
        this.categories.put(name, result);
        return result;
}

public synchronized Item createItem(String name, int price, int quantity)
    throws ItemExistsException {
        TackItem result = new TackItem(this, nextCatalogNo++, name,
            price, quantity);
        if (this.items.contains(result)) {
                throw new ItemExistsException();
        }
        this.items.add(result);
        inventorySize = inventorySize + quantity;
        return result;
}

public synchronized void declassify(Item item, Category category) {
        List items = category.getItems();
        items.remove(item);
}
```

```
public synchronized void decreaseInventory(Item item, int amount)
    throws InventoryUnderflowException {
        inventorySize = inventorySize - amount;
        sales = sales + amount;
        int nq = item.getQuantity() - amount;
        if (nq < 0) {
                throw new InventoryUnderflowException();
        }
        ((TackItem)item).setQuantity(nq);
}

public void destroy() throws IOException {
        String cfn = this.name + FILEEXT;
        File cf = new File(cfn);
        if (cf.exists()) {
                cf.delete();
        }
}

public synchronized Category getCategory(String name) {
        Category result = (Category) this.categories.get(name);
        return result;
}

public synchronized void increaseInventory(Item item, int amount) {
        inventorySize = inventorySize + amount;
        if (amount < 0) {
                throw new IllegalArgumentException();
        }
        int nq = item.getQuantity() + amount;
        ((TackItem) item).setQuantity(nq);
}



public synchronized List getItems() {
        accesses++;
        return this.items;
}

public synchronized void removeCategory(Category category)
    throws NoSuchCategoryException {
        removeCategory(category.getName());
}
```

```
public synchronized void removeCategory(String name)
        throws NoSuchCategoryException {
        Category category = (Category) this.categories.remove(name);
        if (category == null) {
                throw new NoSuchCategoryException();
        }
}

public synchronized void removeItem(Item item)
    throws NoSuchItemException {
        boolean exists = this.items.remove(item);
        if (exists == false) {
                throw new NoSuchItemException();
        }
        inventorySize = inventorySize - item.getQuantity();
        removeItemFromCategories(item);
}

public synchronized void removeItem(int catalogno)
    throws NoSuchItemException {
        boolean removed = false;
        Iterator i = this.items.iterator();
        while (i.hasNext()) {
                Item item = (Item) i.next();
                if (item.getCatalogNo() == catalogno) {
                        this.items.remove(item);
                        inventorySize = inventorySize -
                            item.getQuantity();
                        removeItemFromCategories(item);
                        removed = true;
                        break;
                }
        }
        if (removed == false) {
                throw new NoSuchItemException();
        }
}

private void removeItemFromCategories(Item item) {
        Iterator i = this.categories.keySet().iterator();
        while (i.hasNext()) {
              String category = (String) i.next();
              declassify(item, (Category) this.categories.get(category));
        }
}
```

```
        // TackCatalogMBean Methods

        public boolean isAutoCheckpointing() {
                return this.autoCheckpoint;
        }

        public synchronized void setAutoCheckpoint(boolean autoCheckpoint) {
                this.autoCheckpoint = autoCheckpoint;
        }

        public void doCheckpoint() {
                if (this.autoCheckpoint == true) {
                        checkpoint();
                }
        }

        public synchronized void checkpoint() {
                // this method would write the data from the
                // catalog into a database
        }

        public int getStats(String statName) {
                if (statName.equals("NumberOfItems")) return items.size();
                else if (statName.equals("InventorySize")) return inventorySize;
                else if (statName.equals("getTotalSales")) return sales;
                else if (statName.equals("Accesses")) return accesses;
                else return 0;
        }

}
```

Here is the MBean implementation for `TackCatalogSS`:

```
package jnjmx.ch9;

import java.io.Serializable;
import java.io.IOException;

public interface CatalogManagerMBean  {

        public TackCatalogSS load(String name)
                throws IOException, ClassNotFoundException;
        public boolean isAutoCheckpointing();
```

```
        public void setAutoCheckpoint(boolean autoCheckpoint);
        public void doCheckpoint();
        public int getNumberOfItems();
        public int getTotalSales();
        public int getAccesses();
        public int getInventorySize();
}
```

Here is the MBean implementation for `CatalogManagerMBean`, `CatalogManager`:

```
package jnjmx.ch9;
import java.io.IOException;

public class CatalogManager implements CatalogManagerMBean {
        // TackCatalogMBean Methods
        TackCatalogSS catalog;

        public CatalogManager (Catalog inCatalog) {
                catalog = (TackCatalogSS)inCatalog;
        }

        public TackCatalogSS load(String name)
            throws IOException, ClassNotFoundException{
                return (catalog.load(name));
        }

        public boolean isAutoCheckpointing() {
                return catalog.isAutoCheckpointing();
        }

        public synchronized void setAutoCheckpoint(boolean autoCheckpoint) {
                catalog.setAutoCheckpoint(autoCheckpoint);
        }

        public void doCheckpoint() {
                if (catalog.isAutoCheckpointing() == true) {
                        catalog.doCheckpoint();
                }
        }

        public int getNumberOfItems() {
                return catalog.getStats("NumberOfItems");
        }
```

```
    public int getInventorySize() {
            return catalog.getStats("InventorySize");
    }

    public int getTotalSales() {
            return catalog.getStats("TotalSales");
    }

    public int getAccesses() {
            return catalog.getStats("Accesses");
    }
}
```

The instance of MBeanInfo generated by the MBeanServer would be the same as before:

- Attributes:

```
TotalSales
NumberOfItems
TotalSales
Accesses
InventorySize
AutoCheckpoint
```

- Operations:

```
load()
doCheckpoint()
```

- Notifications: none

Dynamic MBeans are suitable for this design as well. Dynamic MBeans should be used when the application doesn't follow the JavaBean design pattern or when you might not know the exact management interface during development. Dynamic MBeans allow their MBeanInfo to be set during development or runtime. One common scenario is to create dynamic MBeans to represent management functionality already developed in an existing management application. In such cases, as management objects or managed resources in the existing application are instantiated, a DynamicMBean implementation is instantiated as well. The MBeanInfo instance would be created by introspection of the existing management object or managed resource.

Suppose that we already have a management application for a Web server farm that uses three different brands of Web servers. We could create a dynamic MBean for the Web server in general. As each Web server was instantiated, the `MBeanInfo` instance specific to that server would be created. Here is the `TackCatalogDD` example using a separate, external dynamic MBean; it is essentially the same as `TackCatalogSS`. The real differences come in `CatalogManagerDD`:

```
package jnjmx.ch9;


import java.io.File;
import java.io.FileInputStream;
import java.io.FileNotFoundException;
import java.io.FileOutputStream;
import java.io.IOException;
import java.io.ObjectInputStream;
import java.io.ObjectOutputStream;
import java.io.Serializable;
import java.util.ArrayList;
import java.util.HashMap;
import java.util.Iterator;
import java.util.List;
import java.util.Map;
import java.lang.reflect.*;
import javax.management.*;

// Separate Dynamic MBean Example

public class TackCatalogDD implements Catalog, Serializable {

        private static final String FILEEXT = ".catalog";
        private final String name;
        private boolean autoCheckpoint = false;
        private Map categories;
        private List items;
        private int nextCatalogNo = 1;
        private int accesses=0, sales=0, inventorySize=0;

        public TackCatalogDD(String inName) {
                this.name = inName;
                this.categories = new HashMap();
```

```
            this.items = new ArrayList();
    }
    public static TackCatalogDD create(String inName) throws IOException {
            String cfn = inName + FILEEXT;
            File cf = new File(cfn);
            if (cf.exists()) {
                    cf.delete();
            }

            TackCatalogDD catalog = new TackCatalogDD(inName);
            ObjectOutputStream db =
                    new ObjectOutputStream(new FileOutputStream(cf));
            db.writeObject(catalog);
            db.flush();
            db.close();
            return catalog;
    }

    // load is exposed in TackCatalogMBean

    public Catalog load(String name)
            throws IOException, ClassNotFoundException {
            String cfn = name + FILEEXT;
            File cf = new File(cfn);
            if (cf.exists() == false) {
                    throw new FileNotFoundException(cfn + " doesn't exist");
            }

            ObjectInputStream db = new ObjectInputStream(
                new FileInputStream(cf));
            TackCatalogDD catalog = (TackCatalogDD) db.readObject();
            db.close();
            return catalog;
    }


    public synchronized Map getCategories() {
            return this.categories;
    }


    public synchronized void classify(Item item, Category category) {
            List items = ((TackCategory) category).getItems();
```

```
        if (items.contains(item) == false) {
            items.add(item);
        }
}

public synchronized Category createCategory(String name)
    throws CategoryExistsException {
        TackCategory result = new TackCategory(this, name);
        if (this.categories.get(name) != null) {
            throw new CategoryExistsException();
        }
        this.categories.put(name, result);
        return result;
}

public synchronized Item createItem(String name, int price, int quantity)
    throws ItemExistsException {
        TackItem result = new TackItem(this, nextCatalogNo++, name,
            price, quantity);
        if (this.items.contains(result)) {
            throw new ItemExistsException();
        }
        this.items.add(result);
        inventorySize = inventorySize + quantity;
        return result;
}

public synchronized void declassify(Item item, Category category) {
        List items = category.getItems();
        items.remove(item);
}

public synchronized void decreaseInventory(Item item, int amount)
    throws InventoryUnderflowException {
        inventorySize = inventorySize - amount;
        sales = sales + amount;
        int nq = item.getQuantity() - amount;
        if (nq < 0) {
            throw new InventoryUnderflowException();
        }
        ((TackItem)item).setQuantity(nq);
}

public void destroy() throws IOException {
        String cfn = this.name + FILEEXT;
```

```
            File cf = new File(cfn);
            if (cf.exists()) {
                cf.delete();
            }
    }

    public synchronized Category getCategory(String name) {
            Category result = (Category) this.categories.get(name);
            return result;
    }

    public synchronized void increaseInventory(Item item, int amount) {
            inventorySize = inventorySize + amount;
            if (amount < 0) {
                throw new IllegalArgumentException();
            }
            int nq = item.getQuantity() + amount;
            ((TackItem) item).setQuantity(nq);
    }


    public synchronized List getItems() {
            accesses++;
            return this.items;
    }

    public synchronized void removeCategory(Category category)
        throws NoSuchCategoryException {
            removeCategory(category.getName());
    }

    public synchronized void removeCategory(String name)
        throws NoSuchCategoryException {
            Category category = (Category) this.categories.remove(name);
            if (category == null) {
                throw new NoSuchCategoryException();
            }
    }

    public synchronized void removeItem(Item item)
        throws NoSuchItemException {
            boolean exists = this.items.remove(item);
            if (exists == false) {
```

```
                throw new NoSuchItemException();
            }
            inventorySize = inventorySize - item.getQuantity();
            removeItemFromCategories(item);
    }

    public synchronized void removeItem(int catalogno)
        throws NoSuchItemException {
            boolean removed = false;
            Iterator i = this.items.iterator();
            while (i.hasNext()) {
                Item item = (Item) i.next();
                if (item.getCatalogNo() == catalogno) {
                    this.items.remove(item);
                    inventorySize = inventorySize - item.getQuantity();
                    removeItemFromCategories(item);
                    removed = true;
                    break;
                }
            }
            if (removed == false) {
                throw new NoSuchItemException();
            }
    }

    private void removeItemFromCategories(Item item) {
            Iterator i = this.categories.keySet().iterator();
            while (i.hasNext()) {
                String category = (String) i.next();
                declassify(item, (Category) this.categories.get(category));
            }
    }

    // TackCatalogMBean methods

    public boolean isAutoCheckpointing() {
            return this.autoCheckpoint;
    }

    public void setAutoCheckpoint(boolean autoCheckpoint) {
            this.autoCheckpoint = autoCheckpoint;
    }

    public void doCheckpoint() {
            if (this.autoCheckpoint == true) {
```

```
                checkpoint();
            }
    }

    public void checkpoint() {
    }

    public int getStats(String statName) {
            if (statName.equals("NumberOfItems")) return items.size();
            else if (statName.equals("InventorySize")) return inventorySize;
            else if (statName.equals("getTotalSales")) return sales;
            else if (statName.equals("Accesses")) return accesses;
            else return 0;
    }

}       // class
```

Here is the Dynamic MBean (CatalogManagerDD) for TackCatalogDD. Notice that no separate interface is necessary:

```
package jnjmx.ch9;
import java.io.IOException;
import java.lang.reflect.*;
import java.util.Iterator;
import javax.management.*;

public class CatalogManagerDD implements DynamicMBean  {
        // TackCatalogMBean methods
        TackCatalogDD catalog;

        public CatalogManagerDD (Catalog inCatalog) {
                catalog = (TackCatalogDD)inCatalog;
        }

        /* MBean methods */
        public Object getAttribute(String attributeName)
            throws AttributeNotFoundException,
                   MBeanException,
                   ReflectionException
        {
                if ( attributeName.equals("AutoCheckpointing") )
                        return new Boolean(catalog.isAutoCheckpointing());
                if ( attributeName.equals("NumberOfItems") )
                        return new Integer(catalog.getStats("NumberOfItems"));
```

```
        if ( attributeName.equals("Accesses") )
              return new Integer(catalog.getStats("Accesses"));
        if ( attributeName.equals("TotalSales") )
              return new Integer(catalog.getStats("TotalSales"));
        if ( attributeName.equals("InventorySize") )
              return new Integer(catalog.getStats("InventorySize"));
        else throw(new AttributeNotFoundException("Attribute " +
            attributeName + " not found in " +
            this.getClass().getName()));
}

public AttributeList getAttributes(String[] attributes) {
        // In this simple example we always return all attributes
        // in a production example, you need to only return the
        // attributes in the list passed in
        AttributeList returnList = new AttributeList();
        if ( (attributes == null) || (attributes.length == 0) ||
             (attributes.length > 0)) {
               returnList.add(new Attribute("AutoCheckpointing",
                   new Boolean(catalog.isAutoCheckpointing())) );
               returnList.add(new Attribute("NumberOfItems",
                   new Integer(catalog.getStats("NumberOfItems"))));
               returnList.add(new Attribute("Accesses",
                   new Integer(catalog.getStats("Accesses"))) );
               returnList.add(new Attribute("TotalSales",
                   new Integer(catalog.getStats("TotalSales"))) );
               returnList.add(new Attribute("InventorySize",
                   new Integer(catalog.getStats("InventorySize"))) );
        }
        return returnList;
}

public void setAttribute(Attribute newAttribute)
    throws AttributeNotFoundException,
         InvalidAttributeValueException,
         MBeanException,
         ReflectionException
{
        String attributeName = newAttribute.getName();
        if ( attributeName.equals("Autocheckpointing") )
               catalog.setAutoCheckpoint(((Boolean)
                   (newAttribute.getValue())).booleanValue());
        else if ( (attributeName.equals("NumberOfItems")) ||
                       (attributeName.equals("TotalSales" )) ||
                       (attributeName.equals("Accesses" )) ||
                       (attributeName.equals("InventorySize")) ) {
```

```
                throw(new AttributeNotFoundException("Attribute " +
                    attributeName + " not updateable in " +
                    this.getClass().getName()));
        } else
                throw(new AttributeNotFoundException("Attribute " +
                    attributeName + " not found in " +
                    this.getClass().getName()));
    }

    public AttributeList setAttributes(AttributeList newAttributes) {
        AttributeList returnList = new AttributeList();
        if ( newAttributes == null || newAttributes.isEmpty() )
            return returnList;

        for ( Iterator I=newAttributes.iterator(); I.hasNext(); ) {
            Attribute newAttribute= (Attribute)I.next();
            try {
                setAttribute(newAttribute);
                returnList.add(new Attribute(newAttribute.getName(),
                        newAttribute.getValue() ) );
            } catch ( Exception e ) {
            }
            return returnList;
        }
        return returnList;
    }

    public Object invoke(String operationName, Object[] parms, String[] sig) {
        try {
            if ( operationName.equals("doCheckpoint") ) {
                catalog.doCheckpoint();
            } else if ( operationName.equals("load") ) {
                try {
                    return catalog.load((String)(parms[0]));
                }
                catch (Exception e) {
                    System.out.println("Load of TackCatalog failed");
                }
                return null;
            } else {
                throw new
                    ReflectionException(
                    new NoSuchMethodException(operationName),
                    "Cannot find the operation " + operationName +
                    " in TackCatalog");
            }
```

```
        }
        catch (ReflectionException e) {
              System.out.println("Load of TackCatalog failed");
        }
        return null;
  }

  public MBeanInfo getMBeanInfo() {
  /* attributes: boolean AutoCheckpointing r/w,
  int numberOfItems r/o,
  int Accesses r/o,
  int Sales r/o
  int InventorySize r/o */
  /* operations: void saveCatalog,
  Catalog load,
  void doCheckpoint */
  /* notifications: none */
        String catDescription = "Tack Catalog Dynamic MBean";
        MBeanAttributeInfo[] catAttributes = new MBeanAttributeInfo[5];
        catAttributes[0] = new MBeanAttributeInfo("AutoCheckpointing",
                  "java.lang.Boolean",
                  "AutoCheckpointing: boolean value if checkpointing " +
                        "of catalog is done automatically",
                  true,true,false);


        catAttributes[1] = new MBeanAttributeInfo("NumberOfItems",
                     "java.lang.Integer",
                     "NumberOfItems: number of items in the catalog",
                     true,false,false);

        catAttributes[2] = new MBeanAttributeInfo("Accesses",
                     "java.lang.Integer",
                     "Accesses: number of time items in the catalog " +
                            "database have been listed",
                     true,false,false);

        catAttributes[3] = new MBeanAttributeInfo("TotalSales",
                     "java.lang.Integer",
                     "Sales: number of items sold",
                     true,false,false);

        catAttributes[4] = new MBeanAttributeInfo("InventorySize",
                     "java.lang.Integer",
```

```
                "InventorySize: Total number of all items currently " +
                    "in inventory",
                    true,true,false);

        MBeanConstructorInfo[] catConstructors =
            new MBeanConstructorInfo[2];
       Constructor[] constructors = catalog.getClass().getConstructors();
        catConstructors[0] = new MBeanConstructorInfo(
                    "tackCatalog(dbName): Constructs a tackCatalog " +
                    "from an existing database",
                    constructors[0]);

        MBeanOperationInfo[] catOperations = new MBeanOperationInfo[2];
        MBeanParameterInfo[] params = new MBeanParameterInfo[0];
        catOperations[0] = new MBeanOperationInfo("doCheckpoint",
                    "doCheckpoint(): saves the catalog to a file",
                    params ,
                    "void",
                    MBeanOperationInfo.ACTION);
        params = new MBeanParameterInfo[] {
                    (new MBeanParameterInfo("name",
                    "java.lang.String",
                    "Tack Catalog name"))};

        catOperations[1] = new MBeanOperationInfo("load",
                    "load(dbName): loads the catalog from a file",
                    params ,
                    "void",
                    MBeanOperationInfo.ACTION);

        MBeanNotificationInfo[] catNotifications =
            new MBeanNotificationInfo[0];
        String className = this.getClass().getName();
        MBeanInfo catMBeanInfo = new MBeanInfo(className,
                                    catDescription,
                                    catAttributes,
                                    catConstructors,
                                    catOperations,
                                    catNotifications );
        return catMBeanInfo;
    } // getMBeanInfo
}
```

Dynamic MBeans are also interesting as separate MBeans when the application has a separate management class. It is easy to write a dynamic MBean that reflects everything in the separate management class. In fact it is possible to take a `TackCatalogDD` application with a `CatalogManager` class and write a dynamic MBean implementation that sets its `MBeanInfo` directly from `CatalogManager` using reflection at runtime.

Model MBeans are best suited to being separate MBeans for the application. They are already implemented and have a built-in ability to delegate operations to the application. Chapter 4, on model MBeans, gave an example of this approach. Here is the `TackCatalog` application using model MBeans:

```
package jnjmx.ch9;


import java.io.File;
import java.io.FileInputStream;
import java.io.FileNotFoundException;
import java.io.FileOutputStream;
import java.io.IOException;
import java.io.ObjectInputStream;
import java.io.ObjectOutputStream;
import java.io.Serializable;
import java.util.ArrayList;
import java.util.HashMap;
import java.util.Iterator;
import java.util.List;
import java.util.Map;

import java.lang.reflect.*;

import javax.management.*;
import javax.management.modelmbean.*;

// Separate Model MBean Example

public class TackCatalogMM implements Catalog, Serializable {

      private static final String FILEEXT = ".catalog";
      private final String name;
      private boolean autoCheckpoint = false;
      private Map categories;
      private List items;
```

```
private int nextCatalogNo = 1;
private int accesses=0, sales=0, inventorySize=0;

public TackCatalogMM(String inName) {
        this.name = inName;
        this.categories = new HashMap();
        this.items = new ArrayList();
}
public static TackCatalogMM create(String inName) throws IOException {
        String cfn = inName + FILEEXT;
        File cf = new File(cfn);
        if (cf.exists()) {
              cf.delete();
        }

        TackCatalogMM catalog = new TackCatalogMM(inName);
        ObjectOutputStream db =
              new ObjectOutputStream(new FileOutputStream(cf));
        db.writeObject(catalog);
        db.flush();
        db.close();
        return catalog;
}

// Load is exposed in TackCatalogMBean

public Catalog load(String name)
    throws IOException, ClassNotFoundException {
        String cfn = name + FILEEXT;
        File cf = new File(cfn);
        if (cf.exists() == false) {
              throw new FileNotFoundException(cfn + " doesn't exist");
        }

        ObjectInputStream db = new ObjectInputStream(
            new FileInputStream(cf));
        TackCatalogMM catalog = (TackCatalogMM) db.readObject();
        db.close();
        return catalog;
}


public synchronized Map getCategories() {
        return this.categories;
}
```

```
public synchronized void classify(Item item, Category category) {
        List items = ((TackCategory) category).getItems();
        if (items.contains(item) == false) {
               items.add(item);
        }
}

public synchronized Category createCategory(String name)
    throws CategoryExistsException {
        TackCategory result = new TackCategory(this, name);
        if (this.categories.get(name) != null) {
               throw new CategoryExistsException();
        }
        this.categories.put(name, result);
        return result;
}

public synchronized Item createItem(String name, int price, int quantity)
    throws ItemExistsException {
        TackItem result = new TackItem(this, nextCatalogNo++, name,
            price, quantity);
        if (this.items.contains(result)) {
               throw new ItemExistsException();
        }
        this.items.add(result);
        inventorySize = inventorySize + quantity;
        return result;
}

public synchronized void declassify(Item item, Category category) {
        List items = category.getItems();
        items.remove(item);
}

public synchronized void decreaseInventory(Item item, int amount)
    throws InventoryUnderflowException {
        inventorySize = inventorySize - amount;
        sales = sales + amount;
        int nq = item.getQuantity() - amount;
        if (nq < 0) {
               throw new InventoryUnderflowException();
        }
        ((TackItem)item).setQuantity(nq);
}
```

```
public void destroy() throws IOException {
        String cfn = this.name + FILEEXT;
        File cf = new File(cfn);
        if (cf.exists()) {
                cf.delete();
        }
}

public synchronized Category getCategory(String name) {
        Category result = (Category) this.categories.get(name);
        return result;
}

public synchronized void increaseInventory(Item item, int amount) {
        inventorySize = inventorySize + amount;
        if (amount < 0) {
                throw new IllegalArgumentException();
        }
        int nq = item.getQuantity() + amount;
        ((TackItem) item).setQuantity(nq);
}

public synchronized List getItems() {
        accesses++;
        return this.items;
}

public synchronized void removeCategory(Category category)
    throws NoSuchCategoryException {
        removeCategory(category.getName());
}

public synchronized void removeCategory(String name)
    throws NoSuchCategoryException {
        Category category = (Category) this.categories.remove(name);
        if (category == null) {
                throw new NoSuchCategoryException();
        }
}

public synchronized void removeItem(Item item)
    throws NoSuchItemException {
        boolean exists = this.items.remove(item);
        if (exists == false) {
```

```
                throw new NoSuchItemException();
            }
            inventorySize = inventorySize - item.getQuantity();
            removeItemFromCategories(item);
    }

    public synchronized void removeItem(int catalogno)
        throws NoSuchItemException {
            boolean removed = false;
            Iterator i = this.items.iterator();
            while (i.hasNext()) {
                Item item = (Item) i.next();
                if (item.getCatalogNo() == catalogno) {
                    this.items.remove(item);
                    inventorySize = inventorySize - item.getQuantity();
                    removeItemFromCategories(item);
                    removed = true;
                    break;
                }
            }
            if (removed == false) {
                throw new NoSuchItemException();
            }
    }

    private void removeItemFromCategories(Item item) {
            Iterator i = this.categories.keySet().iterator();
            while (i.hasNext()) {
                String category = (String) i.next();
                declassify(item, (Category) this.categories.get(category));
            }
    }

    // TackCatalogMBean Methods
    public boolean isAutoCheckpointing() {
            return this.autoCheckpoint;
    }

    public void setAutoCheckpoint(boolean autoCheckpoint) {
            this.autoCheckpoint = autoCheckpoint;
    }

    public void doCheckpoint() {
            if (this.autoCheckpoint == true) {
                checkpoint();
```

```
        }
}

public void checkpoint() {
}

public int getNumberOfItems() {
        return items.size();
}

public int getInventorySize() {
        return inventorySize;
}

public int getTotalSales() {
        return sales;
}

public int getAccesses() {
        return accesses;
}

ModelMBean createCatalogMBean() {
  ModelMBean catalogMBean = null;
       try {
             catalogMBean = new RequiredModelMBean();
             catalogMBean.setModelMBeanInfo(createCatalogMBeanInfo());
             catalogMBean.setManagedResource(this, "ObjectReference");
       }
       catch (Exception e) {
              System.out.println("Creating Tack Catalog MBean failed: " +
                  e.getMessage());
       }
       return catalogMBean;
}

ModelMBeanInfo createCatalogMBeanInfo() {
        ModelMBeanInfo info = null;
/* attributes: boolean AutoCheckpointing r/w,
int numberOfItems r/o,
int Accesses r/o,
int Sales r/o
int InventorySize r/o */
/* operations: void saveCatalog,
Catalog load,
```

```
    void doCheckpoint */
    /* notifications: none */
            String catDescription = "Tack Catalog Dynamic MBean";

            Descriptor catDescriptor =
                    new DescriptorSupport(
                            new String[] {
                                    ("name=TackCatalog"),
                                    "descriptorType=mbean",
                                    ("displayName=TackCatalogManager"),
                                    "type=jnjmxch9.TackCatalogMM",
                                    "log=T",
                                    "logFile=jmxmain.log",
                                    "currencyTimeLimit=10" });

            ModelMBeanAttributeInfo[] catAttributes =
                new ModelMBeanAttributeInfo[5];

            Descriptor catDescAuto =
                new DescriptorSupport(
                        new String[] {
                                "name=AutoCheckpointing",
                                "descriptorType=attribute",
                                "displayName=AutoCheckpointing",
                                "getMethod=getAutoCheckpointing",
                                "currencyTimeLimit=10" });

            catAttributes[0] =
                new ModelMBeanAttributeInfo("AutoCheckpointing",
                     "java.lang.Boolean",
                     "AutoCheckpointing: boolean value if checkpointing " +
                          "of catalog is done automatically",
                     false,true,true,
                     catDescAuto);

            Descriptor catDescItems =
                new DescriptorSupport(
                        new String[] {
                                "name=NumberOfItems",
                                "descriptorType=attribute",
                                "displayName=NumberOfItems",
                                "getMethod=getNumberOfItems",
                                "currencyTimeLimit=10" });
```

```
catAttributes[1] = new ModelMBeanAttributeInfo("NumberOfItems",
               "java.lang.Integer",
               "NumberOfItems: number of items in the catalog",
               true,false,false,
               catDescItems);
Descriptor catDescAccess =
       new DescriptorSupport(
               new String[] {
                      "name=Accesses",
                      "descriptorType=attribute",
                      "displayName=Accesses",
                      "getMethod=getAccesses",
                      "currencyTimeLimit=10" });

catAttributes[2] = new ModelMBeanAttributeInfo("Accesses",
              "java.lang.Integer",
              "Accesses: number of time items in the catalog " +
              "database have been listed",
              true,false,false,
              catDescAccess);

Descriptor catDescSales =
       new DescriptorSupport(
               new String[] {
                      "name=TotalSales",
                      "descriptorType=attribute",
                      "displayName=TotalSales",
                      "getMethod=getTotalSales",
                      "currencyTimeLimit=10" });

catAttributes[3] = new ModelMBeanAttributeInfo("TotalSales",
                      "java.lang.Integer",
                      "Sales: number of items sold",
                      true,false,false,
                      catDescSales);

Descriptor catDescInv =
       new DescriptorSupport(
               new String[] {
                      "name=InventorySize",
                      "descriptorType=attribute",
                      "displayName=InventorySize",
                      "getMethod=getInventorySize",
                      "currencyTimeLimit=10" });
```

```
catAttributes[4] = new ModelMBeanAttributeInfo("InventorySize",
                "java.lang.Integer",
                "InventorySize: Total number of all " +
                "items currently in inventory",
                true,true,false,
                catDescInv);

ModelMBeanConstructorInfo[] catConstructors =
       new ModelMBeanConstructorInfo[1];
Constructor[] constructors = this.getClass().getConstructors();

Descriptor tackConstDesc =
       new DescriptorSupport(
               new String[] {
                      "name=TackCatalogMM",
                      "descriptorType=operation",
                      "role=constructor" });

catConstructors[0] = new ModelMBeanConstructorInfo(
               "tackCatalog(dbName): Constructs a tackCatalog" +
                      " from an existing database",
               constructors[0],
               tackConstDesc);

ModelMBeanOperationInfo[] catOperations =
       new ModelMBeanOperationInfo[2];
MBeanParameterInfo[] params = new MBeanParameterInfo[0];

Descriptor catDescCP = new DescriptorSupport(new String[] {
               "name=doCheckpoint",
               "descriptorType=operation",
               "class=TackcatalogMM",
               "role=operation" });

catOperations[0] = new ModelMBeanOperationInfo("doCheckpoint",
               "doCheckpoint(): saves the catalog to a file",
               params ,
               "void",
               MBeanOperationInfo.ACTION,
               catDescCP);

params = new MBeanParameterInfo[] {
               (new MBeanParameterInfo("name",
               "java.lang.String",
               "Tack Catalog name"))};
```

```
            Descriptor catDescLoad = new DescriptorSupport(new String[] {
                    "name=load",
                    "descriptorType=operation",
                    "class=TackcatalogMM",
                    "role=operation" });

            catOperations[1] = new ModelMBeanOperationInfo("load",
                     "load(dbName): loads the catalog from a file",
                     params ,
                     "jnjmxch9.Catalog",
                     MBeanOperationInfo.ACTION,
                     catDescLoad);

            ModelMBeanNotificationInfo[] catNotifications =
                     new ModelMBeanNotificationInfo[0];
            String className = this.getClass().getName();
            info = new ModelMBeanInfoSupport(className,
                                               catDescription,
                                               catAttributes,
                                               catConstructors,
                                               catOperations,
                                               catNotifications );
            try {
                    info.setMBeanDescriptor(catDescriptor);
            } catch (Exception e) {
                    System.out.println("CreateModelMBeanInfo failed with " +
                    e.getMessage());
            }
            return info;
        }
}       // class
```

Here we have created a model MBean, but it is not registered with an MBeanServer at this point. In Section 9.2.3 we will look at ways to register this MBean with an MBeanServer. Notice that we have added the get and set methods as operations that the attributes now point to. This example does not take advantage of any of the model MBean's features like caching, logging, and persistence. But it does illustrate how to organize the MBean implementation. As we saw in Chapter 4, it is much easier to create instances of `ModelMBeanInfo` from XML files.

9.2.3 Publish-Only MBeans

Some applications have management information that they need to expose to a management system, but they are unable or unwilling to be interrupted to get current values of attributes or invoke operations. This situation may arise for several reasons—for example, if the application is real-time, highly distributed, performance critical, can only initiate communications and cannot receive asynchronous communications, or runs on a small device that can only send data or receive solicited data. Examples of applications that fall into the last category are browsers and many applications on pervasive devices like PDAs (personal digital assistants). Figure 9.4 shows how an application can set attributes and invoke operations on its MBean, without being affected by the changes in the MBean.

MBeans for these types of applications can be created and registered by another program outside the managed resource. Then the MBeans have a lifecycle that is not tied to the managed resource. The application can find and reuse the MBean while it is executing. The application would be responsible for updating the MBean whenever a configuration or metric attribute was updated. The `getAttribute()` methods would always return the current stored value and not go to the application to get a value. There would be no `setAttribute()` methods available to the management system. The only operations would be those associated with `getAttribute()` methods. The application would use the MBean to send notifications.

Model MBeans are well suited for this pattern of usage. They already support caching of attribute values in the MBean.

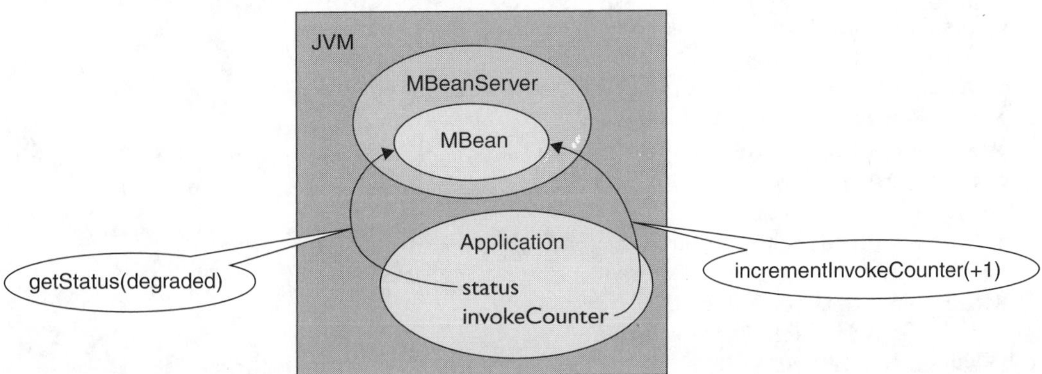

Figure 9.4 A Publish-Only Application

Here is an example of a publish-only application that uses a model MBean. For every attribute, the application updates the value in the model MBean. The model MBean returns the cached value and does not ever invoke any methods on the application. No get or set methods are defined for the attributes because they are not invoked:

```
package jnjmx.ch9;


import java.io.File;
import java.io.FileInputStream;
import java.io.FileNotFoundException;
import java.io.FileOutputStream;
import java.io.IOException;
import java.io.ObjectInputStream;
import java.io.ObjectOutputStream;
import java.io.Serializable;
import java.util.ArrayList;
import java.util.HashMap;
import java.util.Iterator;
import java.util.List;
import java.util.Map;

import java.lang.reflect.*;

import javax.management.*;
import javax.management.modelmbean.*;

// Publish-Only Model MBean Example

public class TackCatalogPO implements Catalog, Serializable {

      private static final String FILEEXT = ".catalog";
      private final String name;
      private boolean autoCheckpoint = false;
      private Map categories;
      private List items;
      private int nextCatalogNo = 1;
      private int accesses=0, sales=0, inventorySize=0;
      ModelMBean catMBean = null;
      ObjectName dynTackMBean = null;
      MBeanServer mbs;
```

```
    public TackCatalogPO(String inName) {
            this.name = inName;
            this.categories = new HashMap();
            this.items = new ArrayList();
            try {
                  dynTackMBean = new ObjectName("Chapter9:id=TackCatalogPO");
                  this.catMBean = this.createCatalogMBean();

            ArrayList mbservers = MBeanServerFactory.findMBeanServer(null);
            if (mbservers.size() == 1)
                    mbs =  (MBeanServer)mbservers.get(0);
            else
                    System.out.println("Creation of Management Bean " +
                        "failed: too many MBeanServers");
            mbs.registerMBean(catMBean, dynTackMBean);
            } catch (Exception e) {
                    System.out.println("Creation of Management Bean failed");
            }
    }

    public static TackCatalogPO create(String inName) throws IOException {
            String cfn = inName + FILEEXT;
            File cf = new File(cfn);
            if (cf.exists()) {
                    cf.delete();
            }

            TackCatalogPO catalog = new TackCatalogPO(inName);
//          Should write to a file here
//          ObjectOutputStream db =
//                  new ObjectOutputStream(new FileOutputStream(cf));
//          db.writeObject(catalog);
//          db.flush();
//          db.close();

            return catalog;
    }

    public Catalog load(String name)
        throws IOException, ClassNotFoundException {
            String cfn = name + FILEEXT;
            File cf = new File(cfn);
            if (cf.exists() == false) {
                    throw new FileNotFoundException(cfn + " doesn't exist");
            }
```

```
            ObjectInputStream db = new ObjectInputStream(
                new FileInputStream(cf));
            TackCatalogPO catalog = (TackCatalogPO) db.readObject();
            db.close();
            return catalog;
    }


    public synchronized Map getCategories() {
            return this.categories;
    }


    public synchronized void classify(Item item, Category category) {
            List items = ((TackCategory) category).getItems();
            if (items.contains(item) == false) {
                    items.add(item);
            }
    }

    public synchronized Category createCategory(String name)
            throws CategoryExistsException {
            TackCategory result = new TackCategory(this, name);
            if (this.categories.get(name) != null) {
                    throw new CategoryExistsException();
            }
            this.categories.put(name, result);
            return result;
    }

    public synchronized Item createItem(String name, int price, int quantity)
        throws ItemExistsException {
            TackItem result = new TackItem(this, nextCatalogNo++, name,
                price, quantity);
            if (this.items.contains(result)) {
                    throw new ItemExistsException();
            }
            this.items.add(result);
            inventorySize = inventorySize + quantity;

            /* Update cached value in ModelMBean model MBean */
            try {
```

```
                ModelMBeanInfo localInfo =
                    (ModelMBeanInfo)catMBean.getMBeanInfo();
                Descriptor newNum =
                    localInfo.getDescriptor("InventorySize","attribute");
                newNum.setField("value", new Integer(inventorySize));
                localInfo.setDescriptor(newNum, "attribute");

                Descriptor newNumI =
                    localInfo.getDescriptor("NumberOfItems","attribute");
                newNumI.setField("value", new Integer(items.size()));
                localInfo.setDescriptor(newNumI, "attribute");
                catMBean.setModelMBeanInfo(localInfo);
        } catch (Exception e) {
                System.out.println("Update of Management data failed");
        }

        return result;
}

public synchronized void declassify(Item item, Category category) {
        List items = category.getItems();
        items.remove(item);
}

public synchronized void decreaseInventory(Item item, int amount)
    throws InventoryUnderflowException {
        inventorySize = inventorySize - amount;
        sales = sales + amount;

        try {
                ModelMBeanInfo localInfo =
                    (ModelMBeanInfo)catMBean.getMBeanInfo();

                Descriptor newNum =
                    localInfo.getDescriptor("InventorySize","attribute");
                newNum.setField("value", new Integer(inventorySize));
                localInfo.setDescriptor(newNum, "attribute");

                Descriptor newNumS =
                    localInfo.getDescriptor("TotalSales","attribute");
                newNumS.setField("value", new Integer(sales));
                localInfo.setDescriptor(newNumS, "attribute");

                catMBean.setModelMBeanInfo(localInfo);
        } catch (Exception e) {
```

```
                System.out.println("Update of Management data failed");
            }

            int nq = item.getQuantity() - amount;
            if (nq < 0) {
                throw new InventoryUnderflowException();
            }
            ((TackItem)item).setQuantity(nq);
    }

    public void destroy() throws IOException {
            String cfn = this.name + FILEEXT;
            File cf = new File(cfn);
            if (cf.exists()) {
                cf.delete();
            }
    }

    public synchronized Category getCategory(String name) {
            Category result = (Category) this.categories.get(name);
            return result;
    }

    public synchronized void increaseInventory(Item item, int amount) {
            inventorySize = inventorySize + amount;
            if (amount < 0) {
                throw new IllegalArgumentException();
            }

            try {
                ModelMBeanInfo localInfo =
                    (ModelMBeanInfo)catMBean.getMBeanInfo();
                Descriptor newNum =
                    localInfo.getDescriptor("InventorySize","attribute");
                newNum.setField("value", new Integer(inventorySize));
                localInfo.setDescriptor(newNum, "attribute");
                catMBean.setModelMBeanInfo(localInfo);
            } catch (Exception e) {
                System.out.println("Update of Management data failed");
            }

            int nq = item.getQuantity() + amount;
            ((TackItem) item).setQuantity(nq);
    }
```

```
    public synchronized List getItems() {
            accesses++;
            try {
                    ModelMBeanInfo localInfo =
                        (ModelMBeanInfo)catMBean.getMBeanInfo();
                    Descriptor newNum =
                        localInfo.getDescriptor("Accesses","attribute");
                    newNum.setField("value", new Integer(accesses));
                    localInfo.setDescriptor(newNum, "attribute");

                    Descriptor newNumI =
                        localInfo.getDescriptor("NumberOfItems","attribute");
                    newNumI.setField("value", new Integer(this.items.size()));
                    localInfo.setDescriptor(newNumI, "attribute");
                    catMBean.setModelMBeanInfo(localInfo);
            } catch (Exception e) {
                    System.out.println("Update of Management data failed");
            }
            return this.items;
    }

    public synchronized void removeCategory(Category category)
        throws NoSuchCategoryException {
            removeCategory(category.getName());
    }

    public synchronized void removeCategory(String name)
        throws NoSuchCategoryException {
            Category category = (Category) this.categories.remove(name);
            if (category == null) {
                    throw new NoSuchCategoryException();
            }
    }

    public synchronized void removeItem(Item item) throws NoSuchItemException
{
            boolean exists = this.items.remove(item);
            if (exists == false) {
                    throw new NoSuchItemException();
            }
            inventorySize = inventorySize - item.getQuantity();

            try {
                    ModelMBeanInfo localInfo =
                        (ModelMBeanInfo)catMBean.getMBeanInfo();
```

```
                Descriptor newNum =
                    localInfo.getDescriptor("InventorySize","attribute");
                newNum.setField("value", new Integer(inventorySize));
                localInfo.setDescriptor(newNum, "attribute");

                Descriptor newNumI =
                    localInfo.getDescriptor("NumberOfItems","attribute");
                newNumI.setField("value", new Integer(items.size()));
                localInfo.setDescriptor(newNumI, "attribute");
                catMBean.setModelMBeanInfo(localInfo);
            } catch (Exception e) {
                System.out.println("Update of Management data failed");
            }
            removeItemFromCategories(item);
    }

    public synchronized void removeItem(int catalogno)
        throws NoSuchItemException {
            boolean removed = false;
            Iterator i = this.items.iterator();
            while (i.hasNext()) {
                Item item = (Item) i.next();
                if (item.getCatalogNo() == catalogno) {
                    this.items.remove(item);
                    inventorySize = inventorySize - item.getQuantity();

                     try {
                        ModelMBeanInfo localInfo =
                          (ModelMBeanInfo)catMBean.getMBeanInfo();
                        Descriptor newNum = localInfo.getDescriptor(
                          "InventorySize","attribute");
                        newNum.setField("value", new
                          Integer(inventorySize));
                        localInfo.setDescriptor(newNum, "attribute");

                        Descriptor newNumI = localInfo.getDescriptor(
                          "NumberOfItems","attribute");
                        newNumI.setField("value", new
                          Integer(items.size()));
                        localInfo.setDescriptor(
                          newNumI, "attribute");
                        catMBean.setModelMBeanInfo(localInfo);
                     } catch (Exception e) {
```

```
                        System.out.println(
                            "Update of Management data failed");
                    }

                    removeItemFromCategories(item);
                    removed = true;
                    break;
                }
            }
            if (removed == false) {
                throw new NoSuchItemException();
            }
    }

    private void removeItemFromCategories(Item item) {
            Iterator i = this.categories.keySet().iterator();
            while (i.hasNext()) {
                String category = (String) i.next();
                declassify(item, (Category)
                    this.categories.get(category));
            }
    }

    // TackCatalogMBean Methods

    public boolean isAutoCheckpointing() {
            try {
                ModelMBeanInfo localInfo =
                    (ModelMBeanInfo)catMBean.getMBeanInfo();
                Descriptor newNum = localInfo.getDescriptor(
                    "AutoCheckpointing","attribute");
                newNum.setField("value",
                    new Boolean(this.autoCheckpoint));
                localInfo.setDescriptor(newNum, "attribute");
                catMBean.setModelMBeanInfo(localInfo);
            } catch (Exception e) {
                System.out.println("Update of Management data failed");
            }
            return this.autoCheckpoint;
    }

    public void setAutoCheckpoint(boolean autoCheckpoint) {
            this.autoCheckpoint = autoCheckpoint;
            try {
                ModelMBeanInfo localInfo =
                    (ModelMBeanInfo)catMBean.getMBeanInfo();
```

```
                Descriptor newNum = localInfo.getDescriptor(
                    "AutoCheckpointing","attribute");
                newNum.setField("value", new
                    Boolean(this.autoCheckpoint));
                localInfo.setDescriptor(newNum, "attribute");
                catMBean.setModelMBeanInfo(localInfo);
            } catch (Exception e) {
                System.out.println("Update of Management data failed");
            }
    }

    public void doCheckpoint() {
            if (this.autoCheckpoint == true) {
                checkpoint();
            }
    }

    public void checkpoint() {
            // This method should save the catalog to a file
    }

    ModelMBean createCatalogMBean() {
           ModelMBean catalogMBean = null;
           try {
                catalogMBean = new RequiredModelMBean();
                catalogMBean.setModelMBeanInfo(createCatalogMBeanInfo());
                catalogMBean.setManagedResource(this, "ObjectReference");
           }
           catch (Exception e) {
                System.out.println("Creating Tack Catalog MBean failed: " +
                    e.getMessage());
           }
           return catalogMBean;
    }

    ModelMBeanInfo createCatalogMBeanInfo() {
            ModelMBeanInfo info = null;
    /* attributes: boolean AutoCheckpointing r/w,
    int numberOfItems r/o,
    int Accesses r/o,
    int Sales r/o
    int InventorySize r/o */
    /* operations: none */
    /* notifications: none */
            String catDescription = "Tack Catalog Dynamic MBean";
```

```
Descriptor catDescriptor =
        new DescriptorSupport(
                new String[] {
                        ("name=TackCatalog"),
                        "descriptorType=mbean",
                        ("displayName=TackCatalogManager"),
                        "type=jnjmxch9.TackCatalogPO",
                        "currencyTimeLimit=-1" });
                        // return cache values

ModelMBeanAttributeInfo[] catAttributes =
        new ModelMBeanAttributeInfo[5];


Descriptor catDescAuto =
        new DescriptorSupport(
                new String[] {
                        "name=AutoCheckpointing",
                        "descriptorType=attribute",
                        "displayName=AutoCheckpointing",
                        "currencyTimeLimit=-1" });
                        // return cache values
catDescAuto.setField("value", new Boolean(this.autoCheckpoint));
// initial value

// not writable
catAttributes[0] =
        new ModelMBeanAttributeInfo("AutoCheckpointing",
                "java.lang.Boolean",
                "AutoCheckpointing: boolean value if " +
                "checkpointing of catalog is done automatically",
                false,false,true,
                catDescAuto);

Descriptor catDescItems =
        new DescriptorSupport(
                new String[] {
                        "name=NumberOfItems",
                        "descriptorType=attribute",
                        "displayName=NumberOfItems",
                        "currencyTimeLimit=-1" });
                        // return cache values

catDescItems.setField("value", new Integer(0));
                        // initial value
```

```
catAttributes[1] = new ModelMBeanAttributeInfo("NumberOfItems",
        "java.lang.Integer",
        "NumberOfItems: number of items in the catalog",
        true,false,false,
        catDescItems);
Descriptor catDescAccess =
        new DescriptorSupport(
                new String[] {
                        "name=Accesses",
                        "descriptorType=attribute",
                        "displayName=Accesses",
                        "currencyTimeLimit=-1" });
                        // return cache values
catDescAccess.setField("value", new Integer(0));
// initial value

catAttributes[2] = new ModelMBeanAttributeInfo("Accesses",
        "java.lang.Integer",
        "Accesses: number of time items in the catalog "  +
        "database have been listed",
        true,false,false,
        catDescAccess);

Descriptor catDescSales =
        new DescriptorSupport(
                new String[] {
                        "name=TotalSales",
                        "descriptorType=attribute",
                        "displayName=TotalSales",
                        "currencyTimeLimit=-1" });
                        // return cache values
catDescSales.setField("value", new Integer(0));
// initial value

catAttributes[3] = new ModelMBeanAttributeInfo("TotalSales",
        "java.lang.Integer",
        "Sales: number of items sold",
        true,false,false,
        catDescSales);

Descriptor catDescInv =
        new DescriptorSupport(
                new String[] {
                        "name=InventorySize",
                        "descriptorType=attribute",
```

```
                                   "displayName=InventorySize",
                                   "currencyTimeLimit=-1" });
                                   // always cache
               catDescInv.setField("value", new Integer(0));
               // initial value

               catAttributes[4] = new ModelMBeanAttributeInfo("InventorySize",
                      "java.lang.Integer",
                      "InventorySize: Total number of all items currently " +
                      "in inventory",
                      true,false,false,
                      catDescInv);

               ModelMBeanConstructorInfo[] catConstructors =
                      new ModelMBeanConstructorInfo[1];

               Constructor[] constructors = this.getClass().getConstructors();

               Descriptor tackConstDesc =
                      new DescriptorSupport(
                             new String[] {
                                   "name=TackCatalogPO",
                                   "descriptorType=operation",
                                   "role=constructor" });
               catConstructors[0] = new ModelMBeanConstructorInfo(
                      "tackCatalog(dbName): Constructs a tackCatalog" +
                      "from existing database",
                      constructors[0],
                      tackConstDesc);

               ModelMBeanOperationInfo[] catOperations =
                      new ModelMBeanOperationInfo[0];

               ModelMBeanNotificationInfo[] catNotifications =
                      new ModelMBeanNotificationInfo[0];

               String className = this.getClass().getName();

               info = new ModelMBeanInfoSupport(className,
                                   catDescription,
                                   catAttributes,
                                   catConstructors,
                                   catOperations,
                                   catNotifications );
```

```
            try {
                info.setMBeanDescriptor(catDescriptor);
            } catch (Exception e) {
                System.out.println(
                    "CreateModelMBeanInfo failed with " + e.getMessage());
            }

            return info;
    }

}       // class
```

In this case we are creating a model MBean that exposes attributes with no get methods, no setters, and no operations. The values for the attributes are cached in the descriptor of the attribute by the application. The model MBean is registered with the MBeanServer. Whenever one of these attributes is updated, the model MBean's cached value in the descriptor is updated as well.

9.2.4 Facades for Distributed Applications

Complex applications may have management operations scattered across many different classes. For distributed applications, the instances of the managed resources may be scattered across several JVMs or even remote JVMs. Operations may need to reach some or all of these diverse classes or distributed targets. In such cases, an MBean can be a very convenient management facade for your application. The MBean can have references (see Figure 9.5) to all of the managed objects—local or remote—or it can discover them at runtime. The MBean can then invoke the operations on the right objects on the right systems.

Model MBeans were designed specifically to perform this function, as the examples in Chapter 4 illustrate.

9.3 MBean Registration and Lifecycle

Now that you have MBeans for your application, they need to be registered with the MBeanServer. There are several ways that you can do this: having the application register the MBean, having a third party register the MBean, having an adapter register the MBean, and having the MBeanServer register the MBean.

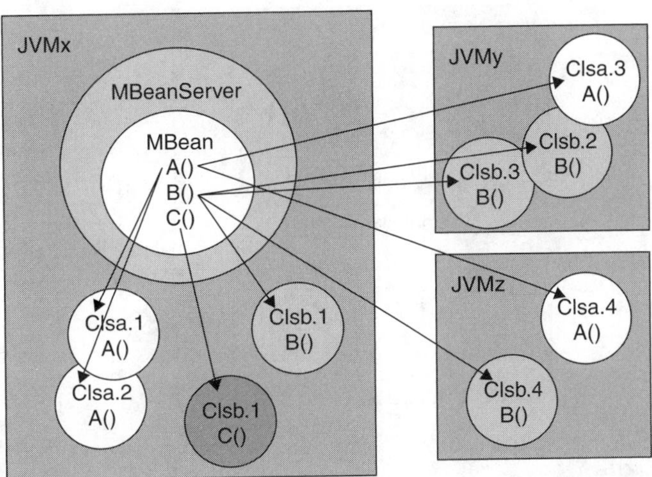

Figure 9.5 A Facade MBean

9.3.1 Registration by Application

The managed application or component can instantiate its own MBean and register it with the MBeanServer during initialization of either the application or the component (See Figure 9.6). In this case the MBean runs in the scope of the application. There are pros and cons to this mode of MBean registration. The pros are that the application can always count on the existence of the MBean, and it can keep a reference to the MBean. If an application has a reference to the MBean it has created, updates of attribute values can be done much more efficiently because they don't have to go through the MBeanServer.

One of the cons to this approach is that the MBean exists only if the application is already up. First let's examine the case in which the application always creates a new MBean during initialization and removes the MBean during destruction. Therefore the MBean cannot stop the application without being destroyed, and obviously the MBean cannot start the application. So if you need application lifecycle control with your MBean, this approach won't work. Another consideration is the life of the application's metrics. Often metrics are running counters that should not be reset to 0 every time the application is stopped and restarted. Because the MBean goes away, the metrics will be reset to 0 when the application starts again. One way to avoid this is to persist the MBean's data from time to time, or at least before destruction.

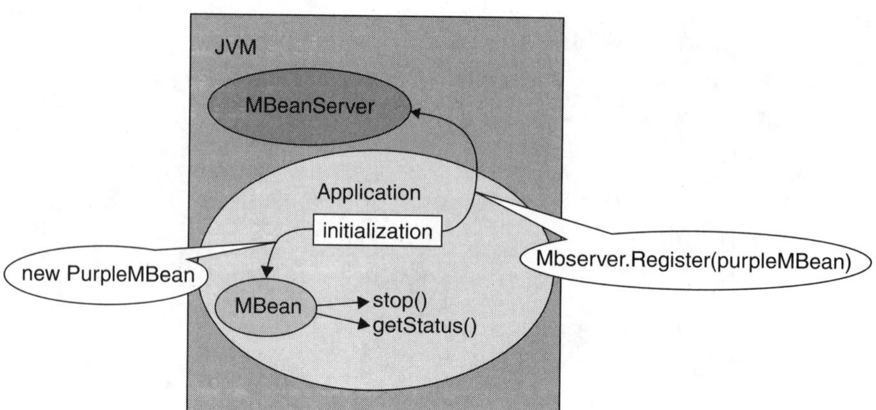

Figure 9.6 The Application Creates the MBean Locally and Registers It with an External MBeanServer

A final consideration against this approach is that there is no way for a management system to query the set of MBeans registered with the MBean-Server and be able to determine which applications are down. It would know only that the application was "down" because the MBean is not registered. A management system would have to compare the list of MBeans that *are* registered with the list of MBeans that *should* be registered and declare the missing MBeans as down applications. This means not only that someone has to keep an accurate list of which MBeans or applications should be available in a JVM or system, but also that the assumption that missing applications are down may be an inaccurate conclusion. A generalized management system may not even know to look specifically for the existence of the MBean.

One solution to this lifecycle problem is to have the application create the MBean and *not* remove it during destruction. The application must only create the MBean on subsequent initializations if there is not already one registered with the MBeanServer. Now the MBean can be used to stop and restart the application, and metrics will continue to accumulate beyond the lifecycle of an instance of the application. However, the initial start of the application must be provided for without the MBean. The application should use the MBeanServer as a factory for instantiating the MBean, as shown in Figure 9.7, instead using the `MBean's constructor` to instantitate the MBean for reliability reasons. As long as the MBeanServer is not in the scope of the application, you should be all set. Now, the MBean is always listed by the MBeanServer, even if the application is not currently up. The management system does not have to try to guess that the MBean is missing and that this

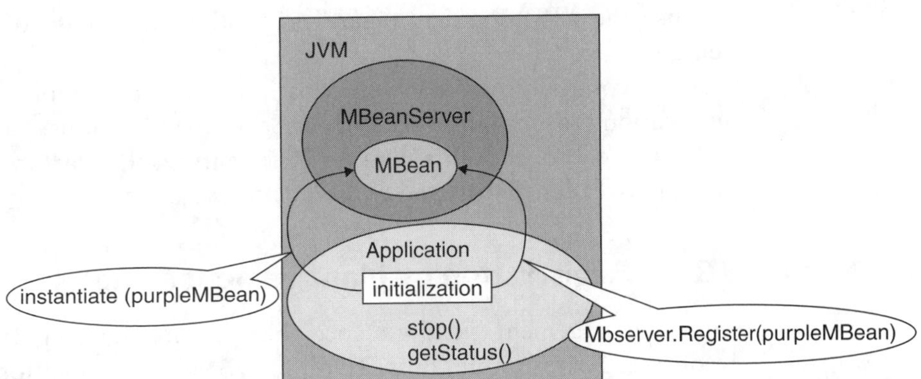

Figure 9.7 The Application Creates the MBean within an External MBeanServer

means the application might be down. Don't forget that the application's `uninstall()` or `stop()` method must clean up the MBean by deregistering it from the MBeanServer.

9.3.2 Registration by Third Party

In this approach a separate application is responsible for instantiating the MBean for the application and registering it with the MBeanServer, as shown in Figure 9.8. This is better than the application's instantiating its own MBean

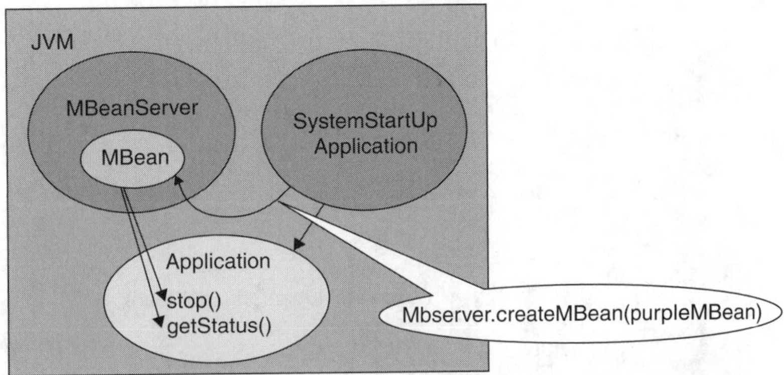

Figure 9.8 A Third-Party Application Creates the Application and the MBean in an External MBeanServer

because the MBean exists regardless of the availability of the application being managed.

One common third-party application is a system initialization or startup application that initializes the MBeanServer, applications, and MBeans in the JVM. If the application is distributed in nature, the startup application may also discover the distributed components and create sessions with them.

9.3.3 Registration by Management Adapter

Many management vendors specialize in managing particular types of resources. For example, both Tivoli and BMC have solutions for managing databases. For these solutions, databases themselves have to create any specific management instrumentation. Most of the management is done from "outside" the database. If the database were to be managed through a JMX MBean, Tivoli's MBean and BMC's MBean would probably look nothing alike, especially considering that they compete in the amount and quality of function they provide. Therefore, each vendor would want provide its own MBean to manage the resource. Each vendor would also need to provide its own adapter from JMX to its proprietary management infrastructures. In this case it makes the most sense to have the management system's adapter instantiate its own version of the MBean for the targeted managed resource, as shown in Figure 9.9.

This approach has the advantage that the semantics of the MBean are well understood and supported by its contributing management system. In addition, management systems can dynamically add new management capabilities.

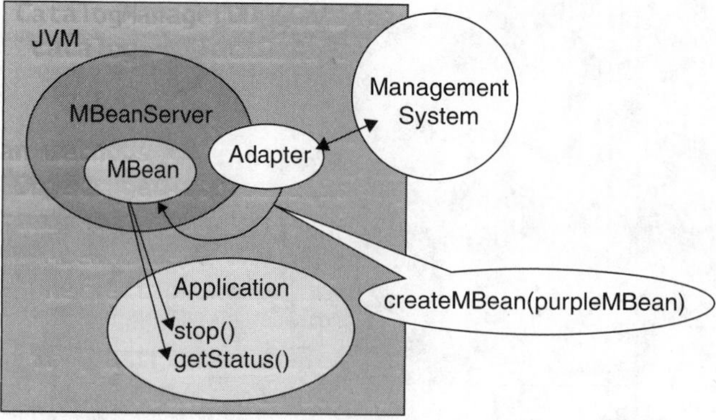

Figure 9.9 A JMX Adapter Creates the MBean

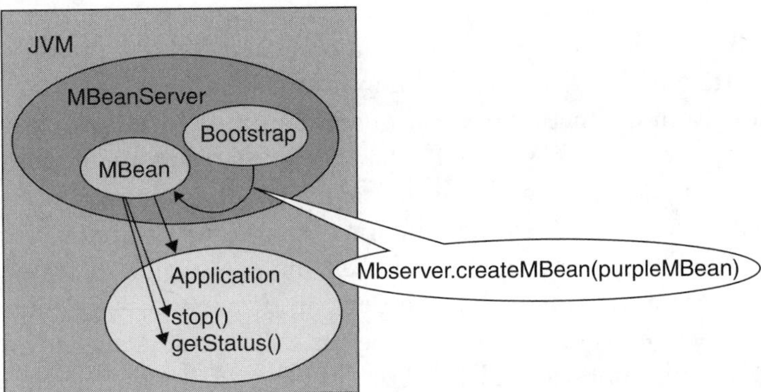

Figure 9.10 A Bootstrap Program Creates the MBean, Which Starts the Application

9.3.4 Registration by MBeanServer Bootstrap

In this case the MBeanServer may have a bootstrap mechanism that creates a set of predefined MBeans. Although the JMX specification does not define a bootstrap mechanism, nearly all the decent JMX implementations do, and you should take advantage of it. If you use the bootstrap, when the MBeanServer starts, the application MBeans will be instantiated and registered as well, as shown by Figure 9.10. This is an especially elegant solution for MBeans that need lifecycle control over the application or MBeans whose initialization starts the application itself. Generally, the bootstrap mechanism is driven by configuration files that today are often XML formatted. Other ways to provide bootstrap information are through database access and environment variables.

9.4 Best Practices

Not all of the lessons we have learned with JMX are easily classified in the lifecycle of an MBean or MBeanServer. This section contains the miscellaneous advice we wanted to present to you, so the subsections here are independent of each other.

9.4.1 MBean Granularity

An MBean should be created to represent a functional component of your application. You should not end up with one MBean per component or class in your application, unless your components are very coarse-grained.

When looking at your application and trying to decide how many MBeans you need for which components and classes, resist the temptation to create an MBean for each component. Step back and look at your application from a functional view, remembering that MBeans can manage across components. Ask yourself what those who are managing this application while it is running will want to manage, check the status of, and reconfigure. What would they say the functional areas of your application are?

Let's look at our tack catalog example. In the tack catalog we had an item, category and catalog, but we developed manageability only for the catalog. Now let's expand the tack catalog for online shopping (remember this is a fictitious and simple example) and see how we chose which components to manage. Now we have the following functions that we need to provide to customers:

1. **Catalog**, which allows a customer to
   - List products
   - Check availability of a product
2. **Shopping Cart**, which collects items to be purchased from the Catalog and allows them to be purchased and shipped.
3. **Order Status Check**, which allows a customer using a browser to check the status of the following items related to an order:
   - Product item number and price
   - Order shipping cost shipment number
   - Ordered product status: in stock, back-ordered, picked, packed, shipped
   - Status dates: picked date, packed date, shipped date, estimated arrival date, back-order date.
4. **Shipper Status Check**, which allows a customer using a browser to track the shipment from the warehouse through depots to the delivery trucks.

We have seen an example of a catalog application having the following business operations:

```
public interface Catalog  {
      public Category createCategory(String name)
             throws CategoryExistsException;
      public Category getCategory(String name);
      public Map getCategories();
      public void removeCategory(Category category)
             throws NoSuchCategoryException;
      public void removeCategory(String name)
             throws NoSuchCategoryException
      public void classify(Item item, Category category);
```

```
        public void declassify(Item item, Category category);
        public void increaseInventory(Item item, int amount);
        public void decreaseInventory(Item item, int amount)
                throws InventoryUnderflowException;
        public Item createItem(String name, int price, int quantity)
                throws ItemExistsException;
        public List getItems();
        public void removeItem(Item item)
                throws NoSuchItemException;
        public void removeItem(int catalogno)
                throws NoSuchItemException;
}
```

Let's look at the Shopping Cart application in more detail. It could have components and methods like these:

- **Cart:**
  - `addItem(itemNumber, quantity)`
  - `deleteItem(itemNumber)`
  - `listItems()`
  - `calculateCartTotal()`
  - `resetCart()`
- **Purchase:**
  - `setShipmentAddress(cart, Name, Street, City, Zip, Phone)`
  - `setCreditCardInfo(cart, Name, CardNumber, ExpiryDate)`
  - `calculateShipping(cart)`
  - `calculatePurchaseTotal(cart)`
  - `checkWarehouse(cart)`
  - `cancelPurchase(cart)`
- **Credit Card Validation:**
  - `authorize(Name, CardNumber, ExpiryDate, Amount)`
- **Order Fullfillment:**
  - `checkWarehouse(cart)`
  - `submitOrder(cart)`
  - `shipOrder(cart)`

In this case you should create MBeans for the Catalog and Shopping Cart applications. You don't really need an MBean for the Order Status Check and Shipper Status Check functions because they are managed as part of the Shopping Cart application. We've already seen the following catalog `MBeanInfo`:

- Attributes:

```
TotalSales
NumberOfItems
TotalSales
Accesses
InventorySize
AutoCheckpoint
```

- Operations:

```
load()
doCheckpoint()
```

- Notifications: none

Other information that could be part of `MBeanInfo` data includes some time-related attributes about response times:

- `AverageProductListResponseTime`
- `ProductListResponseThreshold`

You could also have operations to put the catalog online or take it offline:

- `enable()`
- `disable()`

And you could have notification from the catalog for events that require attention from an administration—for example,

```
"Item list response time exceeded maximum allowable."
```

The Shopping Cart `MBeanInfo` could have similar types of information, operations, and notifications:

- Attributes:

```
NumberOpenShoppingCarts
AverageAgeOfShoppingCarts
AverageTimeInPurchasePhase
AverageDeliveryTime
```

```
PercentageLateDeliveries
DeliveryThreshold
ShoppingCartAgeThreshold
```

- Operations:

```
listOpenShoppingCarts()
listShoppingCartsOlderThan(days)
listLateOrders()
expediteOrder()
cancelCart()
checkOrderStatus()
checkShippingStatus()
```

- Notifications:

```
"Credit card validation application unavailable"
"Order delivery date exceeded allowable delivery delay"
```

As these examples show, the information you are tracking for the application consists of aggregations rather than instances of carts. This information helps you determine if the application is accessible and functioning well enough to keep customers from feeling restless. This section was meant to stress that there does not need to be a direct correlation between MBeans and important objects or concepts in your application. But rather, you need to decide what the appropriate level of management granularity for your application is, in this case by catalogs and shopping carts.

9.4.2 Application Self-Management

Self-management means that an application's MBeans completely manage the application, requiring no third-party or enterprise management system. There are two granularities here: First, the application is accompanied by a JMX-based application-specific management application. Second, the application instantiates MBeans, monitor MBeans, and adapters to handle its management. This management can happen entirely local to a particular MBeanServer.

9.4.2.1 Application-Specific Manager

JMX was designed to be a single instrumentation able to feed both enterprise managers and application-specific managers. Most applications of any complexity will need to be accompanied by a management and administrative application. JMX can provide the necessary infrastructure. The advantages of providing an application-specific manager are that you can create a much more intuitive and detailed presentation to the administrator and you can provide much more detailed configuration and recovery support. It is not uncommon for some of the MBeans' attributes to be managed exclusively by the application-specific manager. A subset, often the more coarse-grained or aggregated data, is exposed to enterprise managers.

If the management application is running in the same JVM, you don't even need an adapter to interact with the MBeanServer. If the management system is running in a separate JVM, you will need at least a simple RMI or HTTP adapter to communicate with the remote MBeanServer.

If you write your own application-specific manager, you should consider providing the following functionality:

- **Application configuration management**, to display and update application configuration attributes. These attributes should be in one or more MBeans.
- **Application operational management**, to display application management operations, allow the specification of parameter values, invoke the operation, and display the response. You should at least provide for lifecycle control: start, stop, and refresh configuration. These operations should be in one or more MBeans.
- **Status display**, to display the current status of the application as a whole, as well as its components. This status display should be influenced by notifications received. The status can be as simple as "up" or "down" shown as green and red. It may also provide variations in between, yellow and orange for degradations. Degradation can be detected when monitor notifications or application-specific notifications are received.
- **Notification** or **notification log display**, to display the history of notifications received or notifications for a time period. Like status displays, notification displays can be color-coded by severity.
- **Management configuration**, to display the configuration values, both read-only and modifiable. The configuration manager can handle all modification of values, but then it must be sure to implement those changes in the managed application. Some management configuration includes
  - MBean configuration (caching, persistence, logging)
  - Monitor MBean configuration (frequency)

  - Notification forwarding and filtering
  - Notification automated response
- **Monitor MBean control**, to start and stop configured monitor MBeans.

Of course, you can pick any subset of this functionality as well, depending on your application, its criticality, its complexity, and how much you like writing management applications.

9.4.2.2 Local Monitoring and Recovery

Every JMX MBeanServer supports monitoring, timers, and notifications. This means that every MBeanServer is capable of monitoring its local applications and responding to notifications. If you are going to use local monitoring, you can instantiate monitor MBeans (see Chapter 7) to watch values of specific attributes of specific MBeans. These monitor MBeans, as well as your application-specific MBeans, may send notifications. This means that you need to have an instance of `NotificationListener` implemented. A notification can be another MBean; an adapter to a local manager, e-mail sender, or pager; or just a class of your choosing.

The `NotificationListener` class that you implement can react any number of ways to a notification. It can do one or more of the following:

- Send the notification to a log
- Display the notification to an operator via a console or e-mail message
- Page an operator
- Forward the notification to a management or correlation system
- Interact with the managed resource to correct the problem indicated by the notification
- Interact with the system to correct the problem indicated by the notification

There is a trade-off between self-management, or local management, and enterprise management. Local management is attractive because it works regardless of the state of the network and has many fewer dependencies on other applications. Because there are fewer dependencies, there are also fewer points of failure in management and recovery. This makes the management much more reliable per failure. You can also monitor and react with a much higher frequency because you do not incur the overhead of going between JVMs on a system or over networks.

The Achilles' heel here is that if the local host is failing, there may not be an external manager to recover any of it. In addition, local management actions have only local knowledge. They cannot know the state of the entire application or enterprise. It may not always be appropriate to recover a resource if other parts of the enterprise are stressed. Another issue to be aware of is double management. This is the case where there is local management, which the enterprise manager is not aware of, and enterprise management. Effectively you end up with two sets of monitors and potentially two duplicate, different, or even conflicting responses.

Our advice here is to use JMX to instrument your application for your own management system as well as enterprise managers. To reduce IT resource use, perform monitoring in the local host. Automatic responses to notifications should be implemented locally only if a larger context is not required to ensure the operation is correct. To reduce redundant management, provide a means to "turn off" management functions that execute locally in favor of that responsibility being taken over and provided by an enterprise management system. Obviously there are trade-offs for each of these decisions, but these are fair guidelines.

9.4.3 Resource Schema

JMX is a model-less manageability architecture. This means that JMX does not require you to use any particular naming conventions for your attributes or operations. Nor does it provide you any standard way to represent management data. The lack of an explicit resource model makes JMX very flexible. It is possible to represent nearly any resource type and data in JMX MBeans. You do not have to try to fit your existing information into someone else's model. Nor do you have to figure out how to extend an existing model when your application doesn't fit neatly into the existing model.

The downside of not having a resource model is that because there is no standard, accepted vocabulary for common management terms and relationships, every MBean may have its own variation for the same type of data. For example, a basic `state` variable can be named `state`, `status`, `currentState`, or `availability`. Its values can be `boolean`, strings as in "up/down" or "available/unavailable", or even multivalued, as in "up/degraded/failed/down". It can become *very* difficult for a management system to realize that all of these represent the same kind of data and they can all be normalized and used to update colors in a topology screen. It may also be hard for the system to determine how to aggregate the status to get a broader system status. This lack of consistent terminology for management systems ends up requiring custom integration of every MBean and its meanings into management systems through the JMX adapter to that management system. Sometimes this can require some custom integration in the management application itself.

One of the goals of JMX was to enable the development of general-purpose management applications that can "understand" the MBeans presented to it without custom development. You can see that the lack of a common model seriously jeopardizes this goal.

More than a few management data models are being developed by standards bodies—for example, SNMP MIBs from the IETF, and CIM from the DMTF. Of these, CIM is probably the best suited as a basic model for building MBeans. CIM is a closer match to JMX in the concepts of operations, attributes, notifications and metadata. SNMP MIBs represent attributes and events well, but the operations concepts can be difficult to translate intuitively.

CIM addresses the device, system, and networking disciplines very well. The models there are fairly complete, stable, and easy to extend. It is reasonably easy to figure out where your device or system belongs relative to the model. If you are developing an application or middleware, it is more difficult to use the CIM model. Although not yet complete, the models for the application are under active development.

It requires quite a bit of work to understand the CIM model and understand the best way to extend it for your own purposes. Even so, we recommend that you use the CIM model as much as you can. If you cannot use the model as is, at least use the CIM vocabulary for variable names and relationships. For example, CIM uses `status` for status or state; if at all possible your MBeans should use `status` for status as well. Following this approach increases the odds that management systems will be able to understand and manage your MBean appropriately. This approach may decrease the amount of development you have to do in JMX adapters or in management applications.

If you have a mismatch in terminology or names but the semantics are very close, you can use the `ProtocolMap` object in the model MBean descriptors (see Chapter 4) to tell the adapter to relate the attribute in the MBean to the attribute in the CIM model.

If you find a CIM model that is close to your needs, it is relatively easy to generate MBeans from the model. There are tools available from Sun that generate MBeans from both CIM models and SNMP MIBs.

Figure 9.11 shows a CIM UML diagram of the core model and the managed system element taken from the "Common Information Model (CIM Core) Model, Version 2.4" white paper (available at http://www.dmtf.org/standards/documents/CIM/DSP0111.pdf).

`ManagedSystemElement` is a basic class that most other CIM classes eventually derive from. Here is a standard-MBean interface that could be generated for `ManagedSystemElement`:

```
public interface ManagedSystemElementMBean {
      String getName();
      void setName(String newName);
      String GetStatus();
      void SetStatus(String newStatus);
      DateTime getInstallDate();
      void setInstallDate(String newDate);
}
```

`ManagedSystemElement` MBeans can be members of `component` and `SystemComponent` relationships MBeans for starters. We would represent these relationships, or CIM associations, by creating new JMX relationship MBeans. In conclusion, using CIM models as the basis for your MBeans is not a trivial effort. But it yields the following benefits: You are future-proofing your MBeans, you are increasing the odds that your MBeans will be understood by other management systems, and you may get new ideas from the CIM model to improve your management design.

9.4.4 Notifications and Logging

It is important to recognize the difference between messages that should be logged and messages that should be notifications. If you have an existing application, it can be tempting to send a notification for every logged message, but doing so could flood your MBeanServer, adapter, and management systems with notifications that are just thrown away or merely logged again. Messages that should be logged should be logged not only to record problems and failures, but also to provide an audit trail, record the progress of transactions, and record the use of features or invocations of functions.

Logged messages are used later—usually not while the application is running—to do problem determination, root failure analysis, usage analysis, and performance analysis. All of these analyses can be used to tune the network, system, or application to improve performance of the more highly used or critical functions. Some of these logged messages should be JMX notifications. Messages about failures or events that require automated responses or recovery, or operator action, should be JMX notifications.

There are several ways that you can send messages from your application as JMX notifications. First, if your application *is* the MBean, you would simply implement the `NotificationBroadcaster` interface or extend the `NotificationBroadcasterSupport` class and send the notification from your application where appropriate. You would find a `sendNotification()` method invocation wherever you logged a critical message. Another common pattern is to instrument a logging application to send the notification.

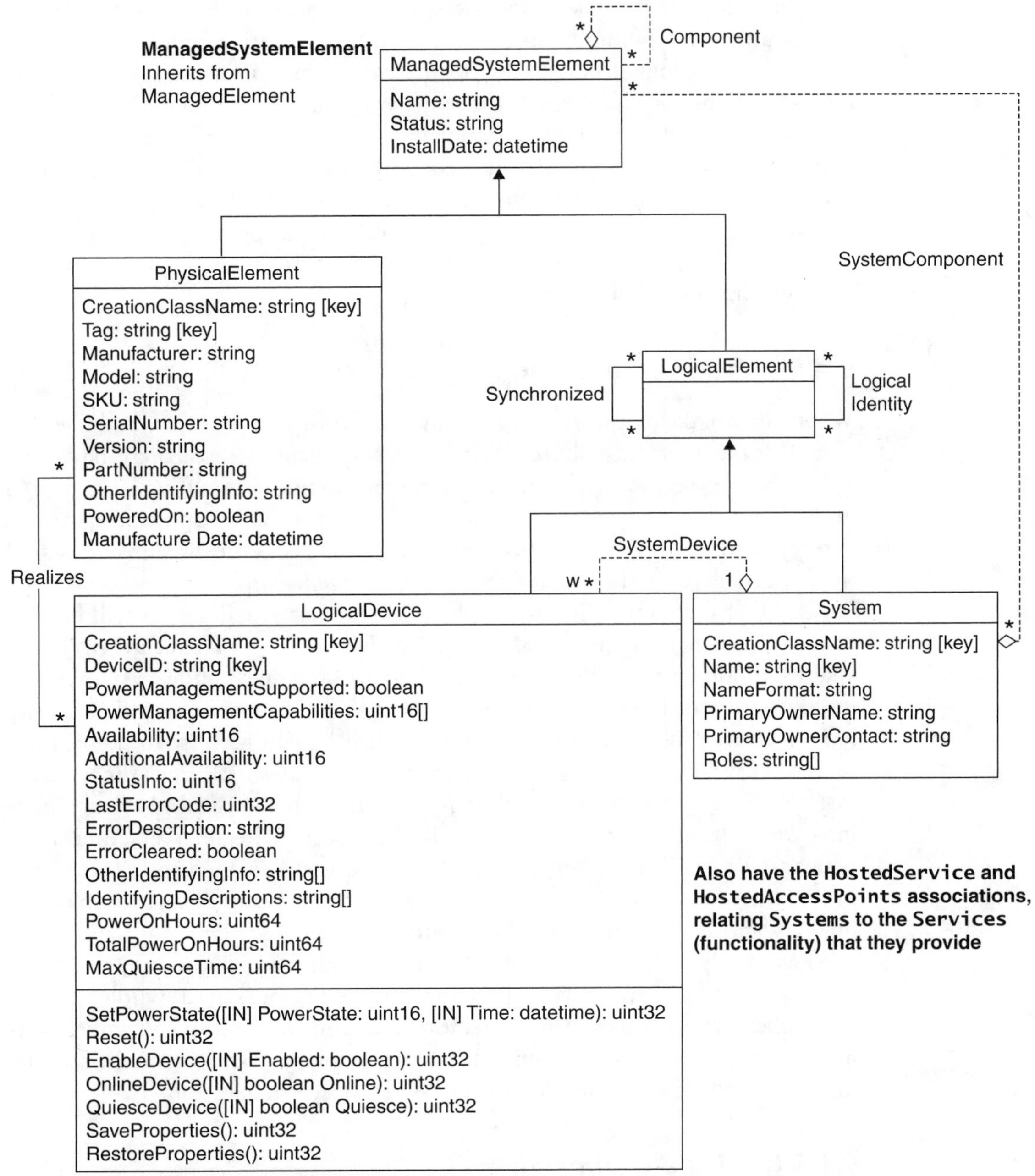

Figure 9.11 The Core Model and the Managed Element

Many complex applications use special logging components or utilities. Such a utility can be modified to send a JMX notification when certain messages are being logged. Or JMX logging can be based on the severity of the message. If you have control of the code, you can modify the logging component to accept a flag to indicate if the message should be a notification or not. Some analysis tools run relatively frequently (every hour or so). If the notifications do not require a response immediately or in real time, you can build the sending of JMX notifications into these types of log analysis tools. Daily analysis tools run probably too infrequently for it to make sense to send JMX notifications from them.

9.4.5 Federation Options

When you are developing distributed applications, you may need to have several MBeanServers distributed across your application. You may have one MBeanServer per JVM, host, or functional component. When you try to build your management application, or represent your application to an enterprise manager, you will need to locate and access the MBeans across all the MBeanServers. This is called MBeanServer *federation.*

Another common scenario in which MBeanServer federation will be necessary is when you are building applications that will execute in JMX-enabled middleware, like application servers and messaging systems. The middleware will have at least one of its own MBeanServers, and you may have your own MBeanServer for your application. In fact, in an application server every application that is executing may have its own MBeanServer instance. The application server's management system will need to recognize its own MBeanServer, as well as all the guest MBeanServers and their MBeans. You will need to deal with MBeanServers designed to talk together in the distributed-application case, as well as those being absorbed unknowingly by another MBeanServer in the middleware case.

Basically you have to decide what your application or manager is going to "see": one MBeanServer—perhaps the local one—or a whole raft of MBeanServers with well-defined relationships. In this section we will examine the single-agent view, along with several implementation models, and the multiple-agent view for implementing MBeanServer federation.

9.4.5.1 Single-Agent View

With a single-agent view, the application or manager interacts with one MBeanServer. Application and manager development is much easier because they don't have to find the right MBeanServer to make a request on an

MBean. That MBeanServer is responsible for aggregating all of the MBeans in the MBeanServers with which it is federated. This is very convenient because the application or manager can interact with a local MBeanServer that has services and adapters to interact with other local or remote MBeanServers. The location of the federated MBeanServers does not change how the application or manager is programmed to interact with its MBeanServer. For the sake of this discussion, we will refer to the single-agent MBeanServer as the *master* MBeanServer. The MBeanServers that the master interacts with (and the application does not) will be referred to as *subordinate* MBeanServers.

You can choose from several federation patterns to support a single-agent-view topology. In fact, applications and managers can't tell the difference among any of the single-agent-view implementations. In all cases they get a large list of MBeans when they invoke the MBeanServer's `queryMBeans()` method, and then they use the MBean name with the local MBeanServer to access the target MBean.

The following list describes the single-agent-view topologies:

1. **MBean propagation via proxies:**
   In this pattern, shown in Figure 9.12, the subordinate MBeanServers have an adapter that listens for MBean lifecycle notifications for creation and deletion. When a new MBean is created, the adapter communicates with the master MBeanServer and creates and registers a proxy for the new MBean in the master MBeanServer. Likewise, when an MBean is removed or deleted, the adapter removes or deletes the proxy in the master MBeanServer. The MBean proxy is designed to communicate with the subordinate MBeanServer and the original MBean so that it stays a mirror image.

   Applications, adapters, and managers also treat the proxy MBeans just like local MBeans. The proxy can be created and controlled in one of two ways:

   (1) All of the federation development is done in an adapter on the subordinate MBeanServers. This means that the subordinate MBeanServers have to be configured with or able to discover which MBeanServer is the master MBeanServer and create their proxy MBeans there. The master MBeanServer treats the proxy MBean like any other MBean and doesn't really know that it is potentially invoking a remote MBean owned by another MBeanServer. It also means that the subordinate adapter may need to invoke the master MBeanServer from a remote JVM. The implication here is that the master MBeanServer must have an adapter that permits remote invocations.

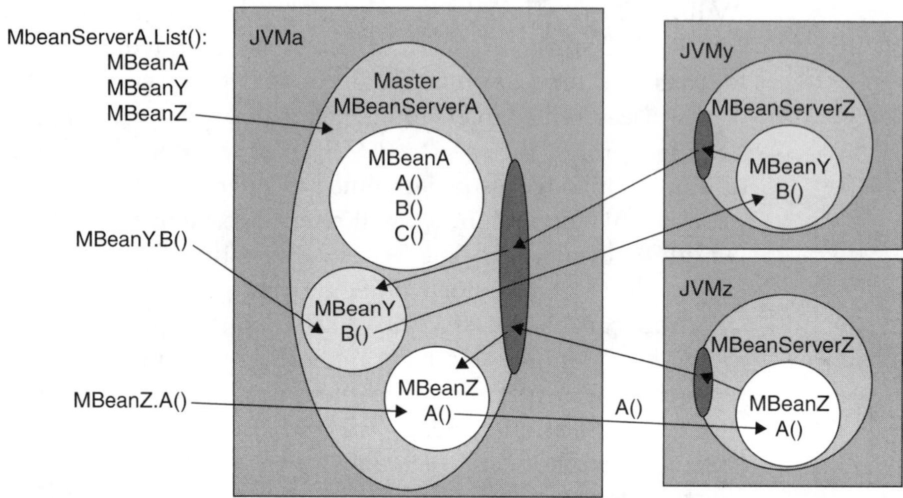

Figure 9.12 MBean Propagation from Downstream MBeanServers

(2) All federation is done in the adapter on the master MBeanServers. The master MBeanServers are configured with or able to discover subordinate MBeanServers, and the subordinate MBeanServer doesn't know that it is being federated. In this case the subordinate MBeanServers must have an adapter that permits remote invocations from master MBeanServers. Usually this adapter will be an RMI adapter, but it could also be a simple HTTP or SOAP-over-HTTP adapter.

The drawback to this pattern is that there can be scalability issues. If there are many proxy MBeans, managers dealing with the master MBeanServer may find searches and dealing with lists of MBeans unwieldy because of the shear volume of MBeans. MBean naming can become critical in these situations to provide some structure for dealing with the MBeans. MBean names should be used to create application domains and resource type groupings.

2. **Request propagation via broadcast:**

In this pattern the master MBeanServer forwards requests to MBeans to the subordinate MBeanServers, as illustrated in Figure 9.13. In this case no representation or proxy of the MBean is registered with the master MBeanServer. In contrast to MBean propagation, the master MBeanServer is specifically built to take care of federation, and the subordinate MBeanServers are not aware that they are in a federated topology. Once again, because the MBeanServers can be in different JVMs, the subordinate MBeanServer must at least have an adapter that gives the

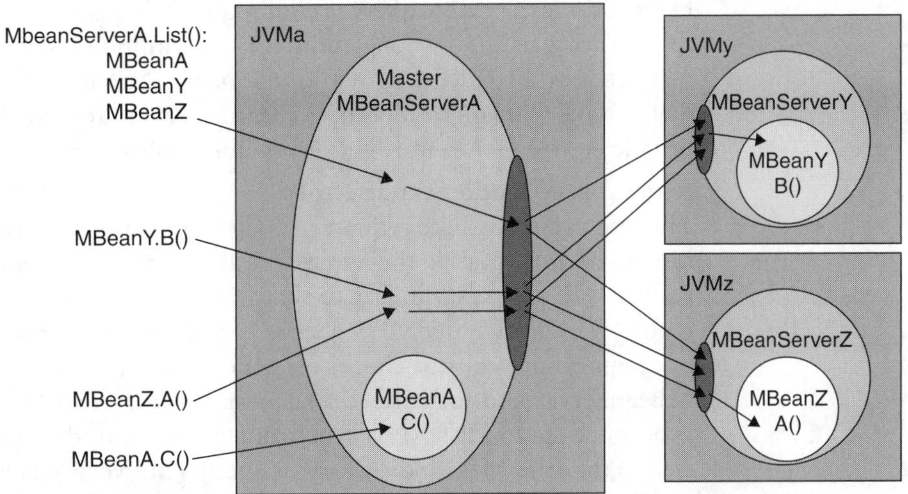

Figure 9.13 Broadcast of Requests by the MBeanServer

master MBeanServer access. As with the previous topology, this adapter will usually be an RMI, HTTP, or SOAP/HTTP remote MBeanServer adapter.

Because the request is broadcast to multiple subordinate MBeanServers, the master MBeanServer needs to deal with multiple responses. It may choose to return any of the following:

- The first one it gets back (fastest performer), and throw away the rest
- An aggregate of the responses in some way: sum, average, median
- An array of all the raw responses: numbers or strings

There are a few drawbacks to this pattern. Although the pattern works well for finding MBeans by name and invoking operations on MBeans whose names you have, it makes listing MBeans more complex because all the MBeans from all the federated MBeanServers need to be retrieved and combined. If there are a lot of subordinate MBeanServers or many requests, request broadcasting can seriously increase the amount of network bandwidth being used for management rather than "real work." It also adds to the total overhead of the system because several MBeanServers may unnecessarily execute the request simultaneously.

In some situations you can use request broadcasting without a defined master MBeanServer. If you have a master MBeanServer, then all requests come from it and are returned to it. The subordinate MBeanServers do not do request forwarding or broadcasting unless they forward to a completely disjointed set of MBeanServers instead of the master's set.

Having a master MBeanServer eliminates the possibility of circular request forwarding—a long-running, slow, infinite loop. If you implement request broadcasting without a master MBeanServer, you must devise a mechanism to identify MBeanServers that have already been broadcast to for the entire set of possible MBeanServers.

3. **Request propagation via directory:**
This pattern is just like request propagation via broadcast, except that instead of broadcasting the request to all MBeanServers, any MBeanServer forwards the request directly to that MBean's MBeanServer. As shown in Figure 9.14, when any MBeanServer gets a request for an MBean that is not registered locally, it checks an MBean directory to find the correct MBeanServer and forwards the request to the correct MBeanServer. This process implies a discovery, synchronization, or update mechanism to ensure that the MBean directory's contents are very accurate.

One way to do this is to make sure that all MBeanServers in the federation have adapters that register new MBeans in a central MBean directory. This arrangement implies that all the MBeanServers know which directory they should be registered with.

Another methodology would be to have the directory periodically list all the MBeans on each MBeanServer to synchronize the directory with the MBeanServers. This approach implies that the directory knows all the MBeanServers it is responsible for.

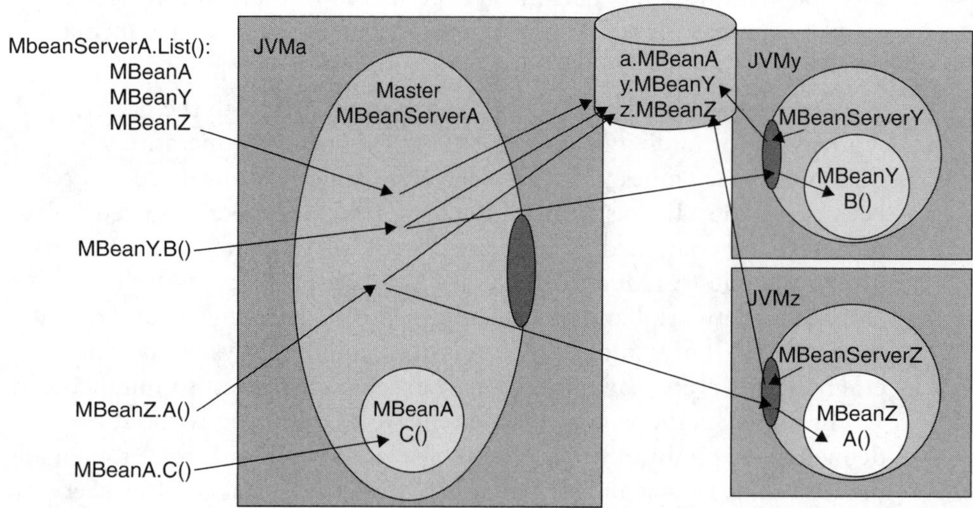

Figure 9.14 MBean Location through Central Directory

A third approach would be to have the directory application dynamically discover all the MBeanServers in all the JVMs and then list all the MBeans. This approach requires the least preconfiguration, but it is not trivial to implement. It presumes that there is a way to discover all JVMs on a system and a way to remotely invoke the `findMBeanServer()` method in it.

One nice feature is that it is possible to create a masterless topology of MBeanServers because they all look up from the same directory and forward to the correct MBeanServer. There is no chance of circular request forwarding. This is convenient in that any MBeanServer will give the exact same view of the MBeans. Therefore, you can have multiple management consoles with little or no impact on your MBeanServer federation topology.

The drawback to this approach is the overhead in maintaining an accurate directory of MBean and MBeanServer associations. The directory also introduces the risk that some newly created MBeans will not be discoverable for a short time, and conversely, that someone might invoke methods on MBeans that no longer exist.

To be fair, there are ways to use directed request forwarding without using a directory. The MBeanServer itself can maintain an association between an MBean name or MBeanServer domain and the subordinate MBeanServer. It may use another mechanism to discover, at runtime, which MBeanServer has the MBean registered with it. The runtime discovery mechanism may be as simple as a naming convention for the MBean that contains the MBeanServer name, host name, and port. New MBeanServers to be forwarded could be configured in at runtime. Without a central MBean directory, it is much more desirable to use a master MBeanServer again. Using a master MBeanServer simply limits the number of MBeanServers that have to maintain their own independent map of MBeans.

9.4.5.2 *Multiple-Agent View*

The multiple-agent-view approach to federation, as shown in Figure 9.15, puts the onus for aggregation on the application or manager. This approach adds complexity to the applications managers that use it. They must now deal with finding remote MBeanServers, figuring out which MBeanServer owns the MBean it wants, performing broadcasts if necessary, and aggregating the results. On the other hand, this approach requires no special adapters in subordinate MBeanServers, nor does it require a master MBeanServer that understands how to communicate with and aggregate MBeanServers.

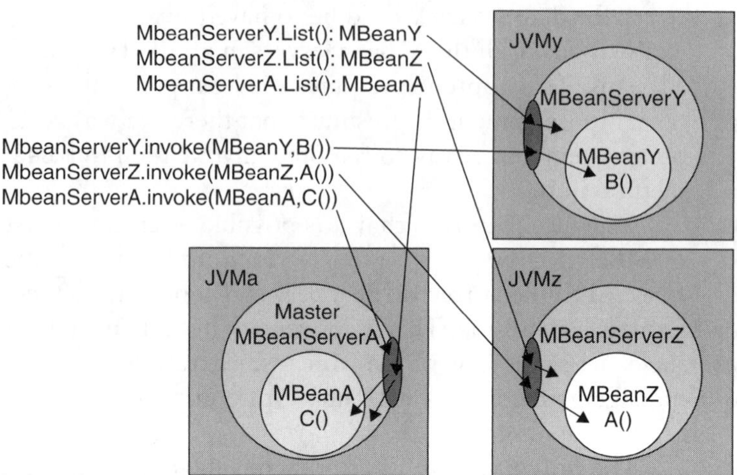

Figure 9.15 Multiple-Agent View

If you decide to have your application see all the MBeanServers, you must have a well-defined mechanism to be able to find all the MBeanServers it should communicate with. This mechanism could be configured into the application, or it could be discovered during runtime. One approach would be to add a small adapter to all MBeanServers that update a simple registry as they initialize.

We recommend implementing a single-agent view for federation. Which implementation option you choose depends on your requirements. If you anticipate having an enormous number of MBeanServers and MBeans, you should use the request propagation via a directory model because it is the most scalable. If you require ease of implementation, the request propagation via broadcast is the easiest to implement reliably. Request propagation via proxy is a good trade-off of performace for ease of implementation.

9.5 Summary

Like any other Java technology, the best way to learn the nuances of managing resources with JMX is to experiment with it. You should take opportunities to use JMX to instrument your manageable resources and applications, develop a custom management console for your application, and make your application manageable by enterprise managers. This chapter has addressed some of the design and implementation choices available to you, but it will take practice to pick the optimal solution.

PART III

Application of JMX

CHAPTER 10

J2EE and JMX

10.1 Java 2 Enterprise Edition

Previous chapters have concentrated on describing JMX[1] as it is generally defined in the base specification: a framework suitable to instrument and manage any software application. The managed application can be a cell phone network, an office suite, an operating system component—any program that can be represented as a collection of JMX MBeans. In fact, it is quite possible that the Java Virtual Machine itself will include a JMX agent as a standard component in one of the next revisions.

This chapter describes how JMX is used for management of a specific class of programs that are becoming more and more essential in the universe of the Internet and e-business. These classes of programs are called *application servers*. Although there are several forms of application servers, the most rapidly growing segment of this market consists of application servers that conform to the Java 2 Enterprise Edition (J2EE)[2] specification.

There are several books that cover all of the details incorporated in J2EE and how to create applications that can be served by compliant application server programs. We won't attempt to duplicate all of that information in this book, but it is important to present a basic overview of J2EE before discussing how JMX will be used to manage J2EE application servers.

From its beginning, the cross-platform portability of Java[3] has made it an attractive language for developers of applications that had to be usable in an "enterprise" environment. Such environments frequently have been built up by the combination of many heterogeneous computer networks consisting of a variety of computing platforms. The ubiquity of the Java Virtual Machine (JVM) hides a lot of the difficult system-level code details from the application developers and allows them to concentrate on creating the business logic for the application.

Even though the Java language itself became a de facto industry standard, there were many different extension libraries for building the distributed systems used in an enterprise environment. The Java 2 Enterprise Edition specification began as an effort to provide a unified, standard definition of the distributed services needed in this environment, as well as a component model for building applications for such an environment. J2EE has become a kind of umbrella specification that incorporates a whole series of subspecifications. The specification starts with the base Java 2 Standard Edition (J2SE)[4] and builds on top of that by adding extension libraries that must be supplied and supported by any compliant application server vendor. Some of the better-known parts of the J2EE specification include Enterprise JavaBeans (EJB),[5] servlets and JavaServer Pages (JSP),[6] Java DataBase Connectivity (JDBC),[7] and Java Message Service (JMS).[8]

Many products on the market comply with the J2EE specification. J2EE application servers must pass an extensive suite of compliance tests (the J2EE Compatibility Test Suite, or CTS) and are then officially designated to conform to J2EE. This means that applications designed to execute in one of these products can be easily deployed in a competing J2EE-compliant application server. Application portability between server products keeps the market competitive and puts the power of choice in the customer's hands, where it belongs (at least according to the widely held philosophy that has been part of the Java revolution since its beginnings).

10.2 J2EE Management

Although all J2EE application server products must adhere to the specifications and pass the compliance tests, the details of their internal architecture and implementation are all quite different. Some server products employ many processes to create a virtual application server; others use a single process for a server. Some are 100 percent Java implementations; others include significant doses of native platform code.

These architectural differences are important because it is in this area where vendors have the opportunity to demonstrate the value of their product over other compliant servers. The fact that the same application can run in many different application servers does not imply that it will run with the same efficiency or reliability in all of them. So J2EE application server vendors are always struggling to find areas where they can excel without straying from the specification and breaking application portability. One of these areas is product and application management.

The lack of a common management service definition in J2EE did not significantly affect early adopters. Most people were consumed with understanding the details of how to use the specification to create applications that were portable and had the proper architecture to perform well under heavy use. However, as the specification matures and more companies have followed it as their application development standard, the lack of any common tools for management has become a more troublesome issue.

The first step toward a common application server management system is to define a management model that all vendors can agree on. This is the motivation behind the J2EE Management specification (JSR 77).[9] This specification represents a model of the J2EE application server, and its subcomponents, that all J2EE-compliant application vendors are required to expose. Regardless of their true internal architecture, all application server vendors will have to expose a set of management objects that follow the JSR 77 model.

According to the base J2EE specification, application servers consist of special *containers* that provide an operating environment for the application components deployed in the server. Application component examples are the EJB module that contains Enterprise JavaBeans, and the Web module that contains servlets and JSP (Web application components). Prior to the J2EE Management specification, there was no common representation of the EJB module for external management. Some versions of some application server products did not expose the EJB module at all.

The JSR 77 management model includes a representation of the EJB module, as well as all of the other relevant components that logically make up an application server. So when JSR 77 becomes a required subspecification under J2EE 1.4, all compliant application server vendors will expose a representation of the EJB module (and every other object defined by the JSR 77 model). A management tool that can access and manipulate components of one J2EE 1.4 application server product will be able to manage all other compliant application servers.

One detail that may not stand out from a casual reading of the J2EE Management specification is that JSR 77 requires an underlying implementation of JMX (JSR 3). JSR 77 is built on top of JMX. JMX classes and interfaces are included in required interface definitions that are part of JSR 77. The JSR 77 compliance tests use classes defined by JMX. So JSR 77 can be thought of as a specification that takes the general management framework of JMX and defines how it will be used to manage a specific application domain—that of the J2EE application server.

10.3 Management Tool Access: The MEJB

Before covering all of the application server components that are represented in JSR 77, let's discuss the mechanism by which management tools will connect to and communicate with application servers. There is no standard defined in JSR 3 for what JMX connectors look like or how code in one JVM can remotely access the JMX agent in another JVM and its registered MBeans. Any remote access mechanism is beyond the scope of the JMX 1.0 specification.

Because every J2EE-compliant application server product is required to support Enterprise JavaBeans functionality, it made sense to the JSR 77 expert group that application server products would be able to support the use of an EJB to remotely access the management system. This means that the only remote access mechanism that is explicitly required by JSR 77 is the Management EJB (MEJB), a session EJB that exposes JMX MBeanServer methods to remote clients.

An important part of the J2EE Management specification is that there are provisions for managing application servers using other management systems besides JMX, such as WBEM[10] and SNMP.[11] Although the implementations of these other access mechanisms are not defined by JSR 77, it is reasonable to assume that most vendors will build protocol adapters from these other systems to JMX, rather than provide a completely separate route to the management functions in parallel with JMX.

10.4 J2EE Management Models

10.4.1 The Base Managed-Object Model

As shown in Figure 10.1, all objects modeled in JSR 77 inherit from the `J2EEManagedObject` model. So regardless of the specific attributes and operations they provide, all managed resources include at least an `objectName` `String` attribute and three `boolean` attributes that give a little more information about the capabilities of the object (see Table 10.1).

The `objectName` attribute for `J2EEManagedObject` is a subclass of the Java `String` type that complies with the JMX `ObjectName` format. The `objectName` attribute is used to locate the managed object within the J2EE

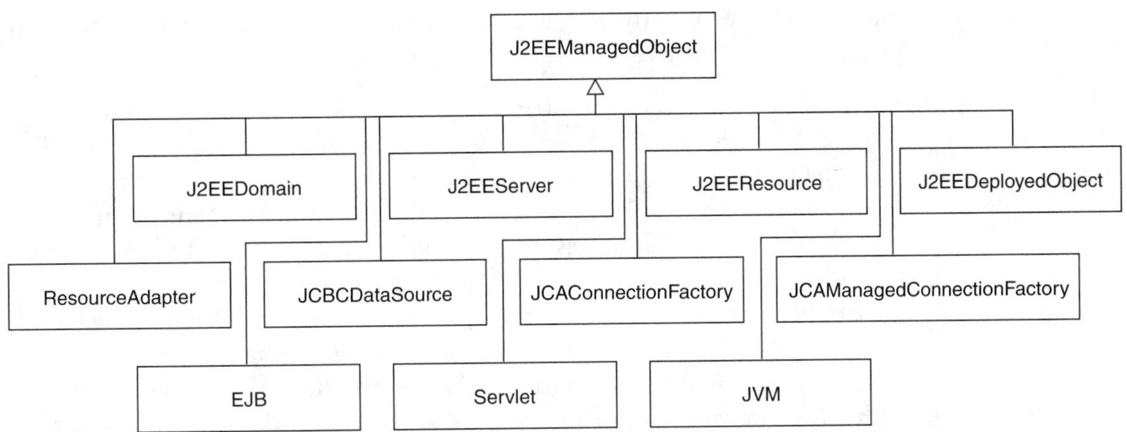

Figure 10.1 Overview of the J2EE Managed-Object Model

Table 10.1 `J2EEManagedObject` Attributes

Attribute	Type
`objectName`	`OBJECT_NAME (String)`
`stateManageable`	`boolean`
`statisticsProvider`	`boolean`
`eventProvider`	`boolean`

management domain, so application server vendors must ensure that it is unique within that domain. Like any other instance of the JMX `ObjectName` class, this one contains a *domain* part and a *properties* part.

The domain part of the name identifies the scope of the management system. If the management program is connected with two or more J2EE environments, this attribute can be used to distinguish the managed objects that belong in one environment from those that belong in the other. JSR 77 does not specify how this domain identifier is calculated or structured—only that it cannot contain characters that are used as separators in JMX `ObjectName` syntax. The restricted characters are the colon (:), comma (,), equal sign (=), asterisk (*), and question mark (?).

There are several properties required by JSR 77 that the application server vendor will set for all managed objects in their domain. These required properties further identify the managed object, as well as place it within the containment hierarchy of the J2EE management domain:

- **`j2eeType`**. The `j2eeType` property identifies the specific subclass of `J2EEManagedObject` that this managed object implements. The JSR 77 model includes 23 specific `j2eeType` properties, such as `J2EEServer` and `EJBModule`. This `objectName` property allows management programs to understand the capabilities of the specific managed object to which they hold a reference.
- **`name`**. The `name` property identifies the specific instance of a managed object, to distinguish it from other instances that share the same `j2eeType` property. For example, if there are three `J2EEServer` objects in the domain, the `name` property distinguishes one from the others. If the managed object is a `J2EEDomain` object, then the `name` property is special. In that case it is required to be the same as the domain part of all of the object names in the management domain.
- **Parent properties**. The properties that identify the parent of a particular object have the form `type=name`, where the type is the `j2eeType` value of the parent object and the name is the name of the parent object. These properties help position the managed object within the JSR 77 model hierarchy. For instance, all `J2EEApplication` objects deployed into an application server will have a parent property that identifies the server. Table 10.2 lists the parent properties that each managed object is required to supply as part of its `objectName` property list.

Table 10.2 `J2EEManagedObject` Parent Properties

`j2eeType`	**Parent Property**
`J2EEDomain`	None
`J2EEServer`	None
`J2EEApplication`	`J2EEServer`
`AppClientModule`	`J2EEServer, J2EEApplication`
`EJBModule`	`J2EEServer, J2EEApplication`
`WebModule`	`J2EEServer, J2EEApplication`
`ResourceAdapterModule`	`J2EEServer, J2EEApplication`

j2eeType	Parent Property
EntityBean	J2EEServer, J2EEApplication, EJBModule
StatefulSessionBean	J2EEServer, J2EEApplication, EJBModule
StatelessSessionBean	J2EEServer, J2EEApplication, EJBModule
MessageDrivenBean	J2EEServer, J2EEApplication, EJBModule
Servlet	J2EEServer, J2EEApplication, WebModule
ResourceAdapter	J2EEServer, J2EEApplication, ResourceAdapterModule
JavaMailResource	J2EEServer
JCAResource	J2EEServer
JCAConnectionFactory	J2EEServer, JCAResource
JCAManagedConnectionFactory	J2EEServer
JDBCResource	J2EEServer
JDBCDataSource	J2EEServer, JDBCResource
JDBCDriver	J2EEServer
JMSResource	J2EEServer
JNDIResource	J2EEServer
JTAResource	J2EEServer
RMI_IIOPResource	J2EEServer
URLResource	J2EEServer
JVM	J2EEServer

Note that the application server vendor may include additional `objectName` properties beyond what is required for JSR 77. These properties would be used by the server vendor's internal implementation, and you should not count on any properties other than those defined by JSR 77 to be available to portable J2EE management programs.

As for the remaining J2EEManagedObject attributes, stateManageable lets the management program know whether this object can have its state altered through explicit operations such as start() and stop(). The statistics-Provider attribute lets the management program know that this object returns performance statistics in the form defined in JSR 77 for the type of object. The eventProvider attribute lets the management program know that this object generates events for significant situations that occur during the lifecycle of the object.

We'll look at the details of the standard management functions for state management, statistics, and events later in this chapter. Right now, let's focus on the rest of the managed resources represented in the model.

10.4.2 The Management Domain Model

JSR 77 contains an object hierarchy. The top object in the hierarchy is J2EEDomain. J2EEDomain is the entry point to the application server management system. It is the object from which all other managed objects are obtained by the management tool.

J2EEDomain is intended to represent a complete management domain for the application server environment. This domain may contain one or many application servers. The domain may span networks and computer systems, or it may encompass only a single operating system process. The application server vendor determines the scope of J2EEDomain.

Methods on the J2EEDomain object allow management tools to query the object in order to learn how many servers are part of the domain.

Table 10.3 contains the attributes defined in JSR 77 for the J2EEDomain object. As illustrated in Figure 10.2, the J2EEDomain object can provide a management tool with the list of all J2EEServer instances in that management domain.

10.4.3 The J2EE Application Server Model

With its contained resources and components, J2EEServer provides a topological view of the management environment. It is meant to represent the server

Table 10.3 J2EEDomain Attributes

Attribute	Type
servers	OBJECT_NAME[] (String[])

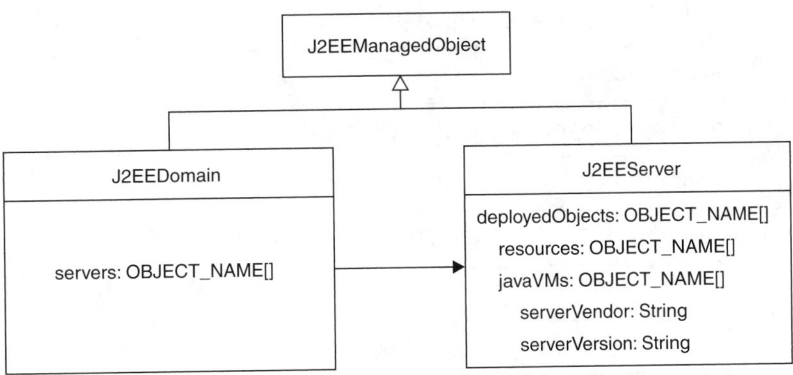

Figure 10.2 Top-Level Model Hierarchy of JSR 77

runtime components. `J2EEDeployedObject` (described in Section 10.4.4), and its subparts, provides an application-centric view of the environment. Taken together, management programs have a lot of flexibility for how they query the application server, display its data, and navigate its various levels of management detail. Figure 10.3 illustrates all of the `J2EEServer` subcomponents.

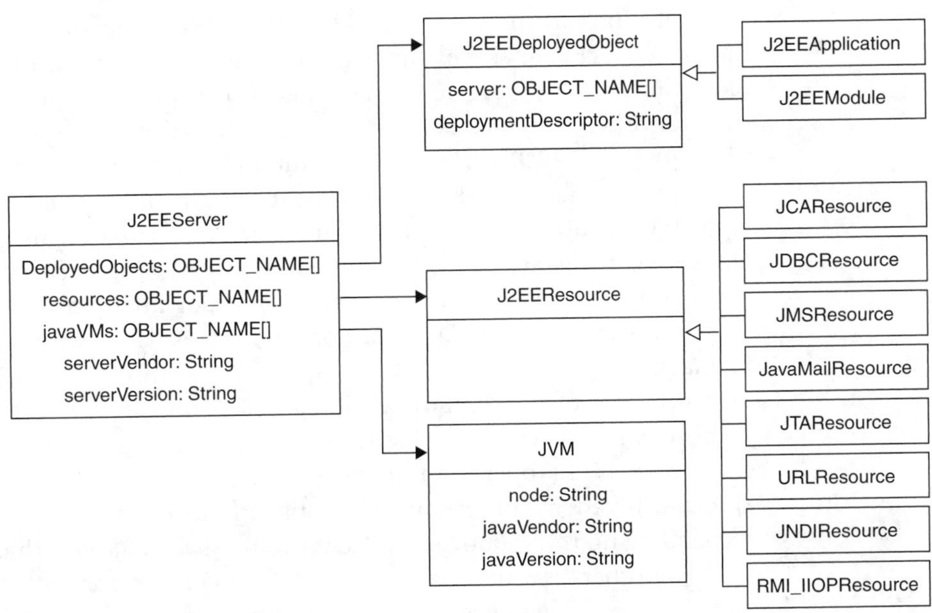

Figure 10.3 `J2EEServer` Subcomponents

Table 10.4 `J2EEServer` Attributes

Attribute	Type
`deployedObjects`	`OBJECT_NAME[]`
`resources`	`OBJECT_NAME[]`
`javaVMs`	`OBJECT_NAME[]`
`serverVendor`	`String`
`serverVersion`	`String`

Table 10.4 contains the attributes defined in JSR 77 for the `J2EEServer` object. It is important to understand that the JSR 77 models are abstract representations of how the vendor has implemented the application server product. A particular application server product may not have a single `J2EEServer` object. The functions represented by the JSR 77 `J2EEServer` objects may be spread out among several different objects in the product architecture. But a compliant application server must find a way to direct management requests addressed to `J2EEServer` to the real managed resources in the product. That's the challenge to platform vendors.

Let's look at the details underneath the `J2EEServer` object. The JSR 77 model for `J2EEServer` includes three required attributes, the JVM, the vendor name, and the version of the application server. The platform vendor sets the `serverVendor` and `serverVersion` properties. These properties identify the server. If `J2EEDomain` supports multiple versions of the server runtime, then these different `J2EEServer` instances can be recognized through their `serverVersion` attributes. If the management program maintains a list of `J2EEServer` instances from different domains, the servers can be distinguished from each other by their `serverVendor` attributes.

Two parallel sets of information are encapsulated within `J2EEServer`. A management program can take an application-centric view of the domain, or it can take a physical runtime view of the domain. The lists maintained in `J2EEServer` support either view.

There is an operation defined on `J2EEServer` that returns a list of `J2EEDeployedObject` instances (applications or application components, depending on the vendor implementation) associated with that server.

The other lists maintained by `J2EEServer` are for more physically oriented objects. There are operations to return a list of Java Virtual Machines (one or more, depending on the product) associated with this server. And another operation provides a list of J2EEResource objects that are used by the server or applications running within the server.

10.4.4 J2EE Application Component Models

J2EEDeployedObject is the base class model for all application module components. Table 10.5 lists the attributes of this base class.

We assemble J2EE applications by combining several application modules. The application modules are sets of application components of the same type. For instance, EJBModule is a collection of one or more Enterprise JavaBeans. WebModule is a set of servlets, JSPs, and Web application content items. Java 2 Connector architecture implementations are packaged as instances of ResourceAdapterModule. Application client code is separated from the server-side logic into instances of AppClientModule.

All J2EEDeployedObject subclasses provide the base attributes for server and deploymentDescriptor. The server attribute is the objectName String attribute of the J2EEServer on which the object is deployed. The deploymentDescriptor attribute is the String representation of the standard J2EE deployment descriptor, an XML file that includes all of the information covering the details of how the application component is configured.

An instance of J2EEDeployedObject can represent an entire application or a single module of an application. As Figure 10.4 shows, there are specific subclasses of J2EEDeployedObject for each type of module and one for the overall application.

A J2EEApplication object represents the overall application. This object provides a list of all of the modules that make up the application.

Table 10.6 shows the attributes for the J2EEApplication object. The list of modules returned by J2EEApplication (in the modules attribute) may include any of the various module types. Those types are all subclasses of the J2EEModule type.

Table 10.5 J2EEDeployedObject Attributes

Attribute	Type
Server	OBJECT_NAME
DeploymentDescriptor	String

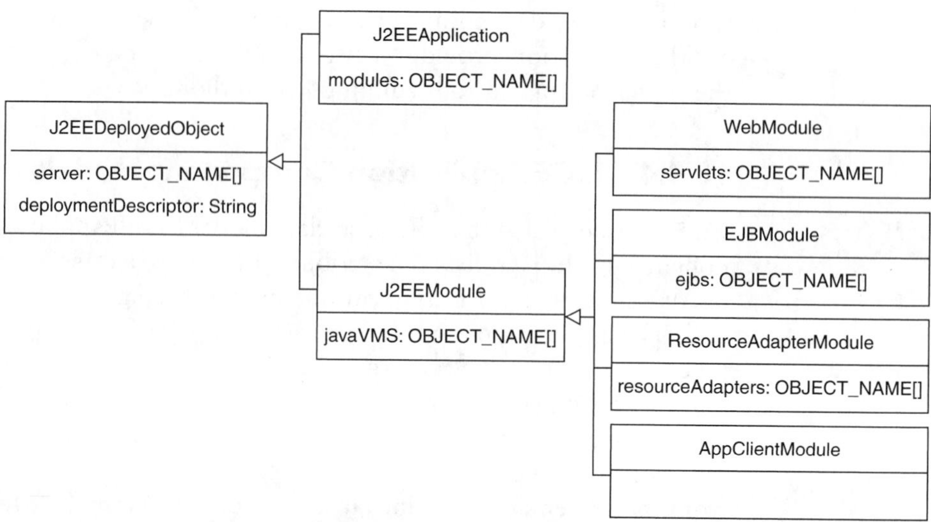

Figure 10.4 `J2EEDeployedObject` Subcomponents

Table 10.6 `J2EEApplication` Attributes

Attribute	Type
`Modules`	`OBJECT_NAME[]`

As shown in Table 10.7, every module provides a list of the JVMs on which it is running. We will look at the JVM managed object model in more detail later in this chapter. There are four subclasses of `J2EEModule`: `WebModule`, `EJBModule`, `ResourceAdapterModule`, and `AppClientModule` (see Figure 10.4).

`AppClientModule` has no attributes defined by JSR 77. However, as with all other JSR 77 models, vendors may extend this managed object to expose proprietary attributes that may be of interest to management programs.

Table 10.7 `J2EEModule` Attributes

Attribute	Type
`JavaVMs`	`OBJECT_NAME[]`

A J2EE Connector architecture (JCA)[12] ResourceAdapterModule contains one or more JCA resource adapters. *Resource adapters* provide the logic to link an application with some back-end enterprise information system (EIS) resources. Examples of such EIS resources are customer information control system (CICS) applications, database systems, customer relationship management (CRM) programs, or any kind of resource manager that returns data of use to the J2EE application.

ResourceAdapterModule maintains a list of the resource adapters that are deployed as part of that module. This list is exposed as the resourceAdapters attribute (see Table 10.8).

WebModule represents a Web application. Web applications are composed of servlets, JSPs, and other content that is delivered to a Web browser over an HTTP connection. The JSR 77 WebModule subclass of J2EEModule, supports an attribute that is the list of servlets contained in the module (see Table 10.9).

An EJBModule instance encapsulates one or more Enterprise JavaBeans (EJBs). EJBs come in a variety of types. EntityBean EJBs represent persistent data stored in a database. SessionBean EJBs represent an interactive session between the application client and the application logic in the server. And MessageDrivenBean EJBs represent the listener end of a messaging system, and provide a mechanism by which requests from an asynchronous messaging system can be delivered to the system. SessionBean is further subdivided into *stateful* and *stateless* types, depending on whether persistent data is associated with the client session.

The EJBs that are combined in one instance of EJBModule may be of different EJB types. Instances of SessionBean and EntityBean can be mixed in the same module. MessageDrivenBean instances can be part of the same

Table 10.8 ResourceAdapterModule Attributes

Attribute	Type
resourceAdapters	OBJECT_NAME[]

Table 10.9 WebModule Attributes

Attribute	Type
servlets	OBJECT_NAME[]

Table 10.10 EJBModule Attributes

Attribute	Type
ejbs	OBJECT_NAME[]

Table 10.11 J2EEModule Subclasses and Application Components

Subclass	Application Component(s)
AppClientModule	None
WebModule	Servlet
ResourceAdapterModule	ResourceAdapter
EJBModule	EJB (EntityBean, MessageDrivenBean, StatefulSessionBean, StatelessSessionBean)

module also. The ejbs attribute of EJBModule (see Table 10.10) returns a list of all of the EJBs deployed in the module, regardless of EJB type.

Table 10.11 lists the various J2EEModule subclasses and the application components that each module type may contain.

10.4.5 J2EE Server Runtime Components

The J2EEDeployedObject model provides the management tool with an application-centric view of the system. The topology represented covers all of the information related to applications that may be running within the management domain.

The other perspective on the domain is one oriented toward the physical resources in use to provide the operating environment in which the applications are served. The JVM class and subclasses of the J2EEResource model provide this server runtime view of the system.

In addition to a list of deployed objects, J2EEServer provides a list of JVMs and a list of J2EEResource instances. Table 10.12 shows the attributes of the JVM object. Each application server is associated with at least one Java Virtual Machine (JVM). Some application servers run in several JVMs

Table 10.12 JVM Attributes

Attribute	Type
javaVersion	String
javaVendor	String
node	String

concurrently. The JSR 77 models provide for this implementation by exposing the JVM attribute of the server as a list rather than a single object instance.

The JVM model includes attributes for identifying the version of the virtual machine and the vendor that implemented the JVM. The node attribute of JVM is the fully qualified host name of the system on which the JVM is executing.

The J2EEResource objects represent system resources that are used by the server or its applications. These can be external resources, such as databases, messaging systems, transaction monitors, naming directories, or mail servers. J2EEResource instances can also be internal to the server, such as the object request broker (represented by the RMI-IIOP model in JSR 77). Figure 10.5 illustrates the set of J2EEResource instances defined in the specification.

The JSR 77 management models do not include much detail for the various subclasses of J2EEResource. Most application server vendors are likely to extend these models with specific implementations that match their internal runtime. The importance of the J2EEResource classes is to provide a structure for management programs to navigate the server runtime. The J2EEResource classes also provide an important hook for exposing performance data that will be discussed in Section 10.5.

The following list covers the J2EEResource subclasses, including an explanation of what each model represents:

- **JCAResource.** JCAResource represents a resource manager that adheres to the Java Connector architecture specification. These resource managers typically control access to nonrelational information systems such as CICS or CRM systems.
- **JDBCResource.** Relational databases are typically accessed through JDBC data sources. The JSR 77 JDBCResource represents the resource managers for such information systems.
- **JMSResource.** The Java Message Service (JMS) is the component of the system that provides asynchronous messaging support.

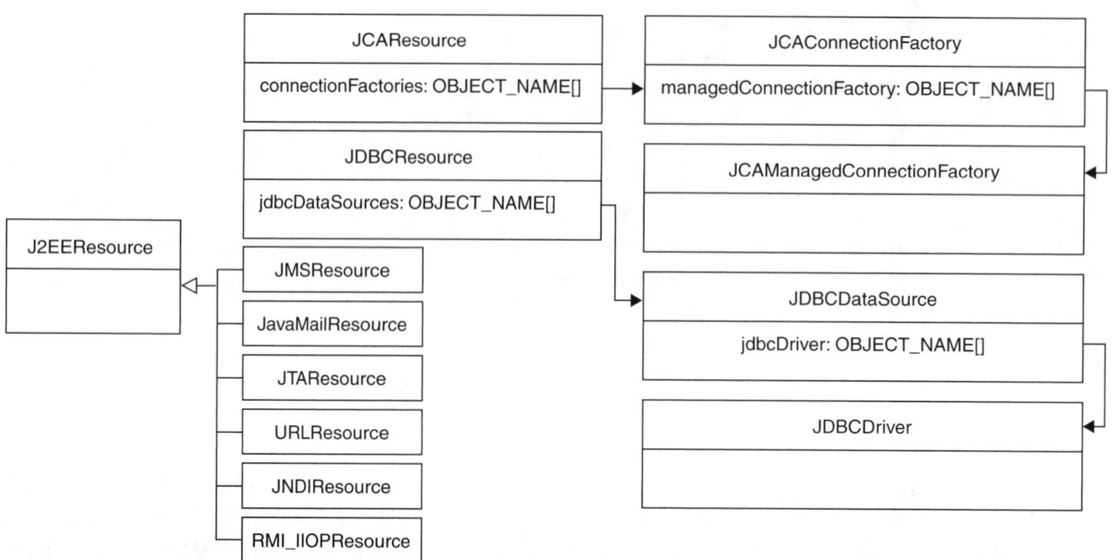

Figure 10.5 Subclasses of `J2EEResource` Defined in JSR 77

- **`JavaMailResource`.** The J2EE specification requires that all compliant application servers include support for e-mail applications with the Java-Mail API.
- **`JTAResource`.** Transactions are an important aspect of the application server system, and the `JTAResource` model represents the Java Transaction API (JTA) resource within the server runtime. In many application server implementations, `JTAResource` is a managed object that is supported by the transaction manager component.
- **`URLResource`.** One of the simplest resources defined by J2EE is the URL. Application components can declare their use of a URL in the `resource-ref` element of their deployment descriptor. URL resource references are bound to an object managed as a instance of `URLResource` in the JSR 77 models.
- **`JNDIResource`.** The Java Naming and Directory Interface (JNDI) is a service provided by the application server runtime to support a common registry of elements that need to be located by other code within the system. The component most likely to support the JSR 77 `JNDIResource` model is the naming server within most application servers.
- **`RMI_IIOPResource`.** This resource represents the runtime component that supports the RMI-IIOP protocol implementation. For most application servers this is really the object request broker (ORB).

10.5 Standard Management Functions

All JSR 77 models inherit from the base `J2EEManagedObject` model. That base model provides a way for any managed object to advertise whether it supports some or all of the three standard management functions defined in the specification: state management, performance monitoring, and event generation. We'll look at the details of each.

10.5.1 State Management

Being able to start and stop a managed object seems like a fundamental requirement for manageability. But many managed resources in a J2EE application server may not be capable of independent starting or stopping. The `stateManageable` attribute of the `J2EEManagedObject` base class indicates whether a managed resource can be started and stopped.

If the `stateManageable` attribute is set to `true`, then the `J2EEManagedObject` supports the `StateManageable` model of attributes and operations. If the attribute is set to `false`, then the object does not support the `StateManageable` model and presumably does not support having its state changed dynamically through the JSR 77 mechanisms. Tables 10.13 and 10.14 show the attributes and operations, respectively, defined by the `StateManageable` model.

By supporting the `StateManageable` model, a component of the application server is really advertising that it follows the finite state machine defined in JSR 77 and illustrated in Figure 10.6. The object stores a value for its state

Table 10.13 `StateManageable` Attributes

Attribute	Type
`state`	`int`
`startTime`	`long`

Table 10.14 `StateManageable` Operations

Operation	Return Type
`start()`	`void`
`startRecursive()`	`void`
`stop()`	`void`

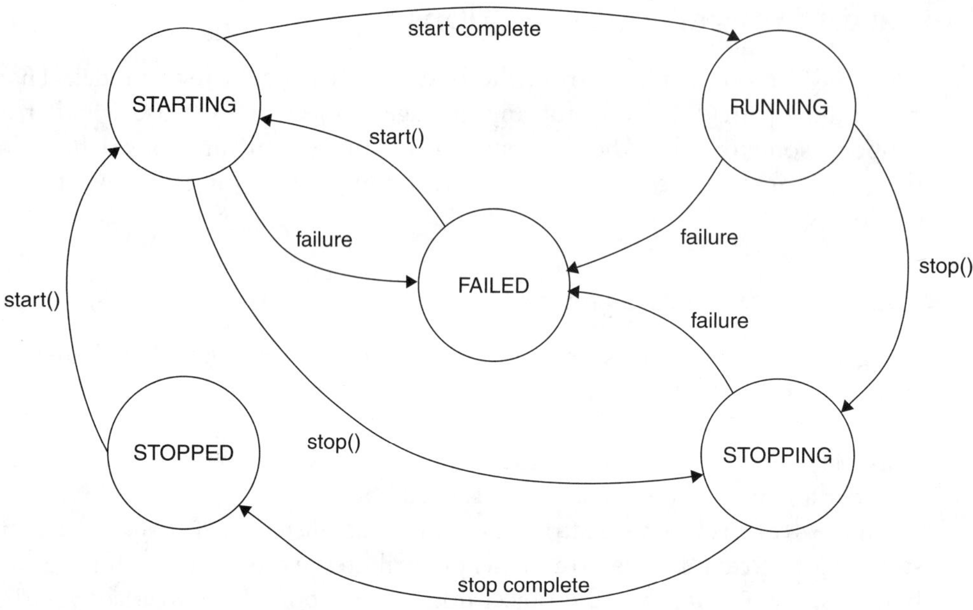

Figure 10.6 State Machine Defined by the `StateManageable` Model

independently from the rest of the system components, and returns its current state to management programs at any point in time.

There are five possible states in which an instance of `J2EEManagedObject`, supporting the `StateManageable` model, can exist: `STARTING`, `RUNNING`, `STOPPING`, `STOPPED`, and `FAILED` (see Table 10.15). As `StateManageable` objects make the transition from one state to another, they may generate events to notify interested parties of the change in their state. Some notifications are required by the specification, and others are optional. Section 10.5.2 covers the event notification mechanism defined by JSR 77, so we will present details there.

The required notifications for `StateManageable` objects are `j2ee.state.running`, when an object transitions into a `RUNNING` state; `j2ee.state.stopped`, to be generated when the object moves to the `STOPPED` state; and `j2ee.state.failed`, to be issued when an object enters the `FAILED` state. Optional state transition events are `j2ee.state.starting`, issued when the object enters the `STARTING` state; and `j2ee.state.stopping`, to be generated when the object enters the `STOPPING` state.

Let's assume that the `StateManageable` object begins in the `STOPPED` state. The management program can invoke a `start()` operation on the object, which will cause the object to enter the `STARTING` state (and optionally issue

Table 10.15 `StateManageable` States

State	Meaning
STARTING	This object is in the process of getting to the RUNNING state.
RUNNING	This object is in its normal running condition in the server.
STOPPING	This object is in the process of getting to the STOPPED state.
STOPPED	This object is not running but is ready to be started.
FAILED	This object has unexpectedly stopped running.

a `j2ee.state.starting` event). The object will remain in the `STARTING` state until it makes the transition out of that state under one of two possible conditions: (1) It may succeed in initializing and move to the `RUNNING` state (at which time it must generate a `j2ee.state.running` event), or (2) it may fail to initialize and enter the `FAILED` state (when it must issue a `j2ee.state.failed` event).

If the management program needs to stop an instance of an object that supports the `StateManageable` model, it will invoke a `stop()` operation on the object. The `stop()` operation causes the object to move to the `STOPPING` state, and it may optionally issue a `j2ee.state.stopping` event. The object leaves this state through one of two paths: It may succeed in stopping and enter the `STOPPED` state (and issue a `j2ee.state.stopped` event), or it may fail to cleanly stop and enter the `FAILED` state (issuing an event at that time).

The `StateManageable` object provides a `startTime` attribute that tells the management program the time that the object entered the `RUNNING` state. Different managed objects within the same application server process may have different `startTime` values.

`StateManageable` objects also support a `startRecursive()` operation that is intended to tell the object that the managed objects that are its children, and that support the StateManageable model, should be started in addition to the target object. There is no corollary operation for stopping a managed object. The `stop()` operation on a managed object stops all child objects in addition to the original target.

10.5.2 Event Generation

Most useful management programs need to know the states of the systems they are managing. But polling for attribute changes is an inefficient technique for monitoring the condition of a server. So JSR 77 has incorporated the asynchronous event notification mechanism defined by JMX. This system allows the management program to register as a listener for only the events that are of interest. When, if ever, the significant event occurs, the registered management program will receive a callback notification.

All `J2EEManagedObject` subclasses that support the `eventProvider` model (note that this set implicitly includes all `StateManageable` objects) provide an `eventTypes` attribute that is a list of the types of notifications that the object produces. Event types are dot-separated strings that identify the event that caused the notification to be generated. There are eight standard event types defined in JSR 77, and server vendors generally extend that set with proprietary notifications. Server vendors cannot reuse the type prefix *j2ee*, however, because that is reserved for the specification-defined events. The set of standard event types defined by JSR 77 is shown in Table 10.16.

When an event is generated within the system, all listeners registered for that event will receive a `Notification` model object. The `Notification` object contains the information needed by the management program to understand what occurred and when it occurred.

Table 10.16 Event Types Defined by JSR 77

Event Type	**Meaning**
`j2ee.object.created`	Issued whenever a new managed object is created.
`j2ee.object.deleted`	Issued whenever an existing managed object is removed.
`j2ee.state.starting`	Issued whenever a `StateManageable` object enters the `STARTING` state.
`j2ee.state.running`	Issued whenever a `StateManageable` object enters the `RUNNING` state.
`j2ee.state.stopping`	Issued whenever a `StateManageable` object enters the `STOPPING` state.
`j2ee.state.stopped`	Issued whenever a `StateManageable` object enters the `STOPPED` state.
`j2ee.state.failed`	Issued whenever a `StateManageable` object enters the `FAILED` state.
`j2ee.attribute.changed`	Issued whenever an attribute of a managed object changes.

Table 10.17 `Notification` Model Attributes

Attribute	Type
source	OBJECT_NAME
timeStamp	long
sequenceNumber	long
type	String
message	String
userData	Object

Table 10.17 lists the attributes of the `Notification` model. The `type` attribute will always match one of the event types for which the listener has registered. The `source` attribute provides identification of the specific managed object that issued the notification because many different objects may be capable of issuing the same notification event. The `timeStamp` attribute tells the management program when the event occurred. And `sequenceNumber` allows this event to be correlated with other events that may be related, issued by the same object. Additional information about the event can be obtained from the `message` attribute and the optional `userData` attribute.

10.5.3 Performance Monitoring

In addition to monitoring the state of an application server and its components, management programs typically gather specific performance data about how well the system is running. Such data allows the management program to understand if parts of the system are under stress and even anticipate failures before they occur.

The J2EE Management specification includes an entire performance data framework to provide this type of information about application servers to management systems. The framework is composed of three components:

1. The `StatisticsProvider` model is what managed objects support if they are going to deliver performance data to external management programs.
2. This performance data for an individual managed object is packaged into a set called `Stats`. A `Stats` object is a set of accessor methods that expose a group of related metrics.

3. The data types of the metrics that are contained within the Stats object must be one of the Statistic model subclasses defined by JSR 77.

For example, a JavaMailResource managed object supports the StatisticsProvider model if the value of its statisticsProvider attribute is set to true. The StatisticsProvider model includes one attribute: stats. JavaMailResource returns this attribute as an object that is a subclass of the Stats model: the JavaMailStats object. The JavaMailStats model includes only one Statistic accessor—the getSentMailCount() operation—which returns an object of type CountStatistic (a subclass of the JSR 77 Statistic model).

In similar fashion, other managed objects that claim to support the StatisticsProvider model return a collection of one or more Statistic objects. The entire collection of Statistic objects for a given managed object is its Stats set. And each Statistic instance in the Stats set has a specific named accessor method.

Note that the defined Stats set of metrics for a particular instance of J2EEManagedObject does not have to be supported completely for the object to be a compliant StatisticsProvider model. The server vendor may elect to provide accessors to a subset of the JSR 77 Stats set for any managed object type. Management programs should always obtain the list of Statistic instances that the object supports by invoking the getStatisticNames() method defined for the Stats model. The list that is returned by the instance of the Stats subclass implemented by a particular vendor is the real set of metrics that the object can provide. The Stats definition in JSR 77 is really just a list of the possible Statistic objects relevant to a managed object type.

Server vendors may augment the Stats definitions for an object. Any metrics returned along with the metrics defined by JSR 77 will be one of the Statistic subclasses. These additional Statistic objects are included in the list returned by the getStatisticNames() method.

All metrics returned to management programs from JSR 77 StatisticsProvider instances are one of the Statistic interface subclasses, which are listed in Table 10.18. These interfaces are defined in the javax.management.j2ee.statistics package.

Each type of J2EEManagedObject has a set of Statistic objects collected into a Stats interface specific to that type of object. Table 10.19 lists the Stats interfaces that apply to the various managed objects.

Table 10.18 `Statistic` Interface Subclasses

Class	Description
`Statistic`	Base class that includes accessors for name, unit of measure, time stamps, and description.
`TimeStatistic`	Time measurement statistic that has accessors for minimum, maximum, and total time values.
`RangeStatistic`	Provides lowest, highest, and current value of a metric.
`BoundaryStatistic`	Provides the limit of upper and lower values of a metric.
`BoundedRangeStatistic`	Provides the high, low, and current values, along with boundary limits, of a metric.
`CountStatistic`	Simple counter statistic that has one accessor for count value.

Table 10.19 `Stats` Interfaces

Managed Object	Interface
`JVM`	`JVMStats`
`JTAResource`	`JTAStats`
`EJB`	`EJBStats`
`EntityBean`	`EntityBeanStats`
`MessageDrivenBean`	`MessageDrivenBeanStats`
`SessionBean`	`SessionBeanStats`
`StatefulSessionBean`	`StatefulSessionBeanStats`
`StatelessSessionBean`	`StatelessSessionBeanStats`
`Servlet`	`ServletStats`
`JavaMailResource`	`JavaMailStats`
`URLResource`	`URLStats`
`JCAResource`	`JCAStats`
`JDBCResource`	`JDBCStats`
`JMSResource`	`JMSStats`

10.5.4 Stats Interface Details

The Stats interfaces are also part of the javax.management.j2ee.statistics package. They are strictly accessor definitions for the underlying application server implementation. As such, they include no attributes as part of their definitions.

The base Stats interface has accessor methods to retrieve the list of statistics for this object in one call, and also to retrieve an individual Statistic object identified by its name (see Table 10.20). The getStatisticNames() method returns an array of the entire set of statistic names that the object exposes. This list includes both statistics defined by JSR 77 and vendor-specific statistics.

The JVMStats class provides accessor methods to retrieve the current JVM heap size and also the amount of time that the JVM has been running (see Table 10.21).

The Stats subclass for JTAResource provides methods to obtain the count of active transactions under the control of the resource (see Table 10.22). The number of committed transactions and number of rolled-back transactions is also available from the JTAStats interface.

The EJBStats interface is the base interface for all types of Enterprise JavaBean managed objects. This base interface exposes methods to access the number of times the create() method on the EJBHome interface has been called, as well as the number of times the remove() method has been called (see Table 10.23).

Table 10.20 Stats Interface

Accessor Method	Return Type
getStatistic(String sname)	Statistic
getStatisticNames()	String[]
getStatistics()	Statistic[]

Table 10.21 JVMStats Interface

Accessor Method	Return Type
getHeapSize()	CountStatistic
getUpTime()	CountStatistic

Table 10.22 JTAStats Interface

Accessor Method	Return Type
getActiveCount()	CountStatistic
getCommittedCount()	CountStatistic
getRolledbackCount()	CountStatistic

Table 10.23 EJBStats Interface

Accessor Method	Return Type
getCreateCount()	CountStatistic
getRemoveCount()	CountStatistic

In addition to the base EJBStats data, the EntityBeanStats interface provides a RangeStatistic value for the number of instances of the bean in the ready state, as well as the number of instances in the pooled state (see Table 10.24).

The Stats subclass for MessageDrivenBean provides a count of the number of messages received by MessageDrivenBean (see Table 10.25).

The SessionBeanStats interface exposes the method to obtain the number of instances of this bean that are in the method-ready state, in addition to the base EJBStats data (see Table 10.26).

Table 10.24 EntityBeanStats Interface

Accessor Method	Return Type
getReadyCount()	RangeStatistic
getPooledCount()	RangeStatistic

Table 10.25 MessageDrivenBeanStats Interface

Accessor Method	Return Type
getMessageCount()	CountStatistic

Table 10.26 `SessionBeanStats` Interface

Accessor Method	Return Type
`getMethodReadyCount()`	`RangeStatistic`

`StatefulSessionBean` objects can be passivated to disk, so the `Stats` subclass for this managed object augments the `SessionBeanStats` and `EJBStats` data with an accessor to get the number of beans that have been passivated (see Table 10.27).

No standard accessor methods are defined for the `StatelessSessionBeanStats` interface. However, server vendors can implement this interface and use it to expose extended statistics beyond those defined in JSR 77.

The `ServletStats` interface provides one piece of information: the time taken to execute the servlet's `service()` method (see Table 10.28).

The `JavaMailStats` interface provides access to the number of mail messages sent by this managed resource (see Table 10.29).

There are no standard accessor methods defined for the `URLStats` interface. Server vendors can implement the interface and provide any statistics that they deem relevant.

Table 10.27 `StatefulSessionBeanStats` Interface

Accessor Method	Return Type
`getPassiveCount()`	`RangeStatistic`

Table 10.28 `ServletStats` Interface

Accessor Method	Return Type
`getServiceTime()`	`TimeStatistic`

Table 10.29 `JavaMailStats` Interface

Accessor Method	Return Type
`getSentMailCount()`	`CountStatistic`

Table 10.30 `JCAStats` Interface

Accessor Method	Return Type
`getConnections()`	`JCAConnectionStats[]`
`getConnectPools()`	`JCAConnectionPoolStats[]`

The `JCAStats` interface is really an entry point for JCA performance measurements. This top-level interface provides operations to obtain a list of `JCAConnectionPoolStats` objects. Alternatively, a list of `JCAConnection-Stats` objects can be retrieved. Details of these two `Stats` subclasses are provided in Table 10.30.

The `JCAConnectionStats` object represents the statistics associated with a single JCA connection. This interface provides a mechanism for management programs to obtain the handle to its `connectionFactory` managed object and also its `managedConnectionFactory` object (see Table 10.31). Those objects exist in the `J2EEResource` topology and may be used to adjust the system if the performance data from the JCA connection represents a problem in the system.

The amount of time spent by the JCA connection waiting for a connection and the amount of time spent using that connection are available as `TimeStatistic` attributes of the `JCAConnectionStats` interface.

The `JCAConnectionPoolStats` interface represents a pool of connections rather than a single connection (see Table 10.32). Several pool-related metrics are available from this interface: size of the connection pool, number of free connections, number of client threads waiting to obtain a connection from the pool, number of times a connection was created, and number of times a connection is closed.

Table 10.31 `JCAConnectionStats` Interface

Accessor Method	Return Type
`getConnectionFactory()`	`OBJECT_NAME`
`getManagedConnectFactory()`	`OBJECT_NAME`
`getWaitTime()`	`TimeStatistic`
`getUseTime()`	`TimeStatistic`

Table 10.32 JCAConnectionPoolStats Interface

Accessor Method	Return Type
getCloseCount()	CountStatistic
getCreateCount()	CountStatistic
getWaitingThreadCount()	BoundedRangeStatistic
getFreePoolSize()	BoundedRangeStatistic
getPoolSize()	BoundedRangeStatistic

Like JCAStats, the JDBCStats interface is really an entry point for accessing more detailed Stats interfaces for JDBC resources. A list either of individual JDBC connections or of JDBC connection pools may be returned by the interface (see Table 10.33).

The JDBCConnectionStats interface is structured much like the JCAConnectionStats interface. It provides the object name string for the JDBCDataSource resource that supports this connection, as well as the waitTime and useTime counts for the connection (see Table 10.34).

The JDBCConnectionPoolStats interface (see Table 10.35) has the exact same accessors to data as the JCAConnectionPoolStats interface (compare Table 10.32).

Table 10.33 JDBCStats Interface

Accessor Method	Return Type
getConnections()	JDBCConnectionStats[]
getConnectionPools()	JDBCConnectionPoolStats[]

Table 10.34 JDBCConnectionStats Interface

Accessor Method	Return Type
getJdbcDataSource()	OBJECT_NAME
getWaitTime()	TimeStatistic
getUseTime()	TimeStatistic

Table 10.35 `JDBCConnectionPoolStats` Interface

Accessor Method	Return Type
getCloseCount()	CountStatistic
getCreateCount()	CountStatistic
getWaitingThreadCount()	BoundedRangeStatistic
getFreePoolSize()	BoundedRangeStatistic
getPoolSize()	BoundedRangeStatistic

The `JMSStats` interface is another entry point to more detailed `Statistic` structures related to Java Message Service resources. It returns a list of `JMSConnectionStats` objects (see Table 10.36).

The `JMSConnectionStats` interface supports a `boolean` flag to indicate if the resource is a transactional one. It also returns a list of `JMSSessionStats` objects (see Table 10.37).

`JMSSessionStats` allows access to lists of producers and consumers of messages associated with the JMS resource (see Table 10.38).

The destination data provided by the `JMSProducerStats` interface represents the identity of the message destination (see Table 10.39). `JMSProducerStats` extends the `JMSEndpointStats` interface, so it also provides all of the data associated with that interface.

Table 10.36 `JMSStats` Interface

Accessor Method	Return Type
getConnections()	JMSConnectionStats[]

Table 10.37 `JMSConnectionStats` Interface

Accessor Method	Return Type
getSessions()	JMSSessionStats[]
isTransactional()	boolean

Table 10.38 `JMSSessionStats` Interface

Accessor Method	Return Type
`getProducers()`	`JMSProducerStats[]`
`getConsumers()`	`JMSConsumerStats[]`
`getDurableSubscriptionCount()`	`CountStatistic`
`getExpiredMessageCount()`	`CountStatistic`
`getMessageCount()`	`CountStatistic`
`getMessageWaitTime()`	`TimeStatistic`
`getPendingMessageCount()`	`CountStatistic`

Table 10.39 `JMSProducerStats` Interface

Accessor Method	Return Type
`getDestination()`	`String`

The `JMSConsumerStats` interface also extends the `JMSEndpointStats` interface. In addition to the end point data provided, the identity of the message origin is available through the `getOrigin()` accessor method (see Table 10.40).

`JMSEndpointStats` is the base interface for both message producers and message consumers. Statistics are available for the number of messages expired, exchanged, and pending (see Table 10.41). The wait time before a message is delivered is exposed also.

Table 10.40 `JMSConsumerStats` Interface

Accessor Method	Return Type
`getOrigin()`	`String`

Table 10.41 `JMSEndpointStats` Interface

Accessor Method	Return Type
`getExpiredMessageCount()`	`CountStatistic`
`getMessageCount()`	`CountStatistic`
`getMessageWaitTime()`	`TimeStatistic`
`getPendingMessageCount()`	`CountStatistic`

10.6 Application-Specific Extensions

Application server vendors will all extend the JSR 77 model in some way or another. This is natural because JSR 77 represents the baseline for management functionality in a J2EE-compliant product. The specification specifically allows for this, and it would be difficult to imagine an application server product that did not include at least some management function above and beyond that included in the JSR 77 models.

Besides the application server vendors themselves, applications designed to run in J2EE environments may now expect to be able to extend the management system of the application server to include application-specific services.

10.7 Areas Missing from J2EE Management

The 1.0 J2EE Management specification is a great start down the path toward a time when J2EE management tools will be "write once, manage anywhere." Obtaining agreement on the management model for application servers is a major step.

There are some significant items missing from the first J2EE Management specification, however. The following list includes some of those missing management functions and reasons why they were left out of JSR 77:

- **Security**. Security is a discipline closely related to management. Management functions are used to configure and enable security. Security functions are used to protect the management systems from unauthorized use. However, most security implementations in J2EE server products are considerably different from one another. This situation is changing and improving with new security-related JSRs. But there was too much divergence in the implementations for security when the JSR 77 expert group was working to allow for standardization in this area.

- **Configuration**. Although configuration of managed resources is a fundamental component of any management system, the range of different implementations for J2EE application server products made the selection of common configuration properties a difficult point on which to reach agreement between all of the different vendors involved in writing the JSR 77 specification.

  So a specification for common configuration properties for all compliant J2EE application server products has been left for a subsequent JSR. This may prove to be a long process because even implementations of the same product on different platforms (such as WebSphere/390 versus WebSphere for distributed systems) have different configuration properties.
- **Load balancing**. Individual application servers are limited in the number of requests that can be served. Most production systems provide a mechanism for grouping or clustering individual servers into a coordinated set so that higher volumes of requests can be serviced. The techniques for accomplishing multiserver coordination are proprietary; in fact, they are a source of competitive advantage between products. The representation of server clusters was not addressed in JSR 77 because of the issues of product differentiation and because a good amount of innovation is still occurring in this technology.
- **Audit**. The JSR 77 model for event notification is a good one for a system that includes a live monitor that registers for all of the important events and is available to receive and process the events when they occur. In practice, most production systems include some form of persistent logging to maintain a history of the events that occur over time. These audit trails are vital when something goes wrong so that support staff can track down the sequence of events that played out as parts of the system failed. As it stands today, every application server product supports auditing and logging in a different way.

10.8 The Vision

After exploring the details of the J2EE Management specification, it's worth taking some time to think about why this specification is important.

If the future of computer application delivery is really one of applications—built from component building blocks and served to clients out of industry-standard containers—then sooner or later those containers will need to be managed in an efficient, standard way. The vision of JSR 77 is that the same program can manage diverse J2EE application server products concurrently—a philosophy referred to as "write once, manage anywhere."

By identifying common management models that all standard application servers will provide, JSR 77 frees the management tools to begin addressing the more difficult issues of scale and volume. Imagine a grid computing network that has the capability to dynamically add or reduce server capacity to meet demand. Such a system is much easier to implement if the management of all application servers in the system is the same. We can achieve a common management approach if we stick with a single server vendor, but the J2EE approach is to enable applications to run in any compliant server.

Although JSR 77 is only a beginning, the vision is that it will lay the groundwork for building more complex distributed systems that can be managed regardless of vendor platform.

10.9 Sample JSR 77 Code

The following code provides an example of using JSR 77 to perform some management of a J2EE application server product. In this example a list of servers is obtained and their states are displayed. If one of the servers is not already stopped, an operation is invoked to stop it. This code assumes that `J2EEServer` supports the `StateManageable` interface. Most instances of `J2EEServer` will support `StateManageable` because otherwise there would be little point in providing access to the server:

```
// Obtain an MEJB reference
Context ic = new InitialContext();
java.lang.Object objref = ic.lookup("ejb/mgmt/MEJB");
javax.management.j2ee.ManagementHome mejbHome =
      (ManagementHome)PortableRemoteObject.narrow(objref,ManagementHome.class);
javax.management.j2ee.Management mejb = mejbHome.create();

// Query to obtain a J2EEDomain object representing a management domain
ObjectName query = new ObjectName("*:j2eeType=J2EEDomain,*");
Set domainSet = mejb.queryNames(query);
Iterator domains = domainSet.iterator();
ObjectName domain = (ObjectName)domains.next();

// Get the list of J2EEServer objects in the domain
OBJECT_NAME[] servernames = (OBJECT_NAME[])mejb.getAttribute(domain, "servers");
```

```
// Iterate over the server list, print the state of the server,
// and stop the server if it isn't already stopped
for (int i=0; i<servernames.length; i++) {
      ObjectName serverhandle = new ObjectName(servernames[i]);
      int serverstate = mejb.getAttribute(serverhandle, "state");
      System.out.println("The state of server: " + servernames[i] + " is: " +
          serverstate);
      if (serverstate != STOPPED) {
            mejb.invoke(serverhandle, "stop", null, null);
      }
}
```

The following code example iterates over the list of servers, registers to receive events generated by the servers, and starts each server (presumably resulting in a `j2ee.state.starting` event from each server):

```
// Obtain the event listener registry
javax.management.j2ee.ListenerRegistration listenerReg =
mejb.getListenerRegistry();

// Create event listener, filter, and handback instances
javax.management.NotificationListener listener = new
javax.management.NotificationListener()
{
      public void handleNotification(javax.management.Notification ntfyObj,
          Object handback)
      {
            System.out.println("Got notification: " + ntfyObj);
      }
};

NotificationFilterSupport filter = new NotificationFilterSupport();
filter.enableType("j2ee.state");
String handbackTag = "myId";

// Iterate over the server list, register to receive events from the server,
// and start the server
for (int i=0; i<servernames.length; i++) {
      ObjectName serverhandle = new ObjectName(servernames[i]);
      listenerReg.addNotificationListener(serverhandle, listener, filter,
          handbackTag);
      System.out.println("Starting server: " + servernames[i]);
      mejb.invoke(serverhandle, "start", null, null);
}
```

The next code example iterates over the servers, obtains their associated Java Virtual Machine(s), and uses the `StatisticsProvider` interface to obtain and display the heap size for the JVM(s):

```
// Iterate over the server list, get the JVM(s) for each server and
// display the heap size for each JVM
for (int i=0; i<servernames.length; i++) {
      ObjectName serverhandle = new ObjectName(servernames[i]);

      // Get the list of JVMs in the server
      OBJECT_NAME[] jvms =
          (OBJECT_NAME[])mejb.getAttribute(serverhandle,"javaVMs");

      // Iterate over the JVM list and print the heap size
      for (int j=0; j<jvms.length; j++) {
            ObjectName jvm = new ObjectName(jvms[j]);
            JVMStats jvmStats = (JVMStats)mejb.getAttribute(jvm, "stats");
            BoundedRangeStatic heapSize = jvmStats.getHeapSize();
            System.out.println("Heap size for JVM: " + jvm + " is: " +
                heapSize.getCurrent());
      }
}
```

10.10 Summary

Mission-critical enterprise systems written in Java have become standardized with the release of Sun's Java 2 Enterprise Edition specification and the many compliant application server products from which developers can choose. But enterprise class applications need to be carefully managed. Part of J2EE 1.4 will include the J2EE Management specification (JSR 77), which describes how all J2EE application server products are to be managed. This chapter provided a brief overview of the J2EE application architecture and programming model. Then the J2EE Management specification (JSR 77) was described in detail, along with examples of how the specification works in real-world application server products. We discussed the philosophy behind the J2EE Management specification, along with some of the shortcomings of the current specification. We also looked at code examples of various management functions implemented according to the JSR 77 specification.

10.11 Notes

1. Source: "Java Management Extensions (JMX) Specification," JSR 3, http://www.jcp.org/jsr/detail/3.jsp, which was led by Sun Microsystems to create a management API for Java resources.

2. "Java 2 Platform, Enterprise Edition (J2EE 1.4) Specification, JSR 151, http://www.jcp.org/jsr/detail/151.jsp, a specification led by Sun Microsystems to define an enterprise-quality platform for serving applications.

3. Java and all Java-based marks are trademarks or registered trademarks of Sun Microsystems, Inc., in the United States and other countries.

4. Java 2 Platform, Standard Edition, "J2SE 1.4 Release Candidate," JSR 918, http://www.jcp.org/jsr/detail/918.jsp.

5. Source: "Enterprise JavaBeans 2.0," JSR 19, http://www.jcp.org/jsr/detail/19.jsp, a specification to define a distributed application component architecture.

6. Source: "Java Servlet 2.3 and JavaServer Pages 1.2 Specifications," JSR 53, http://www.jcp.org/jsr/detail/53.jsp, a specification to define a Web application architecture.

7. Source: "JDBC 3.0 Specification," JSR 54, http://www.jcp.org/jsr/detail/54.jsp, a specification to define a Java API for relational database access.

8. Java Message Service is a specification led by Sun Microsystems to define a Java API for message systems. More information is available at http://java.sun.com/products/jms.

9. "J2EE Management," JSR 77, http://www.jcp.org/jsr/detail/77.jsp, a specification to define the management model for J2EE-compliant application servers.

10. WBEM stands for Web-Based Enterprise Management ("WBEM Services Specification," JSR 48, http://www.jcp.org/jsr/detail/48.jsp), which is Sun's Java implementation of the Distributed Management Task Force's WBEM and CIM operations specifications for accessing CIM data through HTTP.

11. SNMP stands for Simple Network Management Protocol, which is an Internet Engineering Task Force (IETF) standard. More information on SNMP is available at http://www.ietf.org.

12. Source: "J2EE Connector Architecture," JSR 16, http://www.jcp.org/jsr/detail/16.jsp, a specification to define an architecture for integrating J2EE applications with existing back-end enterprise information systems.

CHAPTER 11

Web Services and JMX

Web services technologies and implementations are gaining acceptance in the e-business space. These technologies are being used to implement and deploy mission-critical applications that directly affect the bottom line. Managing Web service execution environments and applications will quickly become part of the management landscape. This chapter briefly describes Web services and their management issues. It then illustrates how JMX can be used by a Web services execution environment and by the Web service itself to make Web service–based applications manageable.

Note that all the examples in this chapter are available to be downloaded from the book's Web site (http://www.awprofessional.com/titles/0672324083).

11.1 Web Services Overview

The Web service movement is an amazing technology to watch take off. One of the most interesting things to keep in mind about Web services is that they just use technologies we already had—XML and HTTP[1]—to create the foundation for an evolutionary shift in how corporations do business on the World Wide Web. But the impact of Web services does not limit itself to between businesses over the Internet; it is also revolutionizing application integration inside the enterprise. This section will provide a brief overview of Web service concepts and technologies. If you are familiar with Web services, you may want to skip this section and go directly to Section 11.2.

So what are Web services?[2] To the business person, Web services are a powerful integration architecture that enables applications to interact dynamically across networks, through the use of open Internet technologies.[3] To a programmer this really means that Web services are software components described via WSDL[4] that are capable of being accessed via standard network protocols such as SOAP[5] over HTTP. Because a Web service's programming interface and access information is described in WSDL, which is a language-independent XML description file, we can say that Web services are interface oriented. This means that they present a modular face and behavior to their clients. Internally, the implementation of the service may be very well designed and modular, or it could be a thin facade over existing or legacy software that is hardly modular. The point is that the client doesn't have to know how it is implemented, just that it supports this nice modular-looking interface.

Another benefit of a service being described is that the description can be published in a directory and then found by clients later. The client uses the binding information in the WSDL service description to invoke the Web service. The description and binding information also makes it possible to compose a Web service as part of another Web service. This all creates a marvelous loose coupling between the service and the clients that use it. Clients are loosely coupled both to how the service is implemented and to when the service was implemented and published.

We'll review what SOAP and WSDL are later in Section 11.1.2. First let's understand the roots of the Web services architecture, the service-oriented architecture.

11.1.1 Service-Oriented Architecture

Service-oriented architectures (SOAs), as illustrated in Figure 11.1, have been around in academia for some time. There are also standards and products—CORBA, for example—that support SOA-style interactions. Web services are a realization of the service-oriented architecture with cross-industry momentum. Web services add XML-expressed interfaces, flexible communication choices, flexible registry choices, searchable registries, and Internet support to the existing CORBA realization of SOA.

In a service-oriented architecture you, a service provider, have a software component you wish to make available to your clients over a network. That software component is the *service implementation*. You now create a service description for it. There are two types of information in the complete service description: functional and nonfunctional. The *functional description* is used directly by the client and describes the mechanics that a client must know to

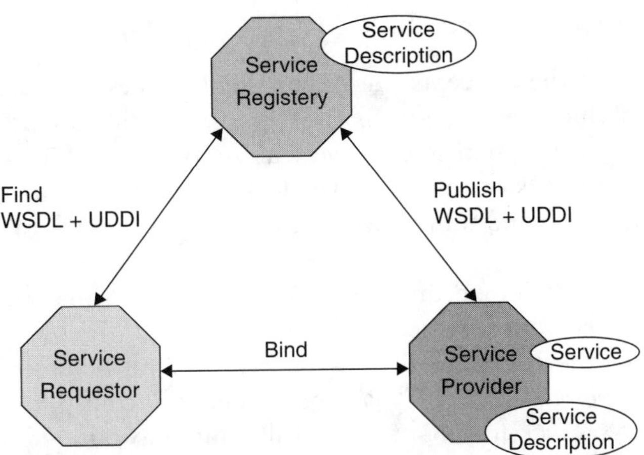

Figure 11.1 Service-Oriented Architecture

invoke your service—that is, the interface and binding data. You may also want to include additional functional description to detail to your clients your security requirements and perhaps how long they should wait before a timeout, among other things. The *nonfunctional description* is the rest of the information that clients will need to find your service and decide to use your service. The nonfunctional metadata should at least include what business owns and runs the service, and what the categorization taxonomy of the service is. You might also include additional interesting information, such as the cost of using your service.

The description of your service is used to publish it in a registry, directory, or repository of service descriptions. After publication, the registry also has a copy of your service description. Later a service requester needs to use a service just like yours. The service requester, or client, finds your service in the registry and retrieves the WSDL from the registry. Now the client developer can write code to invoke the service based on the WSDL. The fact that clients for Web services can be written and deployed long after the service gives us lifecycle decoupling. Given the development tools that are currently available, the client development environment will generate a stub (or proxy) for the service. These stubs would usually completely hide the WSDL and SOAP transport from the client developer. This stub would do the actual bind to the service provider and then invoke the service. The use of client stubs is already supported by JAX-RPC,[6] AXIS,[7] IBM's WebSphere Application Developer and Web Services Tool Kit,[8] and Sun's Sun ONE.[9]

11.1.2 Web Service Stack

Let's look at the concepts and technologies necessary to create a service-oriented architecture for e-business. It is easier to talk about this in terms of a Web service conceptual stack;[10] we will use IBM's stack to illustrate this discussion. The stacks from other vendors all have very similar layers, sometimes rearranged and sometimes split into three stacks: wire, description, and discovery.

In the stack shown in Figure 11.2, the lower three boxes are grouped together. These boxes represent the interoperable Web service stack: the network layer, the XML-based messaging layer, and the description layer. The *network layer* can be any TCP/IP-based network transport. Realistically, the transport you pick for your service will limit who can find and use your service. If you use a widely deployed transport like HTTP, your service is available to a vast number of potential clients and your cost of entry is very low; that is, the cost of access to the Web and a Web server is low. If you use a proprietary transport, such as WebSphere MQ,[11] then only WebSphere MQ clients can access your Web service. This is OK if your potential clients are all within your enterprise and already run MQ clients. Basically you need to pick a transport according to the location from which you think the service will be accessed, the degree of interoperability required, existing network and messaging infrastructure in place between you and your potential clients, and the degree of reliability and security that is required.

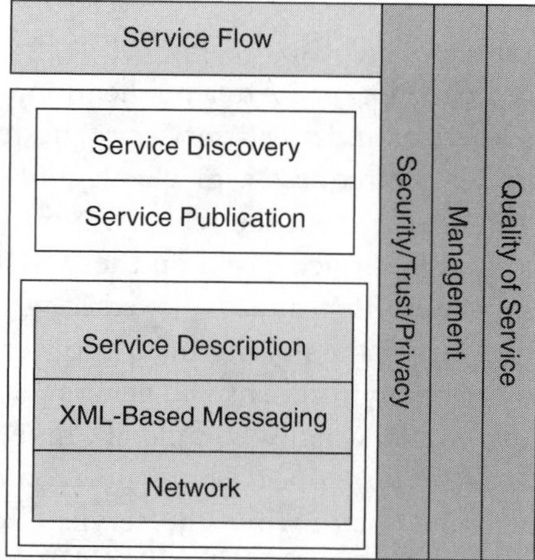

Figure 11.2 Web Service Conceptual Stack

Now we layer on the transport an *XML-based messaging layer.* Today this is predominantly SOAP. SOAP is a simple, standardized enveloping mechanism for communicating document-centric and remote procedure calls using XML. SOAP is a very flexible protocol because of the way it defines the ability to incorporate orthogonal extensions to the message using SOAP headers.

The *Web services description layer,* shown in Figure 11.3, uses XML to describe both the service interface and the service implementation. The service interface is composed of `dataType` designations that are used to compose `message` definitions. These `message` definitions are used to define the `input`, `output`, and `failure` messages of an `operation`. Sets of operations are used to define a `portType` element. The `portType` is conceptually equivalent to a Java interface. A `binding` definition defines how the messages in the operations are actually put on the wire. A `port` definition associates a `binding` element with a location where the service can be accessed. A set of `port` definitions can be aggregated into a `service` definition. `Port` aggregations can be created for various reasons; for example, all `port` elements for all bindings to the same `portType` definition may be a service, or a set of `portType` instances, which may all use the same `binding` definition, that work together to support a service. Services are typically what are published.

The *publication layer* loosely defines publication to be *any* way that a Web service description has been made available to a client. It can be be as crude as sneakernet, where the file is copied to a disk and walked or mailed to your potential clients. Or it can be e-mailed directly to your clients. Alternatively, you can make your WSDL description available at an FTP site or at a URL. You would still need to publish the URL in these cases. This URL could also be used to publish to a WSIL document,[12] which simply lists all the WSDL URLs available on a system. In more sophisticated publications,

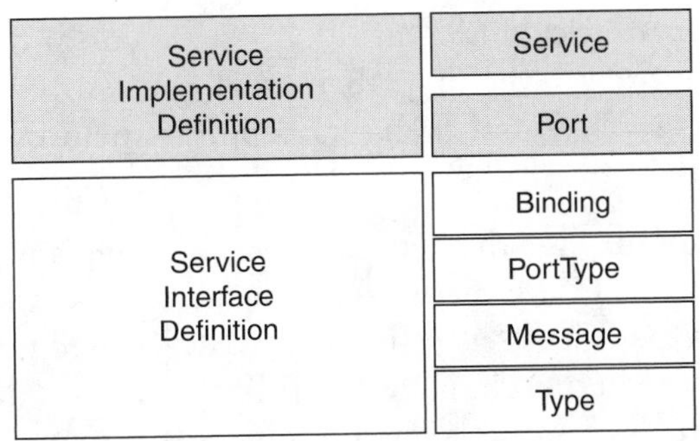

Figure 11.3 Description Stack

you can publish to a searchable registry or directory like UDDI[13] or a repository like ebXML's Registry and Repository.[14]

The *discovery layer* is defined as loosely as the publication layer. For files on disks, discovery can mean simply accessing those files locally. For FTP sites or URL publications, it just means doing a get to retrieve the WSDL document. For UDDI, you would need a UDDI client to be able to query the registry to find the WSDL document you need. Discovery can be done during development or by the software while it is executing.

The *service flow layer* allows service composition and flow definition. The interface-oriented nature of Web services makes it easy to build new Web services that use existing ones. It also makes a service a natural "activity" in a work flow. BPEL4WS[15] is a work flow description language available from IBM, BEA, and Microsoft. The vertical bars represent functionality that needs to be addressed at all layers of the stack. Keep in mind that the solution for one layer may be completely independent of a solution at another layer. For example, the Security/Trust/Privacy vertical in Figure 11.2 will need to be addressed at the networking layer, SSL,[16] as well as the XML messaging layer, ws-security.[17] This will potentially cause additional information to be added to the description. Security at the publication and discovery layers would include requiring logons to the service registry or selecting a registry whose integrity you trust. Likewise, other qualities of service are required at different layers of the stack. For the network layer, you might require a reliable network, like that provided by WebSphere MQ or specified by HTTP-R,[18] a reliable messaging protocol using HTTP.

This chapter is not intended to be a tutorial on Web services or the technologies used to implement them. A significant amount of material available in books, in articles, and on the Web provides a more in-depth education on this topic. Recommended reading includes the "Web Services Conceptual Architecture"[19] white paper, "Building Web Services with Java,"[20] and "Programming Web Services with SOAP."[21]

The Management vertical in Figure 11.2 is the focus of this chapter. Let's take a look at it layer by layer first; then we'll concentrate on how to use JMX to enable Web services and Web service infrastructures to be managed. Here are the layers:

- **Network.** We can manage the network layer by using a network management system for the TCP/IP network. Some network managers—for example, HP's OpenView—also support JMX. We will not address network management in this chapter.
- **Description.** The description layer could include management metadata, or it could include the description of a separate management port for a service. We will discuss this in detail in the next section.

- **Publication and discovery.** Managing the publication and discovery layers would include ensuring that the important service registries and repositories are active, available, and performing well. This is similar to managing name servers today. We will discuss the instrumentation and management of registries in this chapter.
- **Work flow.** Work flows typically have applications to execute them and generally a management application to manage them. This application may use or expose JMX MBeans. In the Web services area, work flows will be exposed as Web services, so the discussion on managing Web services applies to managing a work flow. We will not specifically address the management of work flows in this chapter.

Remembering the SOA triangle, we will look at how to manage the registry and the service. Services typically run in a Web service execution environment, like AXIS, JAX-RPC, IBM WebSphere Application Server, or BEA WebLogic, so we will also look at how to manage the execution environment. We will look at how to manage each of these components from two points of view: the owner of the component and the user of the component.

11.2 Web Service Registry Management

Service registries are typically accompanied by their own management application. This management application may be JMX based, or it may provide JMX MBeans that expose the registries' management information and operations. If it does not provide a JMX interface but does provide programmatic access to its management functionality, you may be able to develop your own registry management application by developing your own MBeans that invoke those APIs.

11.2.1 Registry Owner

There are two levels of registry ownership: (1) owning the registry implementation code and (2) owning and controlling a registry application. In the second case you have purchased the application, like UDDI, from a vendor and are executing it within your environment.

When you own the registry implementation code, you can instrument the registry directly for manageability. What should you instrument it with? You should expose

- Identification information:
  - Product name
  - Version

  - Install date
  - Maintenance level
- Configuration information:
  - IP addresses
  - URLs
  - Current status
- Metrics that will help operators gauge its responsiveness and usage:
  - Number of entries in the registry
  - Number of get requests
  - Number of search requests
  - Rate of access
  - Average response time for a get
  - Average response time for a search
  - High and low watermarks for get response times
  - High and low watermarks for search response times
- Notifications to warn operators that the registry
  - Is degraded
  - Is running out of space
  - Is about to fail
  - Has failed
  - Has experienced security access failures
- Operations to
  - Start the registry
  - Stop the registry
  - Run a backup operation to save the current registry data to a backup database or file

You may also expose additional metrics, configuration, notifications, and operations that are specifically useful for your registry implementation.

Here is a sample UDDI registry MBean interface that could be exposed by the UDDI registry itself:

```
public interface UDDIRegistryManagerMBean {
      // identity
      String getName();
      void setName(String name);
      String getVersion();

      // configuration
      String getURL();
      void setURL(String url);
      String[] getURLs();
```

```
        void setURLs(String[] secureURLs);
        String getStatus();

        // metrics
        int getNumberOfEntries();
        int getNumberOfGets();
        int getNumberOfSearchs();
        int getAverageSearchTime();
        int getAverageGetTime();
        int getHighSearchTime();
        int getHighGetTime();
        int getLowSearchTime();
        int getLowGetTime();

        // operations
        int start();
        int stop();
        int backUpRegistryData();
}
```

A simple implementation of this interface is available from the download Web site for this book (http://www.awprofessional.com/titles/0672324083). Because this example relies on the UDDI registry exposing management interfaces, the examples rely on `UDDIRegistryData` and `UDDIRegistryController` classes to be implemented by the UDDI registry. Therefore the examples don't actually interact with a UDDI registry. All of these examples use the UDDI4J[22] UDDI client implementation available from IBM's open-source projects on the developerWorks Web site (http://www-124.ibm.com/developerworks/projects/uddi4j) and IBM's Web Services Tool Kit available on IBM's alphaWorks Web site (http://www.alphaworks.ibm.com/tech/webservicestoolkit).

If you are in control of the executing registry application, what should you be managing? You should start by monitoring the network availability and operational availability. If the registry is instrumented with JMX, you can use monitor MBeans along with the registry's MBean to monitor performance. You should register for failure notifications as well.

If the registry does not support JMX, you will have to write your own MBean to interact with the registry to get performance data. You should try to monitor performance characteristics, like the number of entries in the registry, the rate of access, average response time for a get, and average response time for a search. Armed with this information, you can tune your registry implementation to be sure your registry responds quickly and accurately. For example, if it is backed by a database, you can expand the database if the number of entries is getting very high. If the registry is itself accessed as a Web service, you can get some of these performance numbers from the Web service execution environment as you would for any business service. We'll see more on this in Section 11.3.

There may also be other operations and performance information exposed to you by the registry that you might want to consider adding to your registry MBean. These will vary pretty widely depending on the registry type and implementation.

Here is a sample UDDI registry MBean interface that could be exposed for a third-party UDDI registry that you are executing:

```
public interface UDDIRegistryRuntimeManagerMBean {
      // identity
      String getName();
      void setName(String name);
      String getVersion();

      // configuration
      String getURL();
      void setURL(String url);
      String[] getURLs();
      String getStatus();
      void setStatus(String avail);

      // metrics
      int getNumberOfEntries();
      int getNumberOfGets();
      int getNumberOfSearchs();
      int getAverageSearchTime();
      int getAverageGetTime();
      int getHighSearchTime();
      int getHighGetTime();
      int getLowSearchTime();
      int getLowGetTime();

      // operations
      long checkAvailability(String businessName);
      long checkNetworkAvailability();
      int start();
      int stop();
      int backUpRegistryData();
}
```

A simple implementation of this MBean is provided on the download Web site for this book (http://www.awprofessional.com/titles/0672324083). Once again, this example relies on the `UDDIRegistryData` and `UDDIRegistryController` classes to be implemented by the UDDI registry and therefore doesn't actually interact with a real UDDI registry.

11.2.2 Registry User

If you are a user of the registry, as either a publisher of services or a discoverer of services, and you do not own the registry, what can you do? You will still want to know if the registry is available and performing well enough for your application to use. You can develop your own JMX MBeans to manage your connection to the registry. You should develop an MBean to represent the registry and monitor it using monitor MBeans.

At the very least, any registries you are dependent on, inside or outside of your enterprise, should be monitored for availability. Because these registries are available through a network (and if they are not redirected by the hosting company), an old-fashioned ping can be used to check on the registry's network availability. Beyond connectivity you should monitor for functional availability—that is, whether the registry can perform the functions you need when you need them. To check for functional availability you should send an actual operation to the registry, like a logon or a fetch of one of your service entries, to ensure that the registry is functional and returning information that is important to your application or enterprise. In this case your registry MBean should have a `status` attribute, and `checkNetworkAvailability()` and `checkAvailability()` operations. The `checkNetworkAvailability()` method would do a ping and return the number of milliseconds it took for the ping to return. If the ping failed to return, the method would return `-1`. It is convenient to use `checkNetworkAvailability()` on the MBean instead of a direct ping because your management application will always call the same method, even if the implementation of the method is more sophisticated than a ping and could change depending on the type of network through which the service is accessed. The `checkAvailability()` method would do a get of one of your service entries, returning the number of milliseconds it took to get the entry back, or returning `-1` for failures. Status would be calculated from the combination of response times to ping and `checkAvailability()`, and evaluation of notifications from the registry.

Let's look at an example of an MBean for monitoring the availability of a UDDI registry. For UDDI registries, you can use UDDI4J, which is a Java

UDDI client API, to interact with the registry. The getStatus() method for the status attribute should execute both of these methods. If they are both successful, then the status is available. If either fails, the status is unavailable. Now you can create a JMX String monitor to monitor the status attribute for a change to unavailable. Such a change will trigger a notification to your management system.

You can also set up custom monitors that check network availability more often by just executing the checkNetworkAvailability() method. If you have service entries that you have published that are critical to your business, you can monitor that they are returned to you with the checkAvailability() operation. If those entries are not available, you can automatically republish. Automatic republishing is not always the correct correctional response, so you should be sure that it has no ill effects on the registry or your entry before you set up automatic publishing. UDDIRegistryClientManagerMBean is an example of an MBean interface we have been discussing:

```
public interface UDDIRegistryClientManagerMBean {
        String getName();
        void setName(String name);
        String getURL();
        void setURL(String url);
        String getStatus();
        void setStatus(String avail);
        Long checkAvailability(String businessName);
        Long checkNetworkAvailability();
}
```

The constructor for this MBean would need to accept the name and IP address of the registry. These would be retrievable as MBean attributes. If you are going to invoke a UDDI operation in the checkAvailability() operation, then you will also need to pass the UDDI logon name and password into the constructor. For security reasons, these will not be retrievable as MBean attributes.

A full implementation of the UDDIRegistryClientManagerMBean class is listed at the end of this chapter and is available on the book's Web site (http://www.awprofessional.com/titles/0672324083). Because the scenario is that we are managing a UDDI registry we do not own, we do not rely on the UDDI registry to implement or expose any management classes. We do rely on the UDDIRegistryClient implementation to interact with the UDDI registry.

11.3 Web Service Execution Environment Management

Web services naturally execute in a runtime. This runtime is also known as a *service container* or *service execution environment*. The Web service runtime, as shown in Figure 11.4, generally takes care of the details of decoding the SOAP messages, creating the correct Java objects, and invoking the service implementation.

Both Sun's JAX-RPC and Apache's AXIS define and provide service provider runtimes that perform these functions. Many of the application server vendors have also shipped Web service runtime support, including IBM, BEA, Oracle, and HP. Web services are not required to execute in such environments. Certainly a single program could listen on the port and perform all the necessary parsing, business function, and response management. However, this is an unnecessary programming burden, considering the number of execution environments available free, in open source, and in products. Programming to the service port and protocol directly in the service also ties a service implementation to a particular binding and decreases your ability to make the service available from various protocols and bindings. Web services are more easily made available if multiple bindings are used when they are implemented in a Web service execution environment because the Web service's execution environment can also function as a multiprotocol access layer.

AXIS provides the ability to add new transports, although the protocol is fixed in SOAP. SOAP over JMS transport plug-ins is available. Web Services Invocation Framework and Web Services Gateway (available from Apache) are Web service execution environments that support multiple protocols and transports. Because of the pervasiveness of the use of Web service execution environments, it is possible to use these environments for management purposes.

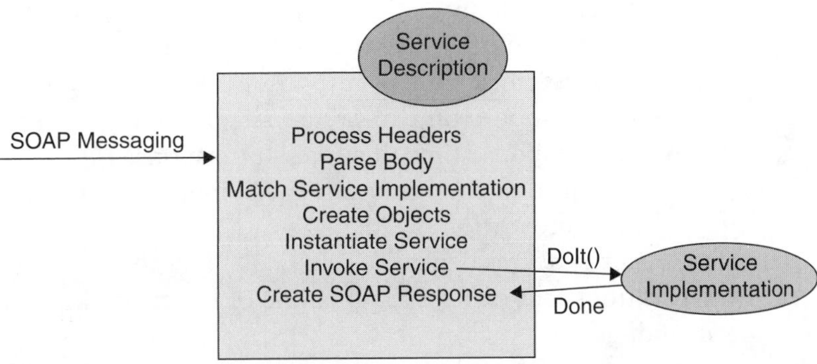

Figure 11.4 Web Service Runtime

Let's look at how we will manage the execution environment, as both an owner and a user. In the next section we will look at how to take advantage of the execution environment to manage the Web services themselves.

11.3.1 Execution Environment Owner

Web service execution environments, or runtimes, are in an optimal position to keep track of some interesting management statistics and provide some important management operations and events[23] for both themselves and the Web services running in them. If you own the execution environment code, you can instrument it to be manageable. How to manage an execution environment that you do not control, but are only using, is covered in the next section. Let's look at the data that should be available from the execution environment about itself. In Section 11.4 we will look at what data the execution environment should track for its Web services.

The execution environment should keep the following information about itself:

- Descriptive information about the implementation running, including
  - Identifier
  - Product name
  - Version
  - Installation date
- Configuration information, including
  - Services deployed
  - Log name
  - URL
- Metrics that indicate the rate of work and responsiveness of the execution environment to them, including
  - Number of requests
  - Number of responses
  - Number of failure responses
  - Average response time of responses
  - Average response time of failure responses
  - Average response time of successful responses
- Notifications that the execution environment can send, including
  - "Service invocation failed"
  - "Security access denied"
- Operations that control the lifecycle of the execution environment, including
  - Start environment

- Stop environment

And the services running in it:

- Deploy a service
- Remove a service
- Enable a service
- Disable a service

Let's look at this lifecycle and how these operations are used. In enterprises, remote software distribution, installation, and deployment software will need to deploy the Web service into the runtime. It must also be possible to write succinct installation scripts for Web services that don't require the installer to be involved in multiple steps. Later, in order to move, update, or discontinue the Web service, it will be necessary to remove a Web service from a runtime. Thus we need deploy and remove operations for adding and removing Web services from the runtime. The disable operation would temporarily block the requests to the Web service without having to remove the service entirely. A disable might be done to allow maintenance on the Web service implementation, network, or backup systems. It might also be done to enforce scheduled availability of a service. For example, the "Technical Support Request" service might be available only from 7:00 A.M. to 7:00 P.M. Monday through Friday. Once the maintenance was finished or the time was 7:00 A.M. again, the `enable` operation would cause the runtime to allow the requests to invoke the Web service again.

As we indicated before, the execution environment should provide management data, metrics, operations, and events for each service. We will discuss service-specific responsibilities in Section 11.4.1.1.

A JMX MBean for the Web service execution environment would publish all of these attributes and operations that applied to the execution environment and send the notifications. Ideally there would also be an MBean for each service deployed in the execution environment. In order to give you functional examples, the samples developed for this section are implemented on the IBM Web Services Tool Kit (WSTK), which includes management support using TMX4J and handlers. Therefore, this MBean for the Web service execution environment is a subset of what is supported by the WSTK. Here is an MBean interface example:

```
public interface WebServiceRuntimeManagerMBean {
       String getName();
       String getType();
       String getVersion();                        // getServerVersion
       Date getStartTime();                        // getStartDate
```

```
    Integer getNumberOfServicesDeployed();  // getServicesCount
    Integer getNumberofRequests();          // getTotalCalls
    String checkAvailability();
    String getServerHostname();            // getServerHostName
    String getServerPort();                // getServerPort
    Boolean getDebug();
    void setDebug(Boolean flip);
}
```

A simple implementation of this MBean is provided at the end of this chapter and on the book's Web site (http://www.awprofessional.com/titles/0672324083). This example works only on the Web Services Tool Kit with TMX4J.

Now that this information is available to you, how do you use it to manage the service? Because the metrics are exposed as MBean attributes, you can create a JMX monitor MBean to watch the attributes that represent the failure rates and response times. The monitor MBean will send a JMX notification. The management systems should get these notifications and react to them with recovery or operator notification. For instance, the management system may deploy a new instance of the service if the failure rate is 100 percent. If the management system is a quality-of-service (QOS) manager, it can react when average response time for methods drops below a defined threshold or failure rate exceeds a threshold. QOS managers typically track and report adherence to QOS agreements and don't adjust the system to improve the QOS. But a QOS manager may interact with a performance, configuration, or operations management system to tune it to improve performance and throughput.

The Web service runtime is also in a position to detect failures and react to or even recover some of them. If certain types of failures are returned—that is, security failures or invalid target service failures—notifications should be sent to management systems. Web service runtimes should send some failures to management systems for recovery rather than do the recovery for themselves because the execution environment may not know about the entire enterprise context in which it executes, and sometimes its own isolated recovery may be inappropriate. In smaller enterprises or single-host environments, however, a sophisticated Web service execution environment that does its own recovery may be appreciated. Recovery may include starting new instances of the Web service implementation if the Web service is not locatable or responding.

11.3.2 Execution Environment User

If your service is running in a Web service execution environment that is not JMX enabled—that is, does not provide you a JMX MBean to manage it—

then you can develop an MBean to interact with the execution environment. How much information you can represent is subject to how much data is made available to you from the execution environment's APIs and log files. The logs may contain audit trails for service lifecycle changes, service invocations, status changes, and failures. You will have to write a program to read the log file, look for the messages, and update the counters or send notifications. Perl, grep, sed, and awk[24] are especially convenient scripting languages for this sort of processing.

Another way you can gather data into an MBean is to take advantage of interceptor or handler support of the execution environment. Handlers are invoked by the execution environment during request processing before the request is dispatched to the service, and during response processing before the response is returned to the requester. Both AXIS and JAX-RPC support these models. You can develop a request and response handler that is also an MBean that supports the runtime and service-specific metrics already discussed. Because it is a handler, this MBean may not be able to detect and publish the configuration information or WSDL URLs for the execution environment. IBM's Web Services Tool Kit contains a JMX management handler for AXIS.

11.4 Web Service Management

Web services are the business logic that must be available to the users; therefore they need to be as well managed as the execution environment. In this section, first we'll look at how you can enable your Web service to be managed and to manage your Web service using JMX. Then we'll look at how you can manage someone else's Web service that your Web service client is dependent on.

11.4.1 Web Service Owner

Web services can be managed through the execution environment and the Web service itself. We will look at what information should be available about your Web service when it is running in an execution environment. We will also look at what information your Web service needs to expose if it is running on its own, outside of an execution environment.

11.4.1.1 Web Service Management through the Execution Environment

As discussed earlier, the Web service execution environment should maintain management information about the services deployed and executing within it.

For each service the execution environment should provide the following:

- Identification information, including
  - Service identifier
  - Service name
  - Service description
- Configuration information, including
  - Access URL
  - WSDL Description URL
  - Configuration files
- Operations to control the service lifecycle; deploy, remove, start, and stop functions are part of the execution environment's operations. They could be moved to the service-specific MBeans, but it's a 50-50 choice, so for these examples they are part of the execution environment MBean.
- Notifications that should be sent by the execution environment for each service, including
  - "Service not deployed"
  - "Service unavailable"
  - "Service failed"
  - "Service deployed"
  - "Service access denied"
- Metrics that help track usage of the service and execution environment:
  - Number of requests
  - Number of responses
  - Number of failure responses
  - Average response time of responses
  - Average response time of failure responses
  - Average response time of successful responses
  - Total elapsed execution time per method
  - Number of invocations per method
  - Average response time of responses per method
  - Average response time of failure responses per method
  - Average response time of successful responses per method
  - Total elapsed execution time per method

As a result of tracking these metrics, the runtime can determine and track availability of a service at a URL and port. This availability status can be set during deployment or removal of the service from the runtime. It can also be set to indicate if all of the responses are returning failures. For more sophisticated systems, like service-level agreement managers, the availability status can be changed when the average response time exceeds or drops below an acceptable response time. Here are some examples of rules:

- When the service is enabled by the runtime or after deployment into the runtime, then the availability should be set to `available`.
- When the failure rate exceeds 50 percent, then the availability may be set to `failing`.
- When the failure rate exceeds 90 percent, then the availability may be set to `failed`.
- When the service average response time is less than 5 seconds, then the availability may be set to `available`, or the average response time value.
- When the service average response time is greater than 5 seconds, then the availability may be set to `degraded`.
- When the service is disabled by the runtime, then the availability may be set to `disabled`.
- When the service is removed from the runtime, then the availability may be set to `removed`.

There should be a JMX MBean for each service running in the execution environment. Because the examples in this chapter are implemented with the support provided by the IBM Web Services Tool Kit, the MBean here won't provide the full recommended support outlined here. The Web service MBean interface for the WSTK would look like this:

```
import java.util.Date;
public interface WebServiceManagerMBean {
       String getName();
       String getVersion();
       void setVersion(String version);
       Integer getNumberofRequests();             //getInvocations
       Integer getNumberofResponses();            // getSucesses
       Integer getNumberofFailureResponses();     // getFailures
       Date getStartTime();                       // getStartDate
       Integer getAverageResponseTimeofResponses();
          // getAverageResonseTimeMs
       String checkAvailability();                // getStatus
       Integer getTotalElapsedExecutionTime();
          // getTotalProcessTimeMs
}
```

An implementation of this MBean is provided at the end of this chapter and from (http://www.awprofessional.com/titles/0672324083).

Using this information, you can determine the usage rate and throughput for your Web service. If you need faster responses, you can tune or configure your service or your execution environment. Alternatively, you can arrange for more instances of the service to share the request load.

Like managing the execution environment, you can create JMX monitor MBeans to monitor the values of the metrics, especially availability and the number of failure responses. When notifications are sent as a result of these monitors, operations can take proactive action to restore the service's availability or start a backup service.

11.4.1.2 Web Service Management Directly with the Web Service

Web services may also need to publish management attributes (configuration and metrics), operations, and notifications that are specific to their own business logic. Therefore, some Web services will need to participate in their own management, even if they have the benefit of management through their execution environment. When designing and developing the management for your Web service, you will need to know if your service will be running in an execution environment.

If you have programmed your Web services to listen directly on a port and parse the raw SOAP message, then your service is running "stand-alone". If it is running stand-alone, then your Web service and MBean will need to support the basic description, configuration, and metrics that your execution environment would have kept for your service: number of requests, responses, failure responses, invocations by method, average execution time for all requests, and average execution time per method. You will also need to provide operations to enable and disable your service to make sure you can temporarily prevent clients from accessing your service without having to uninstall it entirely.

If you have programmed your Web service to run in an execution environment, then it should not listen on a port and should count on the execution environment to invoke its methods with the correct Java objects or XML message. If it is running in a managed execution environment, your Web service should not keep metrics and information for management purposes that are already being tracked by the execution environment, such as a count of method invocations.

In either case your Web service can still expose additional meaningful descriptions, configurations, metrics, operations, and notifications that are specific for your service. Some failures from within the service implementation should cause a notification to be sent from the service or the service's MBean to the management system. In this case, the MBean for the service must be an instance of `NotificationBroadcaster`. You should also make sure that the adapter for your management system is an instance of `NotificationListener` and is listening for this new notification. See Chapter 7 for more information. We recommend that you send notifications whenever the ability of the service to perform its mission is permanently jeopardized. If you send notifications for every hiccup, you may flood your MBeanServer and management system with notifications that they will not have a chance to react to. The result is unnecessary overhead that does not improve how well your Web service is managed.

Web services can publish their own management data in a variety of ways, as described in the sections that follow.

1. The Web Service Manages Its Own MBean

In this approach the Web service creates and maintains its own MBean. The Web service can either instantiate its own MBeanServer or find and use the one provided with the execution environment. Having the service own its MBean is a convenient approach because your Java-based Web service has control over its own management information, can access its MBean locally, and can alter it when appropriate. However, the disadvantage is that it complicates managing the Web service for the management system because the system may have to get two MBeans—the execution environment MBean for the service and the Web service–specific MBean—in order to get a complete picture of the management information for the service.

Here is a sample MBean for Web service–specific management information for a classic Web service: the `StockQuote` service. The `StockQuote` service has one operation on it, `getTradePrice`, that accepts one string value (the stock symbol) and returns one float value (the current stock price). Here is a Java interface for `StockQuote`. The WSDL description from the WSDL specification (http://www.w3.org/TR/wsdl) is at the end of this chapter:

```
interface StockQuote {
    public float getTradePrice (String Symbol, String time);
}
```

The MBean for the `StockQuote` service keeps the URL, and a backup URL, for the stock exchange to be accessed to obtain the current stock price. The implementation of the `StockQuote` service accesses the MBean to get the current stock exchange URL to be used, or the backup URL if access to the primary fails. Here is the MBean interface:

```
import java.net.URL;

public interface StockQuoteManagerMBean {
    URL getStockExchange();
```

```
    void setStockExchange(URL exchange);
    void setBackUpStockExchange(URL exchange);
    URL getBackUpStockExchange();
    void switchStockExchange();
}
```

Here is a simple implementation:

```
import java.net.URL;
public class StockQuoteManager implements StockQuoteManagerMBean {
    URL exchange, backupExchange, newbkup;

    public URL getStockExchange () {
        return exchange;
    }
    public void setStockExchange (URL newExchange) {
        exchange = newExchange;
    }
    public void setBackUpStockExchange (URL newExchange) {
        backupExchange = newExchange;
    }
    public URL getBackUpStockExchange () {
        return  backupExchange;
    }
    public void switchStockExchange () {
        newbkup = exchange;
        exchange = backupExchange;
        backupExchange = newbkup;
    }
}
```

This MBean would be instantiated, registered, and used like the MBeans described in Chapters 3 and 4.

2. The Web Service Augments the Execution Environment's MBean

In this approach the Web service finds, extends, and uses the MBean that the execution environment has created and is maintaining for the service. This approach is more complex for the Web service because it needs to know its MBean's name and locate it from the execution environment's MBeanServer. If the Web service will always be deployed in a known execution environment that is guaranteed to have JMX MBeans for the services, this is fine. However, if the service is going to be running in different execution environments, then the Web service developer will have to address the case in which there is no MBeanServer or preexisting MBean. It also means that the Web service does not have local addressability to the MBean and has to go through the MBeanServer to update it.

On the positive side, this approach makes life a lot easier for the management system because a single MBean represents the management interface to the Web service. Here is the MBean interface for an extended MBean:

```
import java.net.URL;

public interface StockQuoteManagerMBean extends
  WebServiceManagerMBean {
    URL getStockExchange();
    void setStockExchange(URL exchange);
    void setBackUpStockExchange(URL exchange);
    URL getBackUpStockExchange();
    void switchStockExchange();
}
```

Here's the code fragment in which the service constructor finds the MBean from the MBeanServer and instantiates it:

```
public StockQuoteManager () {
  try {
    String wsoname =
      "WebServiceManager:id=StockQuoteManager";
    ObjectName sqName = new ObjectName(wsname);
    ArrayList al =
      MBeanServerFactory.findMBeanServer(null));
    MBeanServer sqMBS = (MBeanServer) al.get(0);
    StockQuoteManager sqMBean =
      new StockQuoteManager();
    ObjectInstance oi = sqMBS.registerMBean(sqMBean,
                                            sqName);
  } catch (Exception e) {
    String errmsg =
      "StockQuoteManager: Could not create MBean";
    System.out.println(errmsg);
  }
}
```

Here's the MBean implementation:

```
import java.net.URL;
import javax.management.MBeanServer;
import javax.management.MBeanServerFactory;
import javax.management.ObjectName;
import javax.management.ObjectInstance;
import java.util.ArrayList;
public class StockQuoteManager implements StockQuoteManagerMBean
                                extends WebServiceManager {
    URL exchange, backupExchange, newbkup;
    ObjectName sqName;

    public StockQuoteManager () {
        try {
              sqName = new ObjectName(
                 "WebServiceManager:id=StockQuoteManager");
              ArrayList al =
                 MBeanServerFactory.findMBeanServer(null);
              MBeanServer sqMBS = (MBeanServer) al.get(0);
              StockQuoteManager sqMBean =
                  new StockQuoteManager();
              ObjectInstance oi =
                 sqMBS.registerMBean(sqMBean, sqName);
        } catch (Exception e) {
               System.out.println(
                  "StockQuoteManager: Could not create MBean");
        }
    }

    public URL getStockExchange () {
        return exchange;
    }
    public void setStockExchange (URL newEexchange) {
        exchange = newEexchange;
    }
    public void setBackUpStockExchange (URL newEexchange) {
        backupExchange = newEexchange;
    }
    public URL getBackUpStockExchange () {
        return  backupExchange;
    }
    public void switchStockExchange () {
        newbkup = exchange;
        exchange = backupExchange;
```

```
        backupExchange = newbkup;
    }
}
```

3. The Web Service Publishes Management portType and port

This approach exposes management information in a Web service paradigm that works regardless of whether JMX is available to the Web service or its execution environment. The Web service would publish management `portType` and `port` definitions, as well as business `portType` and `port` definitions.

It is relatively easy to create an MBean interface that matches the management port's `portType`. JAX-RPC defines how to create Java interfaces from WSDL `portType` elements. Most Web service development tools generate code skeletons from `portType` definitions that can be used to jump-start your MBean development. As shown in Figure 11.5, your MBean will then invoke the Web service management port's operations by using a SOAP API like JAX-RPC or WSIF[25] directly. Alternatively, you could generate a stub for the Web service and invoke the operations from the MBean using the stub. Or you could modify the stub to implement the MBean interface and use the stub as an MBean directly.

If you already have an MBean implemented, you can generate a `portType` element from the MBean interface using the mapping defined by JAX-RPC. Java Web service development tools also support generating WSDL documents from Java classes. A management `portType` for the `StockQuoteManager` MBean of the preceding example might look like this:

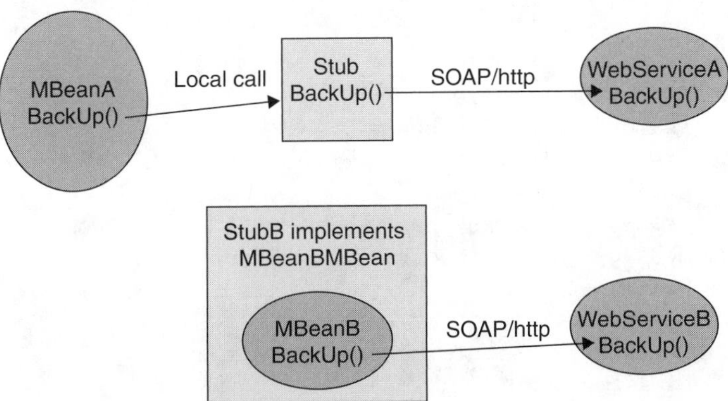

Figure 11.5 Web Service Stubs and MBeans

```
<?xml version="1.0"?>
<definitions name="ManagedStockQuote"
          targetNamespace="http://example.com/stockquote.wsdl"
          xmlns:tns="http://example.com/stockquote.wsdl"
          xmlns:xsd="http://www.w3.org/2000/10/XMLSchema"
          xmlns:xsd1="http://example.com/stockquote.xsd"
          xmlns:soap="http://schemas.xmlsoap.org/wsdl/soap/"
          xmlns="http://schemas.xmlsoap.org/wsdl/">

    <message name="GetTradePriceInput">
        <part name="tickerSymbol" element="xsd:string"/>
        <part name="time" element="xsd:timeInstant"/>
    </message>

    <message name="GetTradePriceOutput">
        <part name="result" type="xsd:float"/>
    </message>

    <message name="SetStockExchangeInput">
        <part name="newStockExchangeURL" element="xsd:string"/>
    </message>

    <message name="GetStockExchangeOutput">
        <part name="exchangeURL" type="xsd:string"/>
    </message>

    <portType name="StockQuotePortType">
        <operation name="GetTradePrice">
           <input message="tns:GetTradePriceInput"/>
           <output message="tns:GetTradePriceOutput"/>
        </operation>
    </portType>

    <portType name="StockQuoteManagerPortType">
        <operation name="GetStockExchange">
           <output message="tns:GetStockExchangeOutput"/>
        </operation>
        <operation name="SetStockExchange">
           <input message="tns:SetStockExchangeInput"/>
        </operation>
        <operation name="GetBackupStockExchange">
           <output message="tns:GetStockExchangeOutput"/>
        </operation>
        <operation name="SetBackupStockExchange">
           <input message="tns:SetStockExchangeInput"/>
        </operation>
```

```
    <operation name="SwitchStockExchange">
       <output message="tns:SetStockExchangeOutput"/>
    </operation>
</portType>

<binding name="StockQuoteSoapBinding" type="tns:StockQuotePortType">
    <soap:binding style="rpc"
        transport="http://schemas.xmlsoap.org/soap/http"/>
    <operation name="GetTradePrice">
       <soap:operation soapAction="http://example.com/GetTradePrice"/>
       <input>
          <soap:body use="encoded" namespace="http://example.com/stockquote"
                encodingStyle="http://schemas.xmlsoap.org/soap/encoding/"/>
       </input>
       <output>
          <soap:body use="encoded" namespace="http://example.com/stockquote"
                encodingStyle="http://schemas.xmlsoap.org/soap/encoding/"/>
       </output>
    </operation>
</binding>

<binding name="StockQuoteManagerSoapBinding"
        type="tns:StockQuoteManagerPortType">
    <soap:binding style="rpc"
        transport="http://schemas.xmlsoap.org/soap/http"/>
    <operation name="GetStockExchange">
       <soap:operation soapAction="http://example.com/setStockExchange"/>
       <input>
          <soap:body use="encoded" namespace="http://example.com/stockquote"
                encodingStyle="http://schemas.xmlsoap.org/soap/encoding/"/>
       </input>
       <output>
          <soap:body use="encoded" namespace="http://example.com/stockquote"
                encodingStyle="http://schemas.xmlsoap.org/soap/encoding/"/>
       </output>
    </operation>
    <operation name="SetStockExchange">
       <soap:operation soapAction="http://example.com/SetStockExchange"/>
       <input>
          <soap:body use="encoded" namespace="http://example.com/stockquote"
                encodingStyle="http://schemas.xmlsoap.org/soap/encoding/"/>
       </input>
       <output>
          <soap:body use="encoded" namespace="http://example.com/stockquote"
                encodingStyle="http://schemas.xmlsoap.org/soap/encoding/"/>
       </output>
```

```
    </operation>
      <operation name="GetBackupStockExchange">
      <soap:operation soapAction=
         "http://example.com/setBackupStockExchange"/>
      <input>
         <soap:body use="encoded" namespace="http://example.com/stockquote"
             encodingStyle="http://schemas.xmlsoap.org/soap/encoding/"/>
      </input>
      <output>
         <soap:body use="encoded" namespace="http://example.com/stockquote"
             encodingStyle="http://schemas.xmlsoap.org/soap/encoding/"/>
      </output>
    </operation>
    <operation name="SetBackupStockExchange">
      <soap:operation soapAction=
         "http://example.com/SetBackupStockExchange"/>
      <input>
         <soap:body use="encoded" namespace="http://example.com/stockquote"
             encodingStyle="http://schemas.xmlsoap.org/soap/encoding/"/>
      </input>
      <output>
         <soap:body use="encoded" namespace="http://example.com/stockquote"
             encodingStyle="http://schemas.xmlsoap.org/soap/encoding/"/>
      </output>
    </operation>

    <operation name="SwitchStockExchange">
      <soap:operation soapAction="http://example.com/SwitchStockExchange"/>
      <input>
         <soap:body use="encoded" namespace="http://example.com/stockquote"
             encodingStyle="http://schemas.xmlsoap.org/soap/encoding/"/>
      </input>
      <output>
         <soap:body use="encoded" namespace="http://example.com/stockquote"
             encodingStyle="http://schemas.xmlsoap.org/soap/encoding/"/>
      </output>
    </operation>
</binding>

<service name="StockQuoteService">
    <documentation>My first service</documentation>
    <port name="StockQuotePort" binding="tns:StockQuoteBinding">
      <soap:address location="http://example.com/stockquote"/>
    </port>
</service>
```

```
    <service name="StockQuoteManager">
        <documentation>My first service manager</documentation>
        <port name=
                "StockQuoteManagerPort"
                binding="tns:StockQuoteManagerBinding">
           <soap:address location="http://example.com/stockquote/mbean"/>
        </port>
    </service>
</definitions>
```

11.4.2 Web Service User

If you are developing a Web service client that depends on a Web service that you do not own, you might be interested in managing that service. This would be similar to managing the registry as a user. You can monitor the service for network availability and functional availability. You can monitor the service either on a regular basis (i.e., every hour) or only when a request to the service fails. If you monitor regularly, you can proactively reconfigure your client to use a different service, open a trouble ticket with the service owner, or send a notification to a help desk. However, monitoring regularly creates resource use overhead that may not be necessary if your client does not run frequently. If you monitor only on failure, you may be able to determine if the service is down permanently and then redirect another request to a different service.

To monitor the service for network availability, you may need to check the availability of the execution environment as well as the service. If the service is running in an execution environment, the service URL may be that of the execution environment instead of the service itself. You can ping that URL to check the network availability of the execution environment. If the execution environment exposes a JMX MBean or a management `portType`, you may be able to get the service status from the execution environment.

To monitor the service for functional availability, you need to invoke one of the operations on the service. You should choose an operation without side effects that uses as little resource as possible, such as a get or read-only operation. If there is a charge for using the service, you might execute this one rarely!

Here is an MBean interface, `WebServiceClientManagerMBean`, for a Web service user:

```
import java.net.URL;
public interface WebServiceClientManagerMBean {
       String getName();
       void setName(String name);
```

```
    int checkAvailability(String serviceURL);
    int checkNetworkAvailability(String serviceURL);
}
```

Here is a simple implementation of `WebServiceClientManager`:

```
import java.net.URL;
import javax.naming.Context;
import javax.naming.InitialContext;
import javax.xml.rpc.Service;

public class WebServiceClientManager
      implements WebServiceClientManagerMBean {
      String wsName;
      String wsURL;

      public WebServiceClientManager (String name,
          String serviceURL) {
              wsName = name;
              wsURL = serviceURL;
      }
      public String getName () {
              return wsName;
      }
      public void setName(String name) {
              wsName = name;
      }

      public int checkAvailability(String serviceURL) {
              Context ctx = new InitialContext();
              javax.xml.rpc.Service sqs = (Service) ctx.lookup(
                              "java:comp/env/DynamicService");
              StockQuoteManager sqm =
                      (StockQuoteManager)sqs.getPort(
                                        wsURL,
                                        StockQuoteManager.class);
              float response = sqm.getTradePrice("IBM");
              if (response != 0)
                      return 1;
                         else
                      return -1;
      }
      public int checkNetworkAvailability (String serviceURL) {
              long respTime = Ping.ping(serviceURL);
```

```
                if (respTime > 0)
                        return 1;
                else
                        return -1;
        }
}
```

This is obviously a simple example that assumes the ping is checking the network availability of the execution environment and the service. The Ping utility is available at the code download Web site for this book.

11.5 Summary

Numerous Java technology–based Web service platforms and development tools are available to developers today. This makes it easy to use JMX to help manage those platforms and services. The IBM Web Services Tool Kit, the Apache AXIS Web service runtimes, and application server products including WebSphere all use JMX to provide manageability of the runtimes. Java developers who need to manage Web service–based applications will need to write some of their own management support today. Web services are still an emerging technology—rapid, but emerging—and it will take a little time for the runtime and management infrastructures to accommodate it.

11.6 Code Listings

11.6.1 UDDIRegistryClientManagerMBean Implementation

11.6.1.1 UDDIRegistryClient Class

```
package jnjmx.ch11;
/** This example requires installation of UDDI4J available from
 *  http://www.uddi4j.org or http://www.ibm.com
 */

import org.uddi4j.*;
import org.uddi4j.client.*;
import org.uddi4j.datatype.*;
import org.uddi4j.datatype.business.*;
import org.uddi4j.datatype.binding.*;
import org.uddi4j.request.*;
import org.uddi4j.response.*;
```

```
import org.uddi4j.transport.TransportFactory;
import org.uddi4j.util.*;

import org.w3c.dom.Element;
import java.util.Vector;
import java.util.Properties;
import java.io.*;

import java.net.*;


public class UDDIRegistryClient {

	String logonID = "";
	String logonPW = "";
	String regName = "";
	String regURL = "";

	/**
	 * Constructor for UDDIRegistryClient.
	 */
	public UDDIRegistryClient() {
	}

	public UDDIRegistryClient(String name, String url, String inLogonID,
		String inLogonPW) {
			System.out.println("instantiating UDDIRegistryClient");
			logonID = inLogonID;
			logonPW = inLogonPW;
			regName = name;
			regURL = url;
	}

	public long ping(String url) {
			// >0 is good, 0 is bad, -1 is unknown host or other exception
			// this ping uses the ping already on the system through the
			// runtime.
			// This will work on a Windows 2000 system with default ping.
			// On a UNIX system or using another ping tool, the parsing to
			// extract the correct average response time may need to be
			// customized.
			long roundTripTime = 0;
			long sendTime, endTime = 0;
			long timeMeasured = -1;
			long pingMS = 0;
			InetAddress uddiIPAddr;
```

```
URL pingURL;
String printstring;

if (url.equals(""))  { url = regURL; }
if (url.equals("")) {
        url = regURL;
       // search for all businesses starting with I ("IBM" should
       // be there)
        url = "http://www-3.ibm.com/services/uddi/" +
               "testregistry/inquiryapi";
}
System.out.println(
    "UDDIRegistryClient:ping ping for url " + url);

try {
        pingURL = new URL(url);
        String hostname = pingURL.getHost();

        String th = (InetAddress.getLocalHost()).getHostName();

        uddiIPAddr = InetAddress.getByName(hostname);
        String hostipaddr = uddiIPAddr.getHostAddress();
        System.out.println("Pinging " + hostname + " at " +
            hostipaddr + " from " + th);
        String[] cmdString = new String[] {"ping", hostipaddr};

        endTime = -1;
        int avgindex, msindex;
        String avgms = null;

        sendTime = System.currentTimeMillis();
        Process pingproc = (Runtime.getRuntime()).exec(cmdString);
        InputStream pingos = pingproc.getInputStream();
        endTime = System.currentTimeMillis();
        BufferedReader rdr = new BufferedReader(
            new InputStreamReader(pingos));
        printstring = rdr.readLine();
        while ((printstring != null) && (avgms == null)) {
                // System.out.println("ping returned: " +
                // printstring);
                avgindex = printstring.indexOf("Average");
                // *Average
                if (avgindex > 0) {
                        msindex = printstring.indexOf(
                            "ms", avgindex);
                       // *Average = xxxms*
```

```
                    avgms = printstring.substring(
                            avgindex+7, msindex); // * = xxx*
                }
                printstring = rdr.readLine();
            }
            if (avgms != null) {
                avgms =  avgms.replace('=', ' ');
                avgms = avgms.trim();       // should leave just
                                            // the digits
                pingMS = (new Long(avgms)).longValue();
            }
            if (pingMS <= 0) {
                // setup url connnection, the url has been
                // redirected to
                HttpURLConnection toUDDI = (HttpURLConnection)
                    pingURL.openConnection();
                toUDDI.setUseCaches(false);
                toUDDI.setRequestMethod("POST");
                toUDDI.connect();
                InputStream is = toUDDI.getInputStream();
                BufferedReader urlrdr = new BufferedReader(
                    new InputStreamReader(is));
                printstring = urlrdr.readLine();
                while (printstring != null)  {
                    // System.out.println(
                    // "url returned: " + printstring);
                    printstring = urlrdr.readLine();
                }
            }

        } catch (UnknownHostException eu) {
            System.out.println("URL " + url + " is unknown");
            return -1;
        } catch (MalformedURLException em) {
            System.out.println("URL " + url + " is malformed");
            return -1;
        } catch (Exception e) { // failed
            System.out.println("Ping failed");
            return -1;
        return pingMS;
    }


    public long test(String url, String businessName) {
        System.setProperty(TransportFactory.PROPERTY_NAME,
            "org.uddi4j.transport.ApacheAxisTransport");
```

```
            UDDIProxy proxy;
            if (url.equals(""))  { url = regURL; }
            if (url.equals("")) {
                    // search for all businesses starting with I
                    // ("IBM" should be there)
                    url = "http://www-3.ibm.com/services/uddi/" +
                            "testregistry/inquiryapi";
            }
            if (businessName.equals("")) {
                    // search for all businesses starting with I
                    // ("IBM" should be there)
                    businessName = "I";
            }
            // System.out.println("UDDIRegistryClient:test for url " + url);

            try {
                    proxy = new UDDIProxy();
                    proxy.setInquiryURL(url);
            } catch (Exception e) {
                    e.printStackTrace();
                    return -1;
            }

            try {
            // creating vector of Name Object
            Vector bizNames = new Vector();
            bizNames.add(new Name(businessName));

            // setting FindQualifiers to "caseSensitiveMatch"
            FindQualifiers findQualifiers = new FindQualifiers();
            Vector qualifier = new Vector();
            qualifier.add(new FindQualifier("caseSensitiveMatch"));
            findQualifiers.setFindQualifierVector(qualifier);
            long findStartTime = System.currentTimeMillis();
            System.out.println("Looking for businesses " + businessName);
            // finding businesses by name
            // and setting the maximum rows to be returned as 5.
            BusinessList businessList = proxy.find_business(bizNames,
                    null, null, null, null, findQualifiers,5);
            // System.out.println("uddi getBusiness return " +
                    // businessList.getBusinessInfos().size());
            long findReturnTime = System.currentTimeMillis();

            Vector businessInfoVector =
                businessList.getBusinessInfos().getBusinessInfoVector();
//           for (int i = 0; i < businessInfoVector.size(); i++) {
```

```
//                      BusinessInfo businessInfo = (BusinessInfo)
                        businessInfoVector.elementAt(i);
//                      Print name for each business
//                      System.out.println(businessInfo.getNameString());
//          }
            if (businessInfoVector.size() > 0) {
                long elapsedFindTime = findReturnTime - findStartTime;
                return elapsedFindTime;
            }
            else {
                 return -1;
            }
            } catch (UDDIException e) {
            System.out.println("UDDIRegistryClient:test UDDIException " +
               e.getMessage());

           DispositionReport dr = e.getDispositionReport();
           if (dr!=null) {

              System.out.println("UDDIException faultCode:" +
                 e.getFaultCode() +
                             "\n operator:" + dr.getOperator() +
                             "\n generic:"  + dr.getGeneric() +
                             "\n errno:"    + dr.getErrno() +
                             "\n errCode:"  + dr.getErrCode() +
                             "\n errInfoText:" + dr.getErrInfoText());
           }
           return -1;
       } catch (Exception e) {
           System.out.println("UDDIRegistryClient:test exception " +
               e.getMessage());
           return -1;
       }
    }
}
```

11.6.1.2 UDDIRegistryClientManagerMBean Interface

```
package jnjmx.ch11;

public interface UDDIRegistryClientManagerMBean {
      String getName();
      void setName(String name);
```

```
        String getURL();
        void setURL(String url);
        String getStatus();
        void setStatus(String avail);
        Long checkAvailability(String businessName);
        Long checkNetworkAvailability();
}
```

11.6.1.3 UDDIRegistryClientManager Class

```
package jnjmx.ch11;

/**
 * @author Heather Kreger: Java And JMX: Building Manageable Systems
 *
 * This class interacts with the UDDI Registry using UDDI4J
 *
 */
public class UDDIRegistryClientManager
        implements UDDIRegistryClientManagerMBean {

        String regName = "";
        String regURL = "";
        String logonID = "";
        String logonPW = "";
        String currentStatus = "available";
        UDDIRegistryClient uddiClient;

        public UDDIRegistryClientManager(String name, String url,
            String logonName, String pw) {
                regName = name;
                regURL = url;
                logonID = logonName;
                logonPW = pw;
                uddiClient = new UDDIRegistryClient(regName, regURL, logonID,
                    logonPW);
}

        /**
         * Constructor for UDDIRegistryClientManager.
         */
        public UDDIRegistryClientManager() {
                super();
```

```
        uddiClient = new UDDIRegistryClient();
}

/**
 * @see jnjmx.ch11.UDDIRegistryClientManagerMBean#getName()
 */
public String getName() {
        return regName;
}

/**
 * @see jnjmx.ch11.UDDIRegistryClientManagerMBean#setName(String)
 */
public void setName(String name) {
        regName = name;
}

/**
 * @see jnjmx.ch11.UDDIRegistryClientManagerMBean#getURL()
 */
public String getURL() {
        return regURL;
}

/**
 * @see jnjmx.ch11.UDDIRegistryClientManagerMBean#setURL(String)
 */
public void setURL(String url) {
        regURL = url;
}

/**
 * @see jnjmx.ch11.UDDIRegistryClientManagerMBean#getStatus()
 */
public String getStatus() {
        return currentStatus;
}

/**
 * @see jnjmx.ch11.UDDIRegistryClientManagerMBean#setStatus(String)
 */
public void setStatus(String avail) {
        currentStatus = avail;
}
```

```
    /**
     * @see jnjmx.ch11.UDDIRegistryClientManagerMBean#checkAvailability(int)
     */
    public Long checkAvailability(String businessName) {
        // System.out.println(
        "UDDIRegistryClientManager:checkAvailability:testing uddi server "
        + regURL);
        long rc = uddiClient.test(regURL, businessName);
        if (rc > 0)
            currentStatus = "available";
        else
            currentStatus = "not available";
        return new Long(rc);
    }

    /**
     * @see
     * jnjmx.ch11.UDDIRegistryClientManagerMBean#checkNetworkAvailability()
     */
    public Long checkNetworkAvailability() {
        // 0 = not available, else returns response time for ping
        // Note, this method will not work if the UDDI registry's URL
        // has been redirected.
        // System.out.println(
"UDDIRegistryClientManager:checkNetworkAvailability:pinging uddi server for " +
regURL);
        long rc = 0;
        Long zero = new Long(0);
        try {
            rc = uddiClient.ping(regURL);
        }
        catch (Exception e) {
            return zero;
        }
        if (rc > 0 ) {
            currentStatus = "available";
            return new Long(rc);
        }
        else {
            currentStatus = "not available";
            return zero;
        }
    }

}
```

11.6.2 WebServiceRuntimeManagerMBean Implementation

```
package jnjmx.ch11;

import java.lang.Class;
import java.util.Date;

public interface WebServiceRuntimeManagerMBean {
        String getName();
        String getType();
        String getVersion();                          // getServerVersion
        Date getStartTime();                          // getStartDate
        Integer getNumberOfServicesDeployed();        // getServicesCount
        Integer getNumberofRequests();                // getTotalCalls
        String checkAvailability();
        String getServerHostname();                   // getServerHostName
        String getServerPort();                       // getServerPort
        Boolean getDebug();
        void setDebug(Boolean flip);
}
```

```
package jnjmx.ch11;

import java.util.Date;
import java.util.ArrayList;
import java.util.Hashtable;
import javax.management.*;

/**
 * Implementing MBean
 *      Date getStartTime();                    // getStartDate
 *      Integer getNumberOfServicesDeployed();  // getServicesCount
 *      Integer getNumberofRequests();          // getTotalCalls
 *      String getAvailability();
 *      String getServerHostname();             // getServerHostName
 *      String getServerPort();                 // getServerPort
 *      Boolean getDebug();
 *      void setDebug(Boolean flip);
 */
public class WebServiceRuntimeManager
        implements WebServiceRuntimeManagerMBean {
```

```
    String rtName = "";
    String rtVersion = "V1R0";
    Date start;
    Integer numDeployed, numRequests;
    String status;
    String hostname="localhost", port="80";
    String rtType = "unknown";
    Boolean debugFlag = new Boolean("false");

    String mbDomain;
    Date mbInit;
    MBeanServer mbs;
    ObjectName runtimeMBName;

    /**
     * Constructor for WebServiceRuntimeManager.
     */
    public WebServiceRuntimeManager() {
            super();
            start = new Date();

            mbInit = new Date();
            ArrayList mbServers = MBeanServerFactory.findMBeanServer(null);
            if (!mbServers.isEmpty())
                    mbs = (MBeanServer) mbServers.get(0);
            else
                    System.out.println(
                        "WebServiceRuntimeManager MBean constructor failed");

    }

    public WebServiceRuntimeManager (String name, String type,
                                     String version) {
            rtName = name;
            rtType = type;
            rtVersion = version;
            start = new Date();
            try {
                    ArrayList mbServers =
                       MBeanServerFactory.findMBeanServer(null);

                    if (!mbServers.isEmpty())
                            mbs = (MBeanServer) mbServers.get(0);
                    else
                            System.out.println(
```

```
                    "WebServiceRuntimeManager MBean constructor " +
                      failed");

            String mbDomain = "SoapManagement";
            runtimeMBName = new ObjectName(mbDomain, "type", "soap");
            // runtime MBeanName

            // need to construct WS MBeanName...
            // namekeys = new Hashtable(4);
            // namekeys.put("type", "soap");
            // namekeys.put("name", wsName);
            // wsMBName = new ObjectName(mbDomain, namekeys);

        }
        catch (Exception e) {
            System.out.println(
              "WebServiceRuntimeManager MBean constructor failed");
        }
}

/**
 * @see jnjmx.ch11.WebServiceRuntimeManagerMBean#getName()
 */
public String getName() {
        return rtName;
}

/**
 * @see jnjmx.ch11.WebServiceRuntimeManagerMBean#getType()
 */
public String getType() {
        try {
                rtType = (String) mbs.getAttribute(runtimeMBName,
                   "ServerType");
        } catch (Exception e) {
                // unable to get attribute, return old value
        }
        return rtType;
}

/**
 * @see jnjmx.ch11.WebServiceRuntimeManagerMBean#getVersion()
 */
public String getVersion() {
        try {
```

```
                rtVersion = (String) mbs.getAttribute(runtimeMBName,
                    "ServerVersion");
            } catch (Exception e) {
                // unable to get attribute, return old value
            }
            return rtVersion;
    }

    public Date getStartTime() {
            try {
                start = (Date) mbs.getAttribute(runtimeMBName, "StartDate");
            } catch (Exception e) {
                // unable to get attribute, return old value
            }
            return start;
    }
    public Integer getNumberOfServicesDeployed() {
            try {
                numDeployed = (Integer) mbs.getAttribute(runtimeMBName,
                    "ServiceCount");
            } catch (Exception e) {
                // unable to get attribute, return old value
            }
            return numDeployed;
    }
    /**
     * @see jnjmx.ch11.WebServiceRuntimeManagerMBean#getNumberofRequests()
     */
    public Integer getNumberofRequests() {
            try {
                numRequests = (Integer) mbs.getAttribute(runtimeMBName,
                    "TotalCount");
            } catch (Exception e) {
                // unable to get attribute, return old value
            }
            return numRequests;
    }

    public String getServerHostname() {
            try {
                hostname = (String) mbs.getAttribute(runtimeMBName,
                    "ServerHostname");
            } catch (Exception e) {
                // unable to get attribute, return old value
            }
```

```
        return hostname;
    }

    public String getServerPort() {
        try {
            port = (String) mbs.getAttribute(runtimeMBName,
                "ServerPort");
        }
        catch (Exception e) {
            port = "unknown";
        }
        return port;
    }

    /**
     * @see jnjmx.ch11.WebServiceRuntimeManagerMBean#getAvailability()
     */
    public String checkAvailability() {
        // this should exercize the Web Service Runtime in some way
        String status = "unknown";
        return status;
    }

    public void setDebug(Boolean dbg) {
        try {
            Attribute newDbg = new Attribute("WstkDebug", dbg);
            mbs.setAttribute(runtimeMBName, newDbg);
        } catch (Exception e) {
            // unable to get attribute, return old value
        }
    }

    public Boolean getDebug() {
        try {
            debugFlag = (Boolean) mbs.getAttribute(runtimeMBName,
                "WstkDebug");
        } catch (Exception e) {
            // unable to get attribute, return old value
        }
        return debugFlag;
    }

}
```

11.6.3 WebServiceManagerMBean Implementation

```
package jnjmx.ch11;

import java.util.Date;
public interface WebServiceManagerMBean {
      String getName();
      String getVersion();
      void setVersion(String version);

      Integer getNumberofRequests();                  //getInvocations
      Integer getNumberofResponses();                 // getSucesses
      Integer getNumberofFailureResponses();          // getFailures
      Date getStartTime();                            // getStartDate
      Integer getAverageResponseTimeofResponses();    // getAverageResonseTimeMs
      String checkAvailability();                     // getStatus
      Integer getTotalElapsedExecutionTime();         // getTotalProcessTimeMs
}
```

```
package jnjmx.ch11;

import java.util.ArrayList;
import java.util.Date;
import javax.management.*;
import java.util.Hashtable;


public class WebServiceManager implements WebServiceManagerMBean {
      String wsName = "";
      String wsVersion = "v1r0";
      String mbDomain;
      Date mbInit;
      MBeanServer mbs;
      ObjectName runtimeMBName, wsMBName;
      Hashtable namekeys;

      /**
       * constructor for WebServiceManager
       */
      public WebServiceManager() {
            mbInit = new Date();
            ArrayList mbServers = MBeanServerFactory.findMBeanServer(null);
            if (!mbServers.isEmpty())
                  mbs = (MBeanServer) mbServers.get(0);
            else
```

```
                System.out.println(
                    "WebServiceManager MBean constructor failed");
        }

        public WebServiceManager(String name, String version) {
                wsName = name;
                wsVersion = version;
                mbInit = new Date();
                try {
                        ArrayList mbServers =
                                MBeanServerFactory.findMBeanServer(null);

                        if (!mbServers.isEmpty())
                                mbs = (MBeanServer) mbServers.get(0);
                        else
                                System.out.println(
                                    "WebServiceManager MBean constructor failed");

                        String mbDomain = "SoapManagement";
                        runtimeMBName = new ObjectName(mbDomain, "type", "soap");
                        // runtime MBeanName

                        // need to construct WS MBeanName...
                        namekeys = new Hashtable(4);
                        namekeys.put("type", "soap");
                        namekeys.put("name", wsName);
                        wsMBName = new ObjectName(mbDomain, namekeys);

                }
                catch (Exception e) {
                         System.out.println(
                             "WebServiceManager MBean constructor failed");
                }

        }

        /**
         * @see jnjmx.ch11.WebServiceManagerMBean#getName()
         */
        public String getName() {
                return wsName;
        }
        /**
         * @see jnjmx.ch11.WebServiceManagerMBean#getName()
         */
```

```
public void setName(String name) {
        // this will change what MBean is used, but it
        // will not change the name of the MBean.
        wsName = name;
        try {
                wsMBName = new ObjectName(mbDomain, namekeys);
        } catch (Exception e) {
                // bad name
        }

}
/**
 * @see jnjmx.ch11.WebServiceManagerMBean#getVersion()
 */
public String getVersion() {
        // version is a local concept, not used by JMX or Web services
        return wsVersion;
}
/**
 * @see jnjmx.ch11.WebServiceManagerMBean#setVersion()
 */
public void setVersion(String version) {
        wsVersion = version;
}
/**
 * @see jnjmx.ch11.WebServiceManagerMBean#getStartDate()
 */
public Date getStartTime() {
        Date initDate;
        try {
                initDate = (Date) mbs.getAttribute(wsMBName, "StartDate");
        }
        catch (Exception e) {
                initDate = mbInit;
        }
        return initDate;
}
/**
 * @see jnjmx.ch11.WebServiceManagerMBean#getNumberofRequests()
 */
public Integer getNumberofRequests() {
        Integer numReq;
        try {
                numReq = (Integer) mbs.getAttribute(wsMBName,
                    "Invocations");
        }
```

```
        catch (Exception e) {
                numReq = new Integer(0);
        }
        return numReq;
}

/**
 * @see jnjmx.ch11.WebServiceManagerMBean#getNumberofResponses()
 */
public Integer getNumberofResponses() {
        Integer numSucc;
        try {
             numSucc = (Integer) mbs.getAttribute(wsMBName, "Successes");
        }
        catch (Exception e) {
             numSucc = new Integer(0);
        }
        return numSucc;
}

/**
 * @see jnjmx.ch11.WebServiceManagerMBean#getNumberofFailureResponses()
 */
public Integer getNumberofFailureResponses() {
        Integer numFailures;
        try {
                numFailures = (Integer) mbs.getAttribute(wsMBName,
                    "Failures");
        }
        catch (Exception e) {
                numFailures = new Integer(0);
        }
        return numFailures;
}

/**
 * @see jnjmx.ch11.WebServiceManagerMBean#getAverageResponseTimeofResponses()
 */
public Integer getAverageResponseTimeofResponses() {
        Integer avgRT;
        try {
                avgRT = (Integer) mbs.getAttribute(wsMBName,
                    "AverageResponseTimeMs");
        }
        catch (Exception e) {
```

```
                avgRT = new Integer(0);
            }
            return avgRT;
    }

    /**
     * @see jnjmx.ch11.WebServiceManagerMBean#getAvailability()
     */
    public String checkAvailability() {
            String status;
            try {
                status = (String) mbs.getAttribute(wsMBName, "Status");
            }
            catch (Exception e) {
                status = "unknown";
            }
            return  status;
    }

    /**
     * @see jnjmx.ch11.WebServiceManagerMBean#getTotalElapsedExecutionTime()
     */
    public Integer getTotalElapsedExecutionTime() {
            Integer procTime;
            try {
                procTime = (Integer) mbs.getAttribute(wsMBName,
                    "TotalProcessTimeMs");
            }
            catch (Exception e) {
                procTime = new Integer(0);
            }
            return procTime;
    }
}
```

11.6.4 StockQuote Service WSDL Document

```
<?xml version="1.0"?>
<definitions name="StockQuote"
        targetNamespace="http://example.com/stockquote.wsdl"
        xmlns:tns="http://example.com/stockquote.wsdl"
        xmlns:xsd="http://www.w3.org/2000/10/XMLSchema"
        xmlns:xsd1="http://example.com/stockquote.xsd"
```

```
        xmlns:soap="http://schemas.xmlsoap.org/wsdl/soap/"
        xmlns="http://schemas.xmlsoap.org/wsdl/">

    <message name="GetTradePriceInput">
        <part name="tickerSymbol" element="xsd:string"/>
        <part name="time" element="xsd:timeInstant"/>
    </message>

    <message name="GetTradePriceOutput">
        <part name="result" type="xsd:float"/>
    </message>

    <portType name="StockQuotePortType">
        <operation name="GetTradePrice">
           <input message="tns:GetTradePriceInput"/>
           <output message="tns:GetTradePriceOutput"/>
        </operation>
    </portType>

    <binding name="StockQuoteSoapBinding" type="tns:StockQuotePortType">
        <soap:binding style="rpc" transport="http://schemas.xmlsoap.org/soap/
http"/>
        <operation name="GetTradePrice">
           <soap:operation soapAction="http://example.com/GetTradePrice"/>
           <input>
              <soap:body use="encoded" namespace="http://example.com/stockquote"
                        encodingStyle=
                            "http://schemas.xmlsoap.org/soap/encoding/"/>
           </input>
           <output>
               <soap:body use="encoded" namespace=
                   "http://example.com/stockquote"
                        encodingStyle=
                            "http://schemas.xmlsoap.org/soap/encoding/"/>
           </output>
        </operation>>
    </binding>

    <service name="StockQuoteService">
        <documentation>My first service</documentation>
        <port name="StockQuotePort" binding="tns:StockQuoteBinding">
           <soap:address location="http://example.com/stockquote"/>
        </port>
    </service>
</definitions>
```

11.7 Notes

1. For more information on HTTP from the World Wide Web Consortium, see http://www.w3.org/Protocols.

2. Source: K. Gottschalk, H. Kreger, S. Graham, and J. Snell, "Introduction to Web Services Architecture," *IBM Systems Journal* (May 2002).

3. Source: IBM Business Definition, "Web Services Technical Architecture" Presentation, H. Kreger, JavaOne 2001.

4. WSDL stands for Web Services Description Language. For more information, see "Web Services Description Language (WSDL) 1.1," W3C Note 15 (March 2001) (http://www.w3.org/TR/wsdl).

5. SOAP stands for Simple Object Access Protocol. For more information, see "SOAP Version 1.2," W3C Working Draft (July 2001) (http://www.w3.org/TR/2001/WD-soap12-20010709).

6. JAX-RPC stands for Java API for XML based Remote Procedure Calls (JSR101, http://www.jcp.org/jsr/detail/101.jsp). Specification: http://java.sun.com/xml/downloads/jaxrpc.html#jaxrpcspec08.

7. Apache AXIS project, SOAP 2.2 implementation (http:/xml.apache.org/axis).

8. IBM's Web Services Tool Kit (WSTK) is available at http://alphaworks.ibm.com/tech/webservicestoolkit.

9. Sun's Sun ONE (Open Net Environment): http://wwws.sun.com/software/sunone.

10. WSCA–Web Services Conceptual Architecture, H. Kreger, http://www.ibm.com/webservices/documentation/wsca.pdf.

11. WebSphere MQ, IBM's messaging product: http://www-3.ibm.com/software/ts/mqseries.

12. WSIL stands for the Web Services Inspection Language specification from IBM and Microsoft: http://www-106.ibm.com/developerworks/webservices/library/ws-wsilspec.html.

13. UDDI stands for Universal Descripton, Discovery and Integration. Information is available at UDDI.org's site: http://www.uddi.org.

14. ebXML Registry and Repository, being standardized at OASIS (at http://www.oasis-open.org) based on the ebXML work on an e-business framework (at http://www.ebxml.org).

15. BPEL4WS stands for Business Process Execution Language for Web Services specification. More information is available at http://www-106.ibm.com/developerworks/library/ws-bpel.

16. SSL stands for Secure Sockets Layer, Secure Sockets specification version 3 (http://www.netscape.com/eng/ssl3).

17. ws-security is the Web services security from IBM and Microsoft (http://www-106.ibm.com/developerworks/webservices/library/ws-secmap).

18. HTTP-R: Reliable HTTP specification, http://www.ibm.com/developerworks/library/ws-httprspec.

19. H. Kreger, "Web Services Conceptual Architecture," http://www.ibm.com/webservices.

20. S. Graham et al., *Building Web Services with Java: Making Sense of XML, SOAP, WSDL, and UDDI*, Indianapolis, IN: Sams, 2002.

21. J. Snell, D. Tidwell, and P. Kulchenko, *Programming Web Services with SOAP*, Sebastopol, CA: O'Reilly, 2002.

22. UDDI4J is the UDDI client API for Java, an open-source implementation of UDDI. Specification and source are available at http://www-106.ibm.com/developerworks/webservices/library/ws-uddi4j.html.

23. Source: J. Farrell and H. Kreger, "Web Services Management Approaches," *IBM Systems Journal* 41:2 (June 2002), http://www.research.ibm.com/journal/sj/412/farrell.pdf.

24. Perl (http://perl.language.com), awk, sed, grep, and gnu (http://www.gnu.org) are UNIX operating system tools.

25. WSIF stands for Web Services Invocation Network, a tool developed by IBM. For more information, see http://www.alphaworks.ibm.com/tech/wsif.

APPENDIX

JMX in Products

JMX has been implemented with value-added function and sold as a separate product. JMX has also been embedded in numerous products to provide manageability infrastructure. This appendix gives an overview of the known products supporting JMX at the time of this writing. The appendix is divided into three sections: JMX Agent Implementations, JMX Managers, and JMX-Enabled Products. There is no doubt that there are products that we have missed; this is not intended to be an exhaustive listing.

One note on terminology: Vendors who implement the JMX agent specification must purchase and pass the Technology Compatibility Kit (TCK)[1] in order to claim JMX *compliance*. The TCK must be purchased from Sun, and the price can be substantial. JMX implementations that have not passed the TCK are called JMX *compatible*. We have noted which implementations are compliant. If nothing explicit is stated, you can assume that the products are compatible.

A.1 JMX Agent Implementations

A.1.1 JMX 1.0 Reference Implementation from Sun Microsystems

Version 1.0 of the JMX reference implementation was released in December 2000. The reference implementation source[2] is licensed under the Sun Community

Source License (SCSL). According to the Free Software Foundation (http://www.gnu.org/philosophy/license-list.html#SunCommunitySourceLicense) and numerous editorials at the time of the SCSL release, this license is not well thought of in the free-software and open-source communities. The reference implementation binary is available for free.

JMX 1.1, a maintenance release, is available from the same Web site. For more information and access to the source or binary versions of the reference implementation, see http://java.sun.com/products/JavaManagement.

Sun also provides a Web site called the JMXperience at http://java.sun.com/products/JavaManagement/JMXperience.html, where Sun and other vendors can contribute interesting tools, MBeans, and components for JMX. Sun has contributed a remoting component that provides a remote MBeanServer for use by JMX clients (usually JMX managers) and an Mof2MBean tool that generates MBean skeletons from CIM MOF files.

A.1.2 JDMK 4.2 from Sun Microsystems

JDMK 4.2[3] was released in 2001. It is the only JMX-compliant implementation (having passed the TCK that Sun developed). You must purchase this product from Sun. It contains adapters for HTTP, RMI, and SNMP. The SNMP adapter works only for MBeans generated from SNMP MIBs by JDMK's MIBGen tool. The adapter does not support the "random" MBean. The SNMP adapter supports SNMP versions 1 and 2. JDMK provides a remote-manager component that includes a proxy for the MBeanServer, and proxies for the MBeans, to make the development of JMX managers easier. It also provides a JMX manager and tools to help define and manage the MBeans. For more information, see http://www.sun.com/software/java-dynamic.

A.1.3 TMX4J 1.0 from Tivoli Systems

TMX4J 1.0[4] was released in February 2001. It is a cleanroom implementation of the JMX specification, and it is JMX compatible, not compliant. It is available from IBM's alphaWorks Web site at http://alphaworks.ibm.comtech/TMX4J. The licensing on this software is the standard alphaWorks trial license. However, alphaWorks is now making technologies available for release by products on a per-technology basis. More information is available at http://www.alphaworks.ibm.com/license. TMX4J contains an HTTP and RMI adapter, and support for a logging facility with JLog.[5] It also comes with a very nice tutorial. IBM's products that support JMX use TMX4J, including WebSphere 5.0,[6] WebSphere Voice Server,[7] WebSphere Edge

Server,[8] WebSphere Business Integrator,[9] WebSphere Business Components Composer,[10] and Tivoli Web Component Manager.[11]

A.1.4 AdventNet Agent Toolkit Java/JMX Edition[12]

AdventNet[13] was the first vendor to ship a product with JMX support. Its management agent toolkit supported the JMX 0.8 version before the JMX specification was final. The most recent version has passed the JMX TCK and is now fully JMX compliant. You must purchase this product from AdventNet. This toolkit includes a rapid prototyping and development tool for building JMX agents, and it includes adapters for SNMP, HTML, RMI, HTTP, CORBA, and TL1 (Transaction Language 1). It also supports distributed JMX agents in a gateway or cascading configuration, as well as the building of stand-alone SNMP and TL1 agents in Java. You can get more information at http://www.adventnet.com/products/manageengine/index.html. Other AdventNet products that use JMX are ManageEngine and Web NMS.

A.1.5 AdventNet ManageEngine

AdventNet ManageEngine is a graphical development environment that helps developers expose business- or application-specific management information even after an application is developed and deployed. JMS (Java Message Service) and Web service JMX adapters are also being supported to integrate the management infrastructure with the existing middleware infrastructure. For more information, see http://www.adventnet.com/products/manageengine/index.html.

A.1.6 MX4J

MX4J[14] is an open-source implementation release of the JMX 1.0 specification that is JMX compatible because it has not passed the JMX TCK. This is understandable, given the current licensing arrangements for the TCK. MX4J uses the Apache[15] licensing model. It provides an HTTP, RMI-over-JRMP,[16] and RMI-over-IIOP adapter. It also includes a tool that allows you to generate your MBean interface via XDoclet. Another interesting extension of MX4J is dynamic proxy support for MBeans so that the calls to the MBeans in your programs are more intuitive. The MX4J implementation has a logging facility that makes it fairly easy to redirect the data to another logging facility, such as log4j.[17] MX4J provides some additional service MBeans: a naming MBean that wraps the RMI registry, a mailer MBean that sends e-mail, and a

JythonRunner MBean that runs Jython scripts. You can find more information at http://mx4j.sourceforge.net.

A.2 JMX Managers

A.2.1 Tivoli Web Component Manager

Tivoli Web Component Manager provides performance and availability monitoring of Web applications, including Web servers, Web application servers, and JMX-enabled applications. It also provides a framework to define and execute automated responses to problems. When paired with Tivoli Web Services Manager[18] and Tivoli Web Services Analyzer,[19] which measure and report on the performance and availability of e-business infrastructure from the end user's perspective, it can help you manage performance and availability from the end user through the back-end application server. More information is available from http://www.tivoli.com/products/index/web_component_mgr.

A.2.2 Dirig Software

The Dirig agent with Fenway Management Extensions (FMX) provides management support capabilities for any third-party or custom Java application that exposes its management information via JMX. FMX gives enterprises and service providers the ability to report on, create thresholds for, and take corrective actions on any exposed attribute to maintain performance and availability of JMX-enabled applications across multiplatform Web server environments. You can find more information at http://www.dirig.com.

A.2.3 AdventNet Middleware Manager

AdventNet Middleware Manager manages JMX-enabled applications deployed on J2EE servers like BEA WebLogic Server. It adds JMX instrumentation for application-level information, in addition to using the JMX instrumentation available for the server infrastructure. It provides a unified view of a network of servers, and it monitors the server and application components. It reports on each segment of an end-to-end Web transaction so that performance and availability issues are quickly isolated. You can find more information at http://www.adventnet.com/products/middleware.

A.2.4 AdventNet Web NMS

AdventNet Web NMS provides an open, scalable, carrier-grade management infrastructure platform, with a suite of J2EE- and JMS-based cross-platform development framework, tools, modules, and APIs, as well as prepackaged applications. Web NMS uses Java, CORBA, and other standards to deliver a management solution that communicates with managed systems (network elements, systems, and applications). It supports SNMP, TL1, XML, CORBA, and Telnet/CLI[20] protocols. To integrate with OSS and other decision support systems, Web NMS supports interfaces like CORBA, RMI, JMX, SNMP, TL1, and HTTP. You can find more information at http://www.adventnet.com/products/webnms.

A.2.5 Vigor Soft hawkEye[21]

Vigor Soft's hawkEye enterprise product is a JMX-based management tool. For more information, see http://www.vigorsoft.com.

A.3 JMX-Enabled Products

The J2EE application vendors have been adopting and implementing versions of their products with JMX support for over a year now. The following products currently use JMX for their own management and/or may be managed by JMX-based managers.

A.3.1 IBM WebSphere 5.0

WebSphere 5.0 supports both JMX and JSR 77, which defines the J2EE management model. Through JMX you have access to WebSphere's configuration and performance metrics. You can find more information at http://www.ibm.com/websphere. WebSphere is a trademark of IBM in the United States.

A.3.2 IBM Web Services Tool Kit 3.1

The IBM Web Services Tool Kit is a leading-edge implementation and showcase for Web service technology. It is available from http://www.alphaworks.ibm.com/tech/webservicestoolkit.

A.3.3 IBM WebSphere Voice Server

IBM WebSphere Voice Server allows delivery of voice-enabled Internet applications to wireline and wireless devices using existing Web infrastructures. You can find more information at http://www-3.ibm.com/software/speech/enterprise/ep_1.html. WebSphere is a trademark of IBM in the United States.

A.3.4 IBM WebSphere Business Components Composer

IBM WebSphere Business Components Composer consists of easy-to-use software implementation packages. You can find more information at http://www-3.ibm.com/software/webservers/components. WebSphere is a trademark of IBM in the United States.

A.3.5 BEA Systems WebLogic Server 7.0[22]

BEA WebLogic Server 7.0 provides JMX-based management and manageability. BEA's JMX support is JMX compliant. More information is available at http://www.bea.com/products/weblogic/server/index.shtml.

A.3.6 IONA iPortal[23]

IPortal by IONA is IONA's J2EE application server, which supports JMX. More information is available at http://www.iona.com.

A.3.7 IONA Technologies PLC: Orbix E2A XMLBus Edition 5.3

IONA's XMLBus Edition (part of the Orbix E2A Web Services Integration Platform family) is an integration platform for the integration of heterogeneous applications built with .NET, Java, J2EE, J2ME, and CORBA. This platform provides rapid development tools, deployment infrastructure, and management for deployed Web services using JMX for instrumentation and management. More information is available at http://www.iona.com/products/webserv-xmlbus.htm.

A.3.8 Hewlett-Packard OpenView

OpenView is a network management system, storage management system, and application management system (including Web services) that now supports JMX plug-ins. For more information, see http://www.hp.com.

A.3.9 Hewlett-Packard Core Services Framework

HP Core Services Framework (CSF) is a framework (specification) and the underlying infrastructure that provides a core set of services such as naming and directory services, management services, logging services, and security services. As a Java standards–based framework, HP CSF supports all the resource managers and services that could be required by Java developers, including JMX. For more information, see http://www.hp.com.

A.3.10 JBoss

JBoss is an open-source J2EE application server that is built on a JMX microkernel. It supports HTTP Server, EJB, Java Connector Architecture, JMX, and CMP (Container Managed Persistence). It is *free* and distributed under the LGPL. For more information, see http://www.jboss.org.

A.3.11 Sonic Software SonicXQ[24]

Sonic Software's JMX-compliant SonicXQ by Sonic Software is an Enterprise Service Bus (ESB) that delivers integration through Web services and JCA. SonicXQ also delivers performance, scalability, and manageability. For more information, see http://www.sonicsoftware.com/products/sonicxq.htm.

A.3.12 Pramati Server from Pramati Technologies[25]

Pramati Server 3.0 is a J2EE application server that comes with a management console that supports management of J2EE servers and applications. It provides an MBean viewer and the ability to invoke MBean operations. More information is available at http://www.pramati.com.

A.3.13 Sybase EAServer 4.0

EAServer is an application server that supports all component models, including J2EE, COM, CORBA, C/C++, and PowerBuilder. For more information, see http://www.sybase.com/products/applicationservers/easerver.

A.3.14 Sun Microsystems: Sun ONE Application Server

The Sun ONE application server (formerly iPlanet application server) provides the foundation for delivering application services (J2EE 1.3) and Web services. It integrates an application development environment. It forms the foundation for the Sun ONE services delivery platform. More information is available at http://www.sun.com.

A.3.15 Sun Microsystems: Sun ONE Portal Server

The Sun ONE Portal Server is an identity-enabled portal solution for managing and administering users, policy, and provisioning services, including single sign-on, delegated administration, and Web services. More information is available at http://www.sun.com.

A.3.16 Compiere Open Source ERP & CRM

Compiere Open Source ERP & CRM is the open-source ERP and CRM business solution for the Small-Medium Enterprise (SME) in distribution and service. Compiere provides support for managing inventory, point of sale (POS), and accounting needs. The Compiere server is JMX compliant. All server services for the accounting server, request server, and utility server are implemented as dynamic MBeans. You can manage the MBeans locally and remotely, or integrate with SNMP or CIM/WBEM managers. The Compiere server is based on the JMX reference implementation. For more information, see http://www.compiere.com.

The following products are also JMX enabled:

- Macromedia: Flash MX, http://www.macromedia.com
- Macromedia: JRun 4, http://www.macromedia.com
- Cogency: Cogency Connectors, http://www.manage.com/products/connectors.html
- Resonate Inc: Resonate Commander, http://www.resonate.com
- SpiritSoft: SpiritWave 5.1 , http://www.spiritsoft.com
- Wily Technology: Introscope, http://www.wilytech.com
- XadrA: VelocityAdaptorServer, http://www.xadra.com

A.4 Notes

1. JMX TCK from Sun: *Java Management Extensions Technology Compatibility Kit 1.0* (April 2000), Sun Microsystems, Inc., 901 San Antonio Road, Palo Alto, CA 94303; available at http://java.sun.com/products/JavaManagement.

2. *Java Management Extensions Instrumentation and Agent Specification v1.0* (Final Release, April 2000), Sun Microsystems, Inc., 901 San Antonio Road, Palo Alto, CA 94303; available at http://java.sun.com/products/JavaManagement.

3. Java Dynamic Management Kit 4.2, Sun Microsystems, Inc., 901 San Antonio Road, Palo Alto, CA 94303; available at http://www.sun.com/software/java-dynamic.

4. TMX4J is Tivoli's freely available JMX-compatible JMX implementation. It is available from http://www.alphaworks.ibm.com/tech/TMX4J.

5. log4J is the Java API for logging available from Apache. For more information see http://jakarta.apache.org/log4j/docs/index.html.

6. WebSphere 5.0 supports both JMX and JSR 77, which defines the J2EE management model. Through JMX you have access to WebSphere's configuration and performance metrics. You can find more information at http://www.ibm.com/websphere. WebSphere is a trademark of IBM in the United States.

7. WebSphere Voice Server allows delivery of voice-enabled Internet applications to wireline and wireless devices using existing Web infrastructures. You can find more information at http://www-3.ibm.com/software/speech/enterprise/ep_1.html. WebSphere is a trademark of IBM in the United States.

8. WebSphere Edge Server V2.0 for Multiplatforms (Edge Server) distributes application processing to the edge of the network under centralized administrative and application control. You can find more information at http://www-3.ibm.com/software/webservers/edgeserver. WebSphere is a trademark of IBM in the United States.

9. WebSphere Business Integrator provides a complete and consistent model for both Enterprise Application Integration (EAI) and business-to-business (B2B) integration. You can find more information at http://www-3.ibm.com/software/webservers/btobintegrator. WebSphere is a trademark of IBM in the United States.

10. WebSphere Business Components Composer consists of easy-to-use software implementation packages. You can find more information at http://www-3.ibm.com/software/webservers/components. WebSphere is a trademark of IBM in the United States.

11. Tivoli Web Component Manager (TWCM) is Tivoli's management application that measures the performance of the components of your e-business: operating systems, Web servers, and Web applications. You can find more information at http://www.tivoli.com/products/index/web_component_mgr/index.html.

12. Information about AdventNet Agent Tookit Java/JMX Edition is available at http://www.adventnet.com/products/javaagent.

13. AdventNet markets agent toolkits that support both SNMP and JMX technologies. More information is available at http://www.adventnet.com.

14. MX4J is an open-source community for JMX specification implementations using the Apache licensing model. More information is available at http://mx4j.sourceforge.net.

15. Apache public license information is available at http://www.apache.org.

16. JRMP stands for Java Remote Method Protocol.

17. IBM JLog is a Java logging API that is available at http://www.alphaworks.ibm.com/tech/loggingtoolkit4j.

18. Tivoli Web Services Manager is Tivoli's management application that checks Web site availability and response time from the user's point of view. You can find more information at http://www.tivoli.com/products/index/web_services_mgr/index.html.

19. Tivoli Web Services Analyzer is Tivoli's management application that helps you baseline and improve the true quality of experience Web visitors receive when accessing your site.

20. CLI stands for Command Line Interface.

21. Vigor Soft's hawkEye enterprise product is a JMX-based management tool. For more information, see http://www.vigorsoft.com.

22. BEA WebLogic Server 5.0, 6.0, and now 7.0 have all provided JMX-based management and manageability. More information is available at http://www.bea.com.

23. IPortal by IONA is IONA's J2EE Application server, which supports JMX. According to IONA, the iPortal Application Server has been incorporated into the Orbix E2A Application Server Platform as the Orbix E2A J2EE Technology Edition. More information is available at http://www.iona.com.

24. Sonic Software's SonicXQ by Sonic Software. For more information see http://www.sonicsoftware.com/products/sonicxq.htm.

25. Pramati Server 3.0, by Pramati Technologies, is a J2EE application server that comes with a management console that supports management of J2EE servers and applications. It provides an MBean viewer and the ability to invoke MBean operations. More information is available at http://www.pramati.com.

Index

K

U